# Messages of the Body

# MESSAGES OF THE BODY

*John Spiegel*

Professor of Social Psychiatry

Brandeis University

&

*Pavel Machotka*

Associate Professor of Psychology

University of California, Santa Cruz

THE FREE PRESS

*A Division of Macmillan Publishing Co., Inc.*

*New York*

COLLIER MACMILLAN PUBLISHERS

*London*

The Free Press
A Division of Macmillan Publishing Co., Inc.
866 Third Avenue, New York, N.Y. 10022

Collier-Macmillan Canada Ltd.

Library of Congress Catalog Card Number: 73-10572

Printed in the United States of America

printing number
1 2 3 4 5 6 7 8 9 10

Library of Congress Cataloging in Publication Data

Spiegel, John Paul, 1911-
    Messages of the body.

    Bibliography: p.
    1. Nonverbal communication.  I.  Machotka, Pavel.
II.  Title.  [DNLM: 1.  Kinesics.  HM258  S755m 1974]
BF637.C45S66      153            73-10572
ISBN 0-02-930400-8

To the memory of
Gordon W. Allport
—teacher and model

Our gratitude to Paul Williams—creative collaborator—
whose study elaborated previous findings
and introduced new distinctions

# Contents

# List of Illustrations

# List of Tables

# Illustration Credits

Grateful acknowledgment is given to the sources cited here for permission to use the following illustrations:

Photographie Giraudon, Paris:

Manet: *Le Déjeuner sur l'Herbe* (Louvre, Paris)—Fig. 9, p. 20

Giorgione: *Le Concert Champêtre* (Louvre, Paris)—Fig. 10, p. 21

Correggio: *Jupiter and Antiope* (Louvre, Paris)—Fig. 29, p. 183

Art Reference Bureau, Ancram, New York:

Botticelli: *The Birth of Venus* (Uffizi Gallery, Florence)—Fig. 6, p. 17

*The Medici Venus* (Uffizi Gallery, Florence)—Fig. 7, p. 18

Praxiteles: *The Knidian Aphrodite* (The Vatican Museum, Rome)—Fig. 8, p. 19

*The Judgment of Paris* (Villa Medici, Rome)—Fig. 12, p. 23

The National Gallery of Art, Washington, D. C., Chester Dale Collection:

Picasso: *La Famille des Saltimbanques*—Fig. 22, p. 170

The Tate Gallery, London:

Armitage: *The Remorse of Judas*—Fig. 24, p. 177

The Art Institute, Chicago:

Forain: *Sentenced for Life*—Fig. 23, p. 176

Homer: *Croquet Scene*—Fig. 25, p. 178

The Museum of Modern Art, New York, The Whitney Collection:

Toulouse-Lautrec: *Marcelle Lender*—Fig. 21, p. 167

The New York Public Library, New York, Prints Division, Astor, Lenox and Tilden Foundations:

Marcantonio: *The Judgment of Paris*—Fig. 11, p. 22

Kunstmuseum, Basel:

Gauguin: *Ta Matete*—Fig. 20, p. 162

The Metropolitan Museum of Art, New York, Gift of Harry Payne Bingham, 1937:

Rubens: *Venus and Adonis*—Fig. 27, p. 180

The National Gallery, London:

Titian: *Venus and Adonis*—Fig. 28, p. 182

*The New York Times Sunday Magazine*, New York:

Garbo and Gable: *Susan Lennox: Her Fall and Rise* (Metro-Goldwyn-Mayer film)—Fig. 19, p. 143

The Metropolitan Museum of Art, New York:

Cassatt: *Young Mother Sewing*—Fig. 26, p. 179

# Acknowledgments

We are particularly grateful to Marcia Morse for constructing appropriate line drawings for our studies, a task which involved drafts, corrections, and adjustments, all cheerfully collaborated upon. We also wish to express our gratitude for the help received from colleagues, friends, assistants and the institutional resources of Harvard University during the course of our work.

Special thanks are owed Peter B. Evans for his role, during his undergraduate days at Harvard, in the interview stage of the research and for his help with problems of conceptualization and of statistical analyses. Professor Robert Rosenthal of the Department of Social Relations, Harvard University, helped immeasurably in the handling of methodological problems and in providing us with a critical reading of parts of the manuscript. Similarly, Professor George Miller, now at Rockefeller University, supplied a critique of certain chapters which, we hope, has softened some over-enthusiastic generalizations. Professor Phoebe Ellsworth Diebold, presently at Yale University, gave us valuable critical reactions to portions of the book, particularly those dealing with previous literature. In addition, the efforts of the staffs of the Widener and Houghton Libraries at Harvard in making available the resources of their rare book collections are much appreciated.

In a book of this sort, attention to the details of publication procedures are as essential as the content. To Carol Nordlinger we owe our thanks for her persistence in obtaining the photographs of paintings and the permission for their reproduction. Michael McAnulty secured programs for the processing of statistical data and helped with their arrangement in tabular form. Florence Trefethen displayed surgical skill in reducing a bulky manuscript to one of manageable proportions. Catherine Richardson and Ann Johnson performed untiring services in typing the manuscript and in tracking its various permutations and combinations between the continental span that separated its authors.

In the final stage of proof preparation, Suzanne Reed kindly took on the task of constructing the index, thereby giving the text the sort of close attention that authors may manage only with reluctance.

Finally, we wish to express our appreciation for the financial support given by the National Institute of Mental Health to the Family Interaction Studies Project in the Department of Social Relations at Harvard, of which the research reported here was a by-product. It is a tribute to the flexibility of the N.I.M.H. staff that support continued to be provided for this unexpected and apparent diversion from the original research plan.

# Introduction

When we consider the biological antiquity of communication through the body, it seems surprising that so little is known about it. In part, our ignorance rests on laziness and indifference. The word is endlessly fascinating, while gesture, posture, and the appearance of the body in motion or rest seem prosaic topics, worthy only of occasional attention. Even works which define media as "extensions" of the body do not discuss how the body, that prime mover and original model of all expression, manages to communicate its messages.

Our backwardness derives from a genuine difficulty in discovering how to capture the expressions of the body for observation and study. The phenomena are at once familiar and elusive—a nearly fatal combination. The movements of the body are too various, pass by too quickly, and are read too easily, though we know not what we read.

This book tries to solve some of the observational and conceptual problems that have hindered the investigation of the movements, postures, and gestures of the human body. It suggests a theory as to how these phenomena are perceived and reports some experiments designed to test, at least in part, the theory.

Our thinking in this area seems to reflect a common intellectual preoccupation—one that is not very well defined—with the characteristics of the visual process, with the relation between "looking" and "seeing," between optical stimulation and conscious knowledge. Although behavioral science has shown an interest in perception as process, it has neglected perception's object: the visual display. The arts, on the other hand, have taken a generally casual interest in the problem of "seeing" while continually devising new forms of visual stimulation. At times, the artist seems almost the enemy of the viewer. No sooner has the latter learned, rather shakily, what he is supposed to be seeing than he is dazzled with yet a new and still more incomprehensible display.

Perhaps the indirect and casual approach to the relation between the specific properties of a visual presentation and its apperception derives from the opinion among all concerned that, whatever the problem consists of, it probably belongs to someone else. Of course, there are exceptions. The need to understand at the same time how and what we see is compelling enough to have led a few hardy souls out of their safe professional habitats onto the squashy ground of inter-disciplinary collaboration. Gombrich (1960), art historian, has tried to deduce processes of esthetic perception from historical changes in modes of representa-tion. Arnheim (1954), Gestalt psychologist, had contributed incisively to the study of esthetic perception by starting from the opposite pole—the rich contri-butions of Gestaltists to the study of perception. More recently, Kepes (1965), an artist and Professor of Design at M.I.T., has brought together a group of artists, photographers, architects, engineers, biologists, and psychologists and has persuaded them to muse on the characteristics of the visual process. Carpenter Center for the Visual Arts at Harvard embodies in le Corbusier's concrete-and-glass castle the hope that amateurs and professionals, students and teachers, of different backgrounds and temperaments, can work together in constructing and analyzing the visual object and the perceptual process.

But collaborative attempts are still subject to the familiar conceptual problems of behavioral science. Not surprisingly, a large part of the difficulty—the peculiar combination of apathy toward and fascination with the visible, in contrast to the auditory, world—is due to the words which have been used to define the process of seeing. Our scientific language comforts and frustrates us by making us feel that we know more than we actually do. We talk of "perception," "cognition," "communication"; of "signals," "signs," and "symbols"; of "form," "content," and "style," and of their resolution in "esthetics"; of "primary process" (very symbolic) and of "secondary process" (very logical); of "the good Gestalt," of "openness," "embeddedness," and "closure," to say nothing of the reversal of "figure" and "ground." We hear of "stimuli" and of "responses," conditioned either by "classical" ("Pavlovian") or by "operant" ("Skinnerian") contingencies in the environment. There is said to be an internal "mental representation," or "schema," which hooks up with an environmental "display," or "stimulus con-figuration." The architects say that a building "makes a statement," whereas the linguists proclaim that a statement is a "pattern" which has a "multi-level structure."

The problem here is not jargon. It lies rather in knowing how to extract the useful information packed into so many seemingly incompatible groups of labels. If one begins with a certain amount of naïve curiosity about the visual process, the litany of the various schools of thought produces confusion rather than en-lightenment. Therefore it seems wiser, at least to begin with, to avoid profes-sional language and concepts for describing cognitive processes and to concentrate instead on the characteristics of visual displays, capitalizing on one's status as a naïve observer.

We first became concerned with the amount of slippage in the interpretation of visual data during the course of other researches. With some colleagues, one of us (Spiegel) was studying the relation between mental illness in a child and the family interactions to which he was exposed, in a group of Italian-American, Irish-American, and "Old" American families. The families were frequently seen in their homes and other settings. Each family was seen by several members of the research team, but not by all.

As the research went along, we were often surprised and frustrated by the amount of variation among research staff members seeing the same family in reporting the physical behavior—even the physical appearance—of family members. Since we began with the assumption that the physical behavior of the parent was significantly related to the child's capacity to cope with his environment, these discrepancies were troublesome. It was manifestly impossible to make systematic observations if two or more observers could not agree about the chief visual features of the behavior being observed—to say nothing of its meaning.

After some time, it was decided that the problem was mainly conceptual. Filming family interactions would only have thrown the problem into the combined laps of the whole research group. If two or three persons could not agree about what they had seen, how could a larger number reach consensus? Since we were then attempting to classify all observable family interactions within one or another category of social role, we "solved" the problem by developing a new role category—"Body Management Roles." It seemed evident that, along with Age Roles and Sex Roles, Body Management Roles represented a species of highly patterned behavior which varied from culture to culture. Furthermore, like Age and Sex Roles, Body Management Roles had to be maintained in proper order at every moment, day and night, throughout one's life. They were not like the roles, say, of "student" or "husband," from which one could take a vacation now and then.

For a long time we were much satisfied with our "solution." We talked freely about Body Management Roles, not minding that we could not quite say what they were. Having a name for our problems seemed to soften the anxiety and discord which had previously characterized our discussions.

Anticipating that the time would arrive when a labeled concept would fail to satisfy unless it were given some content, Spiegel took responsibility for further conceptualization. He proceeded along lines of inquiry that asked how we see and classify the visible appearance and movement of the body in the process of assigning a "meaning." After looking at hundreds of photographs, drawings, and paintings of the human body in all sorts of situations, watching television with the sound off, inspecting body management in public and private places, and reviewing the literature, he arrived at the results which are reported in Chapters 5 through 8, the theoretical chapters of this book. The theoretical approach is based on the assumption that the process of perception and interpretation, like the structure of thought in general, is polyphonic and systematically stratified. If this assumption is to be taken seriously, then the interrelated themes and levels must be clearly specified and the functioning connections between themes and levels must be laid out for inspection and testing.

Meanwhile, the other of us (Machotka) had for some time been interested in the esthetics of visual forms. He had carried out research on the criteria by which children judge painting and had been impressed by the apparent closeness of the child's esthetic judgments to his intellectual level of development (Machotka, 1966). For example, during certain years, the child judges paintings primarily by the subject matter they represent—and he ignores, and most probably is not capable of making perceptual use of, the more formal properties such as style and composition. After a certain age, these formal properties become "visible" to him; this milestone in his esthetic development is significant on the one hand because it is related to certain intellectual milestones, and on the other because it becomes integrated, perhaps in a hierarchical fashion, with the preceding levels. The adult who seemingly judges a painting solely by its formal properties is also responding, more or less consciously, to its subject matter.

The results of this study argued for the importance of subject matter even in highly esthetic responses to paintings. Since the subject matter is frequently human, interest in the meanings of body positions followed quite naturally. There were other sources of this interest. One was Machotka's interest in adult esthetics and psychology, particularly in perceptual processes and the psychoanalytic theory of esthetic motives (Machotka, 1967, 1970a and b). In the study of perception, one runs very quickly into the nativist–empiricist controversy, and, even when one has leanings toward Gestalt theory, one cannot help but entertain questions about cultural and historical differences. If human movements are "expressive," how closely do observers agree on their meaning? What information do they need before they can "see" meaning in a configuration? What is the role of "context" in the perception of meaning?

The contributions of psychoanalytic theory to understanding esthetic processes have emphasized subject matter rather than the formal properties of works of art—at least until recently. Current psychoanalytic thinking focuses more on form, partly as a result of a shift of interest away from unconscious contents toward ego processes. But content is not thereby downgraded: It continues to play a role in theorizing, and comes up with insistence in empirical work. For instance, in classroom experiments where students were asked to write down and accumulate free associations to their favorite works of art, a strong and complex involvement with the content of the work was universal. The content had many meanings, some general, others quite personal; very frequently, it involved body positions and images.

The two of us were well acquainted before our common work began, but were not aware of the way in which our interests might intersect. Our collaboration began when Spiegel showed Machotka the theoretical considerations he had systematized, asking whether they might not lead to fruitful research. For about a semester, we discussed the framework and what we might do with it, and Machotka began to conduct interviews with students in which he asked for their detailed reactions to selected paintings. Our work began in earnest during the following summer when Machotka, with an assistant (Mr. Evans), conducted more interviews, this time using paintings that were carefully chosen for the body positions they represented. The three of us met weekly to discuss the results we had obtained and their relevance to the initial theoretical framework. Some of the results of this work are reported in Chapter 9. Since our interest centered on substantiating certain ideas, rather than merely offering them for others to take up, we had to devise methods by which we could systematically vary the stimuli and precisely measure changes in their meaning. For this part of the study, we obtained the collaboration of Marcia Morse, who patiently listened to our wishes, translated them into visual forms, and cheerfully submitted alterations until all of us had what we wanted. The results form the subject matter of Chapters 10 through 16. They were not investigated, however, in the order of their presentation; initially, we studied four problems (The Arms of Venus, Direction of Gaze, Arm Position and Dominance, and Acrotropic Inequality); later we refined one of them (Venus Clothed), added another (Male–Female Encounter), and restudied still another (Direction of Gaze); finally, we complemented the Venus study with that of the arms of Apollo.

During the year when the first drafts of these chapters were being written, Paul Williams, who previously studied with Machotka, and who has since become a film director, decided to write his undergraduate honors thesis on a topic relevant to this book. We were interested in finding out whether similar results would be obtained if the method used here were reversed, that is, if subjects were asked to create body positions in response to verbal instructions, rather than to describe verbally those that had already been created for them. Williams set up the study in this manner, photographed the positions his subjects created, and tabulated them by categories described in our theoretical chapters. In so doing, he refined the categories still further, and produced a complex and important study which we asked him to summarize for this book. His summary is Chapter 17, which follows immediately the study with which it was meant to be compared.

Aside from Chapter 17, the writing of this book was divided according to the primary responsibility taken in developing various parts. The theoretical exposition, Chapters 1 through 8, was written by Spiegel, the empirical elaboration, Chapters 9 through 16 and the final chapter (18) were written by Machotka. Chapter 4 was extensively revised thanks to the merciful but thorough criticism of Phoebe Ellsworth Diebold, who pointed out errors, added new materials, and helped reformulate conclusions. A bulky manuscript was finally tightened by the insightful and empathetic efforts of Florence Trefethen. To all our collaborators, our thanks; to us, the blame for stubborn errors.

It has often been suggested that the gulf between "the two cultures" can be spanned by applying the technology of science to the objects of scholarship or artistic creation, as carbon-14 dating helps historians or as electronic devices provide new musical materials for composers. As felicitous as such collaboration may be, our own satisfaction lies in locating conceptual problems common to both art and science.

The shared object of knowledge that we propose to examine in this study is actually only an aspect of the way the human body is used in communication. It concerns the positioning of the body in space vis-à-vis another person and the arrangement of the parts of the body in relation to the whole. Yet, even in this small compass, the problems that beset the subject matter of body communication, that stand in the way of dealing with it in a rigorous scientific fashion, will clearly emerge. Within this small area, we shall undertake to define the problems and to propose certain solutions. It is our thesis that the problems are mainly conceptual and that they arise from the history of human thinking about communication through the use of the body. On the assumption that the question of methods will be easier to deal with once the conceptual problems are solved, we have devoted most of our efforts to a description of our conceptual approach and to our still incomplete attempts to test its relevance.*

---

* Whether cross-translation and the closing of the intellectual gap between the professions is possible, or even desirable, has been frequently discussed. Arguments, accented by irony or bitterness, occur even between closely related disciplines (Kruse, 1957, Grinker, 1956). An eloquent defense of the desirability of "translation terms from the poetic all the way to the physical" has been made by Karl H. Pribram (1963).

# Part
# ONE

# 1. Various Concepts of Expressive Movement

The fact that men use gestures, postures, costumes, facial expressions, and styles of movement to reveal their thoughts, feelings, intentions, or personalities is perfectly obvious. Yet such use has received remarkably little systematic investigation by the sciences of behavior, and there exists no discipline—no field of inquiry—that corresponds to its subject matter. Because of descriptive need, examples of body communication have been recorded from the earliest times to the present. They abound in the Bible: "A naughty person, a wicked man, walketh with a froward mouth: he winketh with his eyes, he speaketh with his feet, he teacheth with his fingers." (Proverbs, 6:12, 13); in Shakespeare: "Yon Cassius hath a lean and hungry look. He thinks too much: such men are dangerous." (*Julius Caesar*); in contemporary literature: "Apeneck Sweeney spreads his knees/Letting his arms hang down to laugh,/The zebra stripes along his jaw/Swelling to maculate giraffe." (T. S. Eliot, "Sweeney Among the Nightingales.") Nevertheless, the myriad recorded observations strung out over the centuries have not been organized; the information contained in them has not been extracted.

Science has not been wholly inactive in this regard. On the contrary, since the eighteenth century, there have been sporadic attempts to devise a method or to invent an approach that would enable the investigator to discover how men communicate through the physical structure of the body and the visual sense, rather than through words and the auditory sense. These efforts have produced only modest results.

Recently, there has been some increase of scientific enterprise in this area. But the investigations have emerged within different disciplines and have proceeded along disconnected lines of research. To be sure, in the last few years, a series of conferences has drawn this disparate work more closely together and some very comprehensive reviews of the literature within the behavioral sciences have also tended to introduce greater cohesion. But within the field of body communication as a whole tremendous gaps still exist and many of these lacunae are due to differences in approach, in vocabulary, and in the basic concepts used for observation (Davis, 1972; Hinde, 1972).

Whitehead (1953) and Einstein and Infield (1938), and more recently Kuhn (1962), have provided the now generally acknowledged insight that basic pre-suppositions or conceptions about phenomena—the cognitive models used to approach the data—may be erroneous and may, on this account, prevent one from dealing appropriately with the phenomena. The models are usually good enough in their time but gradually outlive their usefulness. Whether of the nature of the universe, of space, of time, or of behavior, such anachronistic models function like distorting lenses, forcing the observer to look for the wrong data.

It seems that something of this sort has occurred with body communication. The anachronistic model has been more implicitly held than explicitly articulated. It has been embodied in the words used to describe body communication and in the *a priori* assumptions that have guided thinking about the phenomena. The words—and the assumptions correlated with them—consist of such phrases as "expressive movement" and "body language." The general assumption can be stated in terms of the formula: $S \rightarrow E \rightarrow I$, where S stands for some item of an inner *state* of the organism, E for the behavior which *expresses* that inner state, and I for the *impression* which the expressive behavior makes on an observer. The arrows indicate merely that there is some type of relationship, to be further specified, between the elements in the formula. But it is assumed that the postures, gestures, and facial expressions probably stand, on the one hand, in an isomorphic relation with something going on inside the subject which is being expressed and, on the other hand, with something in the observer which is sensitive to the behavior and correlates it with the presumed inner state of the subject. In brief, the subject expresses his attitudes or feelings, the observer interprets them from the physical behavior he sees. The expressive behavior is like an imprecise language that can be translated with some difficulty. The scientific problem, then, consists of finding ways to maximize the element of precision in the language.

The reader may wonder what is wrong with this model. It seems to correspond well enough with the facts—as long as the facts are perceived in accordance with the model and its assumptions. But this merely confirms that cognitive models dictate that events be observed in accordance with their own rules. Though the model is not outrageously in error, two of its assumptions invite questions: (1) that there is an exact correspondence between the expressive behavior and the inner state, or between the expressive behavior and the impression or interpretation put upon it by the observer; and (2) that the expressive behavior contains the elements of precision found in a language. It may be that these assumptions have misled investigators.

The assumption that there is a one-to-one correspondence between the expressive behavior and the inner state has encouraged attempts to learn something about the language of expressive behavior by studying its correlation with something in the inner state. Over the centuries, the words used to describe such "inner state variables" have changed with the fashions of descriptive terminology; the "virtues" and "faculties" of the eighteenth century have been superseded by the "emotions," "motivations," or "personalities" of the twentieth century. But the attempt to understand the language by specifying the set of inner variables has been fairly consistent. On the other side of the equation, the much fragmented research has attempted to understand the language of expression by studying the impressions or interpretations of observers, reading backwards, so to speak, from the impression to the behavior. The impressions, however, have been found to be so variable, the responses of observers to the observed stimuli so unreliable, that the investigator has perforce concentrated on the perceptual problem itself—on the accuracy and reliability of judgments and on the perceptual process which leads to the judgment or interpretation.

As a result of both of these methods for arriving at an understanding of the language of expressive behavior, that behavior has itself suffered a peculiar neglect. It has been treated as a stepchild, either of the inner state or of the observer's judgment. With two exceptions, there has been only the barest attempt to study the patterning of expressive behavior, to investigate its formal properties, to discover the way in which its messages are coded. The exceptions lie in the approaches known as "somatotyping" and "kinesics." In both, the communicative activity of the body is treated as a system in its own right, containing the properties of a precise code of language. Since the assumption that body communication employs the precise terms of a language or the formal categories of linguistic phenomena is itself questionable, these approaches must be included among the results of a conceptual model that needs revision.

To say that the communication system of the body is not like a linguistic system is not to deny that it is a set of coded messages; but its code and the program of encoding and decoding its messages probably bears a closer resemblance to music, drama, and the plastic arts than to words and language. If this is so, then the expression "body language" is a metaphor, a figurative way of saying that some communication takes place. But the mode of communication, the categories of which it consists, are not like the nouns and verbs, the suffixes and prefixes, the phonemes and morphemes, the grammar, and the logical syntax of linguistic analysis.

The notion that body communication consists of a set of physical arrangements which directly represent the inner state of the person in a one-to-one system of substitutions—the glaring eye and gnashing teeth for anger, the relaxed countenance for a serene personality—runs straight through the literature both of everyday observation and of scientific investigation. Here and there, another point of view has been advanced. This point of view (or model) discards the notion of *re-presentation*. Instead of assuming that the behavior which is enacted and visualized is a copy—a representation—of what is within the person waiting to be expressed (attitudes, emotions, intentions, motivations), the alternate model asserts that what is enacted in behavior is a *presentation*. The word "presentation" means that the behavior performed and witnessed is not a copy of anything except (possibly) other behavior performed and witnessed. What is presented is a performance, an arrangement and appearance of the body and a pattern of movement. The arrangement is presented to be seen, to have predetermined or accidental effect on the beholder, whether with conscious or unconscious intention. But its connection with an inner state is tenuous and changeable and is established largely on the basis of a learning process. What is important in this point of view is the notion that the *presented behavior* can exist independent of the inner state. What is to be studied, then, is how each varies in relation to the other. Also, how the presentational behavior is formed, in accordance with what laws or rules, with what properties, conditioned by what biological, social, and cultural parameters.

If *presentation behavior* is substituted for *expressive behavior*, then the other side of the original equation can be studied with greater flexibility. The body behavior that is presented will be decoded by the observer in accordance with rules learned from his own experience. In great part, these will be the rules of his culture. In another culture, with variant rules, the interpretation of the same presentation will be different. Nevertheless, whatever the cultural rules, the individual will always, it is assumed, interpret a presentation partly in line with his own, idiosyncratic cognitive processes, and these will vary with his mood, age, and sex, and with other personality processes such as his fantasies, anxieties, and defenses.

The literature in which body movement has previously been studied begins with John Casper Lavater, a Zurich pastor, who, in 1792, published his *Essays on Physiognomy* (see Figure 1). Not the first to claim to read traits of personality in the face and figure of a man, he was the first to systematize observation in the name of science. Throughout his writing, his tone was defensive and pleading as he reiterated the claim that the inner state of man could be translated from his outer appearance on the basis of universal principles. "One of the chief ends I have in view in this work," he said,

**Fig. 1.** *John Caspar Lavater* by Thomas Holloway

. . . is to prove that there is a Physiognomy; to demonstrate that the Physiognomy is true, in other words, that it is the real and visible expression of internal qualities, which are themselves invisible. Rank, condition, habit, estate, dress, all concur to the modification of Man, everyone is a several veil spread over him. But to pierce through all these coverings into his real character, to discover in these foreign and contingent determinations, solid and fixed principles by which to settle what the Man really is: this appears extremely difficult if not impossible. Let us not, however, lose courage. It is true that Man is acted upon by everything around him. But he, in his turn, acts upon all these external objects; and if he receives their impressions, he also communicates his own. (Lavater, p. 178.)

As to how this communication takes place, Lavater, it seems, also originated the analogy to language:

> I do not promise, for it would be the height of folly to make such a promise, to give entire the immense Alphabet necessary to decipher the original language of Nature, written on the face of man and on the whole of his Exterior; but I flatter myself that I have been so happy as to trace a few of the Characters of that divine Alphabet, and that they will be so legible, that a sound eye will readily distinguish them wherever they occur. (Lavater, p. 27.)

But the "solid and fixed principles" and "the immense Alphabet" that Lavater tried to elucidate left the world unconvinced. His method consisted of presenting to the reader an array of faces differing slightly in expression (Figures 2 and 3). Though always hopeful that the visual display itself would bring conviction about his thesis, in the text he pointed out how the nose of one face was noble, the mouth of another weak, the eye of a third cunning. These judgments appeared personal and dogmatic, and Lavater was never able to explain successfully how he arrived at them. His success, however, lay in his program. Though it had many and severe critics, physiognomy had a popular appeal and became for a time almost a parlor game—a practice not discouraged by the author himself. Lavater wished to educate the public in the art of observation, and there is no doubt that he established for future investigators the importance of the comparative method, of making minute observations of easily neglected bodily features, and of training the visual imagination to perceive what is ordinarily passed over or treated as intuition.

Lavater's method was essentially "diagnostic." What he did, in contrast to what he thought he was doing, was to assert the existence of correlations between patterns of facial and bodily configurations and patterns of personality traits. The correlations that he asserted to be "true" were drawn from his personal experience, and this gave his assertions their arbitrary quality, as well as their occasional flashes of illumination. This "diagnostic" method was given a somewhat firmer foundation in contributions from the field of medicine.

Sir Charles Bell, author of *The Anatomy and Philosophy of Expression as Connected with the Fine Arts* (1844), was an anatomist, surgeon, neurophysiologist, and artist. It was as an anatomist that he first became interested in the

**Fig. 2.** *Facial Expressions* by Thomas Holloway after LeBrun

expression of the emotions. But it was his investigation of the functions of the nervous system that fixed his attention on the correlations between various parts of the body, the orchestration of muscular and vegetative functions which gave a particular emotional reaction its characteristic stamp. The discoverer of the distinction between the posterior (sensory) and anterior (motor) been especially impressed with the relation between the twelfth cranial nerve roots of the spinal nerves, and of the functions of the cranial nerves, he had

**Fig. 3.**   Page from Lavater's *Essays on Physiognomy*

and the respiratory apparatus. He observed that all strong emotions—fear, rage, grief, or sexual excitement—are accompanied by alterations in breathing, and in the muscles of the face and trunk as they affect and are affected by the changed respiratory patterns. Thus, to understand the way an emotion was expressed required a detailed knowledge of the anatomy of facial and thoracic musculature. His book is illustrated with sketches (Figure 4), admirably executed by the author, showing which muscles are involved in the expression of one or another emotional state. (Bell, 1844.) [1]

Although Bell had his own theory of esthetics—his chief reason for writing his book—what is of interest here is the theory of emotional expression he enunciated. He justified his "diagnostic" approach on the basis of an assumed priority (or speed) of bodily response over mental response.

> Expression is to passion what language is to thought. It may be too much to affirm that without the cooperation of these organs of the frame the mind would remain a blank; but surely the mind must owe something to its connection with an operation of the features which precedes its own conscious activity, and which is unerring in its exercise from the very commencement. (Bell, 1844, pp. 197–98.)

Since the body projects its message more rapidly and unerringly than the mind with its dependence on words and perceptions, one must learn to interpret the somatic pattern in terms of its own symbols—its anatomical features.

The anatomical–diagnostic approach was simplified and generalized by physicians who followed Bell. Rather than to specific emotions expressed through particular groups of muscles, attention was directed to the relation of the body as a whole to the personality as a whole. Lombroso, who initiated this approach, believed there was a direct relationship between character and body build, the criminal showing degenerative or atavistic physical features, the man of genius displaying highly developed physical features. (Lombroso, 1876, 1891.) Extending the general strategy of diagnostic correlation, Kretschmer (1925) devised three types of body build—the *asthenic* (skin and bones), the *pyknic* (roly-poly),

**Fig. 4.** *Envy* by Sir Charles Bell

and the *athletic* (muscular)—and correlated them with two types of temperament —the *schizoid* and the *cycloid*. Later, Sheldon and others (1940, 1942, 1954) refined and renamed the categories of physique and developed objective methods of measurement for his system of somatotyping. His categories, parallel to those of Kretschmer, were called *ectomorph* (skin and connective tissues), *endomorph* (fatty and digestive tissue), and *mesomorph* (muscular tissue). Each constitutional type was held to correspond to a personality configuration: the ectomorph with a *cerebrotonic* temperament (over-intense, anxious, introverted); the endomorph with a *viscerotonic* temperament (sociable, amicable, complacent); the mesomorph with a *somatotonic* temperament (assertive, courageous, adventurous).

Although the high degree of correlation between body type and personality traits claimed by Sheldon has been challenged by other investigators, the proposition that there is some degree of association between the two is generally accepted.[2] What is interesting is that the middle term, *expression*, has been wholly eliminated from the paradigm of body communication. The medical approach, it would seem, is now so fixed on the empirical process of finding diagnostic correlations that there is no longer a viable concept of an inner state that requires expression. Personality and physique are regarded as but two aspects of the same biological process, controlled on one side by heredity and genetic endowment, and on the other by adaptation to the environment. Somatotyping is thus a detailed system for the reliable recognition of the expected relationship between body type and personality traits. The assumption is that if the observer has learned the system—like learning the system of Morse Code—he will not make errors in interpreting what he sees. The conceptual model states that there is a completely one-to-one isomorphic relationship between the appearance and movement of the body, the expression in behavior of the personality, and the impression or interpretation of the observer. This model, in contrast to $S \rightarrow E \rightarrow I$, could be represented by the formula, $S = E = I$.

The existence of such isomorphism is, as earlier indicated, a matter to be questioned.[3] The biologists, on the other hand, have not joined in the quest for isomorphism, but have approached body communication from an entirely different angle. The question they have asked about expressive movements does not concern a definition of the precise nature of the internal state of the organism. Nor have they been interested in an overall configuration of personality traits. Rather, they have asked what function a given expressive movement serves for both the individual and the species. They begin with the assumption that an expressive body movement has some origin in the history of the species and fulfills some purpose or goal which now has, or once had, survival value for the group.

The comparative biological approach was initiated in 1872 by Charles Darwin with the publication of *The Expression of Emotion in Man and Animals*. It is not surprising that the author of the *Origin of Species* should have been curious about the origin of expressive movements and their relative distribution in higher and lower organisms, nor that the man who proposed the theory of evolution should have produced a set of etiological theories (actually hypotheses) to explain how the behaviors came about. He advanced three "principles" which are still of interest today: [4]

1. *The Principle of Serviceable Associated Habits* states that movements which were functional in their original context are repeated in related contexts where they serve no purpose except expression. For example, a man who vehemently

**Fig. 5.** *Dog Approaching Another Dog with Hostile Intentions* by Mr. Riviere

rejects a proposition closes his eyes and turns his head aside, though there is no relevant visual stimulus he can avoid by performing these movements.

2. *The Principle of Antithesis* states that certain states of mind lead to actions which are of service (functional or adaptive), while opposite states of mind lead to opposite movements which have no function save that of expression. For example, when a dog is in a "savage or hostile frame of mind," intending to attack, he walks stiffly upright, with ears pricked forward, bristling hairs, tail erect, head high, and eyes fixed and staring (Figure 5). The posture and movements are in line with the dog's *intention* (to attack) and are therefore of service. But when he shows friendliness to his master or another dog, his body sinks or crouches and undergoes flexuous movements, his tail is lowered and wags, his hair becomes smooth, his ears are held backwards, and his eyes are elongated rather than round and staring. According to Darwin, none of these movements serves any useful purpose other than the revealing of the intention to be friendly by turning aggressive movements into their opposite. Similarly, in man, shrugging the shoulders and turning the palms outward and upward indicates helplessness, resignation, patience, or indifference because it is the antithesis of the posture of resistance with head high, shoulders square, chest expanded, and hands clenched.

3. *The Principle of Actions Due to the Constitution of the Nervous System* states that, in moods of high emotional intensity, nervous excitation is conducted

to various parts of the body producing effects independent of will or purpose (like the tears of grief or laughter) which are quite expressive though they serve no useful purpose.

Besides describing the wealth of minute observations from which he inductively drew these principles, Darwin wanted to determine which human expressive movements were innate and universal (genetically transmitted), and which were acquired through learning and, therefore, specific to a given culture. Thus, he formulated an empirical problem that has not been resolved for lack of systematic study. In addition, he made a conceptual distinction that he failed to state explicitly, namely, the contrast between expressive movements and useful movements. The distinction makes expressive movements a residual category: everything that can't be described as "serviceable" or directed toward coping with an external, adaptive problem. Such a contrast would no longer be posited by Darwin's present-day followers. For example, Lorenz (1966) shows how modified threat gestures, such as those which occur in the apparently "useless" and highly ritualized "triumph ceremony" among Greylag geese, actually serve to displace aggression between members of the same goose family to outsiders, thus strengthening the bond of attachment within the family. But the distinction survives in the current terminology of social science which discriminates between *instrumental* (goal-directed) and *expressive* (emotional) behavior.

The ethologists and comparative biologists, who have continued Darwin's line of investigation into the modern era, have placed the interest in the function of expressive movement among various species of animals squarely within the context of "communication" and "social interaction." The origin, adaptive significance, and survival value for a given species of particular movements are still under inquiry. But, two new presuppositions have been added to the inquiry: (1) that the function of the movements is to transmit communication between members of same or different species; (2) that the function of communication is to maintain the social organization of animals in good working order. These presuppositions lead directly to the study of three sets of relationships: (1) the connection between specific mutual patterns of movement and specific activities —for example, threat patterns as a preparation for fighting or courtship patterns as a preparation for mating; (2) the function of specific activities, such as fighting and mating, in the maintenance of the social organization (hence, the survival) of the group; (3) the connection between specific movement patterns and the internal drives that produce the movements—for example, grass-pulling among gulls, a "displaced" threat activity, produced by simultaneously evoked drives to attack and to escape. (Tinbergen, 1953.)

In the language of the ethologists, drives are "released" by patterns of visual stimuli—the coloring, configuration, and movements of the body. Among these stimulus patterns (or communications), two classes require attention here:

patterns of *display* and *intention movements*. It is significant that, in the etho-logical vocabulary, the word "expression" no longer appears. Its place is taken by specification of the internal drives (innate action patterns) that are released, the stimuli that release them, and the behaviors (movements, displays) that are activated by the internal drive through an intervening neural mechanism. *Displays*, such as the vertical threat posture of the male stickleback, signal an impending attack but are not themselves part of the movement of the attack. *Intention movements*, such as the threat posture of the gull (slight elevations and extension of the wings), are themselves part of an attack movement which will (perhaps) be initiated; wings are used in beating off opponents. In both cases, whether display or intention movement, the behavior functions like an advertise-ment of things to come, here called *presentation behavior*.

The variant of the original paradigm which emerges from this approach is more complex because it describes an interaction system rather than an isolated organism. The formula now reads: $\underset{A}{I \rightarrow S \rightarrow E} = \underset{B}{I \rightarrow S \rightarrow E} = \underset{A}{I \rightarrow S \rightarrow E}$. The internal drive (S) of animal $A$ gives rise to a display or an intention movement (E) which becomes a stimulus pattern (I) for animal $B$ evoking in it the internal drive (S) which leads to a responsive display or intention movement in animal $B$, which is perceived as the stimulus pattern (I) by animal $A$. Then the process begins a new round. In other words, the process $I \rightarrow S \rightarrow E$ (interpretation to internal state to expressive behavior) in animal $A$ is understood or decoded (by a human observer) by means of the observed process ($I \rightarrow S \rightarrow E$) of response in animal $B$, plus the response to $B's$ behavior in animal $A$. The forward movement of the reciprocal behaviors through time must be assessed by the human observer and placed in some activity series, such as threat and fighting, or courtship and mating. What was previously obscure or implicit is now clear and explicit: There are two systems of coding that must be accounted for, one within the animal participants to the encounter, another within the human observer who classifies the interaction as an example of threat behavior or courtship behavior. Because they are so aware of the double coding problem, the ethologists make great efforts to put aside their own impressions of what the animal may be responding to and take considerable pains to determine by experimentation precisely which elements in the stimulus pattern emitted by animal $A$ animal $B$ is in fact responding to.

The question of a stimulus pattern specificity arises in the field of art history and criticism.[5] This field is broad, its subject matter extending over many topics in vast expanses of time and place, and its vocabulary and traditions incom-mensurate with those so far considered. Yet art historians have examined the details of the human body represented in painting, sculpture, and design with the minute attention to form and movement characteristic of the comparative biologist studying courtship or threat displays. There, the explicit resemblance ends. For in discussing the multiple processing and coding through which the *impression* made by the art object is conveyed, the historian customarily passes freely back and forth between the intention and interests of the individual artist, the techniques available to him, the expressive concepts native to his historical era and particular culture, the conceptual traditions of the past which have influenced him, and the interpretive concepts of the historian himself.

Whether the human body is presented in the round, in relief, or in painting, the choice of attitude or posture is limited by the subject being represented, by the technical means at the disposal of the artist, and by the canons of proportion —the esthetic code—established within particular cultural areas and traditions. Technique and its relation to the artist's capacity to copy nature will not be considered here, since the "representation" issue is too complex.[6] More to the point of this study is the extraordinarily limited repertoire of body postures and movements that artists have chosen to present for viewing. This is apparently because of esthetic considerations, since body positions are arranged in order to display a balance of forces and of lines and planes. Some of the restriction of the repertoire arises from a limitation of subject matter; in any cultural or historical period, only a few themes from the immense range of human activity have been considered worthy of representation. However, even with allowances made for such limitation, the selectivity and control applied to the portrayal of the body suggests that there are factors operating behind the scene that cannot be subsumed under the simple topic, "expression."

What these factors might consist of can perhaps most easily be discerned through examining the portrayal of the nude figure in Western art. This is an excellent subject for the purpose. The absence of clothing requires the observer to form his impression of what is being "expressed" without the help of the standard contextual cues for time, social occasion, and purpose that costume provides. The interpretation, therefore, is highly dependent upon the exact arrangement of the body, either by itself or in relation to another figure. Furthermore, the engagement of the eye by the unclothed body forces the observer to recognize that his response is based partly on aroused erotic feelings, with all the private, personal, and idiosyncratic associations his past experience has provided him with, and partly on a public construction—a socially learned concept—of what the nude figure is doing and what its body position signifies. Finally, a nude figure, precisely because it can only suggest movement or repose, or some transition between the two, forces the observer to examine his own construction; his interpretation is obviously just that—an interpretation with no more status in "reality" than any other type of hypothesis. The figure will not "come alive" or complete its action and prove that it is about to get up or sit down, embrace or repulse. Its intentions remain relatively inscrutable, but its

**Fig. 6.** Botticelli: *The Birth of Venus*

*intention movements* are there to be interpreted. Thus, the question of how one forms one's impression, how one learns to interpret, is an open one. And it is just at this point that the artist, the art historian, the behavioral scientist, and the viewing subject can collaborate.

From the art historian, one learns of the almost incredible amount of visual and presentational transaction between artists and viewing publics which has been incorporated in a given posture or body position. For example, the original position of the female nude figure used for testing in Chapter 10 was taken from Botticelli's well-known painting, *The Birth of Venus* (Figure 6). But the posture of Botticelli's Venus was drawn, with some alteration along Gothic lines, from a copy of a Hellenistic Aphrodite, perhaps the Medici Venus (Figure 7). And this Hellenistic Aphrodite, just emerging from or entering her ritual bath, was derived from a much earlier model—the Knidian Aphrodite of Praxiteles (Figure 8). (Clark, 1959, Chapter 3.)

Similarly, the seated picnicking figures in Manet's *Déjeuner Sur L'Herbe*

**Fig. 7.**   *The Medici Venus*

**Fig. 8.** Praxiteles: *The Knidian Aphrodite*

**Fig. 9.** Manet: *Le Déjeuner sur l'Herbe*

(Figure 9), used in the exploratory studies reported in Chapter 9, are related to the figures seated in the open air in Giorgione's *Concert Champêtre* (Figure 10).[7] More particularly, the arrangements of the nude and clothed figures in the Manet painting derive from a Marcantonio engraving (Figure 11) that is a copy of Raphael's lost *Judgment of Paris*. (Clark, 1959, Chapter 9.) In the lower right quadrant of this picture there are three seated nude figures, two men and a woman, presumably river gods, conducting the casually intimate and contradictory conversation of heads, arms, and legs that Manet recaptured in his painting. But, it seems, Raphael took this arrangement of idly interacting, seated

**Fig. 10.** Giorgione: *Concert Champêtre*

figures almost literally from a portion of a frieze on a Roman sarcophagus (then, as now, incorporated into the garden façade of the Villa Medici in Rome) depicting *The Judgment of Paris* (Figure 12). (Vermeule, 1964.) From the Roman era through the Italian Renaissance to French Impressionism, the two males have been chatting with each other and ignoring the naked charms of the female with the upper parts of their bodies, while (perhaps) conducting a flirtation of legs with her.

What does tracing the history of the posture reveal? Essentially, how much communication and social learning has taken place among artists (and between artist and viewer) in the process of arranging a form of the body that can be placed in a context appropriate to the decoding of its message.[8] In the case of

**Fig. 11.**  Marcantonio: *The Judgment of Paris*

the Venus figure, a whole series of artists has attempted to capture that moment between repose and action, between self-concealment and self-display, and between narcissistic self-involvement and latent interest in others when, because she is most off-guard, the goddess is most accessible to erotic scanning.

Of course, other messages appropriate to a variety of contexts are connected with the covered–uncovered posture of the Venus figure: the ritual relation between the Aphrodite and the water from which she was born, her renowned beauty and power over gods and men, and the interest of classical Greece in the concept of the ideal—of perfection. Obviously, the relation between the presented body posture and the viewer cannot be reduced to the simple notion of an expression of some inner state. The position of the body and its intention movements can be better described as a vast collection of messages, some concerned with the inner state and the needs of the subject, others with her immediate physical situation and with actions which she is about to carry out, still others with responses anticipated from the viewer. To attempt to put all these messages into words and to disentangle them from each other is extremely

**Fig. 12.**  *The Judgment of Paris*

difficult, not only because of their complexity but also because concepts for decoding the messages of the body itself are still lacking.

If this description is correct, then it is clear that $S \rightarrow E \rightarrow I$ does not take into account the range and distribution of the messages transmitted in the visual situation, and will not be a useful formula. Instead, a formula of sufficient scope is needed to take account of the extraordinary array of messages transmitted by the body, ranging from the wishes, moods, and intentions of the subject through the stylized constraints imposed on body movement during different historical epochs in connection with different media of communication, to the anticipation of the moods, wishes, intentions, and fantasies aroused in the viewer.

And central to the formula must be the patterning of the body itself—its formal or morphological structure.

Fortunately, the philosophy of esthetics—or, at least, some of its exponents —can help with this problem. In a book that deals primarily with logic and meaning in the plastic arts and music, Susanne K. Langer has proposed a distinction between discursive and presentational forms, which differentiates between the kind of communication conveyed by a language from that conveyed by visual structures. (Langer, 1942.) Language is defined as a discursive symbolic structure dependent on a temporal order: one word at a time, one idea at a time. Language operates with a fixed vocabulary and syntax, with units that have independent meanings no matter how modified by context. A non-discursive (presentational) symbolic structure, according to Langer, while equally logical and meaningful, operates in a totally different way. A visual presentation of a house or a person, for example, provides all of its information at once rather than in bits strung out over time. There is no apparent way of breaking down the stimulus into units that can be correlated with stable concepts such as the words of a linguisic utterance. Its meaning resides in its form—the patterned configuration of part to whole. The absence of something abstracted from the form to convey or mediate meaning, as words to do in discursive formulations, insures that the meaning is directly present in the immediate experience. At the same time, the absence of discrete mediators of the information makes it somewhat difficult to say, with precision, what that meaning is.

Although Langer's distinction between discursive and presentational symbolization has been much criticized [9] because of its incompleteness and the difficulty of submitting it to detailed analysis and application, nevertheless it seems a useful beginning because of its principal claims that: (1) visual forms convey logical meanings in a different way than linguistic forms—that is, their information is differently coded; and (2) they have a different function within a system of communication, operating not with respect to the precise denotations of words but with "expressive" functions. Despite the novelty and persuasiveness of her approach, Langer finds it no easier than others to put into words exactly what it is that presentational (visual) forms express.

The word *expression* is based upon too many presuppositions. It supplies not one precise denotation but a range of inconsistent and contradictory possibilities. For example, "to express" can mean "to signify" a particular or general meaning by a representation of any sort. In this sense, "to express" means the same thing as "to represent"—that is, to convey a meaning. Yet, there are many contexts, particularly in the history of art and of esthetics, where "representation" is contrasted with "expression." In such a codification, "representation" refers to the replication of real objects in the physical world; "expression," to nuances of style and feeling in the way the artist goes about representing things—

e.g., in a rough-and-ready way or with precision, calmly or dramatically. From this meaning, it is only a step to the idea of "self-expression," which sharpens the contrast between inner and outer, personal and public. A further step elaborates this opposition between subjective and objective as the difference between emotional attitude and information content. Expressive speech or words are said to convey emotion in contrast to the semantic or syntactic aspects of words and speech which are said to impart meaning. Again, one ends up with the antithesis in sociology between "instrumental" (problem-solving) and "expressive" (affective) behavior and, in psychology, with the contrast between "cognition" and "emotion."

Obviously, a word that refers to such contradictory processes ought to be either abolished, kept in the museum of "antithetical words" (that signify both themselves and their opposites),[10] or restricted to one of its meanings. Presumably, it could be made to signify any system of coding whereby meaning in one medium of communication is translated into another,[11] or, if another word is used for this purpose, "expressive" could be confined to the contrast between emotional and cognitive communication. Yet, where body communication is concerned, contrast between emotion and cognition is not sharp. Even the physiognomic distinction between instrumental and expressive behavior, which at times seems quite clear, weakens under close scrutiny. Nowhere is the unreliability of this distinction more evident than in the examination of acting on the stage. How does the actor "express," "represent," or "project" character to the audience?

For this little understood aspect of body communication, Constantin Stanislavski, Director of the Moscow Art Theater and the originator of "method acting" may be considered an authority. His book describing his "system" for attaining truthfulness or lifelikeness on the stage through employing the imagination emphasizes the "art" of acting. (Stanislavski, 1936.) But the approach is mainly analytic and programmatic. The stage is seen as a behavioral science laboratory where the actor can systematically conduct research into the psychological, social, and cultural aspects of the personality he is creating. "The method" approaches craftmanship indirectly; its primary object is to study and to recreate the conditions under which a given form of behavior takes place. If the actor can reconstruct and hold in mind the manifold of internal and external conditions and contingencies bearing upon the situation of the character he is enacting, from moment to moment, the emotionally appropriate behavior —so the theory goes—will emerge, to a large degree in a spontaneous fashion. Vocabulary excepted, *The Actor Prepares* is an impressive demonstration of the principles of classical and operant conditioning. Perhaps it is not immaterial that Pavlov and Stanislavski were contemporaries in time and place.

But what is exceptional in Stanislavski is the conceptualization—the cognitive apparatus—he invented to classify the various contingencies applicable to the actor's situation. He was able to show how the reinforcements that elicited and fixed mood, motive, and action could be discovered if one searched in the appropriate category for the necessary clues.

Anyone who has acted on stage, and most people who have not, know that emotional and instrumental behavior go hand in hand. They are two aspects of the same general movement. A door can be closed angrily, carelessly, calmly, firmly, or tentatively. In each case, the pattern of movement is slightly different, as are the sound effects. Stanislavski pointed out that the movements could be executed on two different bases. The actor could deliberately copy or imitate the movements he had seen others perform when presumably angry, calm, etc. This he called "representative acting." Or the actor could identify himself with the person he was enacting, feeling himself imaginatively into his situation. In this case, both the instrumental and emotional aspects of movement (and, of course, voice and articulation) would occur naturally in the way anyone might behave under identical circumstances of physique, background, current contingencies, and future prospects. The second basis was Stanislavski's preferred "method," although he acknowledged that imitation of a model always had some part in creating the role.

But what Stanislavski called the "creative imagination," by means of which the actor can feel himself into the circumstances of his character, is not something that can be summoned by command or by an act of will. It has to be programmed, and Stanislavski specified how the programming takes place.

> Can one sit in a chair and for no reason at all be jealous? Or all stirred up? Or sad? Of course, it is impossible. On the stage there cannot be, under any circumstances, action which is directed immediately at the arousing of feeling for its own sake. To ignore this results only in the most disgusting artificiality. When you are choosing some bit of action, leave feeling and spiritual content alone. Never seek to be jealous, or to make love, or to suffer for its own sake. All such feelings are the results of something that has gone before. Of the thing that has gone before, you should think as hard as you can. As for the result, it will produce itself. (Stanislavski, 1936, p. 38.)

To choose "some bit of action" on the basis of what has gone before is only part of the program. Stanislavski also demonstrated how the "bit of action" must fit into what is to come, both in the near and far future. The program, constructed in the mind, and perfectly capable of being explicated, move by move, fits together serial bits of action logically related within a time–circumstance sequence. Units in this sequence and goals—the ends toward which the action moves—can also be described. Unfortunately, Stanislavski was not clear about his method for demarcating units and goals. And this remains incompletely resolved in this study, despite struggles with the problem and, perhaps, some progress.

Even without a precise formula for defining units, it is clear that both the "instrumental" and "expressive" aspects of behavior arise from the sequence of events. The impulses to action, as Stanislavski pointed out, originate in the unconscious and present themselves to the consciousness of the actor. (Stanislavski, 1936, pp. 46–49.) It is then his task to use his critical judgment in deciding whether to present them to his fellow actors and thus to the audience. But the behavior to be presented is related to the sequence. This is the key to the definition of *presentation behavior* as it will be used here. The significance of the *presentation* is that it connects what has gone before with what will follow. The problem in the understanding of body movement and communication is how these connections are established—how the presentations contrast with each other and gear into each other—and how the "meaning" of each presentation is logically related to each sequence as well as to the overall patterning or arrangement of sequences.

# NOTES FOR CHAPTER 1

[1] The use of the anatomical–diagnostic approach, based on a medical analogy, has an ancient and honorable tradition. Machiavelli used the medical analogy to describe the diseases of the body politic, and the Renaissance, in general, gave rise to a number of other "diagnostic" versions of technical problems. For example, in entering his proposal for the construction of the tower of the Cathedral at Milan, Leonardo da Vinci wrote, "You know that medicines when well used restore health to the sick, and he who knows them well will use them well when he also knows what man is, and what life and constitution are, and what health is. . . . In just the same way, a cathedral in need of repair requires a doctor–architect who understands well what a building is, on what rules the correct method of construction is based, whence these rules are derived, into how many parts they are divided, and what the causes are that hold the structure together and make it permanent. . . ." (MacCurdy, 1956.)

[2] "To conclude, we cannot doubt the fact that bodily constitution and temperament have some close relationship. They are paired raw materials from which we fashion in part our personalities through learning." (Allport, 1961.)

[3] Actually, in the case of Sheldon, there is little to quarrel with since the principle of isomorphism has broken down of its own accord in his system. In his final systemization (*Atlas of Men*), he has postulated, by empirical sorting of measurement, 88 different combinations of the various degrees of the three somatotypes. These combinations are said to be correlated with 88 different assortments of temperament. In the *Atlas*, each variety of temperament is designated by references to an animal such as "Big Cat," "Little Cat," "Polar Bear," or "Hippopotamus" which, roughly, combines a type of body with a type of behavior. The animal totems are of some help but, in fact, no one can hold in mind 88 different combinations of

somatotypes with temperaments. Accordingly, the system cannot easily be used for making direct translations from S to I.

[4] The three principles are concisely stated in the first chapter and are then profusely illustrated in the rest of the book. For a new edition, with an introduction by Margaret Mead and illustrations of the work of contemporary anthropologists and ethologists interested in expressive movement, see Darwin, Charles (1955).

[5] Although we have consulted a variety of sources, the authors upon whom we have placed the greatest reliance are Sir Kenneth Clark (1959) and Ernest H. Gombrich (1960).

[6] Gombrich (1960, Part One: "The Limits of Likeness") convincingly demonstrates how, in every cultural era, the artist does not literally copy nature but transcribes it by means of a changing system of notation—a code which must be constantly learned afresh by the viewing public. We shall discuss this process further in Chapter 3 under the phrase "The Representative Transformation." For a more sociological approach to this topic, see Kavolis (1968).

[7] This painting has been traditionally attributed to Giorgione. As a result of recent studies, art historians now tend to attribute the picture to the young Titian. However, since it is best known as a work of Giorgione's, we have let the traditional attribution stand.

[8] Mutual influences of an intellectual kind—agreements and disagreements—between artists of the same and different eras have been well documented by contemporary art historians. It is only recently, however, that sociologists and social psychologists interested in the topic of social change have begun to study the mutual influences between artists and their publics— consumers, dealers, critics, official institutions, and the schools in which the young artist is trained. For examples, see the studies of Geraldine Pelles (1963) and of Harrison C. and A. Cynthia White (1964, 1965).

[9] For a review of the general area of expressiveness and style from the viewpoint of theories of esthetic criticism, see Beardsley (1958).

[10] For example, "cleave" (hold on to or split asunder), "let" (obstruct or give way), and "fetch" (send away or bring around).

[11] This usage will be further explored in Chapter 3.

# 2. Stylized Movement:
## THE DANCE

Such forms of stylized movement as the dance and mime, which have undergone an historical process of conventionalized representation, would, one supposes, be useful places to study the relation between expression and interpretation. Their long connection with the theater and the arts promises a body of critical writings about what is expressed and how it is expressed. Their status as art forms guarantees that they are concerned with the projection of meaning and significance as well as with providing entertainment.[1]

But an inspection of the writings on dance and mime has not proved very helpful. The situation has changed little since 1712 when John Weaver—one of the principal dancers and choreographers of the early eighteenth century—wrote in his *Essay Toward a History of Dancing,*

> 'tis a subject scarce ever before fully discussed in any language, that I know of: For while other Arts, and Sciences, have found learned Patrons to rec-ommend them to the World, by showing their Excellence, Use, and An-tiquity; *Dancing* alone has been generally neglected, or superficially handled by most Authors; being thought perhaps too mean a Subject for the in-genious Labours of Men of Letters. . . . (Weaver, 1712.)

Before Weaver, the only extensive writings on dance had been those of Lucian (1905) for the ancient world, and of Arbeau (1925) for dance forms of the sixteenth and seventeenth centuries. Today, the literature of the dance is vo-luminous but it is still seldom characterized by "the ingenious Labours of Men of Letters." Dance and mime have not attained the scholarly status of the Fine Arts, poetry, and drama, nor have they accumulated a tradition of com-parative analysis or a serviceable set of concepts for discussing what is com-municated by one versus another dance form or dance performance.[2]

The question of communication through dance movements has been approached from two directions. The first is *technique;* that is, the precise nature of the movements characteristic of one versus another style, say of classical ballet in contrast to modern dance. The second is *significance;* that is, what limited aspects of the human experience can be effectively dealt with in one style but not in another. Both approaches are necessary, but neither separately nor together are they sufficient. Discussions of technique in the dance literature are of restricted value, because the movements have to be visualized to be understood. Mere verbal labeling of steps, poses, and sequences fails to grapple with the psychological content of dance forms. It cannot put into words what the dancer "projects" to the audience. But, while the literature of technique is too narrow, discussions of significance are usually too broad to attain specificity with respect to what is being communicated by a particular dance style.

The occupational inarticulateness of dancers and choreographers is often blamed for the lack of a useful dance literature. This "tongue-tied" state of affairs may hold true for some dancers. Nijinsky, for example, is said to have been almost incapable of telling the dancers what he wished them to do when he was choreographing *L'Après-midi d'un Faune*.[3] But there are many dancers and choreographers who have tried to put their experience with the dance into words, and their writings clearly reveal their sensitive perceptions. The publications of dance critics and historians are also available.

Still, there is an enormous gap between what is presented visually on stage and its verbal description. If literary facility is not at fault, the trouble must lie elsewhere. The writings often tend toward poetic imagery and romantic generalization, strongly seasoned with social uplift. Lincoln Kirstein, a vigorous entrepreneur and critic of the dance, remarks, for example, that "a dancer actively released in his legible freedom, springing into space, is as satisfactory a witness to the irrepressible and indomitable instinct to human liberty as anyone can find." (Kirstein, 1941.) Isadora Duncan, the great innovator of modern dance, expressed herself in similarly expansive figures of speech:

> There are those who subconsciously hear with their soul some melody of another world, and are able to express this in terms comprehensible and joyous to human ears. . . . Imagine then a dancer who, after long study, prayer and inspiration, has attained such a degree of understanding that his body is simply the luminous manifestation of his soul; whose body dances in accordance with the music heard inwardly, in an expression out of another, a profounder world. This is the truly creative dancer, natural but not imitative, speaking in a movement out of himself and out of something greater than ourselves. (Duncan, 1965.)

One can grasp what she was trying to say: that good dancing is guided by a creative impulse which seeks, beyond the contemporary canons of technique, to exploit the natural capacity of the body to move in infinitely varied ways and to correlate such patterns of movement with psychological content. The reference to "music heard inwardly" and to movement arising "out of something greater than ourselves" probably has to do with the function of unconscious fantasy in the generation of the creative ideas.

Stanislavski, the logician of the theater, noted her rhapsodic way of talking during a visit to Moscow:

> Duncan does not know how to speak of her art logically and systematically. Her ideas come to her by accident, as a result of the most unexpected everyday facts. For instance, when she was asked who taught her to dance, she answered: "Terpsichore. I danced from the moment I learned to stand on my feet. I have danced all my life. Man, all humanity, the world, must dance. This was, and always will be. It is in vain that people interfere with this and do not want to understand a natural need given to us by nature. *Et voilà tout*," she finished in her inimitable Franco-American dialect. (Stanislavski, 1965.)

Isadora Duncan's kind of luminous, gauzy, non-specific talk about what the dancer is trying to do continues to this day.

But the first dancer to write extensively on the topic was reasonable, straightforward, and specific. John Weaver, the originator of the "ballet d'action," wrote:

> Stage-Dancing was at first designed for *Imitation*; to explain Things conceived in the Mind, by *Gestures and Motions* of the Body, and plainly and intelligibly representing *Actions, Manners,* and *Passions*; so that the Spectator might perfectly understand the Performer by these his *Motions*, tho' he say not a word. Thus far the excellence of the *Art* appears; but its Beauties consist in the regulated Motion of all parts, by forming the Body, Head, Arms, and Feet, into such *Positions, Gestures,* and *Movements*, as represent the aforesaid *Passions, Manners,* and *Actions* . . . so that the Spectator will not only be pleased and diverted with the Beauty of the *Performance* but will also be instructed so as to judge of the *Design* of the performer. And, without the help of an Interpreter, a Spectator shall at a distance, by the lively representation of a just Character, be capable of understanding the *Subject* of the Story represented, and be able to distinguish the several *Passions, Manners,* and *Actions*; as of *Love, Anger,* and the like. (Weaver, 1712.)

Though much of what Weaver referred to lay in the realm of mime rather than true dancing, his words are practical and concrete.

Intoxication with the glowing language of art and esthetics set in at the dawn of the Romantic era. In 1760, Noverre, one of the great systematizers of French ballet, published a series of Letters on Ballet and Dancing, the first of which begins "Poetry, painting, and dancing, Sir, are, or should be, no other than a faithful likeness of beautiful nature." (Noverre, 1930.) The equating of dancing with poetry and painting was brought to a fuller development a hundred years later in the writings of Bournonville, the Danish ballet master who had been trained in France:

> Dancing is a fine art because it puts forward an ideal, not only of plastic beauty, but of lyric and dramatic expression. The beauty which it seeks to achieve is founded not on vague principles of fashion or fancy, but on firm natural laws. . . . The aim of art in general and of the theater in particular is to uplift the soul and to invigorate the spirit. . . . Dancing can, with the help of music, rise to the heights of poetry. Equally it can sink to circus tricks through excess of acrobatics. (Bournonville, 1861.)

A contemporary example of this artistic vocabulary is provided by Alwin Nikolais, a leading choreographer of the "abstract" modern style and a composer of "electronic music."

> The early modern dance explored the psyche. Its concepts involved man's concern with the joys and pains of self-discovery. The idea was poetically translated into a kinetic language enacted by the dance character through whom a moment of psychological drama transpired. In the new art, the dance character is no longer dominant. The new dance figure is significant more in its instrumental sensitivity and capacity to speak directly in terms of motion, shape, time, and space. It is the poetry of these elements, speaking directly out of themselves and their interrelationships rather than through a dominant character. The character may be present, but if it is, it is in equilibrium with the aggregate of all the elements in operation. . . . The choreographer of the new period of modern dance is concerned with basic and legitimate elements, and is imbued with an urgency of pursuing the fleeting banshee of the moment of art according to the dictates of his individual vision. (Nikolais, 1966.)

This assessment provides a vague idea of the difference between the earlier "psychological" modern dance and its contemporary "abstract" form.[4] But appeals to the poetry of the elements of motion, shape, time, and space and to the "aesthetic semantics of the event itself" do not materially forward the discussion. Since such expressions are, at best, a shorthand for an immense and unmapped subject matter, they tend to obscure the author's otherwise helpful concern with meaning.

Movement can be transferred to paper in several ways: through detailed, specific literary description; through classification and labeling as in ballet; or through graphic notation. If one understands the context of the movement thoroughly, its significance can be determined most readily from a detailed, non-technical description. One of the most delightful examples of non-technical description was provided by the late James Agee in his essay on the silent screen comedians:

> When a modern comedian gets hit on the head, for example, the most he is apt to do is look sleepy. When a silent comedian got hit on the head, he seldom let it go so flatly. He realized a broad license, and a ruthless discipline within that license. It was his business to be as funny as possible physically, without the help or hindrance of words. So he gave us a figure of speech, or rather of vision, for loss of consciousness. In other words, he gave us a poem, a kind of poem, moreover, that everybody understands. The least he might do was straighten up as stiff as a plank and fall over backwards with such skill that his whole length seemed to slap the floor at the same instant. Or he might make a cadenza of it—look vague, smile like an angel, roll up his eyes, lace his fingers, thrust his hands palm downwards as far as they would go, hunch his shoulders, rise on tiptoe, prance ecstatically in narrowing circles until, with tallow knees, he sank down the vortex of his dizziness to the floor, and there signified nirvana by kicking his heels twice, like a swimming frog. (Agee, 1964.)

In this passage, specific details of movement, clocked off seriatim, allow the reader to visualize the initial upward movement, akin to flight, the middle sequence of downward spiraling, and the final horizontal spasms, all phases of transition balanced within a harmonious episode. Furthermore, the description beautifully traces that triumph of make-believe over reality which transforms pain into pleasure, injury into beneficence, and ugliness into grace. The minimization of pathos and its conversion into happiness results in the saving of emotional energy which Freud called the essence of humor.

Although such pure description has the power to evoke the actual experience of movement, it cannot deal efficiently with comparison and analysis. In capturing the phenomenon, it misses the opportunity to abbreviate and schematize necessary to a survey of the meaning of different forms of dance, or of performances of the same dance by different dancers. Such an aim cannot be accomplished without inventing categories of movement fitted out with suitable labels.

But the categories tend to grow too large and empty or too narrow and dispersed to represent much that is lifelike or real about the phenomenon. The experience of dance is too complex, the motor aspects too intricate, the significance too intangible, and the visual effect too dazzling to be submitted to piecemeal dissection. No matter how inventive the conceptualization, nor how evolved from a particular dancer's method and theory, classification seems to defy ordering and reassembly into a reasonable reference to the phenomenon. One can only hope for the emergence of someone who will do for dancing what Stanislavski did for acting; who will conceptualize and systematize how the dancer or choreographer organizes himself so as to create and project the spontaneity of his dance and its truthfulness to his original vision of movement.

Meanwhile, one can at least examine the nature of the problem with which categorization must deal. The principal difficulty arises from the complexity of context in which any dance movement is set, which seems to demand that the whole be broken into parts. In the literature of dance, the breakdown is accomplished in different ways in various treatises but has never been formally codified. A thorough codification would need to consider eleven interrelated factors, each of which could be expanded into hosts of subcategories and sub-subcategories.

1. *The characteristics of the body.* This would include the range of possible movements, physique, age and sex differences, the conversion of energy or strength into the appearance of force or lightness, the function of breathing both for the conservation of energy and for the projection of mood, timing and control, relaxation, and tension.

2. *The characteristics of gesture.* Gesture arises in four contexts: physical reflexes (the hiccup); emotional responses (shrinking inward in grief); conventional signals (the salute or hand-shake); and movements associated with activities (walking, running, etc.). With certain purely ornamental exceptions, posturing and posing can be treated as either preparation for, interruption of, or completion of one or another activity. In dance, gesture from any source is stylized in accordance with particular dance traditions and choreographic aims. At the same time, and to varying degrees, the gestures are "abstracted" from their original, everyday functions by means of a reorientation of their goal structures. For example, jumping and leaping are not performed merely to overcome physical obstacles or to win competitions, but to establish a character, exemplify a phrase of music, or to serve as part of the architectural composition of the dance group.

3. *The rules of dance style.* If the rules of a particular dance style are made explicit, they then determine which movements are permitted, which are required, and which are excluded from that style. Each rule within a style can be regarded as a set of instructions for the movements of parts of the body or the body as a whole. Classical ballet made considerable progress in standardizing such instructions.[5] In modern dance, correlated as it is with the continuing revolution against classical ballet and with the perpetual change of our times, rules of style are not standardized. A dancer may add a form of movement to what is often called "the vocabulary of dance." But no one is required to execute such movements in order to qualify as a modern dancer, and students are urged to develop their

own styles. Nevertheless, each of these forms of movement can be translated into words as a set of instructions.

Each "pure" style (syntheses of different styles will not be discussed here) contains certain social–psychological possibilities of movement not contained in another style. The elegance and precision of classical ballet, for example, tend to rule out a realistic presentation of contemporary social problems and psychological attitudes in favor of romanticized good-and-evil and comic possibilities. Modern ballet and dance allow for more concern with contemporary problems.

4. *The cultural frame for the style.* Treatises on dance usually distinguish between ballet, modern dance, and "ethnic" or "folk" styles. This classification does injustice to the history, traditions, and cultures of parts of the world other than Europe and the non-indigenous cultures of America. A more transcultural viewpoint would examine the functions of dance within each cultural tradition and formulate categories for cross-cultural comparisons. The correlation of style with socio-economic, race, or other subgroup conflict within the culture would place the style within its historical or dialectical frame. Thus the problems of both "meaning" and "communication" attached to social–psychological factors would emerge in plainer focus.

5. *The correlation of music with dance.* At times, music has been merely incidental accompaniment to the dance. At other times, the music has been dominant, with dance seeking to interpret it. In still other phases, music and dance have been composed together to supplement each other. But the problem of categorization of the two in parallel has hardly been approached. As suitable categories of musical and movement patterns are constructed, the explicit basis of complementarity between music and dance may become clear.

6. *The characteristics of rhythmic movement.* Some dances occur without music, but they always have rhythm. That rhythm is a part of the stylization of movement and occurs quite outside of dance, for example, in "eurhythmics" and calisthenics. Rhythmic movement is the only ground on which the inner correlation of music and dance is explicitly apparent, though it may not be the most significant element in the relationship between music and dance.

Ruth St. Denis, pioneer of modern dance, spoke of freeing dance from "the bondage of the drum." (St. Denis, 1941.) One can understand her stress on "the spiritual" element toward which contemporary dance strives as increasing the distance between the inner rhythm of the music and that of the dance. The separation between movement rhythm and the rhythm of music is always apparent to dancers: The music occurs in one set of beats, so many to the bar; the dance occurs in another set, so many to the phrase of movement. The counting of beats, which is so obsessive a part of the dancer's routine, is oriented to the phrase of movement but it must be correlated with the set time pattern of the music, if only to be in opposition rather than in harmony with it.

It is easy to think of timing as so simple on the cognitive level and so intricate on the neurophysiological level as to be mainly a "physical" matter. Exotic rhythms, from the Orient and from Africa for example, dispute this view. The cognitive programs necessary to an adequate account of the timing of music and of movement have not yet been developed. This would permit understanding of why some rhythmic patterns are martial, some are erotically seductive, some are virile, and some are mincing.[6]

7. *The characteristics of the stage setting.* The special features of any stage setting in which dance occurs are elements to which style and movement must be adapted. The geography of the stage, its position vis-à-vis the viewer, its environment, its scenic design, and its lighting all form separate subcategories impinging on what the dance communicates.

8. *The dancing group.* Dance can be performed by one person, by two persons, or by groups of three or more, arranged in small clusters or massed in chorus formation. Each increment of size imposes a different set of constraints on the architectonic design of movements and poses. The geometrical designs create their own space on stage, shaping it and conditioning the possibilities of further movements. The various forms in which choreographic space is shaped and the transitions from one to another form are guided, on the one hand, by considerations of balance and symmetry, on the other by the social and psychological correlates of the form. A semicircle of still figures all facing a single figure executing a solo dance embraces a different set of psychological possibilities from a single dancer entering one side of a stage toward a cluster of immobile figures facing away from him on the other. Subclassification of such permutations and combinations is necessary.

9. *The costume of the dancer.* How the dancer is dressed and made up is guided by four considerations: (a) the influence of the costume on the freedom of movement; (b) the relation of the costume to the character represented; (c) the relation of the costume to the massed visual effect of principal and chorus and thus to the mood of the performance; (d) the relation of costume to the body images of dancers and audience. The last is the most subtle and influences all the others. The ideal body image one holds for oneself, or the worst body image, can be realized by the dancer. Such images of total body configuration —of how one presents oneself to a viewer—are, for the most part, held outside of conscious awareness; but they have a powerful effect on one's feeling of satisfaction with the self and with others. (Schilder, 1950.) Thus, the partly nude body of the dancer should to a large extent actualize the ideal image (for a particular culture) of most of the audience, unless some choreographic purpose is advanced by distorting its appearance. In addition, costume establishes the social and, thus, the physical, distance appropriate to the movement between dance figures.

10. *Characterization.* Costume, make-up, and body image are closely connected with the establishment of character and personality through dance movement. In some dance forms, the individual personality of a character is lightly delineated; in others, characterization is schematic—a hero, villain, or prince, devoid of personality, is presented; in still others, characterization plays no role in the performance at all. If characterization is to be developed, some degree of miming will probably invade the dance, adapted to the choreography.

11. *Scenario.* Dance presentations may be based on highly involved plots or none at all. Between these extremes, some performances establish the mood surrounding a generalized characterological type with only a hint of story line. Scenario is the most general of all the categories. All the others fit, like Chinese boxes, into each other, and into the overall packaged plot—the way the performance begins and ends because of what it has to tell to its audience.

The inventory of the major categories involved in the construction of dance as a performance is designed to aid in examining the systematic interrelations between the way dance is presented and the way it is perceived by an audience. Although one can learn something immediately vivid and phenomenological from a literary description of movement, the message is slipped into and out of awareness so rapidly that it defies analysis for the most part. This is not much of an improvement over simply watching a dance—an experience that usually results in enchantment rather than a firm intellectual grasp of the communication process.

Although the categories listed above to break down the performance into elements for examination do not represent a final solution to the problem of conceptualization, they can at least allow for dealing with variation. The categories are interdependent. If one varies, all the others will vary, though not to the same degree. Scenario, being the most general category, will determine the greatest amount of variation. Plot or mood will condition characterization, and thus costume, the dancing group, and so on. Costume will constrain style of movement but not to the same degree as scenario.

The goodness-of-fit between categories will have something to do with what is usually considered under "esthetics." For example, the flat, linear profile movements and erotic gestures that Nijinsky designed for the dancers in *L'Après-midi d'un Faune* fit beautifully into the scenario and characterization but badly into the cultural tradition of ballet to that point in its development. Following its opening performance in Paris, there was a violent controversy over its esthetic merits. Next morning, *Le Figaro* ran a front page editorial denouncing it: "Those who speak of art and poetry apropos of this spectacle make fun of us. . . . We have had a faun, incontinent, with vile movements of erotic bestiality and gestures of heavy shamelessness. That is all. . . ." (Calmette, 1912.) But immediately following the performance, Rodin, who had been working on a bust of Nijinsky, came up with tears in his eyes and embraced him, saying, "The fulfillment of my dreams. You brought it to life. Thanks." (Nijinsky, 1934, p. 174.)

Another aspect of variation flows from the manner in which the categories (and subcategories) function in controlled anticipation. Each category contains a program which the viewer expects to be unfolded as the performance moves along. The elements of the program—the subcategories—are usually unconscious. The programs specify what should be happening. A surprise or novelty is something not in the viewer's cognitive program for that particular category. Being unexpected, and thus unsanctioned, it is referred to that part of the mental apparatus which decides whether to accept or reject the unusual. Is it good or bad? Is it an addition to the performance or a fault in it? Such questions come up separately for each category, though in forming final judgments categories are weighed together. Are the gestures clearly defined? Do the costumes project a recognizable body image? Do the gestures with the costumes fit the characterization? If not, can one modify one's pre-existing programs so as to make them fit? If so, where should the change be instituted? In one's concept of style? Or of scenario?

Such questions are illustrative of the mental activity—it could even be called the creativity—that dance performance requires of the spectator. The pleasure of watching consists, in large part, of having one's anticipations confirmed or challenged. If this is the viewer's experience, then the choreographer's problem is to walk the delicate line between assaulting the expectations of the audience with too many novelties or lulling them with too much repetition. His success or failure often depends upon the category of expectations in which he chooses to make his changes felt.

It is quite possible that this process of creative participation on the part of the audience can be specified in greater detail. Dancers who are also choreographers often write about the internal dialogue that accompanies the beginning stages of a new composition. In the act of composing, the dancer seems to divide himself into three parts—sometimes more. There are the two (or more) characters who conduct the dialogue in conscious awareness, plus the part of the mind which listens to the dialogue and, like a third person, experiences first wonder or amazement at what is taking place and then the obligation to translate the conversation into movement.[7]

If this is the case for the dancer, then may not the viewer repeat this process within himself? May not his final participation in the performance occur by way of identification with the movements and roles of the dancers as the scenario unfolds? This would mean that after he completes a certain amount of correlation of the categories listed above, after he had established and accepted for himself the physique of the dancers, their style of movement, the cultural framework, the costumes and body image, etc., then he lets himself go along with the dialogue being conducted by the dancers, the messages accumulating preconsciously and too fast for labeling, but not too fast for enjoyment.

Over a century ago, Ralph Waldo Emerson made an interesting note in his journal after watching a performance of Fanny Elssler: "Her charm for the house is that she dances for them—or they dance for her, not being able to dance themselves. We must be expressed. Hence all the cheer and exhilaration which the spectacle imparts and the intimate property which each beholder feels in the dancer." (Emerson, 1841.) [8]

What is it within us that Emerson thought must be expressed? Certainly not the raw emotion of "catharsis" on the Aristotelian model. If the dancer dances for us because we cannot dance, then we must at least have some glimmer of a notion of what it would be like to dance, if only we had the opportunity and the training. We would then dance out our fantasies and present our own internal dialogue to a viewer. "Dancing out," analogously to "acting out," transforms a wish, a thought, or a mood into an interpersonal encounter and thus externally fixes and codifies what had previously been repressed or concealed within the person. Unlike "acting out," "dancing out" does not tempt the viewer to engage in reciprocal behavior, or does so only to a minor degree. Toes may tap, and limbs twitch as the viewer watches but he does not leap on stage nor join the dancer, unless specifically asked to do so.[9]

Dance consists of movements and behaviors which are not of the everyday world; and these behaviors are sanctioned under the protective covering of make-believe, which is the theater's guarantee that what is fantasy shall remain fantasy, and not be confused with actuality. The dance, then, is the link which separates and joins the fantasies and other internal processes of the choreographer-cum-dancer and those of the viewer. It represents a code that is correlated roughly, never exactly, or symmetrically, with the cognitive processes of the dancers on stage and the viewers in the audience.

## NOTES FOR CHAPTER 2

[1] We shall not consider here areas of stylized movement which are largely confined to entertainment and make little attempt to project meaning beyond their formalized activities. Thus, we have excluded organized sports and athletics despite their being grounded on stylized movement. This is not to say that such activities are totally devoid of meaning. Issues such as fair play in competition, learning physical coordination, and cooperation in team situations generalize beyond the confines of the particular sport and are part of the context of significance to which an audience responds. Still they are narrowly circumscribed and differ little from game to game, or sport to sport. There are other stylized physical activities that claim a wider significance; boxing and fencing, for example, are duels which retain, mostly in an

inhibited form, their original connection with killing. Their Eastern analogues, such as Judo and Karate, have sublimated and generalized their original context of violence into "a way of life." A recent textbook on Judo states, "The study of Judo without the realization of its secrets—that is, its metaphysical side—leaves one in partial mental emptiness. . . . In its most important phases, it constitutes a kind of higher logic developed through practice and the ascension of the true personality: a realization of the spiritual self in the philosophic rather than the religious sense of the word" (Watanabe and Avakian, 1960). Karate, too, is based on ethical principles derived from Zen Bhuddism. An introduction to a recent manual by the Karate Master, Oyama, who is famous for having killed a bull with one blow of his fist, is entitled, "Karate and Moral Culture" (Oyama, 1959). Similarly, the stylized movements of Yoga, while not derived from combat, are associated with a philosophy which "holds not only the answer to all man's problems, but also offers a scientific way to transcend his problems and sufferings" (Vishnudevananda, 1960). Even though the significance of some of these purely physical behaviors has been so broadened as to constitute a total *Weltanschauung*, they retain a narrowness of expression and projection that makes them unsuitable objects of study for our purposes.

[2] We have uncovered only one publication by a psychologist on the subject of dance (Sheets, 1965). Since the author approaches her subject matter from the standpoint of phenomenology and existentialism, she is concerned with a "pre-reflective" description based on "direct intuition." This is an essentially anti-analytical strategy which is incompatible with our approach. It assumes that a whole can't be broken into parts, while we start with the assumption that a study of parts and their functions is the best way to proceed. Considering the relative immaturity of any scientific approach to such a complex subject, no one can say as yet which approach is the more fruitful.

[3] "Unable to analyze or explain in words what he did or why he did it, he could only demonstrate. No wonder that after one hundred and fifty rehearsals of *Faune*, each dancer reflected perfectly the style of their choreographer!" (Van Praagh and Brinson, 1963.) This assessment occurs in a recently published, scholarly review, of choreographic practice. In her 1934 biography of her husband, Romola Nijinsky, who may not be an altogether unbiased witness, attributes the large number of rehearsals of *Faune* (120 according to her count) to the difficulty experienced by the classically trained dancers in learning to execute the unorthodox movements devised by the choreographer. "Almost as if they were children, he showed them the first steps. In *Faune*, there is no dancing in the old sense of the word. It is a consecutive series of movements. All is executed in profile. . . . as one sees in archaic Greek or Egyptian Sculpture." (Nijinsky, 1934.)

In his autobiography, Fokine offers yet another explanation for the large number of rehearsals. Fokine and Nijinsky were quite competitive in their relations with each other, and Diaghilev, in whose Ballet Russe both worked, did little to diminish their rivalry. Fokine was preparing his ballet, *Daphnis and Chloe*, at the same time that Nijinsky was rehearsing *Faune*. Fokine writes: "What extreme efforts were made to assure the success of *L'Après-midi d'un Faune*, this first experiment of his (Diaghilev's) favorite, and what measures were taken to diminish the success of *Daphnis*! Nijinsky had one hundred and twenty rehearsals for a nine-minute ballet. . . . Such luxury was never dreamed of by any ballet master. In contrast to this, I spent sleepless nights trying to find ways to teach the dancers what I had composed at home." (Fokine, 1961.)

The three explanations are not necessarily incompatible with each other but they illustrate the difficulty of using the existing literature to determine the relevant technical features of the way in which dance movements are conceived, learned, and presented to an audience.

[4] The "abstract" dance is not wholly contemporary, having been performed since the time of Ballanchine's "plotless" ballets of the 1930s and 1940s. These ballets, such as *Serenade*, *Ballet*

*Imperial*, and *Concerto Barocco*, were devoid of characterization and consisted of "pure dancing," interpretive of the music. What distinguishes contemporary, "abstract" dance is that the movements are abstracted from gesture, and are frequently broken up and reassembled in odd patterns. In addition, the dance movements are often correlated with "abstract" music, producing an ensemble of musical and kinetic patterns which cannot be placed within any recognizable frame of meaning. The "abstract" dance, therefore, has the effect—at least on first exposure—of "pure" pattern, without sense or external reference.

[5] For a rigorously explicit statement of instructions on carrying out the rules of classical ballet movements and positions, plus a correlated set of illustrations (line drawings) visually demonstrating how the instructions are to be executed, see Kirstein, Stuart, Dyer and Balanchine (1952).

The function of rules and instructions for the cognitive processing of various body movement categories will be discusesd at length in Chapter 6 of this book.

[6] A notable contribution to the issues outlined in points 3–6 (rules of dance style, cultural differences, correlation of music and dance, and characteristics of rhythmic movement) is to be found in the work of Alan Lomax, Irmgard Bartenieff and Forrestine Paulay (Lomax, 1968). Though primarily concerned with cultural variations in song styles derived from folk and ethnic traditions, part of their work has been concerned with dance movements. Looking at song as "danced speech" they have been able to demonstrate the close connection, in the various cultural regions of the world, between work-style and posture, on the one hand, and dance-style and rhythm on the other. Through the use of a modified version of the Laban and Lawrence (1947) effort-shape concept, they developed a "choreometric coding system" for comparing, through computerized statistical analyses, the variables involved in the different styles of dance movements. Their work is rich in observations and findings suggestive of further conceptualization and empirical research.

[7] Mary Wigman, one of the seminal dancer-choreographers of the modern dance, describes a number of her interior dialogues associated with the gestation of a new composition in summing-up her fifty-year dance career in *The Language of Dance* (Wigman, 1966). Putting the process in more condensed terms, Pauline Koner states, "In the creation of art (the dancer) must analyze his own experience, seeing it objectively even as he is feeling it subjectively. He tries to be at once the viewer and the viewed . . . We dancers can identify with the other, with the audience, with the receiver—and the receiver with us—in a closer way because that person has the identical instrument we have: the body" (Koner, 1966).

[8] Emerson took note of the moral as well as the esthetic implications of Elssler's dancing. The journal note quoted goes on to state: "But over and above her genius for dancing are the incidental vices of this individual, her own false taste and her meretricious arts to please the groundlings and which must displease the judicious. The immorality the immoral will see, the very immoral will see that only, the pure will not see it, for it is not obtrusive, perhaps will not see it at all. I should not think of danger to young women stepping with their father or brother out of happy and guarded parlors into this theatre to return in a few hours to the same; but I can easily suppose that it is not the safest resort for college boys who have left metaphysics, conic sections, or Tacitus to see these tripping satin slippers and they may not forget this graceful, silvery swimmer when they have retreated again to their baccalaureate cells." Here, no attempt has been made to deal separately with the moral, as opposed to the esthetic features of dance communication. It is evident that both vary in accordance with the cultural values of particular times.

[9] In "rock operas" such as *Hair* and *Godspell* players mingle with the audience and the audience is invited onstage at certain points in the performance. Though it creates an atmosphere

of pleasant informality, such formal loosening of the boundary between player and audience symbolizes an increasing cultural ambiguity in regard to the line between fantasy and reality. If viewers and performers can exchange roles temporarily, then perhaps viewers can "dance out" their fantasies or feelings, if sufficiently stimulated, without waiting for an invitation from the performers. This has actually occurred at some of the huge, open-air "rock festivals." Partly under the influence of drugs, partly keyed up by the music and the dancing movements of the performers, intensely involved viewers find the separation between the conventionally ascribed roles unbearable. To the dismay of the musicians and the producers, they then force their way to the stage. Though usually controllable, occasionally this unwanted invasion of stage-space produces a chaotic situation which leads to violence, for example during the Alta-mount, California performance of The Rolling Stones in 1969 (recorded in the film, *Gimme Shelter*) and, in a somewhat different context, during the course of the Newport Jazz Festival, Newport, R.I., in 1971.

# 3. Stylized Movement:
## MIME

Miming is the expression in body movement of the general principle of imitation, or mimicry. But the word has a double reference: It means to imitate *and* thereby to communicate without the use of words. The linking of imitation to non-verbal communication results in an exceedingly complex process, difficult to conceptualize, analyze, or even to describe. It has to be experienced.

Still, everyone has experienced it. The interchange of posture and gesture is one of the most effective means of communication available to parents and young children before the development of language. Miming in the theater, in dance, and in everyday life, develops out of this universal imitative gesture. For this reason, it constitutes a sort of basic code—a *lingua franca*—reaching across cultures and historical epochs.

So fundamental is the process of miming to the subject of this book—the messages of the body—that everything discussed here somehow touches upon it. As an art form with a long theatrical tradition, both as a part of acting and dance, and as a fully developed, pure style, mime has a literature and a history which merits some review.

It seems useful, at the outset, to distinguish between the process of non-verbal communication through imitative gesture and the art form which brings this process to its highest development. Here, "miming" will designate the general behavior process, and "mime" its formalization in the theater. This distinction still leaves a semantic problem. In the literature and in everyday usage, "mime" refers both to a performance, as in the case of "dance," and to the performer, as does "dancer." To avoid confusion, "Mime" (capitalized) will refer here to the performance and "mime" to the performer. This convention follows the usage suggested by Dorcy (1961).

Since miming is concerned with imitation, any discussion of it encounters the difficulties that have gathered around the idea of "imitation" in its long journey through the realms of art, philosophy, and science. Plato made imitation not only the basis of his theory of esthetics but of his entire metaphysical position. He viewed art as the imitation of nature. Each separate art sought to copy its natural objects, not in detail, but in accordance with selected features of the pattern or form of which the natural object was a manifestation. The world itself, according to Plato, was merely a copy—a work of art—of a form beyond direct scrutiny.

For Plato, imitation consisted in the copying of a model. This proposition and its relation to the known arts seemed self-evident. Therefore, the philosopher–esthetican should concern himself with the truth–value of the copy, that which is true being identified with the good.[1] Plato's pedagogical, reformist tendencies dominated his thinking so that all the performing arts were judged on the scale of truthfulness (therefore good and deserving preservation) versus distortion (shocking, merely pleasurable, and therefore deserving to be eliminated from the ideal society). Thus, when he came to consider the place of Mime among the performing arts in the ideal state, the problem was quickly disposed of:

> But there is another sort of character who will narrate anything, and, the worse he is, the more unscrupulous he will be; nothing will be too bad for him; and he will be ready to imitate anything, not as a joke, but in right good earnest, and before a large company. He will attempt to represent the role of thunder, the noise of wind and hail, or the creaking of wheels, and pulleys, and the various sounds of flutes, pipes, and trumpets, and all sorts of instruments; he will bark like a dog, bleat like a sheep, or crow like a cock; his entire art will consist in imitation of voice and gesture. . . .
>
> Therefore, when any of these pantomimic gentlemen, who are so clever that they can imitate anything, come to us, and makes a proposal to exhibit himself and his poetry, we will fall down and worship him as a sweet and wonderful and holy being; but we must also inform him that in our State such as he are not permitted to exist; the law will not allow them. (Plato, Republic, III, 397.)

A contemporary reader might well be puzzled by the severity of this judgment. Why was Plato so disturbed by the mime's willingness "to imitate anything"? What can be so bad about imitating creaking wheels and barking dogs? Or flutes, pipes, and trumpets?

Plato's prejudice derived from his concern for clarity, purity, and simplicity. Each art was to imitate only its proper natural object. Any contamination or intermingling among the arts, or even among the various instrumental techniques of the same art, he considered coarsening and unworthy.[2] Similarly, his preference for truth and simplicity led him to take a somewhat ambivalent attitude toward the creative activity of the artist. On the one hand, he considered the artist to be creatively inspired, possessed, by gods or the Muses. On the other hand, the personality of the artist counted for little as he was merely an instrument of transmission for the divine message. Socrates tells Ion, the rhapsodist, "The poet is a light and winged and holy thing, and there is no invention in him until he has been inspired and is out of his senses, and the mind is no longer in him . . . for not by art does the poet sing but by power divine." (*Ion*, 533.)

Plato, apparently, never fully resolved the contradiction between art as inspiration[3] and art as imitation: If the artist is out of his mind when he creates, how can he apply the technical rules of imitation? Whatever the logical status of this contradiction, philosophers of esthetics and practicing artists ignored inspiration while concerning themselves with imitation. The doctrine of imitation was enormously influential, though Plato's strictures against one art imitating the devices of another were wholly disregarded. During and after the Renaissance, painters, sculptors, and poets borrowed freely from the classical repertoire of forms, from each other, and from scientific models of the world. Choreographers enthusiastically endorsed the imitative nature of the dance.

When Carlo Blasis, the early nineteenth-century Italian dancing master who contributed so much to the codification of dance instruction, wanted to boast about one of his best achievements, he described the manner in which he had translated classical sculptural forms into dance movements suitable to ballet:

> In the Bacchanalian group above-mentioned, I introduced, with some success, various attitudes, arabesques, and groupings, the ideas of which I conceived on seeing the paintings, bronzes, and marbles excavated from the ruins of Herculaneum, and by these additional images, rendered its appearance more picturesque, characteristic, and animated. (Blasis, 1830.)

By the middle of the nineteenth century, however, the concept of imitation had lost its hold on theories of esthetics. Romantic criticism picked up the other side of Plato's paradox—the contribution of inspiration to the artistic product. No longer thought of as pure possession, at least not as possession by supernatural beings, inspiration began to be considered in terms of the personality and life experience of the artist. The Romantic idealization of the irrational, of the sufferings of the artist, and of the power of imagination, switched attention from the what and how of imitation to the why.

The current disappearance of imitation as a leading idea in esthetic criticism by no means implies that the issue has been fully settled. Echoes can be heard in the lively debate over the merits of representational versus non-representational or abstract art. Are form and structure more relevant to artistic aims than any actual, existing object? If so, then there is nothing much to imitate. Art consists of the act of communicating through specified media.

But if the object is still of relevance, if the selection of some of its features and the suppression of others is consistent with the purposes of art, then one is faced with a provocative set of questions: How are the relevant features of the object selected for imitation? How are these features then transferred from the medium in which they originally exist to the medium through which they are to be projected? In this view, the medium is part of the communication but the whole process is concerned with the transfer—and the transformation—of the message as it passes from one medium to another. Here, it is relevant to ask: What transformations are produced by the stylization involved in miming, and how are they achieved?

When Fokine was working out the steps of a Bacchanal, he found himself formulating a principle:

> I evolved a concrete theory on the technique of staging dances of ancient Greece and then, checking my quick improvisation against the theory, came to the conclusion that not a single position, not a single movement was in conflict with what I considered a law for the creation of dance on antique themes. All positions were in accord with what we see on bas-reliefs. However, they were not imitations of bas-reliefs, but movements flowing naturally from these positions and terminating in them. In "reading" the bas-reliefs, one must understand what movement it was that resulted in a particular pose. (Fokine, 1961, pp. 144–45.)

The technical principle Fokine alludes to in this passage is of great importance. It was used by Freud (1955) in his interpretation of the Moses of Michaelangelo. In a later chapter, it will appear under the heading of *intention movements*. Viewing the still object, the choreographer imaginatively reconstructed the movements that might have preceded or followed the frozen positions, and instructed the dancers to carry out these movements. Thus, by bringing to life a tableau, he mimed not only the object but also the sequence of which it was a part. This transformation is part of the magical effect of Mime—that it bestows life and presence upon that which is dead or absent.

Reginald Gardner, an English entertainer, used to amuse his audience by imitating wallpaper patterns. He mimed flowery, flowing patterns with elegant or florid swoops and languishings, and Greek Key or Wave edgings with angular or curved progressions and retractions. The audience loved it because of its absurdity—that he bestowed life and presence upon what should have been permitted to remain inanimate and absent. The triumph of the absurd over the real is a second transformation effect of Mime.

When Charlie Chaplin portrayed the Tramp in *The Gold Rush*, he mimed a delicious meal—a feast—using as the culinary high-point an old, boiled shoe. Starved and frozen to near numbness in the wilds of Alaska, he and his somewhat disbelieving partner gorged on shoe laces, filet of leather sole, and shoe nails as succulent bones. In transforming a cooked boot into nutriment, he banished hunger and pain and put fantasy and entertainment in their place. The act of renunciation and the denial of painful reality were perceived by the audience as both pathetic and delightful, bordering on madness but with a saving grace: Reality was delicately transformed through the minutely constructed operations of make-believe.

These qualities—magical beauty, pathos, absurdity bordering on insanity, and fun—are the special transformations that Mime imposes on the messages it transmits. How does the body make those transformations? Perhaps one should begin not with the body but with the act of mimicry that transmits the message, first distinguishing between "imitation," which Plato applauded, and "mimicry" which he despised.

It is useful, here, to use *imitation* only for the process of learning to repeat identical behaviors between members of the same species.[4] If the word is restricted in this fashion, then some other term, such as *representation*, must be used for the transfer of selected features of objects from one medium into another, as occurs in painting, sculpture, and other techniques. These demarcations leave the word *mimicry* for the designation of a separate and special process.

Understanding of the underlying process may perhaps be obtained from biology. Cryptic coloration and other forms of mimicry occur among many different species of plants and animals. In general, the phenomenon seems to have become selected in the course of evolution for the preservation of the species against its predators. The process of disguise is manifested in at least two forms, roughly parallel to the "cloak" and the "dagger" of human concealment operations.

In the "cloak" form of protective mimicry, the organism melts into its environment and becomes invisible. In the "dagger" form, the organism mimics a dangerous, or at least unpleasantly threatening, specimen to which it bears no close, biological relationship. Such "threats" are produced not merely by the physical markings of the organism but also by its movements and postures as well.

There are some obvious similarities and differences in the two methods of avoiding predators. Both conceal the actual identity of the organism. "Cloaking" removes the organism from the environment—it is just "not there." "Threatening" transforms the identity of the harmless organism by copying its behavior and appearance from the model of a dangerous one. These contrasts are matters of emphasis rather than wholly separable phenomena. In "cloaking," stimuli from the organism are presented so as to escape notice and the effect is that an object actually present is made to seem absent. In the aggressive form of mimicry, stimuli from the organism are arranged so that an object actually absent is made to seem present.

If the above descriptions are reasonably accurate for the animal world, then the parallels to human mimicry, and thus to miming, are substantial. The principal analogy is concerned with the disappearance of an object actually present and the presentation of an object actually absent. In miming, the mime, as an individual in his own right, vanishes. He may remain absent, though actually present, or he may be transformed into an object that is not there, or he may summon up objects that are not there. A mime who bumps into a wall that is not there and falls over backward, summons up and brings into some sort of "presence" that absent wall. He produces the illusion of the wall.

To be sure, all these transformations, changes of identity, and illusions require a good deal of collusion on the part of the viewer. But the collusion may, to varying degrees, be conscious or unconscious, and the more unconscious it is, the more magical will be the effect of the transformation. Collusion in miming requires the suspension of critical judgment and reality testing because one wishes to be fooled. In Mime, the obvious costuming, the use of the full- or half-mask, the painted white-face of Pierrot and his clown descendants, the grease-paint mustache of Charlie Chaplin are all giveaways, simultaneously announcing that deception is occurring and inviting the viewer to be deceived.

These basic properties of the deception game account, in fact, for the transformations previously noted. Since these characteristics are and have always been close to common humanity, Mime has tended to be a popular art form. Because cruelty, stupidity, pain, and suffering are so much a part of everyday, near-hopeless situations calling for mastery, Mime has presented an inordinate amount of slapstick, sadistic buffoonery, triumphant stupidity, undefeated villainy, and unrequited love while underlining the inauthenticity of these themes through its obvious make-believe. They are events that ought not to happen and perhaps would not happen in a better arranged world. As they do happen, however, viewers can at least dispel their effects by making them seem trivial, absurd, funny, or magically subject to will.

The circumstances that condition both illusion and collusion have varied considerably in the course of the history of Mime. There have also been variations in the degree to which Mime is accompanied by words or is wholly non-verbal. Since part of the total effect of Mime is precisely the contrast between verbal and non-verbal communication, it will prove fruitful, at this point, to determine the place of words in the process of miming. What effect does the absence or presence of the spoken word have on the phenomenon?

If imitation consists of the reproduction of identical or similar appearances and behaviors between members of the same species (or class of objects, as in the case of modern reproductions of antique objects), and if representation consists of the transfer of selected features of objects from one medium into another, then, from what has been said so far, it is clear that mimicry consists of a combination of imitation and representation in various mixtures. When Charlie Chaplin in *The Gold Rush* mimed ballet with dining table accessories, he actually reproduced the *pirouettes, grands jetés,* and *pas de chat* of the classical repertoire, imitating the movements of the ballerina's legs. Still, the viewer is asked to accept fork and roll as believable substitutes for human leg and foot, a *representative transformation.*

Illusion and Collusion make their entry not with respect to the imitation, which may be merely good or bad reproduction, but with respect to accepting the representation. Here, also, is one of the major points of contrast between art and science. When representation occurs in science, the reader is explicitly told how the transformation is to take place. "Let us represent by the line AB the time in which the space CD is traversed by a body which starts at rest at C and is uniformly accelerated," says Galileo (1956) in stating his first theorem of accelerated motion. To let a line signify time is to accept a ridiculous substitute. But, having been asked so politely by a great authority, the reader can scarcely refuse outright to go along with the transformation.[5] In art, the viewer is seldom explicitly told or asked (except by art critics) anything about the substitution of one medium for another. If he refuses to accept fork and roll for ballerina legs, that is his business. If he goes along with the code, he involves himself in the collusion and is as responsible as the artist for the illusion.

If mimicry uses both imitation and representation and if miming is mimicry by means of the body, its relations to verbal communication can be established. When, as in stage acting, the spoken word is combined with body movement in the normal fashion of people in everyday life, pure imitation is at work, with no use of representation. When spoken words are omitted and the body is the only medium of communication, then, to varying degrees, the body must substitute for the spoken word, or for verbally expressible ideas.

In miming, representations of words can occur in two ways: The movements of the mime can be made to represent a conversation between two people— that is, a sequence of sentences. Or the movements and actions occurring in the Mime can represent a general idea, able to be put into words, but only with some clumsiness and great loss of overall effect. Thus, despite the considerable amount of pure imitation of ordinary body movement taking place in Mime, its representative function is its most important characteristic, all the more prominent because of the absence of the spoken word. Its weight of meaning, the messages characterized by pathos, magic, absurdity and the other general transformations, can be seen to emerge through progressive stylization in the messages characterized by pathos, magic, absurdity, and the other general course of its history. But, until the very recent past, it has not been clear whether the Mime is merely the representative of the spoken word, or whether it approaches its subject matter from a wholly non-linguistic point of departure.

In the earliest, preliterate record of most peoples, Dance, Mime, and Drama were scarcely distinguishable. Dance was part of a religious, tribal ceremonial based on appeals to supernatural powers in connection with those aspects of the ·cycle of nature necessary to the survival of the group. The dancers were usually costumed, frequently wore animal or bird masks or headdresses, and were accompanied by music. Sometimes the dances re-enacted a legend or myth or were directed at appeasing a god or causing him to appear in the midst of the people. Thus, the ceremony simultaneously told a dramatic story, combined the rhythmic displays of music and dance steps, and established a magical mastery of the environment through imitation and representation of supernatural and natural objects.

Where the archeological and historical records are well documented, as in the case of the Greeks, the gradual separation of Mime, Drama, and Dance can be discerned. By the classical era, the formal dance still showed traces of its original mythical origins and of magical re-enactment through mimicry. Animal dances, particularly bird dances, featured adults and children in animal disguise, trooping from house to house, much as in our Halloween fun-making.[6]

Out of one of the Greek dances, the dithyramb, grew the drama. The dithyramb was a song-and-dance performance in honor of Dionysus. Gradually, the song was transformed into the spoken verses of the *tragoedia*—the "goat song" —and the dancing troupe became the chorus in the drama. While the three actors in the tragedy, costumed, masked, and elevated on high boots, recited their verses, the chorus of twelve or fifteen masked men (sometimes simulating women) danced and mimed the action of the play. The miming was characterized by symbolic, conventionalized gesture—the *cheironomia*—so well understood by the audience that a well-trained dancer in the chorus could portray the whole action of the drama without speaking a word. This form of miming, directly tied to a narrative account of the action, more or less translatable into words, is characteristic of the dance. Its gesture language underwent a recodification in connection with ballet during the eighteenth and nineteenth centuries. Etienne Decroux (Dorcy, 1961) called it the *Mime of the dancer*.

The principal actors in the Athenian tragedy chanted, intoned, recited, or declaimed their verses; they did not "act" in the "realistic" sense that the word is used today. But as the actors recited their verses, they emphasized their meanings with dramatic gestures, probably as conventionally patterned as the *cheironomia* of the chorus. This declamatory gesture language has also had a long history, with periods of greater and lesser formalization. It can be called the *Mime of the speaker*. It differs from the Mime of the dancer in that the former is a representation and imitation of a narrative account of a situation which could have been rendered in sentences. The latter, on the other hand, is an amplification or modification of certain words, phrases, and meanings simultaneously uttered in sentences.

Like the tragedy, the Greek comedy developed out of song-and-dance troupes, the *komoi*, featured in vintage revels. It settled into a staging quite similar to that of the Athenian tragedy, with masked and costumed principal actors and a masked, singing and dancing chorus. But, unlike the elevated, usually somber, mythological themes of the tragedies, the plots of the comedies were based on burlesques of mythological characters and events and on savage fun-making at the expense of contemporary personages. The introduction of characters from everyday life—or the reduction of mythical heroes to the common-man level—required that the actors and chorus engage in a somewhat more realistic imitation of the characters they were supposed to represent. Such representations through selective bodily re-enactment of common activities and feelings constitute the *Mime of the actor*.

Contemporaneous with the evolution of Greek comedy, there developed a primitive form of purely mimetic entertainment. The Dorian Mime preserved the spontaneity and low humor of the original song-and-dance processions. The performers danced, sang, and exchanged dialogue, but the chief accent fell on wordless mimicry of persons, animals, or inanimate objects in stock situations.

There was much high jinks, acrobatics, and slapstick knock-about in these popular Mime performances. Gradually the genre crystallized into a number of set plot outlines consisting of mythological and legendary farces peopled with stock characters: an old man with a pointed beard, and old hag-like woman, a fool, a doctor, one or two slaves (who could also be thieves), and a few legendary heroes such as Herakles.[7]

The Mime performances were stylistically elaborated as they spread from the Peloponnesus, their place of origin, to Athens, Syracuse, Alexandria, Southern Italy, and finally to Rome in the period of the early Empire. Great emphasis was placed on improvising lines and stage "business" so that the latest doings of leading political and social figures would receive prompt comment. In this social and political context, some of the transformations already noted as characteristic of Mime were established: the extravagant fun-making, the absurdity, the spontaneity, and the make-believe triumph on behalf of the common man over those persons and forces that governed his destiny.

By the time that the spoken Mime performance had seized the fancy of the popular Roman audience in the first century A.D., a new theatrical genre known as Pantomime was developing and contained a number of performers who combined set lines with ad libbing and spontaneous mimicry. They were essentially plays interlaced with free wit and unexpected episodes of the type that, today, might be called a "happening." The pantomimes, on the other hand, were solo dancers who mimed, to the accompaniment of music, all the parts of a set libretto, without the use of words. In the Pantomime, the performer wore a mask with a closed mouth indicating his speechlessness. Sometimes he changed costume and mask between interludes to take the various roles of the libretto. Some performers became so skilled that they could switch roles on the spot by slight rearrangements of mask and costume. Such performances were not realistic; rather they were symbolically suggestive. In the place of the literal imitations and exaggerations of the mimes, the pantomimes evolved representations, in dance-like movement, of the tragic world of myth. Here lies the origin of the beauty, the magic, and the pathos previously designated as characteristic of mimetic transformations. If these qualities of the Pantomime are combined with the comic triumph of the spoken Mime, the result is for the ancient world what might have been called, following Etienne Decroux's suggestion (Dorcy, 1961), the *Mime of the mime*.

These four types of Mime—of the dancer, the speaker, the actor, and the mime—are seldom found completely separated from each other. And they have all undergone changes in the course of theatrical history. For example, the classical ballet combined the Mime of the mime, the dancer, and the actor. The gesture language that constitutes the Mime of the dancer was already partially codified by the beginning of the eighteenth century. Here are some examples from the scenario of the ballet *The Loves of Mars and Venus*, by John Weaver,[8] produced at Drury Lane, London, March 1717:

*Astonishment.*  Both hands are thrown up towards the skies; the Eyes also lifted up, and the Body cast backwards.

*Anger.*  The left Hand struck suddenly with the right, and sometimes against the Breast; denotes Anger.

*Impatience.*  Impatience is seen by the smiting of the Thigh, or Breast with the Hand.

In laying down this sort of code, Weaver felt himself to be in accord with the ancient tradition. In his book, *The History of the Mimes and Pantomimes* (1728), Weaver wrote, "The Mimes and Pantomimes, tho' Dancers, had their Names from Acting, that is, from Imitation; copying all the Force of the Passions merely by the Motions of the Body, to that degree, as to draw Tears from the Audience at their Representations . . ."

In the nineteenth century, the dancer's conversation of gestures became more highly elaborated. When the Prince in *Swan Lake* first lays eyes on the Swan Queen, he turns to the audience and brushes his hand across his face to indicate that he thinks she is beautiful. The Queen herself has a long mime sequence to tell the story of her enchantment and to reveal that the Lake of the Swans is a Lake of Tears.[9] The codification of gesture language can be pushed to infinite detail.

In the last half of the nineteenth century, the Mime of the speaker underwent extensive stylization. Cultivation of the voice, known as *elocution*, was accompanied by a studied use of gesture. The codification of both "voice culture" and gesture was based largely on the teachings of François Delsarte,[10] who, from about 1839 until his death in 1871, developed and taught "the laws of expression." His "science of applied aesthetics" provided rules for controlling the movements of the body and the voice so as to "express characterization in a natural manner." It was much studied by painters, actors, dancers, and speakers.

Delsarte's rules were quite specific and were repeated in various manuals for effective speaking. For example, in Wilbor's *Delsarte Recitation Book* (1889), one encounters such Delsartean maxims as, "The shoulder, in every man who is agitated or moved, rises in exact proportion to the intensity of his emotion," and "Every agreeable or disagreeable sight makes the body react backward. The degree of reaction should be in proportion to the degree of interest caused by the sight of the object." Later authors of textbooks on elocution tended to simplify and generalize. In Ross's *Voice Culture and Elocution* (1890), the reader is told that gestures terminating below the horizontal line indicate will, determination, and purpose; those terminating on the horizontal belong to the realm of the intellect and are employed in making general allusions; those terminating above the horizontal denote the imagination since they usually imply an unfolding and lifting toward the ideal.

Gradually, however, the self-consciousness of elocution went out of style. "Voice culture" gave way to "public speaking," and what had been adopted in the name of an effective and natural manner of presentation came to seem mannered—a relic of the nineteenth century. But the fact that specific technical programs for modeling the body to produce specific effects had once been formulated and applied is of considerable importance to any study of the messages of the body.

The disappearance of the formal patterning of the Mime of the speaker is partly due to the general shift away from formal rules for behavior in all sorts of contexts during the twentieth century.[11] Contemporary culture prizes informality and personal style. The anthropologist Edward T. Hall (1959) has postulated that every culture (or subculture) transmits its messages, to varying degrees, in accordance with three modes of projection: formal, informal, and technical. Informal systems are characterized by the absence of definite rules. The behavior is learned through the presentation of a model for imitation with the introduction, "Don't ask questions. Keep your eyes open and watch what people are doing."

The absence of specification of what is to be learned results in a great deal of learning outside of awareness. The physicist, Gerald Holton (1965), has used the distinction between formal and informal communication· in differentiating the style of the "classical" lecturer–demonstrator from the "non-classical," in contemporary teaching of physics. The classical lecturer is "tightly programmed" and leaves no room for unplanned events. Through spontaneous subvocal variations and unplanned gestures, the non-classical lecturer provides much opportunity for unintended communications,[12] including possible threats to his dignity. Miming conducted in this informal style injects numerous, small, subliminal cues into the message system, allowing the listener to select from the rich range of meanings those which he can most easily retain. Holton particularly stresses the importance of research on the use of the hands in demonstrating apparatus and making didactic experiments in science teaching, there being some similarity between the hand of the stage magician and the lecturer–demonstrator in calling attention to or away from details of the visual display.

Informality can be pushed to the point where it seems opposed to any form of stylization whatever. The inutility of this extreme position has been stated by Elizabeth Hardwick (1966) in her review of Peter Weiss's ultra-naturalistic play, *The Investigation*. "What you see in the production of *The Investigation*," she said, "is our fear of stylization, of interpretation. . . . Stylization is too personal as an action, and too refined as a conception, apparently. How much safer to trust the simple flow of 'real life,' to fall back on sincerity at the expense of truth, to trust earnestness more than inspiration." As a result of this earnest realism, she stated, the reality of Auschwitz, which the play attempted to depict (by reproducing, literally, the testimony of Auschwitz SS men given at the 1964 trial at Frankfurt), the horror of the concentration camp, never appeared on stage. Horror has to be formulated, stylized; depiction only renders it meaningless.

If the Mime of the speaker has deteriorated in the course of its recent history, the Mime of the mime has suffered odd combinations of killing neglect and stupefying attention. During the Middle Ages, the Church effectively stamped out the secular theater, including both Mime and Pantomime. Some writers hold that Mime nevertheless maintained an underground existence and subtly intruded into the Medieval Miracle Plays. Furthermore, the secular entertainments of the Middle Ages provided by the dancing and acrobatic *jongleurs* featured stock types that harked back to classical Mime.

But formal Mime as a recognized art disappeared until its sudden emergence in Italy about the middle of the sixteenth century in the guise of the *commedia dell' arte*. These troupes of open-air players presented improvised dramas based upon sketchy plots peopled with stock characters. Though there were some set speeches and soliloquies, most of the action and dialogue was improvised, with heavy reliance on miming. All the characters except a pair of young lovers wore masks and costumes symbolic of their personalities.

The players of the *commedia dell' arte* gathered together the main elements of formal Mime already discussed as the mimetic transformation. Since the art was essentially non-literary, little of its actual content has been preserved. Still, that dream-like, magical, fantastic–realistic style has left a powerful if subterranean imprint on the artistic imagination of the West.[13] A document describing the miming of Tiberio Fiorilli, a much-admired Scaramouche (braggart warrior type) of the seventeenth century, says, "Scaramuccia speaks not, and yet he says the finest things in the world." (Nicoll, 1931, p. 289.) This is as much a tribute to the imagination of the viewer as to the skill of the mime.

The *commedia dell' arte* went out of fashion early in the eighteenth century. In England, the Mime of the mime took a new turn when, in 1732, John Rich introduced what came to be known as Christmas Pantomime at Covent Garden Theatre. In the original productions, the Mime scenes, featuring Pantaloon, Columbine, Harlequin, and Clown (all from the *commedia dell' arte* stock characters), occurred between the acts of a regular play. The productions attracted large crowds and "English Pantomime" was quickly established as a national institution. As time went on, the formal drama was eliminated and replaced with musical extravaganza while the Mime was separated and removed to the end of the production as the "Harlequinade." Though the Christmas Pantomime has retained its popularity to this day, its contribution to the art of Mime has been minimal.

The Mime of the mime persisted more vigorously in France, both in ballet and, to some extent, in the theater generally. In the eighteenth century Jean Georges Noverre (1930), the celebrated *maître de ballet*, wrote,

> Action, in relation to dancing, is the art of transferring our sentiments and passions to the souls of the spectators by means of the true expression of our movements, gestures, and features. Action is simply pantomime. In the dancer, everything must depict, everything must speak; each gesture, each attitude, each *port de bras* must possess a different expression. True pantomime follows nature in all her moods. If it deviates from her for an instant, the pantomime becomes fatiguing and revolting. Students of dancing should not confuse the noble pantomime of which I speak with that low and trivial form of expression which Italian players have introduced into France, and which bad taste would have appeared to have accepted.

"That low and trivial form of expression"[14] was, of course, the *commedia dell' arte*. Noverre was a reformer of ballet, and his reforms were in the direction of naturalistic styles. He wished to rid ballet of the use of masks, inappropriate and unrealistic costumes, and inert gestures. The conflict between the formalism of the dance and the dramatic properties of Mime was to be a source of continual tension in ballet, usually to the disadvantage of true miming. In 1855, reviewing a new and unusually dramatic ballet, *La Fonti*, created especially for Carolina Rosati, Théophile Gautier wrote:

> The Ballet belongs to the type known as *ballets d'action* and represents a drama interpreted by gestures rather than a sequence of choreographic poses. It has been translated with talent by M. Mazilier, one of our best producers of mimed action, and well rendered by La Rosati, but we nevertheless continue to hold that the *ballet d'action* does not satisfy the conditions of true dancing. Every art corresponds to a certain order of subjects which it alone can render . . . Ballet must be a kind of painted bas-relief or sculptured painting . . . A few limited gestures, some taken from nature, others from convention, are the only resources with which to paint human passions. Thus the *ballet d'action* has the appearance of a drama played by a troupe of deaf-mutes, especially as French dancers do not follow the music in their miming.[15]

Poet, novelist, and the librettist of the ballet, *Giselle*, Gautier was the dean of French dance critics during the period of the Romantic Ballet. His opposition to the inclusion of formal Mime in the presentation of ballet can be understood as signifying the process through which the Mime of the dancer came into being. If actual Mime is no more than drama played by deaf-mutes, and if, in addition, it interrupts the music and the dance, then the dancer's miming had best be limited to that quantity of conventional gesture language required to move the scenario toward its conclusion. Gautier need not have sought the support of Plato's esthetic imperative—that "every art corresponds to a certain order of subjects which it alone can render"—in order to validate what was in any event an apparently necessary conclusion.[16]

Dramatic pantomime, however, was too firmly established in the dancer's and actor's tradition to be abolished by such edicts. Periodically, a version of formal Mime was revived on the French stage. One such revival by Courtes and Pilar-Morin had a successful tour in the United States in 1895–97. In an interview reported in *The New York Sun*, January 3, 1897, Mlle. Pilar-Morin said, "In pantomime, which by the way in France is the highest art, the whole body is made responsive to the slightest thought. When one has mastered the art of making hands and feet and body tell what is meant, as far as they can do so, then the real work of the pantomimist begins."

Though French pantomime might have been considered the highest art by its enthusiasts, its emergence as an acknowledged art form had to await the work of Etienne Decroux and Jean-Louis Barrault. Between 1931 and 1939, these two actors collaborated in perfecting the principles of miming which Decroux had developed earlier.[17] Their formulation of new principles emerged from their intense dissatisfaction with naturalistic acting. The highly stylized, plastic use of the body, practiced by the now old-fashioned Romantic actor, had been replaced by a minimal repertoire of movement in the interest of realism. In order to escape such a limitation, Decroux and his collaborators restored the use of masks.

> Once the face is concealed, there remains only the body to express our thought and make it understood. What happens to an actor who puts on a mask? He is cut off from the outer world. The night he deliberately enters allows him first to reject everything that hampers him. Then, by an effort of concentration, to reach a void, a state of unbeing. From this moment forward, he will be able to come back to life and to behave in a new and truly dramatic way. . . . Our research in bodily expression was facilitated by our exercises with the mask. We felt instinctively that only in the phase of this bodily consciousness would we be able to achieve the great metamorphoses. (Dorcy, 1961, pp. 12, 29.)

By "the great metamorphoses" was meant the effort to distill and perfect a new plastic line and a new imagery for the movement of the mime. For example, gesture was to function not merely as the representative of a natural movement or a physiological reflex but also as a link with imaginary objects not represented on stage. Furthermore, gesture was seen as having its own cadence, not dictated by external events, such as the tempo of music, nor the rhythm of natural activities such as the speed of a tennis game, but governed by the inner structure of meaning within the Mime form. For example, the mimed tennis match in Antonioni's film *Blow-Up,* with its slightly slowed-down tempo and the slightly enlarged scale of the movements of the tennis players, was governed by the theme of the plot, not by the rhythm of a real game.

Another aspect of the metamorphoses aimed at by these reformers was concerned with a new relation between movement and space. In everyday life, movement traverses space and correlates with time. In the usual theatrical performance, the body creates the form and dimension of space on stage. In the dance, the choreography in general, and the movements of the dancer in particular create three-dimensional patterns—an architecture of space—by the shifts, or translations, from one point on stage to another. But in Mime of the mime, both space and time can be indefinitely contracted or expanded—or dissociated one from the other—by means of the representative transformation. For example, in Jean-Louis Barrault's Mime, entitled *La Mort Verticale,* death is symbolically enacted and realized while time and space are dissociated. The mime, half nude and seated on the ground, suddenly draws himself upright. The right arm extends desperately toward the sky. There is a moment of absolute immobility. The stiffly extended arm is then bent and lowered, palm turned toward the ground, slowly, very, very slowly. The arm passes in front of the head, the neck, the chest . . . slowing blotting out life . . . until it sinks to the ground. As each part of the body "dies," its immobility increases slightly so that at "death" the body is still sitting stiffly upright, a mummy, a monument to the process of death.[18] Thus, the image created in the mind of the viewer is partially detached from the object which reflects it on the stage. The reality of body movement has been transformed by representation and analogy.

Condensation and dissociation takes place in a more light-hearted way in the miming of Marcel Marceau, the foremost pupil of Decroux and Barrault. In *David and Goliath*, he takes both roles, changing instantly from one to another as he passes behind a small screen. In *Bip and the Butterfly*, Marceau enacts his best known characterization—the mildly disoriented, sweet, clownish, senti-mental Bip—chasing a butterfly, catching it, and destroying it in a burst of love and excitement. But the butterfly itself consists of his own fluttering, trembling hands. The dissociation of the hands from the body becomes completely believ-able, while the chase, capture, and demise of the butterfly have taken place with Bip scarcely moving from one spot.

Condensation, dissociation, distortion, displacement, representation, and sym-bolization—the constant features of the mimetic transformation—are also among the fundamental elements of the unconscious, psychological process. Their effects are especially prominent in dream-formation. The superficial parallels between scenic presentations in the dream and in Mime are striking. Though conversation may take place in a dream or in a Mime, in general dreams are silent and Mime-like while Mimes are silent and dream-like. Both have the compelling force of an illusion—that is, while their content is quite unreal, they are nevertheless eminently believable and are experienced as real as long as their spell lasts. Insofar as both include events caused by mysterious forces beyond immediate comprehension, they may both give rise to a magical, uncanny feeling. Along with the magic, both frequently combine seemingly trivial or absurd actions with significant and moving events.

More relevant than the surface similarities are the underlying correspondences of psychological process. But, here, a difficult problem emerges. According to psychoanalytic theory, the dissociations, distortions, and displacements of dreams and delusions can be explained on the basis of the compromise between repress-ing forces and the strong, emotionally laden, repressed currents seeking some form of expression. The details of each particular dissociation or distortion can be traced to their origin through the psychoanalytic method. With this technique, the mystery is undone, the distortions are released, the dramatic though absurd expressions of the body as portrayed in the dream production are restored to their "normal" and intuitively meaningful forms. If a particular technique can accomplish this for the images produced by a dreamer, then there should be a a consistent method for decoding the mimetic transformations. But, the psycho-analytic method, which depends upon painstaking accumulation of evidence provided by the associations and fantasies of the individual dreamer, is inap-plicable to a staged presentation produced by many people and interpreted by the even larger number in the audience.

This discussion of mimicry and imitation in general and of Mime in particular has emphasized the modifications of natural movement—the *representative transformation*—occasioned by the process of stylization. Another approach to the understanding of the psychological process underlying such transformations would attack the problem from the other side—that is, with an attempt to investigate the "normal" basis of bodily expression. If it were possible to estab-lish a reliable system of decoding the meaning of natural movement—provided there is such a thing—then the mechanism by which it is altered for stylistic purposes would be easier to unravel, and its effects upon the viewer made more comprehensible.

There exists within the behavioral sciences a vast literature devoted to tech-nical studies of this sort.[19] Psychology, sociology, cultural anthropology and the newer methods of investigating the process of communication have all concerned themselves to some degree with the problem of developing reliable methods for determining the meaning of the communications of the body. It is this literature which forms the subject matter for the next chapter.

## NOTES FOR CHAPTER 3

[1] "And will he who does not know what is true be able to distinguish what is good and bad? . . . And can he who does not know what the exact object is which is being imitated, ever know whether the resemblance is truthfully executed? . . . May we not say that in every-thing imitated, whether in drawing, music, or any other art, he who is to be a competent judge must possess three things;—he must know in the first place, of what the imitation is; secondly, he must know that it is true; and thirdly, that it has been well executed in words and melodies and rhythms?" (Plato, Laws, II, 668–69.)

[2] "And then as time went on, the poets themselves introduced the reign of vulgar and lawless innovation. They were men of genius, but they had no perception of what is just and lawful in music, raging like Bacchanals and possessed with inordinate delights—mingling lamenta-tions with hymns and paeans with dithyrambs; imitating the sounds of the flute on the lyre, and making one general confusion; ignorantly affirming that music has no truth, and, whether good or bad, can only be judged of rightly by the pleasure of the hearer." (Plato, Laws, III, 699.)

[3] For an account of the pre-Platonic origins of the idea of art as inspiration, see Dodd (1957).

[4] This is the sense in which the word "imitation" is still used in contemporary psychology. See, for example, Miller and Dollard (1941), and Bandura (1962). For an overview of the rise and fall of the concept of imitation in psychology, see Allport (1954).

[5] Scientists are not always so considerate of their readers' resistances. Writing in what James R. Newman calls his "contemptuous vein," Descartes (1956) described his method of transforming geometry into algebra: "Thus, to add the lines BD and GH, I call one $a$ and the other $b$, and write $a + b$."

[6] The history of the dance in Greece, plus the difficulty of establishing exact forms of movements used in the dance, has been documented by Lawler (1964).

[7] See Allardyce Nicoll's (1931) *Masks, Mimes, and Miracles* for a review of the history of Mime from its earliest beginnings through the demise of the *commedia dell' arte* at the end of the seventeenth century. Our discussion is based largely on the work of Nicoll.

[8] The complete scenario is published in Appendix I in Van Praagh and Brinson's *The Choreographic Art* (1963).

[9] This description is paraphrased from an article by the dance critic, Walter Terry, which appeared in *The New York Herald-Tribune*, November 30, 1941.

[10] A description of Delsarte's "laws" is provided by the dancer, Ted Shawn (1963) in his *Every Little Movement*.

[11] There are numerous examples of this shift in textbooks on "Public Speaking" in the second quarter of the twentieth century. A 1931 *Guide to Effective Speaking* (Riley, 1931) states: "Anybody can make effective gestures. To convey thoughts and emotions by bodily action is as natural as speaking. . . . If gestures are fundamentally natural, the primary step in learning effective gestures is to overcome false dignity." In *Speechmaking: Principles and Practice*, Brigance and Immel (1938) advise, "When we express an important idea or a strong emotion, we tend to reinforce the expression by activity of the whole body, and the stronger the emphasis, the stronger the gesture. The beginner in public speaking will probably progress faster in the use of the gesture if he thinks of it in this simple way. Let him become strongly interested in what he is saying and strongly desirous of creating thought responses in the minds of his audience, and he will inevitably find himself impelled to reinforce his vocal utterance with bodily movements." Oliver, Cort and Hager (1946), caution that, "A general step in learning to use bodily action is to free yourself from inhibtions. Fundamentally, every speaker wants to gesture. It is second nature for him to do so. . . . When the body is relaxed and the mind at ease, the inhibition will be minimized." All these authors give suggestions for the use of various simple gestures and body movements in the course of making a speech, but the principal emphasis is placed on naturalness, spontaneity, and individuality.

[12] The subject of "unintended communication," particularly as it affects the design and execution of psychological experimentation with human subjects, has been extensively investigated by Robert Rosenthal and his associates. They have demonstrated how unwittingly executed noddings of the head, smiles, leaning toward or away from the subject influence the course of an interview or experiment and thus introduce an unforeseen and unmeasured bias into the resulting data.

[13] The tendency of the *commedia dell' arte* figures to be revived after periods of neglect, has been documented by Thelma Niklaus (1956).

[14] A certain amount of patriotic bias seems inevitably to creep into this sort of judgment. Writing on the same subject, Weaver (1712, pp. 168–169) also looked down his nose: "Grotesque dancing . . . this superficial performance of the Pantomimes, the ruins of which remain in Italy; but sunk and degenerated into Pleasantry, and merely conceited Representations of Harlequin, Scaramouche, Mezelin, Pasquariel, etc.; but so intermixed with Trick and Tumbling that the design is quite lost in ridiculous Grimace and odd, unnatural Action. Yet are these modern Mimes inimitable, and tho' they have been aped by several in France, (as I have been informed by persons who have seen both the Italian and the French), the French could never come up to their Grimace, Posture, Motions, Agility, and Suppleness of Limbs. . . . I could wish this kind of dancing were now encouraged in England, since I am certain that the English in a little time would at least arrive at so much Perfection in this Science, as, if not to come up to the Performance of the Ancients, they would without doubt excel all that has been performed in this kind by the Moderns."

[15] This passage is quoted in Ivor Guest's (1955) comprehensive review of the Romantic Ballet in France. Not every reviewer agreed with Gautier's strictures on miming, as Guest demonstrates. The dance critic, Fiorentino, was more appreciative of Rosati's Italian manner: "It is incontestable," he wrote, "that neither Fanny Elssler, who is often cited when Rosati is discussed, nor any other mime or dancer among all those we have seen at the Opera, ever approached such perfection."

[16] The difficulties of synthesizing miming, dancing, and music in ballet are extensively discussed by Kirstein (1935) in his history of classical theatrical dancing. "This quarrel," he states, "is a perennial debate, from century to century, down to our own decade. Which is the correct path for the dancer:—dance or meaningful gesture—abstract movement or pure expression? This inherent dualism in the art is at the root of all choreographic discussion, and can never seem to be resolved even by judicious combination."

[17] Our discussion of the principles of the French School of Mime is based on the account given by Dorcy (1961). A simplified popularization of the history of Mime including the most recent developments can be found in the book by Douglas and Kari Hunt (1964) on Pantomime.

[18] This description is a paraphrase of the account given by Dorcy (1961).

[19] There has been only one attempt, to our knowledge, to develop a comprehensive approach to the analysis of natural movement outside the behavioral sciences. This is the work of Rudolph Laban and his colleagues, published in several books, most notably *The Mastery of Movement* (Laban, 1960). Laban was the dancer and choreographer who devised the dance notation system, *Labanotation*, now frequently used for recording dances and other bodily performances. His analysis of expressive movement is based on the concept of "effort" and was inspired, in large part, by studies of the motions of industrial workers and of other "everyday" activities. It contains a number of categories which can be combined in different ways. Laban was rather unsystematic in his attempts to apply his system but the method has seemed promising and work with it is being carried on by a group of his followers (Bartenieff and Davis, 1965; Lamb, 1965).

# 4. Research Strategies in Non-verbal Communication

Six disciplines have made contributions to the topic considered in this study—anthropology, linguistics, psychoanalysis, clinical psychology, social psychology, and sociology. Within disciplines, however, the theories, the methods, and the aims of the individual studies have varied so much that the disciplines themselves cannot be used as a principle of classification.

This "overlapping" of the literature is the result of a multitude of factors (Argyle, 1972). First, of course, is the fact that there is no officially organized field of inquiry concerned with the subject. To be sure, there has been an encouraging increase in research activity in non-verbal communication in the last few years. Until recently, with the exception of Birdwhistell, no one had devoted his professional career to the study of the human body in action. It is interesting to contemplate how much progress might have been made in this field over the last four decades had the physical behavior of human beings received as much attention as that of white rats, to say nothing of three-spined sticklebacks and chimpanzees.

One effect of the haphazard approach to non-verbal behavior has been an imperfect separation of body communication from verbal modes of communication. In many instances, the investigator's approach has required that gesture and movement be studied as a supplement to verbal content or to the expressive qualities of the voice itself. There is justification for this procedure, since, in everyday life, words, tone of voice, and gesture occur in combination with each other in what Birdwhistell (1962) calls "cross-referencing systems." Still, to study the body as an adjunct to other channels of communication is inevitably to reduce its significance.

No less detrimental are the customary modes of observation. So much more is known about words and linguistic structures than about the forms of body communication that the capacity to observe body motion as an independent system is weak. It could almost be stated as a methodological axiom that, in the first instance, one should study expressive body movement quite apart from words and speech or vocal systems of any kind. One needs to train the visual imagination and, for this purpose, the voice is a distraction.

Parallel to the lack of appreciation for the independence of body systems from other channels of communication, the literature displays a somewhat neglectful attitude toward the body as an anatomical unit. Investigators have almost uniformly favored some parts of the body over others. The face and its expressions have won all popularity contests, then the head as a whole, followed by the hands. Upper limbs have received a small amount of attention, legs, feet, and body-as-a-whole consistently less. There has been a sort of implicit assumption that the head and upper limbs are the most expressive parts of the body. Perhaps this is so; but too often—with the exception of some of Ekman's work—the matter was simply allowed to rest upon this assumption.

Cephalic and verbal preferences have biased not only what is to be studied but also the contexts of the investigations. Very often, the context has been that of the interview between two people—a face-to-face conversation featuring the sedentary posture. One scarcely needs to point out how restricted body movements are in such a situation. These contexts have been chosen largely on the basis of convenience rather than reasoned choice. The ease of acquiring body movement data in these circumstances has probably discouraged investigators from designing a setting in which large numbers of persons performing a wider range of movements can be examined.

Another problem in the field is a lack of agreement on the stimuli from the body that are responsible for perceptions of movement or expression. The body emits excessively complex arrays of stimuli that are coded into messages in accordance with an unconscious and as yet unknown program of transmission and of recognition. The first step in the detection of such programs is to be as specific as possible about the stimuli presented to an observer. In any one experimental presentation, it seems preferable to limit the number of foreground stimuli to as few as possible and to reduce background stimulation to the threshold required to maintain the barest contrast between figure and ground.

The choice of stimulus configurations will probably remain a controversial point for some time, since many investigators prefer to work with motion pictures. This preference is based on the reasonable assumption that the best way to investigate expressive movement is to observe actual movements. It is considered that filmed motion offers the advantage of repeated observation of the same piece of action. Plausible as this argument may be, there are advantages to using still pictures and thus limiting the amount of visual stimulation produced. When using films, for example, it is extremely difficult (though not impossible) to design an experiment capable of demonstrating what stimuli produce what effects. There will undoubtedly come a time when the coding system and the programming involved in the transmission of body messages are so well understood that problems of coping with complex and massive stimulation are no longer troublesome. Until then, an approach that limits the perceptual object and arranges for the presentation of a few stimuli that do not move, though they may suggest movement, seems a necessary supplement.

Given these problems which still await final solution, one can now consider the groupings of the studies that have been carried out. They appear to fall into three major classes with considerable variation within each: (1) studies that focus on the expressive characteristics of the actor, what he expresses and how he expresses it; (2) studies that inquire into the characteristics of the perceiver, what expressive meanings he perceives and what his perceptions are correlated with; (3) studies that treat the behavior of both actor and perceiver as parts of some larger system of relations, such as cultural systems, social groups, or paralinguistic structures. Since three comprehensive reviews of the literature (Sommer, 1967; Duncan, 1969; and Mehrabian, 1969) already exist, this study takes the opportunity to choose a different emphasis—to select certain studies for the methodological approach they represent, and to evaluate the approach rather than the substantive findings.

Within the first group, some investigations adopt a strategy encountered in the previous chapter—the diagnostic approach. An effort is made to determine what variable in the person is correlated with what expressive movement. The psychoanalytic literature, beginning with Freud, contains many explanations of the relation between an expressive movement or gesture and an unconscious motive (Deutsch, 1952, 1963; Jacobs, 1973). Feldman (1959) has written a sort of compendium, or dictionary, bringing together his own psychoanalytic observations and those of others, with regard to a long list of expressive movements, such as blinking, fingering the nose, hiding the breasts, crossing the fingers, finger- or knuckle-cracking, loosening the collar, and many other curiosities. The explanations of what motives are associated with what gestures are often intriguing. For example, blinking the eyelids may indicate a desire to conceal something or the desire to hide from others. In children, blinking may represent a desire to conceal that they have masturbated. In adults, especially women, blinking has the sexual connotation of an uncovering of the genitals. Thus, the movements of the eyes and their coverings can take the place of a variety of movements in which covering and uncovering, concealing or revealing are at issue.

Such observations are based on several procedures and conclusions that deserve close scrutiny. The inattention to stimulus detail—a specification of exactly what parts of the body are producing what movements—is a marked characteristic of such descriptions. For example, blinking is poorly differentiated from winking, though the first term usually refers to a flutter of both eyelids while the second describes a single contraction and relaxation of the *orbicularis oculi* of one eye. It may turn out that blinking and winking both correlate with similar motives but this seems unlikely and, in any case, one could not find it out unless they were treated separately. And the correlations themselves are supported either by no evidence or by evidence drawn from the analysis of one or two cases.

As to the actual connection between the motive and the mannerism, although the relationships are seldom made explicit, the explanation would seem to rest upon a symbolic representation, or displacement, of an intention movement. An intention movement obtains its meaning by virtue of its being a fragment of a more complete action to which it bears the relation of *pars pro toto*. In the case of blinking or winking, as described by Feldman, the completed action would be the covering and uncovering of the genitals. A small portion of that activity, it could be assumed, is transferred to the eyelids where it has the same meaning, though now under the guise (or disguise) of a social convention. Such an assumption, however, would have to be tested by methods more explicit than those used by Feldman, in order to determine its validity.

Because eyeblinks can easily be recorded and counted, they lend themselves to procedures in which a more precise effort is made to correlate a body movement with inner state variables, in a larger sample of subjects than the psychoanalyst is able to round up. Kanfer (1960), for example, with a sample of 38 married, female, psychiatric patients found that the rate of eyeblinks rose when the subjects discussed topics that aroused anxiety or tension. The rate also went up whenever the subjects switched to a new topic and fell as they approached the end of a topic. In order to determine whether rate of blinking is correlated merely with a generally high level of energy arousal, with cognitive switching (topic hopping), with a specific emotional state such as anxiety, or with a particular internal activity, such as the effort to suppress a fantasy or wish, Antrobus *et al.* (1964) asked 24 female college students to think of a secret wish and then to suppress it. The subjects were also told to imagine that they were watching a tennis game, and, in another episode, that they were looking at a static object lying on a table. The investigators found that, when subjects were contemplating a pleasurable fantasy or a static imaginary object, eye movements and eyeblinks were diminished. The rate of blinking and eye movement went up when subjects attempted to suppress their wish. Since suppression was accomplished by switching to another mental topic, active cognitive shifting and suppression of a thought were both aspects of a process which was accompanied by a certain amount of anxiety or tension. The fantasy of watching a tennis game was also accompanied by increased movements and blinking. It is clear, then, that the same, externally expressive body movement is correlated with a number of complexly related internal processes.

It would seem that the imprecise methods of the psychoanalyst and the more rigorous methods of the experimental psychologist both lead to the same conclusion—the absence of an isomorphic or invariant relationship between expressed behavior and internal motive. Given this situation, how can the investigator attempting to correlate inner variables with external behavior deal with the problem?

Four possible strategies suggest themselves from a review of the literature. This is not to say that the strategies have been self-consciously devised by investigators in order systematically to clear up research problems, but merely that they seem implicit in what has been done.

The first involves studying a variety of different expressive behaviors performed in a standard manner by a sample of subjects in order to determine along what inner dimensions individuals actually do vary. This was the method of Allport and Vernon (1933), who were interested in determining whether individuals betrayed a self-consistent style of expressive behavior. Their study showed that individuals were consistent across a variety of tasks in manner of expression. The inner variables, which were empirically derived from a statistical analysis, were grouped along three dimensions: (1) areality—the amount of physical space, large or small, the individual required in order to express himself; (2) centrifugality—a tendency for movements to be directed away from from rather than towards the body, a species of expansiveness; and (3) emphaticness—the sharpness and distinctiveness (versus vagueness) with which all movements are made.

This method of procedure appears never to have been followed up or exploited. It would be interesting to determine how the variations in expressive styles which the authors studied in the performance of mechanical motor acts would be correlated with other personality attributes, how they would vary for age, sex, cultural background, and situational context. Allport and Vernon were interested in the consistently patterned behavior encompassed by the word "style," and ignored the more usual subjects of "motivation" and "emotion." But in the areas of personality, "style" is poorly differentiated from both "emotion" and "motivation" as a defining concept. For example, if one is observing an angry young man or an irascible old man, are not anger, sex, age, and life circumstances involved in their expressive styles? It is often said that "style" is concerned more with *form* than with content, a distinction whose usefulness has been questioned. (See Gombrich, 1965.) But, until one has a better grasp of the formal properties of body movement, such definitional problems will continue to be troublesome. Allport and Vernon made a start in the determination of form–properties, which the studies to be reported here seek to continue.

The second strategy begins at the other pole of the inner–outer continuum. Rather than scrutinizing external behaviors to discover what internal factors are common to them, the investigator begins with a known, or ascertainable, internal factor and observes its "expression" in a variety of body movements. It is assumed that a person constitutes a unity; if he is angry, the anger will be expressed not just in a restricted part of the body nor in an isolated movement but in various ways, making use of various body parts.

The use of this strategy, however, to establish consistent relations between an inner disposition and its external bodily expression is much troubled by variability due to individual differences. Two methods have been elaborated for the purpose of detecting or establishing the inner variable with which body movements are to be correlated. In the first, the desired inner state is elicited by the presentation of an environmental stimulus. Krout (1935), for example, in one of the earliest attempts to apply this strategy, asked college student subjects to free associate to certain stimulus words and then observed their movements. He had previously divided gestures into four classes: (1) reflex gestures, such as the startle reaction; (2) conventional gestures, such as the salute; (3) semi-conventional gestures, containing a personal element, such as smoothing or straightening out one's clothes on sitting down or standing up; and (4) autistic gestures, with private and largely inscrutable meanings, such as scratching oneself, or twisting a lock of hair. The aim of administering the stimulus words was to elicit autistic gestures. The investigator asked the subject to report what his free associations had been during the time—usually unnoticed by the subject—that an autistic gesture has occurred. It was found that the autistic gestures were unconsciously produced in relation to an intrapsychic conflict and were usually accompanied by tension. Frequently, though not always, the subject was able to verbalize the conflict. On such occasions, the symbolic relation of the gesture to the conflict was said to be evident. However, since the type of conflict experienced by subjects varied in relation to the same stimulus words, there was no consistent relation between the gesture and the external stimulus. On the basis of subsequent work, Krout (1954) presented evidence on a large group of subjects that similar conflict situations were correlated with similar gestures and proposed a diagnostic system, or lexicon, for translating autistic gestures into conflicts.

Though Krout's experiments were ingenious, their yield of information was low. He focused exclusively on movements of the hands of the seated subject. Some of the hand positions described seem too slightly varied to carry the full freight of interpretation assigned to them. For example, the thumb between two fingers was said to be correlated with a conflict about achievement, while the index finger between two fingers was correlated with a conflict over affection. Some intervening links between the gesture and the conflict situation appear to be missing. What is noticeably absent is an exploration of the *intention movements* preceding the final resting position of the hands, on which their symbolic structure may be based. Presumably, each hand, or even each finger, may present one or another side of an unconscious conflict. But a different and as yet unconducted experiment would have to be performed to explicate the matter. Finally, a related difficulty is the fact that several of the gestures turned out to be correlated with different or even contradictory attitudes.

If an attempt is made to elicit a simpler internal variable through presenting standard environmental stimuli, this situation seems little improved. Coleman (1949), for example, presented subjects with a set of varied stimuli—a snake, an electric shock, a joke, and others—and then photographed the facial expression of the resulting emotions. Here again, in spite of some intersubject consistency, different subjects reacted with different emotions to many of the stimuli. Furthermore, even when the emotions were similar (as subjectively reported), the facial expressions could vary.

One possible cause of the relative failure of the strategy of these studies is the confinement of the observations to just one part of the body. In view of the ubiquity of individual differences, it would be logical to postulate that some persons express an internal variable through one part of the body while others express the same process through another body part or combination of parts. Dittmann's (1962) study focused just on this issue. He studied the pattern of movements composed of interaction between head, hands, and legs for five different moods. The frequency of movement within each of the body segments was estimated from motion pictures of a patient in psychotherapy. The moods were judged in accordance with what the patient was expressing verbally. It was found that anger correlated with increased movement of the head and legs, with hands inactive, while a depressed mood correlated with increased leg motion, both head and hands being quiet. Dittmann reported data on only one subject so that the question of individual consistencies and differences in patterns of segmental activity remains unexplored. And, of course, the subject was displaying the full range of his five moods in the standard, experimental posture—comfortably installed in a chair.[1]

The third strategy for obtaining firmer correlations between an internal variable and a movement expressive of it is the ontogenetic approach. The method consists of investigating how, in the course of the development of the child, an internal response pattern is molded or differentiated in behavioral expression in accordance with both maturational (internal) processes and environmental impacts. Experimental studies of behavioral processes in the first years of life are rather difficult to execute. As a result, studies of expressive movements in neonates and slightly older children, are not really segregated from the investigation of instinctual, emotional, perceptual, and cognitive processes in general. In addition, with infants and very young children who cannot talk, there is a pronounced difficulty over what to call the inner variables and how to determine their presence or absence. Usually, the presence of an inner state variable is inferred from the outer behavior of the infant, which is then said to be an indicator of the inner state.

One set of terms widely used by students of early infant development for internal state variables is "pleasure–displeasure" (or "unpleasure"). Buhler (1930), for example, "correlated" pleasure and displeasure with positively and negatively directed expressive movements. In a study of 69 infants carefully observed over twenty-four hour periods, she found that during the first few months of life movements expressive of displeasure occurred far more often than signs of pleasure. Buhler treated the term "displeasure" in two ways: as a generic label for the vague, internal discomfort which, in neonates, is correlated with generalized, non-specific thrashing movements; and, as the designation for a class of more differentiated internal states such as fear, anger, depression, and negative surprise.

Buhler reported that negatively directed movements associated with fear were of two types: defensive and withdrawal (or flight) movements. With regard to flight, which was treated as an attempt to avoid a painful, unwanted, or frightening stimulus, the newborn makes aimless movements, the one-month-old child arches his head and back, the two-month-old child turns aside his head, the five-month-old child changes his posture, and, at nine months, the whole body withdraws by rolling away or crawling away. Defensive movements begin at four to five months, with the use of the hands to push away unwanted objects and the repertoire of rejection grows rapidly thereafter. Definite signs of anger, such as hitting the hand that presents the unwanted stimulus, appeared only rarely during the first year of life. On the other hand, "passive displeasure," also referred to as depression, appears at the seven-months period and is conveyed by a falling of the corners of the mouth, a lack of lustre in the eyes, and a puckering of the nose.

Positively directed expressive movements, according to Buhler, are roughly coordinated with a pleasurable internal state. What is meant by the word "pleasure" is never specified. Some responses that are easily recognized as pleasurable appear, for example, when a sequence of behavior associated with displeasure is terminated, as when the baby is made warm and comfortable. On such occasions, pleasure is expressed, or is recognized, by a lifting of the corners of the mouth, glowing or gleaming eyes, and a firming of the muscles of the face. By the end of the second month, this pattern of the expression of pleasure develops into smiling and laughing when the infant sees the parents or hears their voice. Similar signs of the expression of pleasure—lifting of the corners of the mouth, actual smiling, or laughing—are associated with "function pleasure." This is an internal state which is correlated with the performance of sequences of movement and probably represents a mastery of motility.

Another internal state coordinate with positive expressive movements is that of "interest," defined as state of passive receptivity or readiness to receive stimuli toward which the infant is disposed by previous conditioning. It first appears during the third month and is correlated with an opening wide of the mouth, tensing of the facial muscles, slight wrinkling of the forehead, pursing of the mouth, and protrusion of the tongue. After six months, movements of the whole body are added to the facial expression of interest—a stiffening of the muscles, prolongation and stretching of the trunk, and a leaning toward the object of interest. The more active the movements in pursuit of the object, the more likely is the inner state to be "attention" rather than simply "interest."

"Positive surprise" is a third type of internal state associated with positive expressive movements. It is said to take various forms, or, perhaps, to be registered in various degrees, thus enabling the observer to distinguish "interested surprise" from "joyful surprise." There are two other classes of pleasure —pure joy (lacking the element of surprise) and desire (an anxious stretching toward a wanted object).

Buhler's findings have been presented in this detail partly to demonstrate the extraordinary variety of expressive movements which appear quite early in the developmental process, but principally to point out that as pure movements the descriptions would be meaningless. The concrete descriptions become informative only when tied to a classification of internal states, such as joy, interest, displeasure, and fear, triggered in behavior sequences. The reader then uses his implicit concepts of cause-and-effect contexts, based on his own experiences, to "understand" the movements. The influence of this process underlying the reader's perceptions is especially prominent because Buhler provides him with no well-formulated criteria for distinguishing the inner states from their outer manifestations. The internal states coordinate with expressive movements are based upon common sense and conventional labeling.

This atheoretical approach is both a strength and a weakness. Since no theoretical system is advanced and no hypotheses are stated, there is little to challenge the quarrelsome or to stimulate the competitive investigator. Balancing this disadvantage, however, is the probability that the absence of a specialized theoretical language and a set of hypotheses made the observers in her studies much more open to the varied phenomena of infantile expressive behavior than are investigators who are pledged to a particular theoretical approach.

That formal scientific theory is paradoxically liberating *and* constricting may be seen in the work of the psychoanalytically oriented investigators whose studies followed Buhler's. They have studied a much narrower range of expressive behaviors but have had much more to say about their significance. Their orientation within psychoanalytic ego psychology has governed the issue to which they have addressed themselves—to check traditional psychoanalytic assumptions about ontogenesis, which were formulated from studies of the neurotic behavior of adults, against the observed behavior of both normal and disturbed children. Since the behavior of very young children is so largely non-verbal, it was inevitable that expressive behavior should come under scrutiny.

The work of Spitz on the genesis of expressive movement in early infancy is probably the most fully elaborated of the rare psychoanalytic contributions to the subject. It is possible to treat Spitz's work as belonging in the third type of investigation—studies which look at both the expression and the perception of behavior as parts of a larger system of communication. Nevertheless, despite a modicum of attention to the behavior of the parent, Spitz is concerned primarily with the fate of internal, innate, biologically determined variables as they are transformed during infant development into meaningful expressive behaviors. He is also much preoccupied with the mutual influences of such transformations on cognitive and executive processes and on object relations, as aspects of ego development.

Spitz's work can best be summarized in terms of the developmental model it presents for consideration. The model assumes that biologically given reflexes (innate releasing mechanisms) appropriate to an early stage of development are, after an interval of quiescence, re-evoked through appropriate environmental influence and reconstituted anew as expressive movements. In their novel form, they attain both social (communicative) and psychological (dynamic) properties. The interrelations responsible for the transformation are quite complex. What is of essence is the single line of development of a biologically given behavior pattern in the process of psychosocial maturation. As the *relevant* or key internal variable, the original biological behavior pattern functions like a tracer, an element that not only persists over developmental time but that orients around it the internal and external processes that go to make up the expressive behavior.

The model is most completely worked out for the expressive behavior of negation—the head-shaking gesture of saying, "No." Spitz postulates that the bodily pattern originates in the reflex horizontal, back-and-forth rooting movements of the neonate at the breast. The movement is a form of searching or scanning—a hunt for the nipple. At this stage, the behavior pattern has the positive meaning of a turning toward the object. Later, rooting behavior itself subsides (though it may be regressively reinstated, as for example, in the negative, cephalogyric motions of severely deprived infants). During the remainder of the first year of life, refusal is expressed by motor avoidance movements—a pushing away of the object with the hands, or the typical "hiding behavior" that accompanies the "eighth month anxiety response" in the presence of a stranger. In the first trimester of the second year, the child begins to imitate the parents, just as the parents imitate the behavior of the child. Through reciprocal identification in the course of such interactions, the child then identifies with the frustrating, nay-saying of the parents, including the taking on of the negative head-shaking. This is a form of "identification with the aggressor" which can subsequently be used *against* the parents, resulting in a significant increment of autonomy for the child. It is also an important step in the development of the capacity for abstraction, since negation can thereafter be abstracted from its particular contexts and used as a general symbol (head-shaking and nay-saying) for all refusals. Finally, the body movement employed is the old "rooting behavior," now revived and used in the service of social interaction.

Whether or not one is convinced by the evidence for such a sequence is not so important as are the general characteristics of the developmental model. For the model supplies a design of postulated interrelationships between innate biological processes, environmental impacts, and mediating psychological processes which could be applied and tested for other expressive behaviors. Its generalizability is both its strength and its weakness. It has the virtue of any explicit model— that of generating further questions and applications for future research. Its weakness is that the concentration on one particular form of expressive behavior —especially one so conventional and abstract—may draw attention away from other, more subtle and less easily defined behaviors expressive of similar inner states. For example, Mittelmann (1954) has pointed out that "saying no" is only one of several interrelated behaviors expressive of the developing autonomy (and stubbornness) of the infant during the first trimester of the second year. Another behavior practiced on behalf of autonomy and integrity is the grabbing and holding close to the body of a desired object, accompanied by the declaration, "It's mine." The concept of "mine" and its correlations with visual space is just as important an abstraction as the concept of "No."

In tracing the ontogenetic relation between internal variables and externally expressive behavior, the psychoanalysts have been concerned—even in the careful examination of filmed sequences—less with the actual observables of expressive behavior than with its implications for the more invisible intrapsychic, developmental process (Kestenberg, 1965, 1966, 1967). However, the use of specified, internal variables as the determinants of what is to be expressed—in the psychoanalytic study of the child, as in the other areas previously reviewed —remains problematical. The chief difficulties are: (1) the considerable amount of individual variability between the expressible factor and the mode of expression in different subjects and within the same subject at different times; and (2) the circularity (or subjectivity) involved in relating an internal variable to its mode of expression. The logic and the utility of making such a distinction *for the purpose of analyzing behavior* are not disputed. Analytical (conceptual) distinctions, only imperfectly separable in the empirical event, crop up everywhere in the behavioral sciences. But it is necessary to be as explicit as possible about the difficulties that lie in the path of the investigator who starts with the internal variables in the effort to analyze expressive behavior.

There is a fourth strategy for dealing with the inside–outside correlation, but because of the manner in which it ignores the necessity of validating statements about the inside independently, it does not perhaps quite deserve to be called a strategy. Nevertheless, the method is used by a large number of students of bodily behavior, and it deserves separate consideration; and, as later chapters will show, this study seems to belong within this group.

The strategy is distinguished by relying on an observer to make the judgment both about *what* is being expressed and *how* it is being done. Thus, the observer may be asked to say which of a series of photographs (of faces, principally, but sometimes of whole body positions or movements) express the emotion "contempt" or the interview situation called "stress." If enough observers agree about the labeling, the experimenter will examine the properties of the stimuli and be in a position to make some statement about "how" contempt or stress is shown externally. This is the method used in the well-known study of Schlosberg's (1952), in which he showed that the emotions that could be reliably judged from photographs could, in addition, be arranged around a circle whose circumference consisted of the names under which these emotions usually went and whose principal diagonals stood for the dimensions that presumably underlay the discrete names—the dimensions being pleasantness–unpleasantness and attention–rejection. One can object to Schlosberg's use of posed photographs, but the objection is not fatal, partly because reliable classification (and the circular arrangement) were achieved by his subjects with several distinct series of photographs of different actors, and partly because there is evidence for cross-cultural agreement about the emotions expressed by posed faces. (Ekman, Sorenson, and Friesen, 1969.)

Evidence for the reliable classification of spontaneous as well as posed photographs is provided by Ekman (1964, 1965, 1969, Ekman and Friesen, 1967, and Ekman, Friesen and Ellsworth, 1972). He has taken films of students and patients in various interview settings; in some cases, the setting could be described beforehand, in other cases it would only be judged afterward. Judges would then attempt to pair selected stills from these films with the situation they were supposed to represent—and the results indicate that quite a number of pairings can reliably be made. In other studies, Ekman showed the films themselves but with certain classes of gestures extirpated for some subjects and left in for others; the resulting differences in judgments of the films would then provide information on the meaning that the extirpated gestures conveyed. Knapp (1965, and Knapp and Ehlinger, 1966) has used entirely different visual presentations

—produced by placing black cardboard silhouettes of figures against a plain background—and analyzed observer's descriptions of the resulting shadow—theater interactions. The advantage of his stimuli was that the same figures could appear in different positions (in varying head inclinations and vertical displacements), so that none but a very limited number of expressive attributes would be manipulated at a time.

There are two possible assumptions behind this strategy, of which the second seems preferable. One is to suppose that the observer can deduce inner states accurately from their outer manifestations. This assumption, however, is open to the objection that, in the absence of an independent criterion of accuracy, all that can be claimed is that observers make a reliable deduction though not necessarily a valid one. Validity can be established in this case only by identifying the inner state separately and accurately, and this, as already seen, can be very problematic in practice. The alternative assumption makes the problem of validity less pressing by shifting the "locus" of meaning of the expressive act. If one assumes that the outer manifestation is less a product of an inner condition, which in some manner presses outward, than an act which is *itself* directed outward—that is, towards other observers—the main research problem becomes one of correlating the physical properties of the manifestations with the observers' interpretations. The earlier problem of "inner" validity is not disposed of, of course, but it is made considerably less urgent by being placed in a more restricted perspective—one that searches for the *meaning* of expressive acts in in the eyes of the beholder.

Carrying this assumption further, one may argue that meaning as attributed by observers must on *a priori* grounds be reasonably correct in the ordinary run of things. Social interaction could not be based on a total misunderstanding of the intentions of others (although successful comedy can be, at least in small doses). And it seems plausible further to assume that human beings rarely engage in mere externalizations of their inner states, even when out of sight of others. From some time after early infancy, they have fairly good knowledge of the reactions their actions can be expected to evoke. It makes more sense, therefore, to say that persons *present* themselves rather than that they *express* themselves.

Two sets of research questions should naturally arise from this shift in theoretical focus, and they may be said to be concerned with two aspects of "outer" validity. The first could concentrate on the conditions of accuracy or inaccuracy in the sender—that is, what types of senders, and in which situations, are apt or inept at behaving in a manner consistent with their intentions. Curiously enough, such questions have been neglected in systematic research, although in psychotherapy they are asked quite often (and solved occasionally), at least on an individual basis. The second set can concentrate on the conditions of accuracy or inaccuracy in the observer; these have been asked systematically, and are next discussed.

The process correlated with the perception of expressive behavior can be broken up into four analytical categories, all interrelated in the empirical event: (1) the cues or stimuli taken into account by the perceiver in reaching his judgment; (2) the cognitive categories, or coding principles, used by the perceiver in matching cues with potential judgments; (3) the unconscious internal needs and defensive processes in the perceiver—his "perceptual style"—which render him impervious to some expressions and delicately attuned to others; and (4) the social context of the perceptive act, whether it takes place in a "real life" situation, or a laboratory situation, as well as the set of instructions, explicit or implicit, under which the perceiver is operating.

Although there is a large and growing literature on the general issues involved in social perception and the process of forming an assessment of others (see Bruner and Tagiuri, 1954; Tagiuri and Petrullo, 1958; Tagiuri, 1958; Allport, 1961), only a small portion of this literature is devoted to the topic of bodily expressions, and this portion, with a few exceptions, is limited to studies of the human face. Furthermore, the investigations of facial expressions center almost wholly on the judgment of emotions.

According to the thoughtful review of Bruner and Tagiuri, the difficulties and contradictory findings of such investigations are due to several overlapping technical problems: (1) the difficulty in determining the physical properties of the stimuli that are taken into consideration in forming a judgment of what the face is expressing; (2) the nature of the discrimination demanded of the subject in distinguishing one emotion from another—e.g. to distinguish disgust from contempt; (3) the nature of the identifying labels that judges are asked to use —for example, agreement is higher if judges can use their own descriptive labels rather than words imposed upon them by the experimenter; (4) the lack of contextual information about the situation in which a given emotion (and its accompanying facial expression) was experienced; and (5) the lack of inter-individual consistency in the mode of expression of an emotion, and (6) the failure of experimenters to sample variations in expressive style over a sufficiently large population.

These critical issues are quite relevant to the types of study reported here. For example, though it is difficult to determine precisely what physical stimuli the viewer takes into account in looking at the moving or still body, it is not impossible. There are several ways one might go about it, depending upon how fine-grained or coarse-grained a method one elects to use. For a fine-grained stimulus, such as the positioning of an eyebrow, one could track eye movements in the viewer and use an elaborate and detailed notation system such as has been proposed by Birdwhistell (1952, 1970). However, fine-grained approaches to the myriads of stimuli emitted by the human body are, at the present time, quite frustrating and confusing. There is no question that the viewer takes note of the smallest and most fleeting stimulus, often outside of awareness, as has been demonstrated by Haggard and Isaacs (1966). But it is still difficult to discover a method for translating these densely packed and subtle cues into stable meanings. Therefore, it has proved more practical to use a coarse-grained approach, that is, a method of confining the stimuli to be noted to the large-scale patterns emitted *in toto* by the anatomical divisions of the body, such as the head, the upper torso and arms, the legs, or the body as a whole in relation to another person.

Bruner and Tagiuri's second and third points can be grouped together since they are both aspects of the cognitive processing of expressive movement. If a viewer is asked to state what "emotion" a face or a figure is expressing, he encounters the vagaries of the labeling problem in the sphere of emotions. The words used to describe emotions (or affects or feelings) are drawn from an everyday language not notable for its precision. Having borrowed them wholesale, psychology has ever since made vigorous attempts, without much success, to discover what they mean. Fear, anxiety, rage, jealousy, pleasure, love, aggression, hate, warmth, withdrawal, and many others have been entered into the lists of attributes subjects have been asked to infer from looking at motion or still pictures, paintings, or "real life" encounters. Such terms are nearly intractable either to definition or scaling because the method by which one infers their existence in behavior is largely unknown. How does one decide that another person is "jealous"? Presumably, by taking into account his immediate situation, the events that preceded it (and possibly his whole life history), his anticipations of the future, and his current behavior, including his statements about himself and others. In short, the word is a referent for an immense vista of interpersonal facts and meanings, an abstraction that almost defies reduction to the concrete settings from which it is abstracted. Yet, the traditions of Western thought force one to regard "jealousy" as an inner thing, a psychosomatic state or process that actually exists somewhere within the individual and could be found, if only there were some way of opening him up to inspection.

If emotion—"that whale among the fishes" (Meyer, 1933)—remains so obdurate to investigation, then it seems reasonable to conclude that it has been erroneously conceptualized. Probably, linguistic traditions are misleading. At any rate, an attempt will be made in the next chapter to reconceptualize what is involved in such behavior so as to bring empirical observation more into line with the flow of human events. It seems that such a reconceptualization is mandatory if the cognitive procedures of the investigator are to be harmonized with those of the naïve viewer.

The question of how to classify emotions is not the only cognitive problem involved in the perception of expressive behavior. In fact, the emotion problem comes up in acute form mainly because the recognition and assessment of expressive behavior have been investigated through presenting judges with faces (as in the Schlosberg study cited above) which are conventionally treated as if they had nothing to express but an emotion. But it is obvious that the face can also express affirmation, negation, understanding, bewilderment, doubt, conviction, denial, questioning, flirtation, and a large number of other interpersonal transactions not ordinarily called emotions. When the rest of the body is taken into consideration, the list of labels and the uncertainty about their conventional status increase. Is a shrug an emotion or does it convey an emotion? How is one to classify activity versus repose, tension versus relaxation, an openly receptive versus a closed-in posture?

Some would suggest that these behaviors be called messages and that they be considered as parts of a system of communication. The proposal itself seems sensible enough at first. Certainly, a shrug is a piece of information transmitted to a viewer, whether or not he is a participant in the system of communication. However, there is an objection to this mode of conceptualization. To treat expressive behavior as wholly embedded within the *system* of communication or interaction is to overlook the directedness and purposiveness of behavior arising within the individual. Although the social system controls the behavior of the individual to a considerable extent, there is no reason to suppose that the system can prevent the individual from determining, consciously or unconsciously, what to present or withhold from it. Expressive behavior is what the individual *presents* to the system of interaction, his contribution to it. Thus, here, *expressive* is not considered the best term; *presenting behavior* is used instead and the formal, stimulus properties of *presentations* in visual space are the properties to be investigated.

Presentations, moreover, whether intended or unintended, are not made merely to a system of communications that sits in some abstract state outside the flow of time and human events. Presenting behavior is made to a system of action that is going somewhere, that has a destination, whether known in advance or not. The *line of action* is a property both of the individual and of the group, which the presentations of the individual can facilitate or block. What is presented either moves the action forward, backward, stalls it, sidetracks it, or breaks it up altogether.

Of course, the system of action, and the separate lines of action within it, being social, are composed not only of people but of their social roles as well. An individual puts forth his presenting (expressive) behavior in the course of taking his social role. He presents himself as someone—say an Iago—subordinate to and respectful of, indeed flattering toward, his superior officer,

Othello. In his role as subordinate and friend, he expresses himself as having no intentions for the future except to support and push forward Othello's interests. But, watch out, for he conceals his "jealousy." Behind the mask, he intends at the least to block and at the most to destroy Othello's relation with Desdemona and his whole future career as a respected figure in the political life of Venice. He can only carry out his unexpressed intentions within his officially allocated and publicly sanctioned roles. Therefore, he must mask his presentations lest he be ejected from the relationships he requires in order to carry them out.

These situational complexities lead to Bruner and Tagiuri's fourth point about the difficulties in research on the recognition of expressive behavior: the lack of contextual information about the situation in which a given emotion was experienced. One is reminded of Stanislavski's advice to the actor–student cited in Chapter 1: "Can one sit in a chair and for no reason at all be jealous? . . . Never seek to be jealous . . . for its own sake. All such feelings are the results of something that has gone before." If a judge is required to interpret the smiling expression on the photograph of a face, without being given any information about the past, present, or future contexts of the person's situation, can he distinguish the smile that masks jealousy from the smile of genuine sympathy? Will he not have to supply an environing situation, or a scenario stretching over time, from his own stock of smiling responses?

The example of jealousy is, of course, extreme, and should not be interpreted to mean that *no* emotion can be judged without knowledge of context. Some emotions seem to be so clearly portrayed that they can even help determine the context, as Frijda (1969) has shown. But many emotions depend largely or entirely on their context for recognition, both at one point in time and in a sequence. At this point, one encounters an ancient dilemma, which appears in various modern guises, about the nature of cognition, and this dilemma sets the stage for one further study of the process of inference.

Two views, it appears, of the cognitive process have opposed each other in the history of philosophy and psychology. In one, cognition is pictured as a step-wise, sequential affair, each step determining and limiting the next, as in logical inferences and mathematical reasoning. This type of cognitive model assumes that the mind can only deal with one thing at a time and that it moves from part to part over time in the process of building a whole—whether that whole is a sentence, a conclusion, a concept, or a painting. The other cognitive model pictures the process of thinking as beginning with a whole—a concept, a schema, or a construct—within which the partial data either of sensation or thought are assembled.

That the problem is not merely a dry, semantic dispute can be ascertained through its entry into several areas of theoretical and practical application: the presumed difference between the intellectual procedures of the sciences and the arts (see Holton, 1964); the appropriateness of various methods for correlating visual imagination and craftsmanship in art, architecture, and design (see Ehrenzweig, 1964, 1965 and Gibson, 1965); and the design of computer programs for problem solving (see Newell, Shaw, and Simon, 1964), and for pattern recognition (see Neisser, 1953, 1967). In all these areas, the authors of the references cited have been able to demonstrate that *both* serial, sequential processing *and* simultaneous, multi-level processing of information are required for the recognition of abstract form and its various concrete, sensory versions. Selfridge and Neisser's (1960) description of a computer program for the recognition of hand-printed letters utilizing multiple, simultaneous, parallel operations, all of which must be carried out before any decision is made, seems a most convincing demonstration of a machine simulation of holistic thinking. Another model for dealing with the simultaneous, hierarchically-structured cognitive–perceptive process, while yet retaining the feature of linear sequence, has been proposed by Miller, Galanter, and Pribram (1960).

If this dichotomy is to be made relevant to studies of the process of perceiving expressive behavior, one must make a further distinction. To conceive of holistic processes in combination with parallel or simultaneous processing seems unnecessary, as does the apparent combination of elemental processes with sequential ones. One can ask quite separately, it seems, whether a given process is sequential or simultaneous, and whether it is holistic or elemental. The first question is probably more difficult to answer, although the evidence previously reviewed indicates that the interpretation of a given behavior may depend on its place in a sequence of acts—which, in turn, suggests that the processing involved is also sequential. This does not mean, of course, that sequential processing is used exclusively or even predominantly, but merely that sequential processing may be assumed to operate in certain circumstances. The second question—whether a process is holistic or elemental—seems more within the reach of current research methods, because evidence for or against one or the other alternative depends on being able to identify the product, rather than being able to observe the process itself. A study by Katz (1964) is relevant here, in that it illustrates the operation of both holistic impressions and the elements that enter into determining them.

Katz was interested in studying what postural configurations (elements) contributed to what he called the "understanding posture" (a whole) of an interviewer. He made use of filmed data of dyadic interviews gathered by Rosenthal (1963) in the course of studying unintentional biasing of experimental data. Judges were first asked to rate the filmed interviewers on the overall presence of "the understanding posture" for two groups of interviewers—experienced and inexperienced. Then, at various points in the film, motion was stopped and judges were asked to rate the interviewers on several stimulus configurations observed during the intervening period—number of glances at subjects emitted by interviewers; number of smiles; amount of head activity; direction of experimenter's gaze; slant and tilt of experimenter's body, toward or away from subject's position, or experimenter's hands· and their specific activity. He put forward the hypotheses that: (1) The principal body movement characteristic of the understanding posture is an activity of the head that denotes attending to another person; (2) as the interviewer gains experience, his use of body cues (as reinforcers) of unintended biasing will increase; and (3) a central cue for such unintended biasing is a body movement toward the subject, conveyed by the two different modalities of forward movement, slant and tilt. Analysis of the data gave strong support for the first hypothesis, weak support for the second, and no support for body slant but strong support for the forward tilt (slouching or hunching versus tilting forward from the upright vertical plane). The study demonstrated, then, that observers could both make holistic judgments *and* identify the elements that went into them.

This attempt to review the issues arising from studies of the perception of expressive behavior has come up against the conceptual and technical problems they generate. A possible reaction to the problems of studying either the expression of emotional meaning or its perception is to study both at once. This likelihood introduces the third major area of review: expressive behavior regarded as a system of action occurring in a social situation. The disciplines that have contributed to this area are sociology, anthropology, and linguistics, or rather, its offspring, paralinguistics and kinesics.

Sociology has contributed very little directly to the study of body movement, though one might have thought that, at least in the area of small-group behavior and microsociology, some attention would have been paid to the topic. With respect to their content, sociology and social psychology appear to be rather disembodied sciences. Their subjects, it seems, are human beings who display their attitudes, enact their roles, occupy their statuses, resolve their conflicts, establish their families, and move up or down within their stratified social systems without ever using their bodies. The dispensability of the body as an object for study in sociology has been repeatedly affirmed. For Durkheim (1951), social man was superimposed upon physical man. For Cooley (1922), society was the collective aspect of personal ideas, and facial expression was merely the "handle" by which such ideas were communicated. Even Mead (1934), whose notion of "the conversation of gestures" suggests a physical interaction, had something else in view. "Gestures," whatever they are, are important only for their symbolic equivalents, for their ability to evoke "organized attitudes." Their specific somatic forms are never described; they are merely the vague and generalized means through which attitudes are internalized. In more recent times, this disdain for the somatic has been put forward with greater strictness as the principle of somatic exclusion (Parsons and Shils, 1951).

There are some significant exceptions to the rule of somatic exclusion in sociology. Simmel (1924) has discussed the implications for the control of inter-personal behavior of unilateral and mutual glancing—the encounter of the eyes. "The eye," says Simmel, "has a unique sociological function." Park and Burgess (1924, pp. 29–93) have discussed the significance of touching for the topics of social contact and social distance. And Goffman (1959) has devoted considerable attention to the manner in which people present themselves to others in the course of daily life. In fact, we are greatly indebted to Goffman for the vivid and detailed way in which he has described presentation behavior in his various publications. But the "sociology of the senses" anticipated by Simmel has never developed (Frank, 1958).

It is true that there have been a few detailed studies of the movements of the eyes occurring between two interacting persons—including direction of gaze, mutual glancing, and avoidance. These studies have demonstrated that the person speaking breaks off eye contact more frequently than the listener (Exline, Gray and Schuette, 1965; Kendon, 1967; and Nielsen, 1962). It has also been estab-lished, at least for a sample of college students, that women maintain mutual eye contact for longer periods than men (Exline, 1963, and Exline, Gray and Schuette, 1965). Ellsworth (1968) has shown that eye contact will produce quite different results when the topic of conversation is pleasant than when it is unpleasant. Renneker (1963) has observed that, in films of psychotherapy inter-views, eye-area movements are first in frequency, head movements second, and other speech-accompanying movements third. Ekman (1964) has demonstrated that, with eye contact omitted, in two-person interactions, the head conveys the emotional quality of the communication, while the body as a whole conveys the information about the intensity of feeling. But these studies, closer to social psychology than to sociology, have for the most part been conducted by psy-chologists.

The contributions of anthropology are another matter. The concern in anthro-pology with body movement has ranged from specialized studies of the physical interactions between family members to broad surveys of the varieties of postural and gestural mannerisms in a large sample of cultures. Mead and MacGreggor (1951), for example, have published a photographic essay of the development of motor habits in Balinese children. They give special emphasis to the way in which the maturation process in the child is patterned by learning in the course of interaction with the parent so as to produce the postural and movement responses characteristic of Balinese adults. Their work is a landmark, not only because of the demonstrative use of filmed sequences of behavior, but also because of the wealth of research questions that are raised—questions that still await exploration and explication.

The general surveys of motoric customs and habits raise a group of problems not easily dealt with in the compass of this review. Some are descriptions of or references to the cross-cultural distributions of limited aspects of body movement such as posture (Hewes, 1957), facial expression (Eibl-Eibesfeldt, 1972) and gesture (Hayes, 1957). Within their restricted contexts, these works serve as dictionaries or lexicons, pointing to research questions with reference to systematic variation of body presentations between cultures. Others, like the surveys of La Barre (1947 and 1964), are fragmented museum collections of bits and pieces of body behavior from all over the world roughly grouped into such categories as styles of walking, greeting, kissing, beckoning, pointing, and sound production such as musical, whistling, and drum languages. In part, the miscellany of motor behaviors that La Barre assembles is meant to convince the unconvinced that such acts are more culturally than biologically determined coding systems that must be learned by the populations of the various cultures. In part—and in this he is surely successful—they are meant to impress the reader with the sheer variability of human custom. Fortunately, other studies (Ekman and Friesan, 1971; Ekman, 1972) have demonstrated that, at least for the face, a certain amount of consistency obtains across cultures.

The question of the significance of variation of movement patterns between cultures is one of the most basic and subtle issues involved in the attribution of meaning to the presentations of the body. It is an issue to which the research to be reported in the following chapters has not been able to address itself, although it is of cardinal importance to any future studies the present investigators may undertake. A series of studies that does take cultural relativity into account has been published by Hall (1955, 1959, 1961, 1966). An anthropologist, Hall singles out data of body movement confined to certain dimensions of physical space. He points out, for example, that different cultures have different norms for the appropriate physical distance to be established between persons involved in conversation and other types of interactions. Hall's conceptualization of physical interactions is embedded in a comprehensive theory of cultural variation as a "silent" but specifiable system of communication, and his distinctions between the formal, informal, and technical aspects of such systems is of considerable interest for both theoretical and applied anthropology.

In a more recent publication, Hall (1963, 1966) provides a set of categories accompanied by a system of notation for a class of events that he calls a "proxemic behavior," or, more simply, "proxemics." It is proposed that proxemic behavior is a function of eight different dimensions with their appropriate scales: (1) postural–sex identifiers; (2) sociofugal–sociopetal orientations; (3) kinaesthetic factors; (4) touch code; (5) retinal combinations; (6) thermal code; (7) olfaction code; and (8) voice loudness scale. Because of the range of interpersonal transactions to be noted, Hall's program comes close to Simmel's appeal for a comparative sociology of the senses, and it is apparent that it transcends the more limited body movement categories reviewed here. The intent of the program is to record, qualitatively and quantitatively, all events occurring between people in space, based on the biological possibilities of action and the various constraints upon these possibilities imposed by cultural variations. Little attempt is made to attribute meaning to the various items in the "dimensions," but the author suggests that, once observers begin to use the categories and the notation system, culturally ascribed meanings of proxemic behavior keyed to the system will be easily discovered. This seems a reasonable proposition and it is to be hoped that the proposed program will be tested in various contexts in order to determine what its advantages and disadvantages may be.

At least two investigators have studied dimensions analogous to those of proxemics, although not with a view to testing this proposed program. Little and collaborators, for example (1965 and 1968), have looked at the relation between personal space and value congruence, to find if "congruent" people are assumed to stand closer than non-congruent individuals. Sommer (1961, 1965a and b, 1966, 1967) has studied the relation of seating arrangements to status; he has tried, for example, to find out whether subjects will seat themselves closer or farther from an empty chair "belonging" to persons of high or low status. His studies are not confined to such simple variables as these, but most of them have been done in naturalistic settings, a fact that lends to their credibility. (It might be pointed out that his work represents one of the rare applications of field experimentation, and that its success in his hands leads one to wonder at its recent neglect.)

It is of considerable interest that a number of the items and their notations in the first four categories proposed by Hall are similar to those this study has arrived at without knowledge of his conceptual experiments. If two attacks on the same phenomenon, starting from different angles of approach, turn out to arrive independently at similar conceptualizations, one tends to be persuaded that the conceptual categories are relevantly geared to the phenomenon.

Hall's method depends largely on the model of structural linguistics, and in this it resembles the work of Birdwhistell, whose work on "kinesics" has represented a pioneering attempt to conceptualize and define the phenomena of body communication. Birdwhistell (1961) has defined kinesics as ". . . a methodology . . . concerned with the communicational aspects of learned, patterned body motion behavior." By "patterned body motion," Birdwhistell (1963) has in mind a quite strict analogy to the conceptual categories of descriptive linguistics:

As I worked with Kinesics, parallel phenomena emerged in the body-motion material. When kines, kinemorphs, and complex kinemorphic constructions (comparable to phonemes, morphemes, and syntactic sentences) were isolated, other behavior extending over varying lengths of kinesic material was revealed. Analogic to the linguistic material, parakinesics, although differing in structure from the microkinesic particles, was patterned and communicational.

A further analogy to descriptive linguistics in Birdwhistell's method has been the development of a system of notation for kines, kinemorphs, and other distinguishable units of body motion, including microkinesic particles that have to do with very small movements in isolated body parts (Birdwhistell, 1952). The format of the notation system is identical with that used for transcription in descriptive linguistics.

The publications on the kinesic approach, up to the present, have been mainly programmatic. No completed illustrations of the application of its descriptive concepts to actual behavior have been published, although partial ones have appeared (Birdwhistell, 1970) and a future publication has been announced in which the kinesic, paralinguistic, linguistic, and psychodynamic approaches will be correlated with each other in the analysis of an interview. (Bateson, Birdwhistell, Brosin, Hockett and McQuown, in press.) A full and concise survey of kinesic concepts—based in part on the yet-unpublished materials, has been published by Hayes (1964). From the evidence so far, it seems safe to predict that the strategy of analysis in this publication will take the form of *explication de texte*, the basic procedure involved in the descriptive linguistic model. If this is the case, then one may also predict that it will eventually be necessary to devise a field of "psychokinesics," parallel to "psycholinguistics," in order to take into account the psychological processes correlated with kinesic phenomena.

Because of the paucity of published, illustrative materials, kinesics, like proxemics, has not yet been widely applied and tested by other investigators. Research conducted in consultation with Birdwhistell, but going beyond the kinesic concepts, has been published by Scheflen (1963, 1964, 1965, 1973). The data of communication used for body movement analysis are derived from psychotherapeutic interviews and are, accordingly, concerned with the positions of seated figures engaged in conversation. The supplementary concepts suggested by Scheflen are of considerable interest, however, since they are designed to discriminate units in the flow of communications which are larger than kinemorphic constructions. If it is assumed that kinemorphs are equivalent to phrases in the lexical system, then Scheflen's concepts carry on the parallels between movement and speech. Roughly, sentences become equivalent to "points" (head, hand, or eye-movement junctures following brief statements), paragraphs to "positions" (sustained body posture followed by shifts when one has made one's position clear), and a "speech" (or a letter or a total conversation) is made the equivalent of a "presentation" (getting up to leave the room at the conclusion of an interaction). Since these notions and the use made of the word *presentation* are in some ways similar to and in others different from the theoretical propositions incorporated into the investigations to be reported in this book, they will be discussed further in the next chapter.

Scheflen makes a very strong case for the strategy here referred to as *explication de texte*. He provides a specification of its operation under the rubric, "contextual analysis" (Scheflen, 1965). What is referred to is a set of discovery procedures for the detection and isolation of units in a communication system, and for the determination of the function of these units in the system. The suggested procedures are practical and may well serve to systematize the rather random and frequently frustrating efforts of those investigators who are studying sound films of interviews without knowing which, among the hundreds of body stimuli encountered, are worth paying attention to. (See Renneker, 1963.) But Scheflen scorns research methods designed to isolate the psychological variables that are correlated with the linguistic and kinesic phenomena. Such methods are denounced as "atomistic" and unsuited to the actual phenomena, which are better treated by natural history methods.

Perhaps one would be less inclined to dispute such a theoretical stance if it were not presented so uncompromisingly. Be that as it may, the linguistic analogy underlying these studies seems unproven and quite likely theoretically constricting. Several serious objections to the analogy may be formulated—serious enough to suggest that a better starting point for research must exist than the analogy with language.

(1) There is high agreement among the users of language about the meaning of its elements and rules for their combination. True, very few users are aware of the elements and rules, but most users respond to changes in the elements in a way that indicates a perceived change in meaning—which, after all, is the linguist's criterion for defining elements in the first place. No comparable degree of agreement is observable for body movements.

(2) Language consists of units that are both stable and discrete. The layman is aware of "letters of the alphabet," words, sentences, and paragraphs; and the linguist treats phonemes, morphemes, and other structures, whose characteristics are clearly defined (and also agreed upon). By contrast, the units of non-verbal communication, no matter how useful for research, are superimposed by investigators on a much more continuous flow of acts. If the units of non-verbal communication were discrete, a satisfactory system for their transcription would very likely have been devised at about the time writing was invented.

(3) Although a few linguistic units (onomatopoeic words) derive their form from the objects or acts they represent, they are a small minority, while, in bodily communication, there seems to be a considerable number of "units" that either denote an obvious act or object (such as bodily protrusions used for pointing, or some obscene gestures) or take the form of parts of the complete act (such as the clenched fist, the frequent "grooming" observable especially in situations involving both sexes, or the forward lean of the torso to indicate closeness, concern, agreement, etc.). The latter type of movement seems to be the more frequent of the two and is discussed more fully in later chapters as *intention movements*. (One must note that Desmond Morris, 1967, emphasizes the importance of intention movements in animal communication.)

(4) Related to the preceding point is the unique ability of language to refer to entities that do not exist in any concrete, immediate, observable sense—such as past or future tenses, gods or demons, silent majorities, and other unobservables. Perhaps this capacity exists because words can be defined purely by their relation to other words (as the existence of pictureless dictionaries will confirm). This is not to say that language could exist entirely without concrete referents, but that linguistic communication can take place with only a minimal awareness of concrete referents. No such property is immediately evident in non-verbal communication.

(5) Language contains not only discrete units but readily discernible rules for their combination. As a result, new utterances can be produced that contain units never before brought together—and be understood. On this point, Scheflen argues specifically that non-verbal communication is similar, although the non-verbal combination rules require more complex methods of recording and analysis which remain to be discovered. He further hypothesizes that the linguistic and non-linguistic parts of communication are themselves linked by language-like rules in one single system of communication. No such system has been discovered, and it is proposed here that a search for it may be unrewarding. The linguistic analogy, when it speaks of a *pattern* of interrelations between elements, or between elements and their context, requires perfect co-occurrences (as in the fact that "all human beings have a heart"). Yet it seems much more likely that linguistic and non-verbal events that co-occur do so with a degree of probability rather than with certainty. At most, individuals may work out their own highly predictable combinations of linguistic and non-verbal communication, but such regularities may differ markedly from person to person.

(6) Finally, non-verbal acts may occur on more than one level simultaneously, either within one communicant, or among two or more, so that messages may contradict each other (when emitted by one person) or pass each other by (when two people are emitting). Language requires considerably more order in

time and, for the sending of contradictory messages, most often seems to resort to stepping outside the system—into non-verbal communication.

All of this detail about the analogy is presented not to dispute the findings of that school of research, but to suggest that the linguistic model is likely to lead to difficulties if applied extensively to non-verbal communication. Some of the most subtle of the observations made by Scheflen and co-workers seem quite unrelated to the linguistic model, a fact that underscores the power of clinical sensitivity over theory.

If crucial differences between linguistic and non-verbal communication may be assumed to exist, that is not to imply that the two systems cannot be meaningfully compared.[3] Aside from the structure of the two systems, important questions arise about the manner in which the elements of each are perceived— or decoded from the acts into which they have been encoded. The following chapters will elaborate certain notions of the appropriate elements, and rules for encoding and decoding non-verbal information.

## NOTES FOR CHAPTER 4

[1] In a subsequent communication, without giving any details, Dittmann (1963) acknowledged that "in looking at other subjects in experimental interviews, we find that patterns of movement in the three body areas vary tremendously from one person to another; and for some people one or another area does not lend itself to frequency counts at all, since movement is almost continuous, while for others one area may remain motionless under all experimental conditions."

[2] In his introductory textbook on social psychology Brown (1965) states this Western predilection in succinct form: "Emotions unlike physical objects present two views, an insider's view and an outsider's view, and we think of the insider's view as the real thing."

[3] On this point Mehrabian (1972) has developed a promising technique for comparing consistent and inconsistent messages conveyed simultaneously by means of verbal, vocal and facial communications.

# 5. The Structure of Events

The preceding review of the literature on the communications of the body particularly criticized the notion that the signaling function of the body is analogous to a verbal language—an assumption that encourages some investigators to classify the subject matter under the heading of "paralanguage." It also questioned the proposition that the body "expresses" some item of a subjectively experienced inner state of the organism, such as an emotion or a motive, and it ruled out the phrase "expressive behavior" for the purposes of this study. No greater merit, however, was ascribed to the opposite injunction: that, in the interests of objectivity, body behavior be regarded as a conditioned response to immediate, external contingencies—the situational stimuli.

In place of these notions, the idea was put forward that the observable actions of the body function as a link between the internal processes and the external situation. Because the behavior of the body participates to some extent in the internal process and to some extent in the external situation, this linkage was called an internal–interface–external transaction.[1] To define the observable actions of the body as interfacial, however, is not to imply that the body's function in the transaction is merely that of a conductor, transmitting messages between the external and internal zones. The body functions as a system also, in as orderly and constrained a way as the internal and external systems function. One of the matters that needs to be determined, then, if understanding of body communication is to be advanced, is the formal, structural aspect of the body as a behavior system.

The description of the body's patterned behavior will have to take into account the fact that this behavior—being transactional—constitutes a part of the external situation. In order to take this into consideration, two intertwined questions need to be dealt with. First, what are the characteristics of the external event (*event structure*)? Second, how is the behavior of the body incorporated into the external event (*presenting behavior*)? This chapter will describe the structure of events and presenting behavior in general terms. In the following chapters, the presentations of the body will be described specifically.

The word *encounter* refers to a confrontation of two or more persons in a physically and temporally bounded segment of space–time. It is a meeting together in the context of some social action. The literature of social psychology, sociology, and anthropology is rich in terminology designed to specify the structure and function of two-person groups, of small, face-to-face, multi-person groups, of institutions, and of large-scale social systems. Each of these disciplines has a large number of units of analysis that it finds useful for particular problems. Yet something is missing, something to which the word "encounter" specifically calls attention.

What is missing is the element of patterned physical action flowing over time; the flow of behavior within and across encounters, its beginnings and endings, its directions and turning points somehow escape the abstractions of the behavioral sciences. The phenomenon of flux, of continuous movement, eludes observation. Guided by their conceptual apparatuses, the behavioral sciences segment the flow of behavior into manageable units of "befores" and "afters" which are then compared with each other. But description of the flow of events in "before–after" terms hardly does justice to the realities of social life, and, while it has produced notable triumphs, one begins to feel the need for some method of describing the physical patterns of interacting behaviors—act upon act upon act—as they proceed in a succession along a course.

The flux of behavior is easier to slice up and reassemble than to fix before the eye of method. Too much passes by too rapidly, and the observer is too implicated in the process itself. Whoever makes the attempt to gather together all the pieces of an event as it slides by is apt to be overwhelmed by trivial detail or else to come up with large banalities. It is no wonder that the pre-Socratic struggle between the followers of Heracleitus and Parmenides was decided against the champion of flux and the connection between opposites, or that Plato made fun of the view set forth by Heracleitus.[2] The task of describing the flow of behavior had best be left to the poets, dramatists, and artists.

Barker and his co-workers (Barker 1963, Barker and Wright, 1955) have approached the problem of examining the flow of behavior by focusing on events and asking how individuals become involved in one or another of them, what sorts of events occur, in what contexts, and with what purposes, and in what forms or patterns. On this strategy, behavior *flow* is understood to be an attribute of the event, not of the behavior of the individual. If one looks only at the individual, what one discerns is a series of encounters with events and the persons involved in them. But when such encounters are described and recorded only from the point of view of one person, without regard to the innate structure of his motives and the structure of the events in which he participates, the product is a discontinuous and quite fragmentary record, displaying neither flow, nor aim, nor form of any sort, but appearing merely as a set of isolated acts.

If it is correct to ascribe flow to the event (the course of events) produced by encounters, then the task of describing behavior flow changes its character. Since events are aspects of social behavior, one would need to decide in what terms to describe the social interaction, using what concepts are already available in the social science literature. Because events are extended in time, it is necessary to find out how they traverse time or, more precisely, what alterations they undergo in their procession through time. Whatever undergoes change must have structures and be divisible into parts. Therefore, one needs to discover what units are involved in the structure of events, and how they differ from each other in their relation to time. Inasmuch as events are variously extended in space, as well as in time, it is important to determine how to differentiate descriptively between large-scale and small-scale events. Finally, events are characterized by direction in space–time and are furnished with starting points and end points and various stages in between through which they run their course, often getting off course or hung-up or otherwise failing to reach their anticipated destinations. Since the expected form of events from beginning through middle to end is the measure against which completeness or incompleteness in human affairs is judged, as well as success and failure, it is important to have some method for describing direction and for measuring the amount of progress in the expected direction.

All of these problems are handled in an approximate fashion in everyday affairs without the aid of science. What science could add to common knowledge, however, is an element of precision and an examination of minute detail that could bring forth knowledge and facts not readily apparent. More may be gained for the behavioral sciences than is suggested in this modest statement. For the issues seem ordinary precisely because they are usually placed in an unrealistic, excessively linear time perspective, with the result that several issues in psychology and sociology that are dependent upon an accurate knowledge of the polyphonic, stratified character of behavior flow are currently being handled in an awkward fashion. This is especially the case for the study of "the emotions," of "emotional" or "expressive" behavior, and of "body communication" in general. This study is concerned only with a small part of the larger issues involved in the structure of events, that part which deals with the entry of body behavior into the event through the encounter between persons. This limited concern has generated some suggestions for a conceptual framework appropriate to some of these issues.

It is apparent that events are characterized by a number of systematically varying, interrelated structural elements: (1) progress through space–time in serial sequence; (2) the specific social occasion that the event is concerned with —what it is "about"; (3) the more general cultural context in which it takes place—its space–time setting; and (4) the number of persons involved and the size of the operation—its scale. The first two structural elements will be dealt with in some detail, the last two merely touched upon.

The progress of events through space–time can be divided into units spatially and temporally. As an event progresses, it may occur in different parts of the physical environment in divisions that can be called "topical" units, referring to the places where they occur. As the events pass through the various topical units, they become connected in time. The time-connection, however, refers not only to the places where the events occur but also to stages in the development of the event.

Since the event begins in a certain place and proceeds on to others, literally and figuratively, its development can be likened to progress along a pathway to a destination. Time and place thus connect the beginning of an event with its ending. How it begins and how it ends—especially how it ends, whether with good fortune or bad—are two of the principal concerns of those involved in it. Because outcome is such a significant feature of the event, the name *exode* will designate the largest unit characteristic of the event. *Exode* does not mean merely the last act, or finale, but all the happenings from the beginning that lead up to the outcome and include it in a continuous process.

Whether all events have definite beginnings and discriminable endings, thus qualifying as exodes, is doubtful. Uncertain beginnings and inconclusive endings, as well as false starts, are familiar experiences. Furthermore, many events— perhaps those in which individuals are most frequently involved—are repetitious and recurrent routines, differing little in outcome from day to day or week to week. Although it is convenient here to treat all such events as varieties of exodes, the question of classification, here as elsewhere in this account, can only be settled by future study.

If the word *exode* refers to the main event in full course from start to finish, completely fitted out with its sequences stratified in time and place, then some other word is needed for the divisions or groupings of sequences and topical units within the exode. It is obvious that exodes do not proceed in a uniform manner—a smooth flow from beginning to end—but are marked by pauses, interruptions, variations in tempo, hitches, conflicts, crises, changes of direction, of place, and of personnel. The word *episode* is used here for all such alterations in the course of an exode. Such usage conforms to the common, everyday meaning of the word, but much empirical study is needed to distinguish varieties of episodes and their significance for the structure of the various types of exodes within which they occur. In everyday speech, episodes are not considered as conclusive; they are thought of as parts of a larger course of action which exhibit a certain coherence. Common observation indicates that episodes follow each other in a reasonable order, possibly with some degree of overlap, in the course of the exode. In some exodes, especially those concerned with public performances and ceremonies, the ordering of episodes is readily discernible. Introductory and preparatory episodes (proposing, planning, rehearsing, announcing, etc.) are followed by the performance, which itself is divided into various episodes having to do with assembling the performers and the audience, the parts of the performance including intermissions, the conclusion, and the departure or disengagement of audience and performers. In most routine exodes, as in the daily life of a household, school, office, or factory, the order of the episodes is also carefully programmed, though there is always room for a surprise—the unexpected incident or fortuitous episode. The programming of episodes into the exode is much more difficult to discern for large-scale events like wars, political campaigns, and social movements. Even in these, however, the episode can be recognized by its coherent form and by its propulsive relation to the exode. Each successive episode moves the exode away from its starting point toward its outcome. Any episode that does not function in this way—one that stalls the action of the exode, goes into reverse motion, or diverges in an unexpected and possibly fatal direction—tends to disrupt the exode, and concomitantly to give rise to the behavior which has been called "emotional."

If the episode has a formal structure in which it coheres over time, then one aspect of that structure must be concerned with the sequence of behavior within the episode. Just as episodes are assembled within exodes, so some serial, interpersonal events must be programmed within the episode. Consider, for example, the assembling episode preparatory to a public performance or ceremony. People arrive singly or in small groups; they congregate at entrance points; they make an entrance, and, after some milling about, arrange themselves in positions vis-à-vis the performance area—a stage, an altar, a boxing ring. In another place, the performers conduct other preparatory rites, assisted by their helpers. If all these activities can be included within the introductory episode, each probably has a propulsive structure of its own. What is this structure and how can its units or parts be designated?

The name *haptode* will serve for such units within the episode, and will signify a joining together of disparate acts along the pathway of an episode. Haptodes join, connect, and convert separate acts into the continuous flow of behavior characteristic of the episode. These conversions are concerned with beginnings and endings, with transitions between different segments of the episode, with arrangements and rearrangements of order within the episode, and with progress in a straight line, whether in the right or wrong direction. The joining together consists of a coupling process in which the front end of one haptode is fitted into the rear end of the next.[3] This copulative function within and between haptodes has two forms: immediate and delayed coupling. Immediate coupling takes place on the basis of contiguous or shared acts. Contiguous acts are geared together in a lock-and-key fashion, as when one person hands another person an object, or when one person bends down so that another person can leap-frog over him. Most stimulus–response set-ups in psychological experiments are in the form of contiguous acts. A shared act produces immediate coupling by belonging simultaneously to one haptode and its successor. In this case, if haptode *B* follows haptode *A*, then the last act of haptode *A* is also the first act of haptode *B*. For example, three people climb down a ladder from a dock to enter a rowboat. As the last man steps into the boat, he also pushes it away from the dock, thus disembarking the boat. For the first two men, filing down the ladder is one haptode; entering the boat and seating themselves in a balanced arrangement is a second haptode. For them, the coupling between the two haptodes consists of the act of stepping into the boat. In a more general sense, the act of making an entrance in all sorts of occasions and places conjoins topically placed haptodes.

Delayed couplings of haptodes are more complex, because the delay may be brought about in different ways. In some cases, the delay is "natural"; that is, some physical event must occur before the coupling can be effected—night must fall, a key participant must arrive, the wind must die down—before action can proceed. Delayed coupling involves a waiting game, giving rise to occasions for boredom or impatience. The delay, however, may be "artificial" in the sense that no physical process interferes with the coupling. The delay may be introduced into a potentially smooth-flowing haptode or haptode sequence by one of the participants to the encounter who backs out, pauses, repeats himself, or blocks the action in some way. Delayed coupling, varying in length of time consumed, is correlated with the issue of "timing" in all interpersonal process. "Timing," however, is also correlated with the ordering of the haptode sequence within the episode—that is, where and when a particular haptode is to be inserted into the sequence.

Coupling is obviously concerned with goodness-of-fit between successive haptodes. In part, goodness-of-fit is related to the question of direction within the episode. If haptode *A* could be succeeded by haptodes *B*, *C*, or *D*, but if only one of the three can follow for a given sequence, obviously a choice must be made. Usually, each possible choice leads in a different direction. Such choice points are occasions for conflict and they bring into play the steering mechanisms available to the group participating in the event, its decision-making processes and control procedures.

In this connection, a formal distinction can now be made between the haptode and the episode. The arrangement of haptodes within the same episode can vary in a number of different, serial patterns. There is room for flexibility, rearrangement, trial-and-error. The sequence of episodes within an exode is relatively fixed in order. With the exception of initial and terminal haptodes—such as saying "Amen" at the end of a prayer—the choice of haptode sequence within an episode can follow the maxim that there is more than one way to skin a cat. In contrast, once an episode has been completed—the battle won, the performance finished—options for succeeding episodes are vastly diminished. Turning points have been reached that cannot be retraced. Haptodes can be tried on for size, practiced, and rehearsed, to be retained or discarded or placed in a different position in the sequence. They can be undone, canceled out, or highlighted. The outcome of an episode can be modified by subsequent episodes but its effects are registered permanently on the course of the exode.

This serial progress of events through space–time can be called *parodic*, since the structure is observed by following alongside the pathway of the event. Many questions concerned with parodic structure remain unanswered; clearer definitions still need to be constructed; illustrative materials have been too sparse. But the parodic structure will serve as a tentative framework for the inspection of events from a number of different angles. Another angle of inspection that has been mentioned above [4] is the social nature of the event, what it is "about." The way in which the event parades along its various space–time dimensions to reach its outcome is determined by the parameters of the social situation. Unfortunately, there exists no convenient classification of social situations. But the theory of social roles as it has been developed in the literature of social science offers a potential method for grouping various social situations.

In his previous studies of family process, one of the present authors proposed a definition of the social-role concept and a classification scheme which has proved useful for the study of small-scale interpersonal events (Spiegel, 1956, 1957, 1964). The definition states that a social role is a goal-directed sequence of acts patterned in accordance with cultural value orientations for the position a person holds in a social group or social situation. This formula provides for several contingencies related to role structure. It assumes that roles can be described as sequences of acts moving toward a target outcome—the goal—which also describes the function of the role. Thus, one can discuss the activities of a mother, a teacher, or a salesman in terms of their goal–functions. But it has has been well demonstrated that the exact pattern of acts for these (and all other) roles varies in different cultures and subcultures in accordance with the values of the culture. Therefore, a precise layout of the value orientations of the culture (Kluckhohn, 1961; Spiegel, 1959, 1972) is a prerequisite to specification of the norms for role patterning that are internalized by members of a culture. Finally, the definition stipulates that roles are not distributed at random in social systems but are allocated for the position a person holds in a group or situation. One cannot simply choose to be a teacher or salesman without regard to social rules that relate the person to the role. Roles do not occur in a vacuum and are seldom held solo. On the contrary, in a role system, one must present behavior that is reciprocal or complementary to that of one's role partners. Teachers have to respond seriatim to the responses of students and vice versa so that complementarity can be maintained and the classroom events in which they both participate can move forward.

The social structure of the event, then, is provided by the social positions and roles of which it is composed. A comparative analysis of social situations, however, requires a taxonomy of role systems. Without some way of classifying roles in genera and species there would be little to compare. The classification scheme mentioned previously is set forth in Table 5–1, which arranges roles in strata from the most general to the most specific. For example, formal roles are more general than informal roles because they encompass wider segments of behavior. Similarly, within the category of formal roles, the biological roles are more general than the semi-biological or institutional roles. The biological roles

TABLE 5–1.  General Classification of Social Roles

| | | Goal Structure | |
|---|---|---|---|
| *Form* | *Order* | *Class* | |
| Formal | Primary Biological Roles | Body Presentation<br>Age<br>Sex<br>Primary Kinship | |
| | Secondary Biological Roles | Kinship Secondary<br>Ethnic<br>Class–Caste | |
| | Institutional | Educational, Occupational, Religious, Intellectual–Esthetic, Political–Economic, Recreational | |
| Informal | Transitional Roles | Sick, Dead, Mourner, Criminal, Traveler, Visitor, Guest, Host, Stranger, Messenger, Friend, Enemy, Exile, Leader, Follower, Informant, Interviewer, etc. | |
| | Character Roles | Hero, Villain, Fool, Weakling, Prankster, Sadist, Masochist, Exhibitionist, Liar, Seducer, Victim, Rescuer, Comedian, etc. | |
| Fictive | Mythological Roles | Gods, Spirits, Scapegoats, Ghosts, Witches, Dragons, Poltergeists, Superman, and Spaceman, etc. | |
| | Imaginary Roles | Any of the Preceding Classes of Roles | |

of age, sex, and body presentations pattern the behavior of all people, at all times, in all situations. One is never free to step out of behavior appropriate to one's age, sex, or body-type—at least not without severe repercussions from the social environment. Institutional roles, on the other hand, occur in lesser spheres of behavior, transitional and character roles in even more restricted circumstances, while fictive roles are appropriate only in very special situations.

The various uses to which these categories can be put have been described elsewhere. (See especially Spiegel, 1964.) Here, it is only necessary to point out that the participants in any particular social situation occupy only a few roles selected from the total array of possibilities in the formal and informal role categories; and, by these selections, their social functions are recognized and the approximate behavior expected from them is predicted. Any observer of the social scene in question—unless he is from a totally alien culture—will recognize the cues for the various kinds of roles and will know how to classify and predict—within limits, of course—the behavior to come. If he does not recognize the cues, or is supplied with too few of them, he will ordinarily make up roles for the participants out of his imagination. In so doing, he unconsciously inventories the stock of role assignments stored in his memory and selects an assortment fitting the few cues that are available. The inventory process always begins with age, sex, and body-presentation roles, which have to be established first because of their anchoring position as the most general of all roles.

The inventory process triggered by the visual stimuli of age, sex, and body appearance is vastly aided by the verbal tags or "titles." Titles are names for types of events, for specific events, and for the role-encumbents participating in the event. If an observer is presented with only the visual stimuli of an untitled event about which he has no specific prior information, then he will try to attach event and role tags to the stimuli, beginning with the primary, biological roles, in the construction of a hypothesis of what the event is about. For example, *pretty, young, girl, stretched out on couch, graceful but thin and coughing frequently, pale:* Sick? T.B.? *The man sitting beside her, attentive:* Doctor? Lover? Armand? These are cognitive programs constructed with the aid of entitling. The strategy may involve a run through a list of formal, informal, and fictive roles. The list of roles is not put together at random. It is stratified by a set of connections in depth, probably proceeding from the most general to the most specific roles. The choices made at the most general levels limit the kinds of choices that can be made at more specific levels. Since such vertical stratification is combined with the horizontal segmentation of the event in terms of its haptode structure—where it is in its own time and place—it is obvious that no simple, linear time perspective of before and after, stimulus and response, or input and output can come to grips with its complexity. Consider, for example, how much information search regarding time, place, and title is required in order to relate Doctor–Lover–Armand to the tubercular heroine of *La Dame aux Camélias*.

The further the event is removed in space–time from current affairs, the more historical or cultural information is required by the observer in order to successfully relate stimuli to role possibilities. As earlier stated, this is the third structural element needed for event description. The relation of space–time setting to body communication will be especially pertinent to such matters as costume (dress and ornamentation), cosmetics, posture, and gesture. These matters function, in the first instance, as cognitive maps for role assignments allocated to the participants in an encounter. To be properly dressed and made up is to be prepared for one's role, so that others can be notified as to what is likely to happen. Taking a proper stance and arranging one's face becomingly—whether as Roman Emperor facing one's legions or as American President facing one's television camera—is a prerequisite to getting the proceedings headed in the right direction. But the differences in management of the body in Rome, on the one hand, and in Washington, on the other, are as significant as the similarities.

Considerations of size and number call attention to the fourth structural element: the scale of events. Here, the issue involves differences in effects produced by variations in size of the same type of event—a small skirmish versus a battle, a small private funeral versus the ceremonies for the death of a national hero. These, of course, represent gradings within continua rather than simple polar opposites. The effect of scale varies along different dimensions for the different personnel making up the encounter but all share in one effect: The bigger the event in space–time, the more impressive it is, both for those who participate and for those who observe. The explosion of visual and auditory stimuli emanating from large-scale events, the compression and overlapping of episodes, the difficulty in scanning and comprehending all that goes on—all such out-of-the-ordinary aspects of the encounter contribute to the sense of insignificance that the individual is likely to experience.

The aspect of large-scale events that is most closely associated with body communication has to do with crowding. No matter how spread out in space they may be, if huge numbers of people congregate, there will be some reduction of the usual distance one person keeps from another, especially from a stranger. Enforced closeness in a crowd has several effects. The difficulty of verbal communication, of transmitting messages, and in making one's wishes known or effective, confines behavior to the more excitable or emotional levels; occasion for communication through physical action is increased. Not only has the individual less control over his own options for conduct through verbal communication but, even in the physical plane, his freedom of action is more limited than usual. He is blocked, hemmed in, channeled, anything but his own man. Blocking of individual action contributes to the "raw temper" of crowds, and to the celebrated "contagiousness" of crowd behavior. The individual has little choice but to act in concert with others. His movements must conform to the crowd's lest he find himself trampled or crushed. Where his movements go in the parodic structure of the event, his "emotions" and "motivations" are likely to follow. Indeed, constraint of body movement would seem to underlie many of the effects of the crowd on the psychology of the individual—effects that impressed LeBon by their animal-like, almost mystical power to submerge individuality in favor of the crowd's primitive will or "mind," and which Freud (1960), following LeBon's (1952) description, explained on the basis of regression, loss of ego-boundaries, and identification with the leader-as-father and with the crowd-as-brothers. Useful as Freud's explanations have proved to be, they are incomplete. If one studies not only crowds but crowding, not merely the nature of mass behavior but, more pertinently, the physical process through which the individual is drawn into it, then the structure of body movement and the positioning that crowd formation imposes on its members must be examined.

These, then, are the four aspects of event structures proposed for initial, tentative consideration: the parodic structure, which controls the flow of behavior between the start and finish of an event; the interplay between roles and persons, which determines what the event is about; the setting of the event in time and place; and the scale on which the event is unfolded. The interconnections among these four constitute the basic materials of much of art and literature.

In order to introduce a greater clarity in these propositions, it is now necessary to consider as precisely as possible what is meant by the presentational or demand characteristics of behavior.[5] A definition of *presentation behavior* must take into account that it is to be contrasted with what is called a *response*. Response behavior is the activity, given a certain state of the organism (hunger, thirst, etc.), which is elicited by the presentation of a certain stimulus configuration. It has become a habit, or convention, to label almost all behavior as a response to some internal stimulus (drive, defense, or cognition), or to some external stimulus (auditory, visual, verbal), or a combination of all of them. Thus, what is here called *presenting behavior* is usually thought of as a *response*. Such naming obscures an essential difference. A *presentation*, or *presenting behavior*, can be defined, for purposes of this study, as the intentional arrangement of stimuli emitted in the presence of another person (or organism of some species) in order to evoke a desired response. The intention, the manner of arranging the stimuli, and the response that is desired—or any one of these alone—may be either conscious or unconscious at the time that the presentation is made. No matter what its status in awareness, presenting behavior looks to the future and is, in this sense, "purposive." In this sense, also, it falls into sharp contrast with the concept of a response, which is considered to be controlled by the past. A response follows some stimulus; a presentation anticipates some response. Yet, since the data here consist merely of behavior as it flows in experience, then it is obvious that both presentation and response are aspects of the behavior flow within the event.

It is of the essence of a stream to be characterized simultaneously by a point of origin and a destination, so far as an observer outside the stream is concerned. For an observer standing on the bank of a river, any volume of water flowing past him clearly came from somewhere and is going elsewhere. Another observer, trying to swim across or ford the river may have a different experience. He may well find himself more occupied with the speed, force, turbulence, and depth of the water. Though the space–time parameters and goals for the two observers may lead them to characterize the flow in different terms, the various descriptions do not contradict each other. The response aspects of the behavior flow refer to its origins, the presentation aspects to its destinations.

The two aspects of behavior are quite obviously associated with each other by the internal process known as "choice." To any given presentation of stimuli, an individual may experience numerous, competing potential responses. The behavior that he then presents consists of some selection from among them to produce the effect he desires.

A review of the literature about the forms of body movement points up the lack of attention given to the stimulus conditions—the exact formal arrangements of the body—that produce responses. Investigators appear to have been more interested in the verbal or emotional response than in the stimulus configuration. They have looked at the stimuli mostly as a way of getting the response going, and, in fact, tended to judge the stimulus by the internal or external response associated with it. But the body, as a stimulus configuration, has its own properties, deriving from its physical nature and what can be done with it in space with other persons and objects. Such doings constitute the events in which persons become involved through encountering each other. It is from such event possibilities that they must select what they do with their bodies and how they stimulate others. To be able to make systematic statements about these possibilities means examining the body and its possible positions and movements vis-à-vis others in considerable detail, as will be reported later. But it also means taking a hard look at the structure of the events themselves, as they occur in time and space. For persons "respond" not merely to the stimulations of others, but also to the event itself, to its flow, to the way things are going. They keep trying to influence the event through word and act. These attempts are so drastically directed at hoped-for outcomes that one needs a special term for the activity—especially for the physical activity—by which they seek to bring off the desired effect. It is for the sake of having a way of talking in detail about activity intended to have an effect on the event itself that *presenting behavior* and *presentation* are used here. A presentation, then, is a contribution to the future of an event that the usual scientific vocabulary deals with only in a rather roundabout fashion.

If a presentation is defined as an arrangement of stimuli created to evoke a range of responses from others and, thus, to contribute to the course of events, one can ask: To what aspect of event structure is a particular presentation directed? The answer is clear: to all four aspects simultaneously. Presenting behavior is made for the sake of an outcome, within the role structure of the event, oriented to its time–place setting, and to its scale. If it does not fit neatly into all of these parameters, it is recognized as abnormal, bizarre, mistaken, novel, or mysterious. However, the fit or lack of fit of a presentation into an event may not be spread out evenly over all four aspects. It may be erroneously timed or mislabeled—that is, contributed to the wrong haptode within an episode—and, thus, have an unexpected or unfortunate effect upon outcome. It may not fit into the role structure of an event, either because of its lack of correct placement within the values of the group or because it is contributed by some-one who has not established his right to occupy the role within which he makes his presentation. It may have been imported to the time–place setting of the event from another occasion into which it more properly fits. Or it may be out of scale—outsized and overdone or diminutive and underplayed. A thorough-going presentational analysis would examine any piece of presentation behavior for its degree of fit into the four aspects of event structure.

The body's advances toward an outcome, its moves in one or another direction of the exode, its entry into the haptode in some disposition of flexible parts—all these represent stimuli of quite determinate form which are contributed to the flow of behavior. They are the tactics, the physical arrangements, by means of which the body occupies space and time and influences the course of events. But these physical arrangements and their visual stimuli are in need of a detailed conceptualization directed to the forms of the various arrangements that the body is heir to. A morphology and a taxonomy of body behavior is required in order to keep track of what the body does while making its presentations. For this morphology, the term *somatotactics* is here suggested; Chapter 8 will propose some descriptive concepts to deal with its taxonomy. Meanwhile, it is useful to consider the topic of presenting behavior and the structure of events from another perspective—that of the cognitive process that is evoked for the sake of identi-fying the events.

# NOTES FOR CHAPTER 5

[1] For the special sense in which the word "transaction" is used here and elsewhere in this book see *Transactions: The Interplay Between Individual, Family and Society* (Spiegel, 1971) in which "transaction" is distinguished from "interaction." Transaction is conceived as referring to reverberating, multidimensional relations between systems with ill-defined or shifting boundaries. Interaction refers to reciprocal, unidimensional relations between entities with well-defined boundaries.

[2] Plato depicted Socrates as poking fun at Heracleitus for confusing the nature of reality with the words (and their origins) used to describe reality. Socrates points out that abstract words are anchored in the behavior of concrete things and their motions, but claims that such primitive etymologies are misleading, directing the attention of philosophical thought away from fixed and enduring "first principles." Thus, after a lengthy, occasionally hilarious discussion of semantics, Socrates cautions the youthful Cratylus, "Nor can we reasonably say, Cratylus, that there is any knowing at all, if everything is in a state of transition and there is nothing abiding. . . . and if the transition is always going on, there will always be no knowing, and, according to this view, there will be no one to know and nothing to be known. But if that which knows and that which is known exists ever, and the beautiful exists and the good exists, and every other thing also exists, then I do not think that they can resemble a process or flux, as we were just now supposing" (Plato, *Cratylus*, 1953, sec. 440). But it is just this rejection of the primitive orientation of abstract words to bodily behavior that has been responsible for the deep gulf between the arts and the sciences in Western thought. What was gained for logic and reason was lost for perception and cognition, and continuous motion in human events became something untruthful and unreliable.

[3] Our verbal habits produce a small paradox concerning directions in space–time. If haptode $A$ is followed by haptode $B$, then haptode $A$ is going in the direction of haptode $B$. Therefore, its front or forward end in space would immediately precede the beginning of haptode $B$. But the act which takes place at this spatially forward terminus of haptode $A$ is also the last act to occur in haptode $A$. Thus, from the point of view of time, this last act takes place at the rear end of the haptode, at the opposite pole from its beginning or front end. We are forced either to conclude that here, as in the Kingdom to come, the last shall be first, or else to reckon with the possibility that our linguistic structures, as Socrates suggested and as Whorf (1956) came close to demonstrating, seriously skew our perceptions of reality. If time is assumed to be a fourth dimension of a time–space continuum, then, presumably, a direction in time would be different from a direction in space, not merely its polar opposite along a straight line.

[4] A modern Socrates might ask, "Why do we say 'above' when we obviously mean behind (in time)?" If our figures of speech are so carelessly chosen from an unsatisfactory pool of metaphors, how is it possible to provide an accurate description of what we do in the exposition of a subject-matter? In effect, no matter how much we take them for granted, all our descriptions are anchored in physical action. Therefore, we may as well opt for close scrutiny of body movement, laying bare the physical derivations of our thoughtways.

[5] What follows has been much influenced by various authors whose works will not be specifically discussed. The writers who have had an influence on our thinking are Allport (1955), Burke (1950), Goffman (1959), and Langer (1942).

# 6. The Cognitive Aspects of Presenting Behavior

The hero, Achilles, skulks in his tent. Charlie Chaplin shakes his fist at the big bully, trips over a chair, and falls down. Greta Garbo in *Camille* sinks tearfully into the arms of her lover, yielding, under the protection of illness, to an illicit love.

If the reader is familiar with the background and context of these actions, a few words can suggest the enormous range and variety of behavior exhibited in them. But to find words to describe the exact details of the behaviors is another matter. How does one describe skulking behavior? How does Greta Garbo convey her anguish in yielding to her lover's embrace? More mysterious yet, how does she create the ambiguity which makes it hard to decide whether her tears flow from guilt because she is yielding, or relief because she has held out so long?

The answers to such questions have been beyond the reach of psychology. The difficulty in finding a scientific method for dealing with the ambiguity and allusiveness of movement tempts one to leave the topic within the realm of art and sensibility. The actor, one may say, uses his talent, the viewer his intuition. And viewers of Charlie Chaplin's and Greta Garbo's movements receive the message without difficulty, despite the defaults of psychology. Yet it would be interesting and useful to understand how body presentations are related to inner dispositions, to the structure of events, and to the responses of the participants to the encounter.

A presentation is an arrangement of responses selected from a response pool and composed with the intention of eliciting desired responses in others. The arrangement can be called a stimulus configuration, but it is obvious that it is composed in accordance with a plan, an expectation of what effect it will have. Here "plan" and "expectation" refer to a set of rules that connect the stimulus arrangements with the responses. These rules do not ordinarily circulate in consciousness, though some of them can be brought into awareness easily enough. They operate as a dictionary of instructions containing rules to the effect: "If this, then that . . ."; "if an open hand is extended, grasp it"; "if a clenched fist is extended, duck it." Such conditional rules must be shared, at least approximately, by the participants to an encounter if a presentation is to have its anticipated effect. If they are uniformly shared, then the participants may act with precision and in concert. If a considerable number of the rules are not held in common, then problems, mistakes, and misunderstandings will disturb the flow of behavior.

By the time he reaches adult life, any one person must have learned thousands of such rules linking presentations with responses. If on every stimulus occasion he had to retrieve a correct assortment of responses from a huge list of rules, he would be incapable of action. The mind must contain some method of simplifying the operations needed to find the appropriate instruction. And the instructions, in all likelihood, are not stored in verbal codes but in visual–motor imagery. On what sort of coding and filing system could such cognitive operations be based?

Recent research on cognitive processing (thinking and problem solving) offers some help. The research has involved experiments with humans and animals and studies of computer simulation of thought processes. Central to these investigations has been the importance attributed to categorization and concept formation. That the principle of classification is an important element in thinking is certainly not a new idea. The new twist in the current research, however, is the emphasis given to the process of forming categories. Grouping in categories is said to be a basic characteristic not only of thinking and learning but also of perception and response—that is, of behavior in general. Responses, it is true, can be learned by rote through simple conditioning to specific stimuli. But most organisms, even simple ones like the rats used in so many psychological experiments, have the capacity, as Bruner (1957) puts it, of going beyond the immediate information given in the situation. They are able to transfer a type of behavior learned in one situation to a new situation that resembles it but which is not identical to it. In other words, the organism groups the two different situations on the basis of certain common, defining stimuli while disregarding unshared stimuli (Wallach, 1958). The defining characteristics are abstracted from the two situations and placed in one category.

There still remains the question of what it is that is being coded and how the categories are constructed. It is here suggested that, in the visual–motor domain, coding categories are constructed along three dimensions. The first dimension codes the visual stimuli of objects and settings presented to the viewer. It answers the question: What is this thing in this situation, or what is this event? The second dimension is concerned with the program of instructions relating response arrangements to the given event. It answers the question: What do I do in this situation, what is my goal, what is my activity? The third dimension is concerned with the varieties of possible movements, or more exactly, the physical forms of movements. It answers the question: What pattern of movement do I use in order to reach my goal?

Categories for processing the first—the *event dimension*—have been much studied in the literature of experimental and social psychology with respect to "objects." The features of visual stimuli used for recognizing objects and for discriminating among them, have been investigated in various research strategies ranging from stimulus–response approaches through learning, perceptual, and cognitive methodologies. But the characteristics of objects-in-settings used to identify events appear not to have been so extensively studied. Yet the visual categorization of the event—even of the stage it has reached in the haptode or episode—is probably not a different process from the visual categorization of the object alone.

It is here proposed that events are coded by means of categories related to the position of the object in the *role structure*, the *parodic structure*, the *space–time setting*, and the *scale* of the event. The visual specification of the object-in-the-event will depend on the level of the category selected for its identification in the hierarchical arrangement from the more general to the more specific. Levels of generalization have been worked out for role structures (see Table 5–1), and it was suggested that the process of visual recognition through which a human object is assigned to a role might well begin with the examination of cues (stimuli) concerned with the most general categories of role structure—those of age, sex, and body presentation. More specific categories would then be considered by working down the branching pathways of lower-order categories while matching the choices against cues subsequently presented to, or discovered by, the viewer. Before one can proceed with a description of such "verbal referencing," it is necessary to consider how sets of instructions may be collected and assembled into larger categories. For this, it will be necessary to consider the manner in which activities—the second dimension suggested above—are coded.

Activities can be defined as serial movements that relate behaviors to their role structures. But they can be regarded as a dimension separate from roles because their hierarchical categorization proceeds along lines independent of role structures. There are names for many of these categories, such as "eating," "sleeping," "greeting," "walking," "escaping," "playing," "love-making," "roller skating," "stealing," and "skulking," all of which can be considered answers to the question: "What are you doing?" The list could be enormously extended. If there exist thousands of specific instructions (e.g., for sleeping, from the full set for the insomniac—"Get undressed, put on your nightclothes, take your sleeping pill, wash and brush your teeth, get in bed, cover up, close your eyes, relax"—to the minimum for the sleepyhead—"Close your eyes"), there must exist hundreds of activities, varying for person, group, and society. Some are easy to identify because of existing labels; others evade precise labeling but are recognized in phrases.

There are a number of levels in the hierarchy of the *activities dimension*, though their ordering is unclear and in need of thorough study. Each of the activities mentioned above consists of a category containing a set of instructions. But any one of the instructions contained in any one of the activity categories can be broken down into a yet more specific set of instructions. Consider the instruction formulated above as "Take your sleeping pill." This sounds simple when stated as an instruction, but it consists of a large set of lower-order instructions like, "Open the door of the medicine chest; remove the bottle of sleeping pills; unscrew the top of the bottle; tip the bottle slightly; allow several capsules to slip into the palm of your hand; retain one (or two) capsules; replace the remainder; screw on the top of the bottle; replace the bottle in the medicine chest; fill a glass of water; place the capsule in your mouth; take a sip of water; swallow water with capsule." In this program, some essential steps may have been omitted and others placed out of their appropriate order. Such errors can be corrected by observation of the behavior of an actual sample of sleeping-pill users.

Despite specificity of the "sleeping pill" program, it is obvious that each of the steps in that program could be made even more detailed and specific. A whole page of specific instructions, for example, could be written for the more general instruction, "replace the remainder (of the capsules) in the bottle." But an account of the upper levels of generality in the activities dimension is more interesting here.

Activity sequences are assembled on a larger scale in categories programmed for the role structure of the event. Any separate activity can occur in a number of different roles, but it will be given various stresses in different roles. It may dominate the programming of a role, in which case other activities are entered into the program for subsidiary or preparatory purposes. Furthermore, when a separate activity dominates a role, it occupies more time within the program created for the role. For example, "studying" as an activity has a position of dominance in any program created for the role of "student." Yet other categories of activity also enter into the student role, such as receiving the next day's assignments from the teacher and complaining about them to fellow students. Grumbling about the teacher is a verbal activity and thus falls outside the domain of behavior being considered here. Sleeping in the classroom, on the other hand, is a physical activity that suits the present purpose better, especially as it is an example of behavior that does not belong in the student role, and, to take the most benevolent view of it, gets in only by error. One function of role categorization is to specify which activities belong in which role and which are ruled out, are negatively sanctioned. On the side of positive sanctioning, both studying and sleeping enter quite legitimately into a number of other roles where they have a subsidiary or preparatory function.

Activity programs are oriented to their goals. The specific contingencies of the goal control the assembly of all the other movements into the program. In addition, it is the goal that usually governs the selection of the linguistic label for the category. But the goal need not be the final act in the sequence. For example, in the program for "taking a sleeping pill," the user might well swallow the sleeping pills (goal) and *then* screw on the bottle top and replace the bottle in the medicine chest. In this case, one might think of the last two movements (and their related instructions) as "following through" or "completing" the program. If the last two movements were to be omitted, and if the user had been in the process of monitoring his own activity, then the omission would probably be transcribed verbally as, "I forgot," or "I didn't finish what I was going to do."

Here it is suggested that visual–motor categories can be produced in two different ways. Each of these processes of category construction is, in turn, accompanied by a different process of category location. The process of locating response categories will be called *referencing* and the referencing process can be defined as an instruction for bringing one set of response features into correlation with another. Without referencing, the visual–motor features of various responses would exist as a tangled jumble in the mind. Therefore, referencing is the means through which cognitive order is produced.

The first system of category construction is based on the detection of identical elements in otherwise different responses. These identical elements are selected (abstracted) and drawn away from each stimulus arrangement in which they are located to be made the "content" of a category. A number of different categories constructed in this fashion may each, again, share an identical feature, which is selected and abstracted to form yet another superordinate category. The process is repeated with the formation of ever-broader categories, increasingly emptied out of specific features to make up a vertical series. Each superordinate category in the series embraces a feature found in the several categories below it, thus composing the general-to-specific hierarchy mentioned previously.

If categories are to be appropriately constructed—that is, placed or located in this vertical series—the placing and locating will take place through the process of *vertical referencing*. Such a process consists of using the rules that specify how to make the choice at a descending choice-point between one or another subcategory of a general category. Such choices are crucial. They are one source of error in cognitive processing. If one chooses a "wrong" subcategory, then all subsequent choices following that category branch (descending from it) will be "wrong." If one makes a "correct" choice, error may still occur at the next lower branch. Obviously, to be wrong is easy, to be right, a matter for congratulations.

But to be "correct" depends upon the second manner of forming categories. In this method, responses are grouped together and placed within a category not on the basis of identical features, but on the basis of their all being associated with a goal. This association of dissimilar response features in the service of a goal is manifest in the activity category labeled "taking a sleeping pill." The only way in which the various response features are related to each other is that they are all concerned with the response of pill-taking. This system for grouping response features into a category can be called the *associative method*, and can be contrasted with the first system, the *selective method*.

The process set into motion by the associative method is here called *cross-referencing*. It entails scanning a number of different vertical hierarchies of categories in order to pull out—at the appropriate level of generality—the categories that are to be joined with each other to form the sequence required by the associative category. To refer back to "taking a sleeping pill," it is obvious that each of the steps in the program had to be pulled out of some assembly of vertical hierarchies. For example, "open the door of the medicine chest," the first instruction, associates (by cross-referencing) openings with doors and chests. But "openings" are drawn from a selected hierarchy of varied sizes, "doors" from a hierarchy of varied shapes, and "chests" from a hierarchy of varied contents. To be right or wrong on vertical referencing depends on the second manner of category location, namely, cross-referencing. To find the right subcategory for "door" on the vertical hierarchy, one would need the cross-reference to "medicine chest." This would locate a subcategory which, in visual–motor terms, could be transcribed "a door that doesn't look like a door but looks like a mirror while acting like a door." On this same classificatory level, one could probably find a visual–motor category for doors that look like doors but are not; namely, "false doors," such as in Egyptian tombs and mystery stories. Without the first subcategory, one would have difficulty finding "the door" of the medicine chest. Indeed, one may have this problem even with the help of the subcategory, whose instructions may not match "the door" in question.

To return to the discussion of the activity dimension that was interrupted in order to consider the referencing process, both the understanding of others' presentational activities and the grouping of one's own activities in response to them is carried out by means of such a twofold process. But the salient feature of activities to be considered here is their relation to the "objective" world of which they are a part—the *event dimension*. The event dimension must be in continuous association with the activities dimension in order that the organism can present behavior effectively. Activities have to be programmed for the occasion at hand. What is commonly called "adaptation" consists of a progressively improved fit between the objective structure of the event and the responses presented to it. The coding of presented stimuli and of response selection must match each other so that the presentation "makes sense." Further, the matching must take place in a rather precise fashion. Categories selected from the event dimension and identified at a certain level in the hierarchy from general to specific must be cross-referenced with categories drawn from the activities dimension at the same level, and then be checked out to determine whether the two categories so selected belong together. To return to a previous example, if an event is identified as a structure of student roles set within a classroom, and if a particular student finds that a sleeping response presents itself, what will he do? He may have to debate within himself whether to yield to the urge or to suppress the activity as best he can. In the process, he will have considered the presence of other students and the instructor, reaffirmed their current role status by making a mental contrast to several other events more to be desired considering his boredom, reviewed the program for student behavior by recalling what happened to him the last time he went to sleep in class, endowed more desirable activities with a certain gratification in fantasy, decided that the alternatives do not fit the occasion, and that sleeping is too risky.

Cross-referencing of categories from activities to events is so automatic that its operations go more or less unnoticed. It comes to attention when it fails to operate efficiently. Then, a person is said to have made a mistake or, in more serious circumstances, to have displayed maladaptive behavior. In the language of current ego-psychology, it will be said that reality-testing has failed or that the integrative function of the ego has been weakened. It is probable that the integrative function of the ego consists of the simultaneous operation of many vertical and cross-referencing systems, and that reality-testing consists of the precision of match between the "actual" event and the category chosen from the "event" dimension, as well as the response category selected from the activity dimension. Describing a three-way match is probably too simple, since cross-referencing systems are much more complicated than such descriptions allow for, particularly as they involve sensory systems not considered here.

Restricted though it may be, the model is still incomplete with respect to the visual–motor domain. It needs a consideration of the third dimension necessary to visual–motor coding: the categories pertaining to movements of the body considered independently of events and activities.

First, however, it is possible to make a preliminary exploration of how presentations produce their effects. If a presentation is an arrangement of responses composed in order to elicit desired responses in others, one can assume that the connection between the stimulus arrangement presented and the expected response has been established through learning, and takes the form of the instruction: "If this (presentation), then that (response)." Such rules obviously function in both directions—that is, as a transaction—between a person and his environment. Thus, a person may say to himself, alternatively, "If such and such a response in my friend is reinforcing for me (I desire it), then I must make such and such a presentation," or "If I make such and such a presentation, which is reinforcing for my friend (he desires it), he will make such and such a response."

If identical presentations elicited identical responses (in accordance with the rules) on every occasion in which they were performed, then human beings would indeed exist in a social environment as highly regulated and predictable as those of the ants and bees. But the rules refer only to probabilities. Even between two people who have come to know each other well, the same presentation will not elicit the same response on every occasion. The variations that appear are not a disorderly abrogation of the rules, but a sign of complexity, indicating that the instructions connecting the response with the presentation in such an apparently controlling fashion are themselves controlled by a set of contingencies that govern rule-setting and selection. Sometimes, one set of rules connects the presentation with the response; at other times, another.

The variation in the rules is associated with internal and external contingencies. If one makes a presentation to a participant to an encounter when the latter is tired, a different response will be elicited from that which he would probably exhibit if alert. If one makes the same presentation in public, one can anticipate a different response than would be shown if it were made in private. Because these contingencies vary in a systematic fashion, requiring different rules for different occasions, the rules themselves must be systematized or organized in some way which corresponds to the variations in the contingencies that govern them.

Both the instructions connecting stimulus arrangement with response and the categorical grouping of instructions constitute a type of coding. Coding is the process whereby a particular physical signal or stimulus pattern is systematically and reliably associated with (transduced or translated into) another stimulus pattern or a behavior pattern. For example, the dots and dashes of the Morse Code are reliably related to the letters of the alphabet, and the latter constitutes a transduction of the former. Morse Code "means" "the letters of the alphabet." This is the paradigm of "meaning" used here in the description of movement and what it "expresses." In understanding, or deriving the meaning of a message in Morse Code, one refers each pattern of dots and dashes to a letter of the alphabet. It is through the cross-referencing process that meaning in visual presentations is discovered. By means of referencing, one determines of what "presentation" a "representation" is a "re-presentation" in a different signal system.

"Meaning" in the larger course of human affairs is more complicated than this description will allow. But it is complicated by the variations in the contingencies governing rule setting. These contingencies are excessively complex, requiring complicated cognitive systems of vertical and cross-referencing to keep them in order. If meaning is associated with referencing, it follows that a complex system of vertical and cross-referencing will produce a complex meaning. The simple answer to the question of what the Morse Code "means" can be made more complicated. The words "Morse Code" could be cross-referenced with one of several vertically assembled category systems. One could try out, for fun, the general category of "Communication," and run down the branching roots of subcategories, pausing over a choice between "message" and "information." If the former is chosen, then the further cross-referencing will be concerned with the manner in which Morse Code is sent, who sends it, to whom, and through what channel. If the latter is chosen, then the potential program of cross-referencing will assemble "content of message" categories, such as how much information can be packed into Morse Code, what kind of information, used for what purposes.

The preceding description of the cognitive processes through which "meaning" is determined is necessarily incomplete. Partly, this is because the coding (transducing) process, on the basis of which instructions and categories are formed, is correlated with neurophysiological processes that are not yet fully understood and that would range too far afield from this discussion. In addition, the neurophysiological events underlying referencing and programming, which must be correlated with some type of "scanning" process, are not understood at all. Secondly, the incompleteness results because the discussion has been confined to visual–motor coding. Since an encounter between a person and his environment involves the correlation of signals transduced through ocular–motor, auditory, tactile, and kinaesthetic systems, any attribution of meaning or recognition involves a wider set of categories used for cross-referencing than is considered here. Nevertheless, the principles of referencing probably hold true no matter what signal systems are included in the referencing program. If this is the case, then meaning, recognition, representation, and expression are all associated with the cross-referencing process.

Referencing programs can be operated in the absence of any sensory signal system, as in the case of ordinary thinking. Vertical referencing can be cross-referenced with an erroneous (or absent) signal system—as in the case of hallucinations—or a signal system can be cross-referenced with an erroneous category—as in the case of illusions. It is our semantic structures that force us to attribute primary or causal "reality"—however phrased—to one or another location in a referencing system. In an authoritarian culture, one may say of a person who displays defiance that he "needs" to be punished. In an egalitarian culture, one may say of this same defiant person that he has a "need" for punishment. In both instances, the word "need" is used to locate the origin or cause of a behavior process; in the first, as external to the person (the environment which seeks to control or abolish the behavior), in the second, inside the person (who, in accordance with previous conditioning, seeks punishment). A more concise and objective description would picture defiance as an activity that may evoke a punishing response and punishment as an activity that may evoke a defiant response. They are cross-referenced with each other under certain contingencies of social control.

When a large-scale referencing program has been thoroughly learned and standardized, one ordinarily speaks of the operation of cognitive structures and attributes great influence to them as "gestalts" responsible for the immediate perception of external stimuli. Fortunately, the investigator who is exploring a novel area of inquiry is free to tackle the referencing process at any point he chooses, and in terms of any scale, without being bound to previous constructs. This study investigates the way in which the codings of events, activities, and body movements are cross-referenced with each other in the attribution of "meaning" to a visual presentation of the human body.

# 7. *Somatotactics:*

## THE GROUP OF BODY MOVEMENT CATEGORIES

If one attempts to devise an abstract and formal system for dealing with body movement, one encounters a problem that resembles the difficulties surrounding *space* in the history of physics. Space as an abstract reference system with formal geometrical properties was attained only after prolonged struggling with two earlier ideas—first, the notion of *place*, or a succession of places indefinitely extended, later, the Newtonian concept of *absolute space*—a fixed container, alternately empty (void), filled (with the "ether"), or dotted with celestial objects. The current notion of space as a variously curved four-dimensional field was achieved only by divesting the concept of its concrete, contained objects and of its rigid, three-dimensional, box-like properties (Jammer, 1954).

A similar problem of concreteness had to be overcome in the conceptualization of force and motion, at first a matter of pure, brute strength displayed by gods and other supernatural powers; later, properties of an animated nature—a world soul; still later, an external agent, a push, imparting motion to an object. The idea that forces also act at a distance, as in gravitation, was not fully separated from the influence of supernatural powers until Newton's "laws" of mechanics gained acceptance. The new, geometrical, impersonal, clockwork universe excluded any analogy between the motion of physical bodies relative to each other and the willed action of human or superhuman beings (Jammer, 1957).

In conceptualizing the movements of the human body in its physical and human environments, one encounters the problem of concreteness whenever an attempt is made to observe the "actions" of the body. Body movement appears to become manifest only in expressive activity of one sort or another. Apart from human activities, the movements of the body appear as meaningless gestures or inert postures. But, to attain an abstract and formal system of body movement, which can somehow be conceived as generating the more concrete presentations of the body, one must divorce the movements from the everyday activities in which they become manifest. It becomes necessary to search for patterns, for a morphology of movement, embodied in the everyday activities.

There must be a vast though finite number of movements which the human body is capable of performing. There are two ways of conceiving how such a large set of movements could be ordered. One can imagine that there is no definite, intrinsic ordering, apart from the limits imposed by the human frame. On this assumption, the movements assembled into activities are drawn from a huge, random collection of bits and pieces of learned movement available for possible use. The process, in this case, would be like that of the artist who selects pigments for his current painting from a random collection of splotches on his palette. Alternatively, one could suppose that movements, like activities and roles, come to the performer neatly packaged in categories available for vertical and cross-referencing. In this image, the process is like a prior step in the artist's procedure. He has, at some point, carefully mixed the splotches on his palette, combining pigments drawn from neatly packaged and labeled tubes of paint. How is one to decide which model to employ for the conceptualization of movement?

Some help for making the decision comes from examining the features of a concrete activity. For example, in the schedule of instructions for "taking a sleeping pill," there were two items referring to unscrewing the bottle top and screwing it back on again. Both instructions describe a screwing motion, one calling for the reverse of the other. The movements in question consist of grasping the bottle top between thumb and forefinger and then performing a maneuver such that as the forefinger moves in one direction the thumb moves in the opposite direction, the effect a twist that rotates the bottle top slightly. Since the arc of rotation is quite limited, the twisting movement must be repeated several times. The thumb and forefinger thus pass each other in opposite directions repeatedly and with a certain rhythm resulting from the fact that the switches of the two fingers occur at regular intervals in time.

One could conceive of this motion as twisting and untwisting responses waiting to be included in one or another activity where they will be of use. This conception implies that twisting and untwisting are not parts of any particular order of movements, being merely related pieces in a random collection. But one could conceive of the movement as part of a larger movement category consisting of rhythmic, alternating, bypassing of parts of the body. On this assumption, one could search for other movements within this category, such as pill-rolling, snapping of the fingers, massaging, the *entre-chat* of classical ballet (rapid, alternate crossing and uncrossing of feet and ankles in mid-air during a jump).

If it is assumed, tentatively, that movements can be ordered in categories quite apart from their local anatomical features, one must ask several questions: What is the ordering principle? How are levels of specificity and generality organized? Are categories of movement related to events in accordance with any intrinsic meaning or do they obtain meaning only from their inclusion in one or another activity? To put this last question in the vocabulary used here, can the presentation of a movement within its movement category evoke an organized perceptual response independently of its inclusion in an activity program or in a role program? If the answer to the two last questions is positive, this would imply that there exists a *movement dimension* that can be cross-referenced directly with the event dimension without having to pass through the sorting and screening imposed by activities and roles.

In the discussion that follows, and in the tables and notations for classifying body movements, categories have been constructed in accordance with four principles proposed as answers to the above questions, beginning with the physical properties of the human body in its environment. These properties are treated as the most general categorization of movement that can be made. They enter into the programming of all more specific movements. As these categories start with the concept of the human body in its surrounding environment, the organization of the categories is egocentric, beginning with the innermost core of the body and spreading outward. These most general categories are called *personal*.

This concept creates a contrast with a less general, overall category dealing with two human bodies that move in relation to each other. It seems obvious that, in such mutually interrelated movements, all the categories grouped together as personal must be deployed in order to represent the phenomenon. Yet something is added to the phenomenon in the sense that novel properties emerge from the encounter between persons. Categories to deal with these emerging properties are labeled *interpersonal movements* to represent the general feature from which the new properties arise. Finally, the general classification is completed with the category of *multi-personal movements*, not further broken down nor discussed (see Table 7–1). This class refers to the mutual movements of three or more persons relative to each other. It can be expanded to describe extended arrays of persons assembled in massed groupings. Such patterns are based on interpersonal movements, though on a larger scale.

Another principle of classification is concerned with the relation between physical form and the programming of motion. The idea that movements are patterned is not a novelty but the concrete and formal aspects of the patterning have seldom been attended to. If they have recognizable shapes, if they can be given borders and outlines, then these forms ought to be examined in minute detail. These efforts to identify the patterns and to describe them through verbal categories and diagrams are merely designs—that is, something imposed on the

**TABLE 7–1. Somatotactical Categories**

| | | | |
|---|---|---|---|
| **A.** *Personal movements* | *I. Body space* | Anterior, right antero-lateral, right postero-lateral, posterior, left postero-lateral, left antero-lateral | Areal radiation |
| | | Internal, proximal, axial, distal, limbic | Distance radiation |
| | *II. Body action* | Uniform / Compound | Resting |
| | | Uniform / Compound | Moving |
| | | Self / Other | Intending |
| | *III. Motion patterns* | Direct / Curved, circling, spiraling | Straight / Curved |
| | | Right turn, left turn / Weaving, zigzagging, oscillating | Angled / Alternating |
| | *IV. Body areas* | | I / II / III / IV / V |

| | | | | |
|---|---|---|---|---|
| **B.** *Interpersonal movements* | *I. Syntropic patterns* | Diatropic, protropic, paratropic, apotropic, amphitropic, cyclotropic | Horizontal | |
| | | Acrotropic, isotropic, hypertropic, hypotropic | Vertical | |
| | | Ankylotropic, allotropic, asyntropic | Mixed | |
| | *II. Synkinesic patterns* | Approach | | |
| | | Contact | | |
| | | Accession | Approach separation intervals | Positive induction / Positive counter induction |
| | | Intersection | | |
| | | Inclusion | | Negative induction / Negative counter induction |
| | | Manipulation | | |
| | | Extrusion | | |
| | | Separation | | |

**C.** *Multi-personal movements*

phenomena—not a discovery of something universally true of the phenomena. The designs selected may or may not be appropriate and useful for description; others may prove superior.

Two tests have been applied for determining suitability and usefulness. The first is the test of potential programming. For each category, its label, and its notation, it has been asked whether a program of instruction for movement could be written so that the formal pattern would be produced. Thinking up categories constituted an intellectual exercise which, though it had its own rewards, gave no evidence as to the representativeness of the categories. The second test, then, was an attempt to find out whether others might actually be using such categories in their perceptions of the world of body movement. The experiments reported in subsequent chapters were designed to obtain some evidence on this score.

A third principle of category design involves labeling. Labels are meant to highlight the most representative feature of any category—in other words, that selected feature shared by all subcategories. Ordinary English words are used for this purpose whenever possible in order to avoid neologisms. Unfortunately, the English language does not always provide suitable terms—words that pinpoint the feature in question. Where no precise English word is available, a new word from Greek roots has been fabricated on the notion that a Greek neologism is less offensive than an English one.

A final principle of category design applies to the diagramming devised to display those features of the categories which might not be easily recognized from a purely verbal description. Since the diagrams refer to a series of static positional arrangements, they may not seem to be concerned with motion. But since motion is an order of progression through specified positions in space, both the positional arrangements and the order in which they are traversed must be included in any set of instructions constituting the program employed to exemplify the pattern of movement. Space and motion can be considered identical with respect to structure, and the diagrams are made on this basis— that is, a specified progression through successive positions in space—for all the categories included in Table 7–1. But it did not seem warranted to publish all these diagrams, since they merely resulted in showing a pattern easily discriminable on the basis of verbal description.

Diagramming is related to the fully developed systems of notation such as those used for the scoring of music and of dance movements. Of these, the graphic system of *Labanotation* used for recording dance movements is the most recent development.[1] These recording methods employ a set of conventional graphic signs to code a set of specialized performances in program form. The reader familiar with the system may translate their signs into the succession of musical notes, or dance movements constituting a musical performance or a dance. Labanotation is somewhat more generally applicable than musical notation since it can be used to instruct a performer in any sequence of movements in any setting.

The fit between the categories used here and the system of Labanotation is tenuous and essentially unusable. Labanotation treats the topic of movement in accordance with the assumption that movement can be conceived as formed from random bits and pieces of anatomical motion lying about to be assembled in various patterns and sequences. On this view, movement contains neither intrinsic psychological nor social features and its various groupings can't easily be referred to sets of activities or event structures.

This assessment is not a disparagement of Labanotation or of the basic assumption on which it rests. The same strictures could be leveled against the system of musical notation or, for that matter, the alphabet. They are simply codes that lack any intrinsic "meaning." The "meaning" inheres in the pattern of musical sounds,[2] of body movements, and of articulated speech, which the codes instruct the performer to produce. In each case, the graphic signs of the method of notation specify the sequences without placing them in any high-level categorical system.

The developed notation systems are prescriptive and exact. Middle C is always a note of 132 vibrations per second, standing in a definite mathematical relation to all other notes in the twelve-tone scale above or below it. But what is needed here is classification that preserves the element of diffuse relationship and symbolic allusiveness found in ordinary body movement, while still conferring order upon the phenomena.[3] This is here named *somatotaxis*, a word that refers to the arrangement of the body in space. *Somatotactics* denotes the study of this area of behavior, and the adjective *somatotactical* refers to the various categories of the classification system.

Since (see Table 7–1) the most general somatotactical category, Personal Movements, refers to the radial or egocentric orientation of the upright body in space, the first category to be considered involves the structuring of the space within which the body is made to behave. In considering the two subcategories of Body Space, the Topical and the Directional, it is important to clear away some preconceptions derived from the history of Western thought, where the body is thought of on the basis of its bilateral symmetry and of space in terms of three right-angled dimensions. One must remember that they are merely concepts, ways of coding the phenomena presented by transactions with the environment. In addition to the (admittedly striking) right–left, back–front organization of the human frame, there can be perceived a more basic radial pattern, a plan shared with plants, starfish, worms, and other lowly forms of life. Radial symmetry starts from a central core surrounding a prototypical head–tail (or top–base) gradient and spreads outward in all directions, each direction pointing into space like the spoke of a wheel.

The same cautions apply to the ordinary conception of space. In the history of Western thought, much time and energy has been applied to the problem of separating the concept of space from that of place, to abstract and generalize the concept of space as a set of dimensions with fixed properties quite independent of what human beings must be doing with reference to them. Because of the accidents of history, a three-dimensional, 90 degree coordinate system of axes was selected for this purpose. But coordinates of any number of dimensions and degrees might have been selected just as well. According to R. Buckminster Fuller,[4] designer of the geodesic dome, a four-dimensional coordinate system would have served better for many purposes. This would require the replacement of the present 90-degree frame of reference with a 60-degree coordinate system; the rectangles and cubes of the present concept would be replaced by triangles for plane surfaces and tetrahedra for volumes, six triangles about a point in a plane and 20 tetrahedra ranged about a point in space. If space were conceived of as a set of packages bounded by the four sloping sides of a tetrahedron, then spatial dimensions could be coded along the more radially arrangeable axes of 60 degrees.

There is merit in conceptualizing the spatial area around the body as a design that is congruent with the radial symmetry of the body, and also with the bilateral symmetry of the body. The arrangements diagrammed in Figures 13a, 13b, and 13c were conceived to meet these conditions for the areas of the space around the body into which body movement is directed. Since movement into an area of the radially segmented space around the body is the key feature of the construction of the category, this subcategory of Body Space is called *Areal Radiation.*

There is an assumption built into the principle of category design used here that should be made explicit. The assumption is that the primary orientation of the body as it moves into space (from its starting point) is not along a straight line, but towards a place in one of the radiation areas. How that place is reached, whether by a straight, curved, or wobbly pathway, is not a primary issue. Accordingly, it is not the straight lines of the diagram that are of significance to the visual–motor systems, but the placement of an object in one of the areas radiating from the body.

Thus, if one wishes to reach an object, one may have to move directly forward into the anterior radiation area, or turn a bit into the right antero–lateral area. Meanwhile, the object may have moved or remained stationary. In either case, as a result of one's own movements, one's body will have switched around and therefore will require relocation on the ground plan of the radiation areas. In

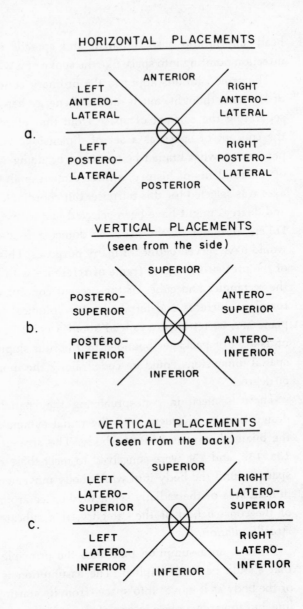

Fig. 13. Areal Radiation

this fashion, movement is steadily programmed in relation to the categories of horizontal placements.

Although it is supposed that the ground plan of the horizontal radiation areas functions as a stable system of reference for the programming of movement, it is not clear how movement into the various anterior, lateral, and posterior areas is learned in the course of development. The usual sequence of horizontal movements consists of "'turning" followed by "straightening," an assumption used in the description of interpersonal movement where mutual turning (*syntropism*) is said to precede mutual movement along a straight line (*synkinesis*).

Radiation areas in the vertical plane for the body in upright position, facing the right side of the diagram, are displayed in Figure 13b. The head is in the superior area, the shoulders and chest in the anteror–superior and postero–superior areas, etc. With trunk held still, the arms can easily swing through the antero–inferior, antero–superior, and superior areas, but traverse the postero–inferior and postero–superior areas with difficulty. The categories of *vertical placements* in body space function as a stable reference system for a class of body movements. They also serve to relate objects in space to body movement in a manner similar to that described for horizontal placements.

A third plane may be drawn through the body, as represented in Figure 13c. This plane would be at 90 degrees to one's line of vision if one were looking directly at the back of a standing person (as in the diagram), or at his front. In this plane, the superior and inferior areas assume the same meaning as in the preceding discussion, but in between them are located the latero–superior and latero–inferior areas, whose meanings differ. The latero–superior area may be occupied, for example, by epaulettes, a pet parrot, or by the face of a person intent on creating discomfort by looking over your shoulder. The latero–inferior area has frequently been reserved for hand-arms but, at greater distance, may be filled by a toddler or a well-trained dog.

The correlation (cross-referencing) between the horizontal and vertical radiation areas—and of object placements in these areas—is a learning task that, presumably, occupies the first eighteen months of life.[5] During that time, the various radiation areas come to be differentially associated with the objects and events "taking place" within them. Such differential effects vary with the life history of the individual and in accordance with cultural prescriptions. For example, in many cultures, events "taking place" in the superior radiation areas will be ascribed greater significance than those occurring in the inferior areas. The existence of such effects independent of the nature of the activities giving rise to them argues for the possibility that some somatotactical categories can be cross-referenced directly with event categories, skipping over precise reference to the activities dimension.

The significance of boundaries and the areas which they demarcate is even more apparent in the case of the *distance* radiations of body space (Figure 14). Distance categories represent ways of coding the "amount" of distance separating the placement of an object or event from the central core of the body. "Amount" denotes a behaviorally conceived rather than a quantitative definition of distance. Internal space, for example, denotes the space between the inner core of the body and the skin. The metrical features of internal space are of some significance especially to the very fat or very lean; but the occurrence of any object or movement within that space is of the greatest significance to the individual

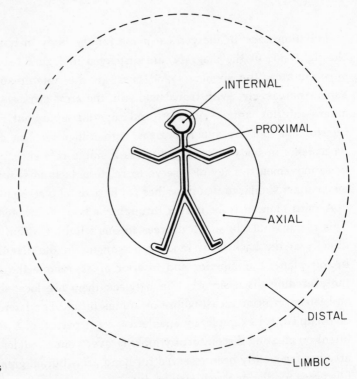

INTERNAL

PROXIMAL

AXIAL

DISTAL

LIMBIC

**Fig. 14.** Body Spaces

concerned, regardless of his corporeal dimensions. Internal space is the most intimate and personal of all the concentrically-arranged areas included in distance categories.

Proximal space is second, consisting of the area between the body and its coverings of clothing, hair, or ornament. In the completely uncovered body, it consists of the physically unbounded but psychologically restricted area immediately adjacent to the skin. Just as internal space can be entered through the natural orifices of the body or invaded through injury at unnatural sites, so proximal space can be entered in several ways: by secretions from internal space, by movements from axial space which glide beneath the clothing, probe within the hair, or strip away the coverings. Unclothed or uncovered sections of proximal space are freely accessible to entry unless covered with the hands or protected (*pro + tegere* = to cover up) [6] by defensive countermoves within axial space.

Of all things that a person may present to the external world, those that occur at the internal–proximal boundary are among the most valuable. Only slightly less value attaches to presentations made from the proximal–axial boundary. Clothes may not make the man but they help and, in extreme situations, are important to survival. Therefore, cleaning, preening, arranging, and rearranging the forms of the proximal–axial boundary are ubiquitous activities in all known cultures, and across species.

Axial space extends from the external boundary of proximal space to the limit of the area controlled by the extended arms and legs. Because the range of movement of the limbs is greater anteriorally than posteriorally, axial space is fluid and irregular in shape. In the anterior, antero–lateral, and postero–lateral radiation areas, its outer extent corresponds to what is commonly meant by the expression "at arm's length." In the posterior radiation area, it is much contracted.

Since various parts of the axial–distal boundary are defined by the position in which the arms and legs are held, these positions constitute presentations that evoke various responses in others. Arms stiffly crossed over the chest, for example, tend to indicate not only a closed up but also a shrunken version of axial space in which there is no room for another person or object. Arms held out in slightly curved position with hands apart tend to define a strong boundary with a definite opening, as if to say, "Come in." The legs similarly can open or close, define or leave indefinite the current status of the axial–distal boundary. All such definings, openings, and closings at the axial–distal boundary repeat, reinforce, or countermand similar presentations which can be made at the internal–proximal and proximal–axial boundaries. The tightly pursed mouth of a woman, saying, in effect, "No entry" may be contradicted by an expanse of unclothed skin or revealing clothing that communicate something like "Hither" or "Available," only to be again neutralized by locked arms and crossed legs conveying either "No" or "Not yet."

It is common knowledge that the messages of the body may contradict or reinforce each other. Nevertheless, whether the presentations are contradictory or congruent with each other, their messages are unclear until they have been fitted into the parodic structuring of events. Did the woman just described purse her mouth, lock her arms, and cross her legs in the presence of a sexually aroused male or in response to a question asked of her by a girlfriend? If in the presence of a man showing sexual intentions, were the woman's definitions of her various boundaries presented before he made an approach—in which case they could have been understood as a challenge—or after his approach, in which case they could have represented a refusal? It is clear, then, that in order to reduce the inevitable uncertainty and ambiguity of the responses called for by the boundary conditions around these spaces, presentations from these boundaries or within these spaces must ordinarily be cross-referenced with activities, with roles, and with the structure of events.[7] By themselves, they imply a broad range of possible responses with no clues as to which particular response pattern is to be chosen.

Broad though they are, their range of possible meaning is not limitless. It is confined to the kinds of behavior possible within a particular area of body space, or required in order to cross a boundary. From this viewpoint, the character of the body spaces alters dramatically on crossing the axial–distal boundary. For distal space, which proceeds from that boundary to a line representing the outer limits of scanning available to the eyes and ears, is vast in comparison to those previously discussed. Furthermore, all presentations made to internal, proximal, and axial space are susceptible of kinaesthetic, tactile, and other forms of immediate sensory processing. Presentations made by others in distal space are more remote, and movements made in that space are less immediately connected with the person. On the other hand, all movements made by a person in the direction of his own distal space are movements into the world of objects and events in the search for encounters.

Distal space embraces the knowable world at any one moment in time. Electronic devices, telescopes, radar, and the like can amplify the range of scanning and thus enormously extend certain parts of the distal–limbic boundary. The limbic space beyond that boundary, however, remains impenetrable for ordinary sensory processing. What movements and events may occur within it have to be supplied by the fantasies of the individual or the group. Events beyond the borders of sensory processing have never lacked description in whatever terms religion or science might suggest.

If these several categories of areal radiation and distance radiation appropriately describe the way space may be coded with reference to the body, one must ask what sorts of body action can occur with reference to these spaces. By *body action* is meant a behavior of the body more specific than movement itself. Thus, *moving* becomes one of three kinds of action the body can display. It may be moving, at rest, or exhibiting an intention to move. When resting, it may show uniform rest, as in sleep, or part of the body may be motionless with respect to body space, while other parts move within one or another of its spaces. In the latter case, one needs to employ the subcategory, *compound*, though this category may be unnecessary if observations are confined to those parts of the body purely at rest or purely in motion.

Although for certain coding purposes it is preferable to use the participle form of the verb to label these categories—e.g., "moving"—for other purposes it is better to use the noun form—e.g., "a move." The verb form is preferable to denote the general principle being referred to; the noun to denote a behavior that has a beginning and an end and thus is to be fitted into an activity or an event. A rest, for example, is a time-limited category. These considerations apply in particular to the category labeled "intending." An *intention* can be defined as an interrupted move but it deserves a category status at the same level of generality as moving and resting. Even though it consists of interrupted movement, it is not a subvariety of moving or resting. For an intention functions as a cue to an activity which may or may not occur. A dog may open its mouth and bare its fangs but never bite or snap. The preliminaries function for their own sake in the presentation of a threat. It is perceived as a threat, however, because it is recognized as a part of an available move of aggression which may or may not be put into action.

There are few intention movements that can't be put into action or subside into rest. A large part of the messages of the body are transmitted by means of presentations of this order. Sitting upright or moving the feet forward while sitting in a chair are intentions to get up. The face is capable of numerous intention movements belonging to total actions of the body but substituting very successfully for them. Many gestures are motions that have gotten locked out of their total pattern of completed movement and thus function as intentions. The sign of the intention is that the part stands for the whole.

Intention movements may come about in two different ways. In the first, the interruption is imposed by the person on himself. Self-interruptions occur in the kinds of intentions under discussion above. But interruptions may be imposed from without. Action may be interfered with by some interposing event, or frozen by painter, sculptor, or camera. Intention movements that are created by external agents have more variety and scope than those produced by self-interruptions. They offer more challenge to interpretation—i.e., what *is* the movement that was in process? Persons who are called "expressive" have a larger repertoire of self-interrupted intending actions available to them than those called stolid or unexpressive.

If one is to inquire into some of the many connotations of the words "style" and "expression"—issues that have been raised in earlier chapters—one will find that the interrelations between resting, moving, and intending form an important point of departure for such an investigation. Personal style can be defined as the ratio of frequency between resting, moving, and intending exhibited by an individual. Over-enthusiastic self-interrupters tend to get disorganized; those who constantly interrupt others produce an inordinate amount of intending action in their environment, something that has its funny as well as its sad aspects. The humor of Charlie Chaplin rests in large part in his ability to get persons or objects to interrupt his moves, which then disintegrate into a stream of dramatic but ineffective intentions. The postponement of the unachieved goal arouses responses in the audience proportionate to their own incomplete actions or unattainable goals.

The contribution of body action categories to "style" and "expression" (or "style of expression") is further evidenced in their modification by *motion patterns*, the next set of categories to be discussed. When the body moves, it will display either a straight, curved, angled, or alternating pattern of motion. Each of these categories alone, or some combination of them, will produce linear or circular movements, turns, spirals, or oscillations. Alone, or in combination, they form frequency ratios by means of which one recognizes individual differences in body actions, that is, ratios characterizing either the rests, moves, or intentions of different persons. Some persons, whether resting, intending, or moving, are all angles and sharp points; others are mainly straight, either forward, or in the vertical plane, and are therefore characterized as forthright, straightforward, downright, or upright. Still others move or rest in curves, softly, sensuously, or deviously. In the burlesque stage tradition well-endowed women move mainly in alternating patterns, their breasts, shoulders, hips and buttocks bobbing rhythmically up and down and to and fro.

There is no need, here, to spell out the relevance of body action and motion patterns for various styles of art. The relation of straight and upright rests to the Byzantine, of curved moves to the Renaissance, and of angled intentions (interrupted from all sides) to the Cubist styles seems obvious. But the coding principles of artistic styles involve not only body movements (and, by analogy, the movements of objects), but are also concerned with the spatial categories of somatotactics. The rules of perspective developed in the Renaissance constitute a finely worked out code for a radially conceived distal space based on lines of sight radiating from (or toward) distant objects. This code was superimposed on the 90-degree, vertical–horizontal coordinate system inherited from the Egyptian and Mesopotamian wall reliefs. Nevertheless, as stated above, body space may be coded in planes and radial projections involving a variety of coordinate axes arranged in accordance with angles other than 90 degrees.[8] The body can be approached from any combination of these alternative coordinate systems and can thus be made to present itself in curved planes and radial projection areas wholly released from the standard, three-dimensional reference system. Contemporary art styles code the human body and impersonal objects in spatial arrangements based on such alternative choices—choices which, for people who have not learned the alternate coding system, are difficult to interpret. For this reason, a thorough-going somatotactical study of artistic style is very much needed.

To return to motion patterns, it is apparent that straight, curved, angled, and alternating movements (plus rests and intentions) represent the basic principles for the coding of all determinate activities. Walking, running, sewing, eating, writing, hammering, sawing, screwing, and unscrewing—all the skilled activities programmed into one or another role category—are made up out of some combination of these motion patterns tailored to attain a goal.[9] The fitting of movement patterns to activities and roles demands a tremendous amount of cross-referencing between the activities dimension and the movement dimension. Yet how easily the fit or lack of fit is recognized in immediate perception. When the Sweeney of T. S. Eliot's poem lets his arms hang down to laugh, one immediately recognizes the behavior as subhuman and probably apelike because hanging arms in the antero–inferior radiation area do not fit into the activity involved in human laughter but do fit into the upright walk and grimacing of the larger apes especially as portrayed in the film industry by human beings cavorting about in ape costumes.

As is evident in this description, cross-referencing is concerned with the areas and parts of the body that are placed in motion. The cross-referencing of activity with body part leads to a consideration of the last category under the Personal Movements classification, *Body Area*, important but not to be discussed here in any detail. Any system of categories for coding the anatomical divisions and parts of the body will vary depending upon the use to which the categories are directed.

The coding system proposed here is concerned with the formal pattern of movement in body space rather than with the anatomical program of movement that produces the pattern. This is in marked contrast with Labanotation which supplies a specific set of instructions for moving the feet, the arms, the head, and other parts of the body, in directions that will ultimately result in a pattern. Neither the graphic signs of Labanotation nor their corresponding verbal instructions can readily be translated into a pattern of movement by simple inspection, just as a person not well versed in musical notation cannot easily discern melody and harmony from an inspection of a musical score. This difficulty in visual decoding applies also to the Birdwhistell system. For this reason, both of these approaches to coding would fall within the activities dimension previously discussed. They are not concerned with movement as pattern or form but with the parts of the body moving in certain directions.

As the categories under discussion here are concerned with the shape of movement and its immediate reference to personal encounters, there is no need for a specialized category system for the parts of the body involved in the movement. Everyday English words for body parts serve as adequate designations for the fine divisions of body areas involved in action and motion patterns. However, in order to have a way of keeping track of the distribution of body presentations along the head–foot gradient (or upper to lower distribution), the body areas shown in Figure 15 are designated so that area I refers to the head and neck, area II to arms and thorax, and so on, with area V referring to the body as a whole. This gross segmentation of body areas is consistent with the approach to somatotactics adopted throughout this book: that in the current, undeveloped state of the field, it is wise to base one's strategy of investigation on the development of categories and methods directed at coarse- rather than fine-grained and complexly interwoven movements. If one can determine how messages from such gross divisions of the body are coded, one will be in a better position to deal with subtle and complicated presentations. Here, no attention is paid to the development of coding categories for those most sensitive of all indicators—the face and the hands acting independently of the rest of

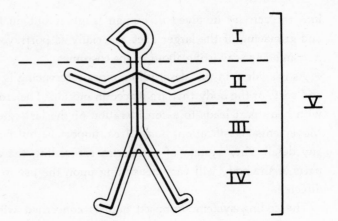

**Fig. 15.**  Body Areas

the body. In some of the experiments to be reported later (Chapter 13), one feature of the face, the eye, and one feature of this organ, the direction of the gaze, are considered. Even this departure, however, is consistent with the design of experiments to deal with only a few categories at a time, each of which can be made to vary independently of the others.

This concludes the discussion of all the subcategories classified as *Personal Movements.* It is apparent that this most general category might just as appropriately be called *Personal Space.* For body space has emerged as a product of body movement. It is a way of coding the places—the planes, boundaries, and radial projection areas—into which the body or its parts may move, given the physical features of the human body. But, the initial proposition can just as well be reversed. Body movement, as defined here, consists of those physically possible combinations of motion and rest that can be made to occur in body space. Space and motion define each other; neither concept is possible without the other. Therefore, both must belong to some more general category referring simultaneously to the shape of motion *and* the shape of space.

There is no word for labeling this more general concept of shaping or structuring which embraces both space and motion. Indeed, it is difficult for the mind to take such a notion seriously. To assert an identity between space and motion may seem excessively abstract, unreal, or even ridiculous. Identity means that feature which space and motion hold in common and which is more general than either of them, namely, their structure or form. But the words, form or structure, do not refer merely to the visual contours or outlines of objects and events, but to *an arrangement*, an ordering of relationships, that embraces both the "inside" and the "outside" of objects and events.

These considerations apply with considerable clarity to the case of the *Interpersonal Movements.* Their arrangements of motion have no "existence" as an object of science nor as a formal event until the patterns of movement created by two or more people moving with reference to each other are coded. But to do this, it is necessary to categorize the shape of the space created by the arrangements of the bodies during rest and motion. For the structure of the space between and around the bodies varies for the different positions of the bodies with respect to each other. Different kinds of events may or may not "take place" because of these varying spatial arrangements. Since the movements of the bodies and the shapes of the spaces are both aspects of the same structural arrangements, only one set of somatotactical categories to refer to either of them is needed.[10]

The movement of one person with reference to another remaining at rest or of both moving simultaneously with reference to each other can be characterized in two ways. The first type consists of turning movements carried out by one with reference to the other, or of both simultaneously with reference to some pivot between them. Such movements emphasize the radial organization of the body, its movements and its spaces. Because of the turning motion, such movements are here called *tropisms,* and since the bodies turn together, or in relation to each other, the overall category is labeled *syntropism.* In contrast to syntropic movements are mutual encounters that feature a moving closer together or farther apart on a line of approach and separation. One may approach another who remains at rest, or both may approach at the same time. The straightness or crookedness of the line of approach or separation are of importance because the line connects the central core of the body of one person with that of the other. Because of the straight-line connection over which the movement travels, this type of motion is here called *kinetic* and the overall category is called *synkinesis.* The positions through which synkinesis travels are called *synkinetic intervals.*

The turning patterns of syntropism can occur in any axis or plane connecting the two bodies but, for the present, only planes that are horizontal or vertical relative to the baseline on which the human body seeks support are to be considered. Sets of horizontal (Figure 16) and vertical (Figure 17) syntropic positions are postulated, each labeled with a prefix descriptive of the pattern. Each of the six positions of horizontal syntropism can be considered a set of initial conditions from which the body may turn, or, alternatively, as a set of final conditions into which the body may turn. The diagrams employ symbols representing the human body as viewed from above after turning into one or another of the positions, or, as with the cyclotropic position, while in process of turning. Since the positions are established by an interrelationship, they can be maintained during rest, motion, or intending action, and the bodies may be seated, standing, walking, or running.

The *diatrope* refers to the face-to-face situation, the most direct confrontation available to humans, which generates a variety of specific activities—love-

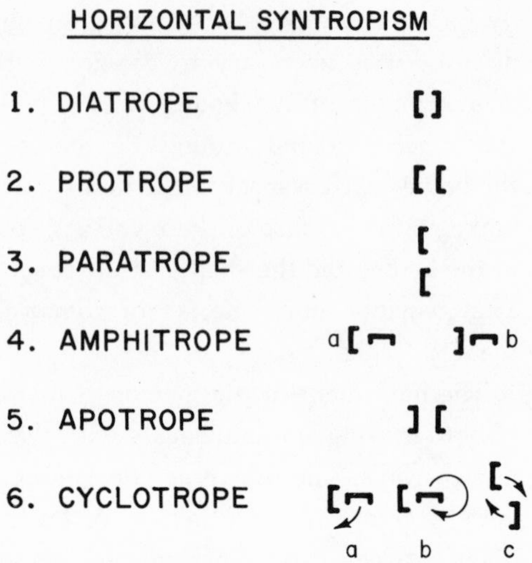

**Fig. 16.**   Horizontal Syntropism

making, fighting, greeting, comforting. (In Western culture avoidance of the diatrope tends to imply evasion or the desire to conceal.)

If interpersonal movement starts with a diatrope and one person turns through an arc of 180 degrees, the *protrope* makes its appearance—the queue line in which people patiently wait "in turn" to be served or the opposite extreme, the chase. Turning in front of another, bypassing others in the protropic order, and struggling to get to the head of the line all have implications for competition. Leadership (and followership), and the ambition to be the first one to arrive at any position of importance, literally or figuratively, are embedded in the protrope.

The *paratrope* implies companionship and togetherness. Side-by-side, in motion or at rest, the persons making up a paratrope can choose whether to remain even with each other or break up the formation by charging into protropic competition. This choice is *de facto* evidence for the potential instability of all the syntropic arrangements. They can be maintained in delicate balance only by mutual consent: Given this attention, the paratrope can be presented as the basis for a united front—a wall of human resistance, an exhibition offering maximum display like a chorus line, or a small group, say of emissaries, representing a larger group before a constituted authority. In the last case, the paratropic group assumes a diatropic position in a multipersonal array.

The *amphitrope* can be easily established by small turns out of the other positions, and is, therefore, the most unstable of any of them. Since the design is based on 90-degree positioning, relative to each other, the persons involved may assume two different versions of the amphitrope. The first is ordinary profiling, which is a compromise between turning away and turning toward. The second is a more dramatically stated disengagement in which one person

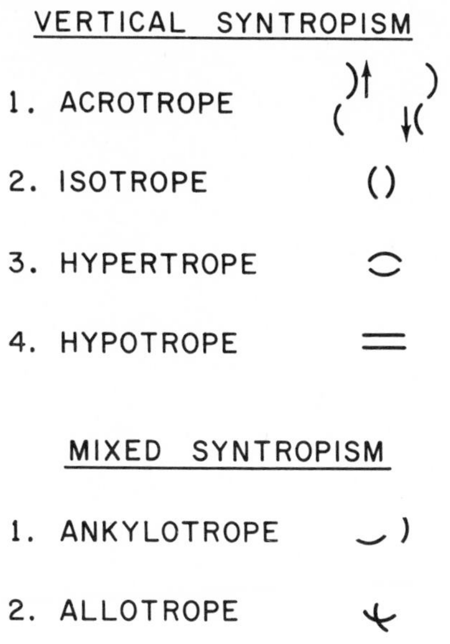

## VERTICAL SYNTROPISM

1. ACROTROPE

2. ISOTROPE

3. HYPERTROPE

4. HYPOTROPE

## MIXED SYNTROPISM

1. ANKYLOTROPE

2. ALLOTROPE

**Fig. 17.** Vertical and Mixed Syntropism

partially turns his back on the other. Such quasi-disengagements occur for a number of different reasons: interrupted transitions between other positions that may contain no meaning at all, or intention movements that betray uncertainty, conflict, or coolness toward the relationship. In some instances, "type *a*" creates the opportunity for the profiler to present certain physical attributes, his "best side," to his partner.

The *apotrope*, featuring a confrontation of posteriors, is the classic statement of a disengagement which is not yet a separation, signaling blind, unspoken hostility, indifference hoping to be cajoled, injury awaiting relief. On the other hand, the apparent opposition may be correlated with fear rather than anger, as when two persons maintain vigilance in potentially hostile territory by surveying opposite sides of the horizon.

The *cyclotrope*, the most varied of the syntropic arrangements, is the most suited to exhibitionistic display. In the first form, one partner stays at rest or pivots in place while the other circles him. In the second form, one stands still while the other rotates in front of him. In the third, they both rotate about a center equidistant from each other. The center may be at rest relative to the ground or may move along the ground as the gyrating partners traverse space. Although a dazzling display runs through all the variations, the purpose of the display does not remain constant. In the first form, circling can be directed at finding a vulnerable point for attack while the one circled displays his immunity or resistance to intimidation. The pivoting performer in the second form may be inviting admiration or participation while the waltzing partners of the third enjoy their visual–motor exhibits. At the same time, the forms of the cyclotrope lend themselves to the close footwork and armwork of infighting, as in boxing, grabbing for wrestling holds, the catches of karate, and the thrusts of fencing.

Vertical syntropism (see Fig. 17) generates more restricted patterns than horizontal. In the diagrams, the human figure is represented by a design indicating the body as viewed from the side. The *acrotrope* features a peaked structure in which the partners move in such a fashion as to maintain one at a higher level than the other. Peaking can be achieved in several ways. In one, no matter how one partner moves, the other manages to rise above him—a form of physical one-upmanship. At the opposite pole, no matter how one partner moves, the other manages to stay below him—a form of physical self-abasement. These two effects, however, are extremes outside the usual, unstable assent to mutual movement built into a syntropic structure. In ordinary acrotropic movements, the partners agree to participate in the elevation of one over the other.

The peaker displays *positive acrotropism* while the abaser shows *negative acrotropism*. Positive acrotropism can be correlated with superiority, authority, majesty, and triumph. Negative acrotropism is associated with inferiority, incapacity, humility, and acceptance of authority. These behaviors are reciprocal and the complementarity thus established between peaker and abaser overcomes an imbalance in the pattern that is different from any seen thus far.

In addition to the general tendency of all the syntropic patterns to break up and be reconstituted, the acrotrope is off balance because of its asymmetry. In the other patterns, the movements of one person are some kind of fair copy of the movements of his partner, and imitation of each other's movements helps to keep these structures intact. But the movements of positive acrotropism are unlike those of negative acrotropism, in spite of which fact the whole structure may be coded (internalized) by both participants. Positive acrotropism includes holding oneself erect, with head high, climbing to a higher position, strutting about in a cock-of-the-walk fashion, and looking over the other person's head or looking down the nose with head held up. The negative movements are also varied, ranging from holding the head bowed, kneeling or prostrating oneself, to averting the gaze, or opening up the axial–distal boundary in the antero–superior plane, with open, raised, and outstretched arms and eyes turned up and opened widely.

The dissimilarity of acrotropic movements is marked. What holds the structure together is the diagonal continuity of space and the dove-tailing of movement within that space. As a result of a dissimilarity which yet preserves complementarity, positive and negative acrotropism can each be recognized apart from the other—that is, in the absence of an actual acrotropic structure. It is in this respect that acrotropism is unlike any of the other patterns in the syntropic series.

Similarity of movement and the uses of imitation reappear in the next vertical syntropic pattern, *isotropism*. The structure requires that the partners to the encounter remain approximately at the same height, executing a performance that might be called "leveling," the physical basis of egalitarianism. As with the other syntropic patterns, its properties emerge with greater salience when a stream of behavior effects a contrast in sequence. For example, when an adult renounces his normal positive acrotropism with respect to a child and descends to the child's level or picks the child up and lifts him to his own level, the resulting isotrope has salience. Similarly, if within a group which has been maintaining isotropism one member suddenly elevates himself to establish an acrotrope, then the switch calls attention to the lost isotrope. *Salient* is here used to designate any interpersonal movement acquisition whose maintenance or loss has become a focus of attention for the participants. In the more usual event, especially in the case of the isotrope, the regnant syntropic pattern is so much a part of the stream of behavior that it comes to no one's attention. This condition may be called *embedded*. Embedded isotropes occur almost universally in everyday affairs among age-mates of similar height. The isotrope becomes salient, however, by being lost in encounters between an average and a very tall or very short person.

In all these categories, movement has been viewed as a property of the human body whose weight is supported by the legs. No effort has been made to provide special categories for seated figures, since the interpersonal aspects of movement in space undergo no great change when the participants sit down. They may still face each other, turn their backs on each other, sit side-by-side or in a row, raise and lower themselves, or offer profiles to each other. Only the cyclotrope disappears and even this may be restored by the swivel chairs of barbers and dentists. What is principally different about the seated figure is the added scope for combinations of different syntropic patterns maintained simultaneously. This versatility results from the increased torsion that the seated body can undergo when the legs do not have to provide the main support. Two persons sitting opposite each other may make a diatrope with their legs, a paratrope with the shoulders and the thorax, and an amphitrope with their heads. Thus, opportunities for the reinforcement or contradiction of messages are more plentiful. In addition, the hands and feet take an increased role in amending and punctuating both verbal and body messages.

If no new categories are required for the seated posture, what is the somatotactical situation of recumbent figures? In a restless and activist culture, it is not easy to investigate the interpersonal aspects of prone or supine behavior. Categories for supine behavior are therefore presented with less confidence than for other postures.

In the recumbent position, weight is distributed all along the longitudinal axis of the body. This diffuse support sharply limits motion in the horizontal plane, confining it to feeble crawling or hunching movement. In the vertical and diagonal planes, on the other hand, motion is less obstructed because a part of the body can be used as a temporary base of support. Thus, rolling over, elevation of a part or the whole of the trunk using the arms and legs as support, or of the arms and legs, keeping the trunk as support are all movements that can be easily executed. To be sure, such movements occur within a relatively restricted space, and vary considerably depending upon whether the anterior, lateral, or posterior surface of the body is used for support. Nevertheless, the vertical plane appears to produce more salience of movement than the horizontal. For this reason, vertical syntropism has been chosen as the key to categorization of recumbent interpersonal movements.

If one looks for the features of vertical syntropic movement involving two or more recumbent people, one's attention is drawn to the shift between two possible arrangements. The partners to the encounter may lie together at the same level or one may lie over the other. The first pattern is called *hypotropic* on the assumption that the aim of the movement is not so much to stay level vis-à-vis each other as to stay "down" or "low" together. The second has been labeled *hypertropic* on the assumption that turning over and above or under and below is the basis of the pattern. If stacking or stratifying is the principle of the hypertrope and flattening out or lowering that of the hypotrope, then the implications of each pattern should flow from these principles. The hypotrope should sponsor activities concerned with the minimization of exhibited (or observed) behavior—that is, mutual behaviors that are not to be witnessed by others. Concomitantly, of course, the hypotrope would be concerned with the exclusion of all activities not immediately related to the participants' interest in each other—in their mutual safety, well being, enhancement of each other, and mutual exchanges of inspection, admiration, criticism, love, or sexual attentions.[11] The intense mutuality of the hypotrope is shared by the hypertrope but with a different accenting. Visibility and activity are more easily generated within the stratified pattern. Mastery, either sexual or aggressive, is associated with the over–under positioning. Because mastery may well invite resistance, the establishment and maintenance of the hypertrope is often a matter of struggle and intense, asymmetrical action. To be put down or pinned down, to overthrow or overturn are introductory haptodes that give the hypertrope considerable salience in everyday life. But mixed in with such movements are actions that derive from the approach–separation series—a set of categories that still remains to be discussed.

Before synkinetic patterns are considered, brief mention should be made of mixed syntropism and asyntropic movements. The 90-degree, angled structure of the *ankylotrope* combines horizontal positioning in one participant with vertical positioning in the other. The implication of this arrangement is an asymmetrical distribution of action featuring activity versus passivity. The horizontal partner in the passive position may be ill, tired, or vanquished. The upright partner may be a caretaker or a victor. No matter what role systems are "expressed through"—i.e. cross-referenced with—the ankylotrope, the violent contrast of horizontal with vertical is required to give them their stamp of helplessness and dependency.

The *allotrope*, on the other hand, is a grabbag of angles and curves into which some encounters may congeal. In spills and upsets, and falls and tumbles involving two or more persons, allotropic arrangements featuring fantastic, amusing, or painful positions and movements may occur. Athletic contests such as wrestling and karate may generate allotropic structures which may seem chaotic to the uninitiated. What appears as disorder, however, may well contain a pattern that is distinguishable from merely random movement. If, on the other hand, a movement involving two or more persons is actually unpatterned—no part of it oriented toward the formation of a somatotactical structure—that state of affairs may be designated an *asyntrope*. Two people may occupy the same social space without relating their movements to each other in any way. Thus, asyntropism denotes release from group formation and the constraint it exercises over body movement.

When a wrestler pins his opponent to the ground in a hypertropic pattern, or a warrior stands triumphant over his fallen enemy, making an ankylotrope, these effects have been brought about by physical operations other than by the simple turning movements ascribed to syntropism. Although they are complex and varied, such operations can be grouped in a graded series of actions characterized by specific movement and body–space features. Since the movements produce a straight line of decreasing or increasing space between the participants, they are categorized with reference to "intervals" in a continuum, one end of which is *approach*, the other *separation*. As in the case of all interpersonal movements, the mutual actions of two or more participants to an encounter are required to produce the pattern established at each interval. Such patterns are located and categorized at eight intervals (Fig. 18), and these eight are presumed to exhaust the possibilities of synkinetic movement.

The precise form of the movements in *synkineses* cannot be adequately described except by reference to the body spaces and their boundaries. An *approach*, for example, may be made in distal space or within axial space. *Contact* may be established at the distal–limbic, the axial–distal, the proximal–axial, or the internal–proximal boundaries. For simplicity, synkinesis will here be considered only with reference to the axial–distal boundary and its penetration. But there is a further complication to be considered. The movements between the partners may be smooth or turbulent. Or, to consider the phenomenon from another angle, the pattern at any interval may be established by consensus or

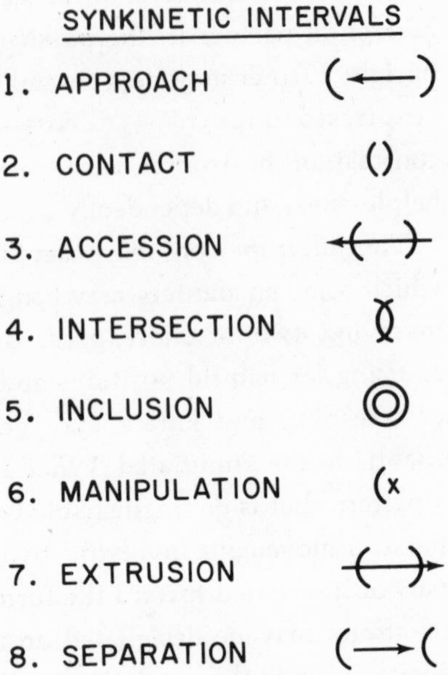

SYNKINETIC INTERVALS

1. APPROACH        $(\longleftarrow)$

2. CONTACT          $()$

3. ACCESSION       $\longleftarrow\!\!\!(\quad)\!\!\longrightarrow$

4. INTERSECTION    $\emptyset$

5. INCLUSION        $\circledcirc$

6. MANIPULATION   $(x$

7. EXTRUSION       $(\quad)\!\!\longrightarrow$

8. SEPARATION      $(\!\longrightarrow\!($

**Fig. 18.**  Synkinetic Intervals

may include a disagreement between the partners over the establishment of the pattern. In the latter respect, synkinesis differs considerably from syntropism. In the absence of consensus, a syntropic pattern simply disappears, being transformed into another syntropic pattern or replaced by asyntropism. But when a disagreement is associated with a synkinetic pattern, a struggle over the establishment of the pattern ensues. Indeed, if disagreement and struggle come to characterize a syntropic pattern, the synkinetic referent of the movement dominates the encounter. For if one person attempts to overcome the reluctance of another toward the establishment of a pattern of whatever design, then he must at some point act directly, in a straight line, in order to secure compliance.

Because of these complexities, a problem arises in the conceptualization of movement over the approach–separation continuum. It has been assumed that each of the synkinetic intervals occurs under one of two conditions: *agreement* or *disagreement*. Each of these conditions is correlated with somewhat different movement characteristics at each of the intervals. In general, agreement is associated with smoothness of action, continuity of movement, and an orderly interweaving of complementary behaviors; disagreement, with a jerky, discontinuous, or interrupted flow of motion in the participants and a wobble in the structural features of the pattern caused by discoordination of complementary movements. These differences are, in turn, associated with two varieties of *induction* and *counterinduction* movements. Under the condition of agreement, induction movements are composed of a smooth, complementary series of *asserting* movements and *accepting* movements, on the one hand, and of *asserting* movements and *refusing* movements, on the other. Refusing movements can be listed under the label *positive counterinductions* since they avoid the establishment of the pattern while keeping to the general context of mutual agreement.

Under the condition of disagreement, *negative induction* consists of *enforcing* movements. One partner's moves are such as to press, shove, drag, pull, or hit the other until the desired pattern is established. As in the case of agreement, there are two complementary series associated with such negative induction. One is *enforcing–acquiescing*, in which the one participant produces a set of "acquiescing" movements such as to conform to the pattern his partner is trying to enforce. In the other series, *enforcing–averting*, enforcing movements are met by *negative counterinduction*. This consists of the production of *averting* movements employed to turn aside, to misguide, dodge, deflect, or, in some fashion, outwit, and minimize the enforcing movements of the other partner.

The behavioral issues covered by the words *agreement* and *disagreement* have not been touched upon, because they are outside the present discussion. They have biological, psychological, and social determinants which must eventually be brought into relationship with the purely descriptive approach being set forth here. Indeed, unless the past history of any agreement or disagreement is brought into the explanation of the behavior at hand, somatotactics will remain a mere refinement—a verbal decoration at the margins of behavioral science. Nevertheless, to enter into these issues at this time would unduly burden a discussion already overloaded with conceptual baggage. The present work will employ a descriptive rather than a causal or dynamic definition of what is involved in agreement and disagreement. *Agreement* is a condition existing between two or more people, such that any pair of potentially complementary behaviors introduced into the encounter is acceptable to (or conforms with) the scale of values that governs the choice between alternatives for each of the participants. *Disagreement* is a state wherein a pair of potentially complementary behaviors inserted into the encounter is not acceptable to the scale of values of at least one of the participants. How the scale of values comes into being, what it consists of, what cognitive, emotional, and experiential factors are associated with it are considerations excluded from the current discussion.

The concept of *induction* takes into account the fact that a movement has a beginning, an end, and an aim. The aim labels what is being induced by a movement when it is still in its initial stages. In the terms of reference given here, induction is aimed at the establishment of a pattern—either in the synkinetic or syntropic series and usually in both at once. An observer (or participant) can usually recognize the aim or intention of a movement from its pattern and context long before it reaches completion; the issue of whether he is in agreement or disagreement with the induction of the pattern being aimed at arises at about the same time as he recognizes the aim. He has time, in other words, to register his agreement or disagreement with the *haptodes* in progress before the sequence reaches the irreversible state called an *episode*. Time is a critical element in the structuring of an induction, more so in its qualitative than in its quantitative aspect. By *qualitative* is mean the ratio of the speed of movement of one participant to that of the other, and the consequences of that ratio in terms of readiness, preparation, and surprise.

If there is *time* (an optimal ratio of speed of movement), then the basic components of induction and counterinduction can be manipulated; that is, arranged or rearranged in various orders and sequences. They can be transposed, for example, so that a counterinduction precedes an induction. The variations in order of sequence, in fact, are correlated with significant judgments of intention. This occurs because the initial stages of an induction are treated as *intention movements*. Thus, the question of who initiates an induction and who responds with a counterinduction, or who initiates a counterinduction before receiving a confirmed induction is an element as important as, and related to, the critical time dimension.

To illustrate these variations, under the condition of agreement, a participant may initiate the counterinduction, *acceptance of approach*, before perceiving a movement indicating, by intention, *assertion of approach*. Open arms, for example, held low in the anterior–superior plane, constitute such a counterinduction anticipating the assertion of an approach by the partner. If the partner had actually initiated an approach, then the open arms would constitute an *accepting movement*, complementary to the *asserting movement* of the initiator. By transposing the sequence, by initiating the complementary behavior before the assertion of approach got started, the person with the open arms "sent" the message ordinarily labeled *an invitation*.

Conversely, an initiator may present a *refusal movement* to an anticipated approach—say, arms crossed over the chest and chest held out and high— before the induction of an approach is produced by a partner. Ordinarily, this behavior is one that discourages advances on the part of the other, and yet makes room for some other synkinetic pattern under the aegis of agreement. It is *not* an averting movement directed against anticipated enforcement of an approach. In the latter case, a transposed counterinduction would take the form, since it is under the sign of disagreement, of an intention movement aimed at getting out of the path of approach, or, alternatively, of placing some obstacle between the participants to prevent an approach. In connection with assigning the *interposed obstacle* to the category of averting movements, one can see how this negative counterinduction applies to the case of Achilles' skulking. Up to his elbows in disagreement with Agamemnon, Achilles initiates and maintains a move which averts an approach: remaining in his tent inaccessible to persuasion.

As regards the first interval in the synkinetic series, an approach is recognized by any movement that reduces space between axial space boundaries. A positive asserting of approach in distal space is initiated with undefined axial boundaries. But, if the movement is accepted, as contact of axial boundaries becomes imminent, the axial boundaries of both participants are likely to be clearly defined by a raising and extending of the arms. The accepting of an approach is reinforced by approaching the approacher, though merely holding still to await the approach with undefined axial boundaries is acceptance enough. Refusing movements, the positive counterinductions, take the form of a closure of axial space with folded arms, or a small movement away from the approacher indicating that the axial boundary is not to be contacted.

In a negative approach, released by averting movements in the partner, the enforcing movements are indicated by several parameters. The speed of movement is either comparatively slow or comparatively fast as regards the partner, or it alternates between the two, producing the unevenness of motion characteristic of disagreement.

Averting movements such as this one are sometimes referred to as *defenses,* acquiescing movements as *surrenders,* enforcing movements as *attacks.* These words, however, put too narrow a construction on a group of complementary movements that cover a range of encounters not necessarily so dramatic and aggressive. In fact, exactly what behaviors are denoted by the word "aggression" is something of a mystery. The experiments reported in the following chapters attempt to acquire data that throw light on what the dimension *aggressive–nonaggressive* means to a group of subjects. The word "attack" is shown to be rather non-specific, referring either to a sharply outlined asserting movement in the context of agreement or an enforcing movement in the context of disagreement. "Defense" also slips around between a denotation of refusing movements (agreement) or averting movements (disagreement). It appears necessary, therefore, to devise categories that provide greater stability in the coding of movement than is found in the everyday words of the common language. Furthermore, the direction of movement as referred to body space changes in a non-uniform fashion, causing the jerky, discontinuous motion referred to above. The physical effort involved in the changing, obstacle-overcoming movements produces somatic effects such as sweating, irregular, rapid breathing, flushing, and the protrusion of muscle and tendon into the proximal–internal boundary noted as *tension.* Finally, there is a simultaneous correlation from all body areas of direct, in-line movement aiming at the partner across space which produces the effect of *concentration.* This is an effect quite at variance with the *relaxation* of a positive approach, in which at least some body areas are not involved in performing the approaching movements.

In real life, the intervals succeed each other in  spontaneous and varying flow patterns, just as the notes of music produce that melody or harmony which is the object of cognition. But for the sake of the expository goal being pursued here, it is necessary to consider each interval in turn, with only a glancing reference to alternative patterns of succession. For example, acquiescence by surrender when no viable plan of escape offers itself also suggests that *negative separation* is a possible successor to a negative approach. Running away is an acquiescing movement complementary to the enforcement of a negative separation. In a negative separation, there is disagreement about parting, one participant trying to make the other go away against his desire to stay. Acquiescing, under these circumstances of enforcement, indicates that the unwanted participant has given in to the instruction to leave. It is quite possible to conceive of a situation in which the enforcement of a negative approach was initiated, to begin with, for the sake of applying the enforcement of a negative separation—as when an intruder has to be caught in order to make him go away. Thus, the flow pattern, *negative approach–negative separation*, can be coded as a generalized category containing a number of melancholy subclasses such as *being chased away*, *being rejected*, or *being exiled*.

Even though the routine description of each interval apart from the others must leave the more interesting matter of flow patterns largely to the reader's imagination, one can note the presence of an intrinsic stepwise or scalar association between the intervals. The intervals of the Approach–Separation Continuum resemble the notes of the musical scale. Each leads into the other in a normal progression of small steps, though the steps can be omitted or combined in larger intervals than occur in the normal scale. The synkinetic steps are conditioned by the relative geometrics of body spaces and body boundaries existing between the two participants. But the movements at intervals fall into two classes, some being oriented by the boundary conditions, others by the interrelation between spaces. Approach, contact, accession, extrusion, and separation are governed primarily by the relationship between boundaries; intersection, inclusion, and manipulation, by the relation between spaces. The rationale of the difference between boundaries and spaces as controlling conditions will later become more evident. Meanwhile, it may be said that a boundary must be penetrated before a space can be occupied.

An approach is always made to a boundary. Despite the "Welcome" sign of accepting movements and the "Keep Out" sign of averting movements, the normal transition is for an approach to lead up to a contact with the boundary of the next space. Boundaries function as checkpoints at which a number of behavioral processes take place. The approacher presents his credentials, so to speak, and takes the opportunity to examine the conditions of the boundary. The partner being approached becomes alerted to his own boundary conditions and examines those of the approacher. Such reciprocal monitoring is cross-referenced with the activity and role structure within which the approach has been made; strangers, for example, are examined under a different set of criteria than friends or enemies. But no matter what the role structure may be, a contacting movement tends to be oriented to the prospect of *accession*—that is, being allowed across or forcing oneself across the boundary into the next space.

In a positive contact, asserting movements and accepting movements are mutually exploratory and often indistinguishable from each other without reference to the previous direction of movement. Contact at the axial–distal boundary, for example, requires that both participants define their axial spaces by raising and extending the arms. Because of the key significance of contact to role structure at this boundary, asserting and accepting movements are ritualized in most cultures for the type of role characterizing the encounter. Handshakes, grasps, salutes, and a variety of attitudes and postures facilitate and conventionalize axial contacts. Such gestures usually form parts of culturally patterned greeting ceremonies, though the full greeting ceremony usually includes more than axial contact, that is, between proximal–axial and internal–proximal boundaries, along with an intersection of axial spaces.

The enforcing movements of a negative contact include grabbing and clinging, either at the axial or at the proximal boundary. The complementary averting movements consist of throwing off, shaking off, or pulling away. Acquiescing to a negative contact is correlated with a peculiar asymmetry in which the person acquiescing makes no reciprocal exploratory moves but, immobile and passive, allows contact to continue. Such counterinductions are sometimes called *passive resistance*, or *non-violent resistance*. They should be differentiated from movements designed to refuse a positive contact, for example, the refusal to touch or grasp an outstretched hand.

Given the soft, unprotected structure of the human body, all of its boundaries are susceptible to penetration. The *accession interval* specifies the conditions under which penetration is effected following the establishment of contact. In a positive accession at the axial boundary, the movement across the boundary is reciprocal to a variety of accepting movements. The prototypical accepting movement is a defined and open axial space, the so-called "open arms" position; closed arms, the refusal. The asserting of positive accession is accomplished by an intention movement whose completion will obviously involve crossing the boundary, and such movements are often made to test boundary conditions. Given "time"—that is, if they are not too rapid relative to the movements of the others—they will instigate either an acceptance or a refusal. Negative accessions, on the other hand, are accomplished by rapid enforcing movements that provide inadequate clues as to their point of impact or overcome resistance at closed off boundaries. To avert a negative accession, one makes use of dodging movements, similar to averting a negative approach, plus a number of procedures designed to reinforce the boundary, especially at its natural openings, such as pursing the mouth and squeezing the eyes shut. By contrast, wide open eyes and mouth are coded as accepting an accession; and, if these movements are made before a positive accession has been initiated, they function as invitations.

Once a boundary has been crossed, body spaces mutually occupy the same physical space. They extend across each other in a relationship which may be called *intersection*. Because of the high degree of access to internal space conditioned by such close quarters, the existence of agreement or disagreement becomes even more sensitive an issue than in the other intervals. *Positive intersection* is established and maintained by virtue of a negotiated agreement among the partners to respect each other's boundaries—that is, to go so far, and no farther, subject to future renegotiations. Of course, continuous monitoring of boundary relations is appropriate only to the foreplay of sexual encounters in which negotiation and renegotiation of exactly what boundary is to be crossed and what body space is occupied is part of the pleasure. In less erotic circumstances, continuous renegotiation is unnecessary, for two reasons. First, cultural patterns standardize distances and overlaps for various role relations.[12] As long as the participants adhere to the cultural prescriptions, they need not concern themselves with the meaning or implication of every move for the intactness of the body and the future of the relationship. Second, when intersection occurs in neutral encounters, the mutual activity is likely to be directed at a goal outside of the circle of overlapping spaces, either literally or figuratively. Joint performances for others, mutual projects, communications about topics unrelated to immediate physical actions all reflect stable boundary states, delicately adapted to intersecting spaces.

*Negative intersection* is the position of battle. Disagreement is transfigured in a struggle for one-sided control of overlapping body space and criss-crossing boundaries. The in-fighting (within axial boundaries) is highly bound up with the intactness of proximal–axial and internal–proximal boundaries. Once these give way, or are controlled by the movements of one participant, the disagreement changes direction and the fight is over. This outcome, however, is usually coordinate with the establishment of a *negative inclusion*—for which one may read, "The enemy has been surrounded and immobilized." As in the case of *positive intersection*, enforcing and averting movements incidental to negative intersection are almost indistinguishable unless one knows the previous history of the encounter—which is the answer to the always-vexed question: Who started the fight? A challenge, for example, can be classified as an *averting movement* which, if presented in advance of a movement enforcing negative intersection, invites that movement to take place.[13]

Positive intersection can flow into *positive inclusion* or *positive manipulation*. In a positive inclusion, the defined axial boundary of one participant completely

**Fig. 19.** Garbo and Gable from *Susan Lennox: Her Fall and Rise*

encircles the defined axial space of his partner, who accepts total embrace. The squeezing and holding of asserting movements are matched by the limp offerings of the accepting movements, and the steady counterpressures of refusing movements. The skill of the actress Greta Garbo in making presentations evocative of both attraction and repulsion—of a tortured acceptance or a wistful rejection of love—lay in her ability to combine accepting with refusing movements in a pattern so ambiguous that the observer could scarcely decide which was which. The photograph on this page is evidence. The right forearm, wrist, and hand exert pressure against the embrace while the right shoulder is pressed forward in an accepting movement. The face refuses a kiss in an extrication movement that paradoxically offers a wide expanse of neck to the approach of her lover's lips. A still picture of the encounter allows one to make such judgments with some degree of assurance. On the screen, the movements pass so rapidly and with such compelling force that one is unable to determine how the effect is produced.

Negative inclusion may be an uncomfortable interlude for all concerned. To have surrounded a hostile, struggling, protesting body is not much better than to be pinioned by an overpowering encirclement. Negative encirclements have an odd way of being temporarily transformed into positive, or at least neutral conditions, like the boxer's clinch, or the respite for mutual repairs incident to states of a siege. This may be due to the rapid exhaustion of resources occasioned by the strenuous vigilance required at this interval.

*Manipulation* can be defined as mutual movement between participants, occurring at the stage of intersection or inclusion, of such a nature that one participant is arranged, rearranged, or disarranged by the other. The active movements of the manipulator are performed by the hands, often with the help of tools, and sometimes of other body parts, such as the legs or mouth. In positive manipulation, the arranging is constructive, amusing, enhancing, or problem solving. Accordingly, the accepting movements involve the offering of various body parts to the hands of the manipulator. In negative manipulation, the movements are disarranging or destructive, such as tearing, breaking, smashing, piercing, or bruising. Negative manipulations that are disarranging and painful but also problem solving, such as the actions of doctors and dentists, must be placed in a special category—one which is difficult to learn.

*Extrication* is exiting, the reverse of accession. Having crossed axial, proximal, or internal boundaries, one or the other partner must eventually remove himself from such intense association. *Positive extrication* is a pattern of complementary, synchronized activity in which the asserting movements involve an outward motion, away from the overlap of inclusion or intersection. What is asserted is an extraction of the body or a body part. The accepting movement is a release. Refusal consists of resistance against performing the release movements. Under the terms of agreement, however, such refusals can only be of short duration. They must give way to release, on the one hand, or a return to positive inclusion or intersection, on the other. *Negative extrication,* under terms of disagreement, consists of the extrusion of a participant from the intimate association. One partner forcibly expels the other, or attempts to. Averting a negative extrication is accomplished by twisting and cork-screwing in the effort to slip under the expulsive movements, while essentially remaining *in situ.* Acquiescing is a dishrag performance in which one allows oneself to be pushed out.

To be pushed or thrown out means, in somatotactical terms, to be forced beyond the point of contact between axial boundaries. It is at this point that the last interval in the series, *separation,* begins. *Out* is beyond contact between axial boundaries and *separation* is a movement that increases the distance between axial boundaries. In positive separation, such an increase may be accomplished by one partner moving away from the other or by both distancing simultaneously. Asserting a separation is merely to move away. Accepting it is to remain still or move away oneself. Refusing is to advance as the other retreats, trying to diminish axial distance. In negative separation, the explosive movements of negative extrication are continued as intention movements, transmitting the get-out-of-here message. Averting movements in a negative separation consists of slowing down a retreat or turning around to take a stand, mainly of defiance against the intention movements of the other. Since the latter may consist of such activities as threatening to throw objects or aim weapons across distal space, averting negative separation may well employ some of the counterinduction used in a negative approach, such as dodging and weaving, while resisting retreat. Acquiescing is the tail-between-the-legs retreat in which the effort is to put as much distance as possible, as quickly as possible, into distal space.

## NOTES FOR CHAPTER 7

[1] A brief history of the various attempts to perfect a system of dance notation as well as a compact exposition of the system developed by Rudolph Laban is provided by Hutchinson (1954).

[2] The relation of pattern in musical sequences (conceived as a probability code) to the issues of "style" and "meaning" has been considered from the viewpoint of experimental psychology (Wallach and Kogan, 1959), and of the psychology of aesthetics (Meyer, 1956). The connection between pattern and "meaning" in music is similar to the connection between body movement pattern and its "meaning."

[3] The notational system most analogous to the approach to be described here is that known as "Solfege" or, more precisely, "Tonic Sol-fa Method and Notation." It is a system of musical notation used by singers. According to the *Encyclopedia Britannica* (1964), "The system is based on 'mental effect,' i.e., the effect on the mind of any note, chord, or progression in relation to a central Tonic or key-note." By making use of the time-honored verbal labels, *do, re, mi,* etc., for the relative position of a note in a scale, the notation conveys the pattern of sounds directly to the mind of the sight reader. This is possible because the tonic or key note symbol, *do,* is movable from key to key and the pattern of sounds, both melody and harmony, remains constant with reference to the *do* no matter in what key it is located. This constancy of relational patterning is not true of conventional musical notation where the same visual pattern will represent different melodies and harmonies for the various keys which are coded separately on the staff lines. In the conventional system, the sight reader must infer the melodic and harmonic pattern by a complicated process of vertical and cross-referencing. In "solfege," the pattern is obtained by simple reference to the key note, which indicates the "interval" to be sounded.

[4] Fuller (1965) states, "If we accept 60 degreeness, we find that instead of getting only four right triangles around a point in a plane, or eight cubes around a point in space, we get six 60 degree angles about the point in the plane, and 20 tetrahedra around one point in space. Furthermore, the circumferential modular frequency of planar or omni-directional patterning will always be in one-to-one correspondence with the radial frequencies of modular subdividing. When we do this, we find we have a model of the spontaneously coordinate structure which nature actually uses." If we overlook a certain quarrelsomeness over whether nature has commissioned her structures on the basis of 90 degreeness or 60 degreeness, it still turns out to be interesting that Fuller's concept of radial structure actually found in living organ-

isms rationalizes the relation between the radius and the boundary of structures, since all stable structures turn out to consist of closely packed tetrahedra, or spheres.

[5] According to Piaget (1954), it is during the first year and a half of life that "the child, starting from a space completely centered on his own activity, manages to locate himself in an ordered environment which includes himself as an element." This is brought about by an intercorrelation of schemata relating objects to movements and displacements in space. As a result of the increased ability to combine and recombine schemata, both objects and space are "desubjectified" according to Piaget. There is some correspondence between the approach being developed here and Piaget's formulations. However, Piaget's interest in logical and objective reconstructions of the environment and in the preservation of "groups" apart from the activity of the operator, lead him to take less interest in the subjective orientations of the body which we have placed at the center of our approach. Piaget's "reality" is constructed out of the child's relation to inanimate objects, not to interpersonal relations.

[6] We insert a word-derivation into the text to illustrate the point previously made that movement categories lie buried in our everyday language and need to be disinterred.

[7] A possible exception to this rule was noted on page 121.

[8] How the 90-degree relation of vertical to horizontal attained its triumph over other coordinate systems in the hands of the Egyptians, and how they used the concept of the square grid to code the proportions of the human figure are described by Giedion (1964).

[9] The complex cognitive controls exercised over even such simple motions as these have been described by Miller, Galanter, and Pribram (1960). They point out that the two physical components of hammering (lifting and striking) are each under the control of a testing procedure which determines when and whether the component will be launched and when it will be stopped. For their analysis of such motions, see pp. 33–37 of their book.

[10] The reader may well wonder why separate categories for space and motion are required for the Personal Movements if they are not needed for Interpersonal Movements. The reason is as follows: For Interpersonal Movements, the referent both for space and motion is another body. For Personal Movements, the external referent system must be physical space or physical motion, as conventionally perceived. The identity of physical space and motion defined in contemporary theories of physics is not widely known or recognized. To have attempted to demonstrate this point would have taken us beyond our range of competence and would have unduly lengthened the discussion.

[11] We have neglected to make further theoretically possible refinements within the category *hypotrope* because of the relative infrequency with which hypotropes occur. But they can be specified quite readily, without the necessity of creating further neologisms; if one tilts the horizontal syntropisms on their side, one can speak of diatropes or paratropes, etc. within the hypotropic situation.

[12] Such cultural patterns have been described in detail by Hall (1966). For a psychological analysis of interpersonal distance, see the work of Little (1965), Little, Ulehla, and Henderson (1968), and Kuethe (1962 a and b, 1964).

[13] Staged fights, such as prize fights, wrestling matches, and exhibitions of fencing, judo, or karate, lie outside of the present discussion. They are correlated with "agreeing to disagree" and are based on occupational or recreational roles in which commercial profit or personal prestige outweighs the specific somatotactical issues being considered here.

# 8. Visual–Motor Coding and Linguistic Coding

Suppose a person looks out the window of a tall office building at the street far below and sees two figures on the sidewalk; one moves at a moderate pace up the sidewalk from the left to the right side of the observer's visual field; the other—further to the left in the visual field—appears to be moving much faster in the same direction along the sidewalk and is closing the gap between the two figures as the observer watches. Given this minimal amount of visual–motor information, how will the observer proceed to code it—that is, to give it meaning?

The visual–motor presentation can be checked out against four major category systems: event, role, activity, and somatotactical categories. Let it be assumed as a rule that the coding of the visual information always begins with the somatotactical categories. In effect, this rule states that what must be established first is the presence or absence of movement and the type of movement being presented. An extension of this rule is that in the presentation of two or more moving objects, one begins with the Personal Movements and then crosses over to the Interpersonal Movements as soon as possible. (See Table 7–1). The practiced eye, engaging a not unfamiliar presentation, can sweep across and down the Personal Movement categories in quick succession, picking out Body Space for Areal Radiation (anterior), for Distance Radiation (limbic); picking up uniform Moving for Body Action, the Straight (direct) categories for Motion Patterns and category V (whole body) for Body Areas. This referencing produces the assembly: two objects moving directly forward in the same line, each with uniform motion at a different speed relative to each other. Now, following the rule of cross-reference, when this assembly is checked through the Interpersonal Movement categories, Syntropic and Synkinesic Patterns may be simultaneously processed. Only the Horizontal Syntropic categories would be run through the procedure since the observer's angle of vision provides little information about

Vertical or Mixed categories. The choice [1] would have to be a Protropic pattern since both objects had been coded previously as moving into their own anterior Areal Radiations (i.e., "forward"). The check through the Synkinesic Patterns, however, would not permit a choice between the Approach or the Separation category, though it could easily eliminate the others. The closing of the gap between the two figures could be coded as either a Positive Approach, Negative Approach, or a Negative Separation. The figure in the rear, in other words, might be attempting to catch up with one in front of him for some agreeable or disagreeable end or he might have violence in mind, wishing, for example, to drive him off the sidewalk or out of the area, while the one in front might be resisting being driven away by showing nonchalance.

It is clear that a choice between these alternatives cannot be made at the level of somatotactical processing, and that only a cross-reference to some other more general category system will straighten the matter out. The question is which category system to switch over to—activities, roles, or events?

Let another rule be proposed, one that is open to several exceptions. As soon as multiple-referencing in the somatotactical categories encounters a choice point at which no decision can be conveniently made, the referencing process is switched over to the role systems. The point of the rule is that, after the observer has made some progress in coding the sort of movement he is being presented with, he must then establish the nature of the moving objects and the roles in which they are displaying the movement. Objects and roles are always conjoined in a presentation: The objects move (or rest) to some end or purpose. The observer leaning out of his office window has not yet decided what the figures whose movements he has been taking note of might be. They might be ants scurrying past. Or dogs. Perhaps children on their way to the movies. Freely available fantasies could indefinitely extend the list. Presumably, the observer is endowed with an ample stock of role categories and his coding problem at the moment is to select the most appropriate category for assignment to the objects whose movements he has been studying.

To relieve him of his fantasies by allowing him more information, let him be assumed to get out his binoculars. He now sees that the leading figure is a woman, the figure to the rear, a child, probably a girl. He assumes that he is being presented with a set of family roles. With the choice of the general role categories for human beings accomplished, further role categorization can be postponed while the multiple-referencing process crosses over to the activity category system.

A switching over to the activity set of categories after assignment of the general object and role categories can be considered obligatory because the choice of further coding categories at all levels depends upon what activities are in process. For example, let us say that, with the aid of his binoculars, the observer notes that the woman in the lead is walking and carrying an armload of bundles, while the child is running with arms free. Having combined walking and carrying packages in his assignment of an activity code for the woman together with running for the child, the observer is now in a position to choose more specific roles for assignment to the two figures. Suppose he chooses the roles of mother and daughter for a more specific designation of the generalized woman–child roles. This choice, taken together with the activity code, would then point to a possible assignment of a category at the level of events—a shopping expedition. Since event categories are divided into haptodes, episodes, and exodes, as indicated in Chapter 5, a tentative assignment of the terminal episode, "return from a shopping expedition," would place the immediate situation comfortably within a string of events.

Thus supplied with a provisional scenario, the observer can refer back to the still unsettled choice between an Approach or a Separation at the somatotactical level. In the absence of more detailed visual information, the rule to be followed is to choose that category which fits more simply and economically—that is, without need for supplementary data—into the scenario as it has been constructed up to that point by the multiple-referencing process. A mother and child beginning to return from a shopping expedition may easily become separated, especially if the mother has her arms full. Periodically, the child must run to catch up with the mother, displaying a Positive Approach. With the assignment of this Synkinetic category, then, the observer completes his coding, feels satisfied that he has "recognized" the visual presentation or that he has grasped its "meaning."

To review, the principal steps in the cognitive process first occur in an obligatory succession: (1) a choice of somatotactical (movement) categories; (2) a selection of object–role categories; (3) the assignment of activity categories; and (4) a choice of event categories. None of these four steps can be brought to completion the first time around. Thus, after the first run-through, the programming is non-obligatory. More specific categories may be selected, tried out, discarded, assembled, and reassembled with a freedom that was only hinted at in the example. The assembly of categories from all levels is a construction, accomplished through the multiple-referencing procedure.[2] The construction ends—or is temporarily satisfied—by the composition of a *scenario*, that is, a story or plot that organizes all the coding categories from the various levels into an event structure.

The manner of construction of the scenario [3] is the major conclusion to which specification of the function of coding categories leads. It is the principal way in which the elements of a complex visual presentation are given meaning. The coding categories serve to transform the visual stimuli into units that can be assembled and reassembled for the sake of one or another scenario. The dramatic "gestalt" of the scenario imparts significance and order to the observed phenomena, no matter how allusive or fragmentary the visual presentation may be. A child running to catch up with his mother, for example, is not a major dramatic event, but it is a story that has form and content, fits into memory, and can be recaptured or "*re*-cognized" under appropriate conditions of programming.

One result of this conclusion is that it abandons the notion of the "visual image" as an entity—as something spontaneously and globally present in perception or awareness. The visual image is a construction, according to the present views, made up of a complex set of coding elements, placed within a scenario. But, if the scenario is the end result of a complicated program of visual–motor coding, if meaning is the sum of all the work that goes into the assembly of categories and the construction of the scenario, then how is this meaning transposed into a linguistic code?

Here, one comes face to face with the lack of information about the substructure of a language. Some aspects of the process, however, are freely available to superficial inspection. It is apparent that the order of recoding in a linguistic program bears no relation to the visual–motor program. For example, if the observer were to be asked by an office-mate, "What are you looking at?" he might answer, "Some people on the sidewalk," or "A child chasing after its mother." The first answer indicates that a general decision about roles (people = human beings) has already been made, but takes no account of movement or activity. The second answer codes movement with more specific roles but omits any reference to the event categories. It is as if the completed scenario with its assembly of categories is treated, for linguistic purposes, as a package. The package can be opened up and different pieces of it brought out to be displayed in linguistic forms. There lies a fantasy behind every verbal utterance. But the linguistic forms are new creations; the categories are newly assembled in accordance with the constraints of syntactic structure; and the order of transposition of various pieces of the package into sentences is quite variable and at the discretion of the speaker.

It is not much help to know that a similarity of programming between visual–motor and linguistic codes which *might* be present is, in fact, not present. Furthermore, a radical dissimilarity between visual–motor and linguistic processing is often assumed. Langer has assumed a marked difference between speech and visual stimuli attributable to the amount of time consumed in delivering the stimuli.

Visual forms—lines, colors, proportions, etc.—are just as capable of *articulation*, i.e., of complex combination, as words. But the laws that govern this sort of articulation are altogether different from the laws of syntax that govern language. The most radical difference is that *visual forms are not discursive*. They do not present their constituents successively, but simultaneously, so that the relations determining a visual structure are grasped on one act of vision (Langer, 1959, p. 86).

It is obvious that the views presented here differ considerably from those of Langer in respect to the nature of this difference. Although there is no argument about the great difference in the time required to code visual and linguistic presentations, it is argued that visual stimuli are not processed simultaneously in one act of vision but require carefully sequenced transformation by means of a complex set of categories, and that the more significant difference rests upon the order of transformation of information and the categories in which the information is conveyed. As Ulric Neisser (1967, p. 146) has so cogently put it, "Imagery is not a matter of opening old file drawers, but of building new models."

It is important to be as clear as possible about the differences between visual–motor and linguistic coding to determine how the visual–motor information is transferred to the linguistic system. It is also important to study the process in reverse—to ask how linguistic information is transposed into a visual–motor presentation. In this connection, consider the following sentences:

The man came too soon.

The man arrived prematurely.

The man was there before the appointed time.

The man showed up early.

The sentences, of course, reveal the number of different grammatical constructions and semantic devices by which the intercoding can be effected. They also illustrate the highly selective reprogramming which is a characteristic of language. Despite the variations, nothing is conveyed of the setting of the event nor of the activity by means of which the man arrived at wherever he arrived. Such information may either be omitted or introduced in a later sequence, whereas it must be coded in proper sequence in an actual visual presentation. The noun with its article, standing at the head of the sentences, provides a human object and a sex role—an example of the rare, point-for-point correspondence of codes. It would have taken "the old man" to convey the age and sex roles which are usually coded together in actual visual observation despite difficulties presented by "unisex" costuming in contemporary scenes. The verb phrase provides very little somatotactical information. The syntropic pattern is omitted. A synkinetic pattern (Approach) is vaguely implied.

But, it is the adverbs and adverbial phrases that are of the greatest interest.

If the categories coded by the word "soon" or its close relative, "early," are noted, it becomes apparent that there is no equivalent category at all in the visual–motor coding of an encounter. These words categorize quite abstract features of a time relationship. The category embraces all events in which, relative to an expected time of occurrence (or normal elapse of time), the actual occurrence takes place in a shorter amount of time. The adverb "too" functions as an intensive, indicating an almost unacceptable shortening of elapsed time. The adverb "prematurely" is a shot at the same abstract target from a different angle. It codes a category grouping together all events characterized by stages of development occurring in succession and in which one stage occurs before its time. Though much too generalized for visual–motor coding, it nevertheless comes somewhat closer to the visual–motor aspects of an encounter insofar as it deals with a succession of stages. "Before the appointed time" approximates what can be coded in a visual–motor system but is still too general because of the abstractness of time.

In the visual–motor system, events are programmed in reference to a *time* which enters only as a succession of haptodes or episodes, within an exode. If a haptode occurs out of sequence—that is, before its expected entry in accordance with the program for the event—it will be coded as occurring before its assigned *place* in the sequence, or as being out of sequence. Or the whole sequence may be perceived as not belonging to the roles being enacted. These are matters of multiple-referencing in accordance with a prearranged or learned schedule. If too much or too little time elapses for the appropriate coupling of haptodes, this too will be perceived—but not as a property of time treated as a category standing by itself. Abstract time lies as much outside the system as abstract space does, both being products of linguistic processing.

To put these matters in other terms, visual–motor codes make no provision for treating their categories as categories in their own right, to be referenced with other categories in the form of a generalization. The visual–motor categories operate silently as *locater systems* making it possible for the physical features of a phenomenon to be cognitively identified. They never call attention to themselves with the clamor and clatter of a verbal generalization.

The observable physical circumstances of an encounter will help to support this assertion. For example, what physical consequences could be described by the sentence, "The man came too soon"? Presumably, the man in question approached something or someone in advance of expectations. To expand this situation in visual–motor terms, one could say that the man made his approach before it was scheduled in the program as learned (or prearranged) by the participants. Now, how would the participants respond to this misplacement?

In a verbal exchange, they might negotiate an adjustment through a discussion of its general features. The man might describe himself as "an earlybird," or apologize, saying that his watch is fast and he is always early. But, in a word-less visual–motor encounter, all such general linguistic accounts of the misplaced arrival would be unavailable. As in pantomime, their place would be taken by body responses and movements indicative of surprise, acceptance, anger, or anxiety on the negative side, or surprise, acceptance, and pleasure on the positive side. Such emotions, feelings, affective responses, or motives are the equivalents, in somatotactical coding, of generalizations in linguistic coding. They constitute the detachable generalized meanings, which are selected from the particulars of the encounter and are recognized as being transferable to (or characteristic of) other, subsequent events of the encounter. Just as time characterizes a general feature of encounters in linguistic terms, so surprise or anger can characterize a general feature of encounters, spreading over all the particulars, in somatotactical terms.

It has already been suggested that the topics of emotion and motivation needed to be reconceptualized, perhaps as presentations oriented to the direction of events, either preservative of present directions (positive) or directed toward producing change (negative). The subcategories of the approach–separation continuum made agreement (positive synkinesis) and disagreement (negative synkinesis) the most general categories governing the patterning at each of the intervals. Agreement and disagreement [4] may now be categorized as the most general of all categories available for visual–motor coding. They are abstract and detachable from the particulars in the same way that the concept of time is abstract in linguistic coding. Operations are conducted to increase or decrease the amount of agreement or disagreement in all sorts of encounters. Agreement and disagreement function as universal principles governing relations between persons, between persons and lower order species, and between persons and things. Just as they operate as universal strategies governing external relations, so they also operate with respect to the internal, cognitive processes. They function as the principles applied in the locating and matching of categories in accordance with a previously learned program and, thus, in the detection and perception of error. Finally, they are at work in that most complicated of all cognitive operations, a conflict of motives.

Internal conflict is not directly relevant here, but it is impossible to consider the visual–motor coding of emotion and motivation without touching on this topic. One recognizes the presence of external conflict from the body movements of persons participating in an encounter. And, as in the example of the presentation made by Greta Garbo (see Fig. 19), one detects the presence of internal conflict through the contradictions and lack of fit between the movements of different parts of the body. Such movements are immediately coded under categories labeled in the linguistic system as emotions or motives. Though the appropriateness of the linguistic labels in current use throughout is always questioned here, there is no doubt that the presence of agreement or disagreement in the encounter is associated with the production of behavior for which various names like "jealousy," "embarrassment," "pride," "anguish," "disappointment," etc., to designate just a few, are used.

A more descriptive name for the category of behavior that occurs immediately below and in connection with agreement and disagreement is proposed here. Instead of emotion, affect, drive, feeling, motive, expressive, etc., let this category of behavior be called *directive*. The behavior in question is to point out the direction in which a person wants events to go—or, not to go. If Bill is envious of Tom, he wants events not to go in the direction of enhancing Tom and, if his envy is sufficiently aroused, he would prefer them to go in the direction of turning Tom into a sorry sight. If Ellen loves Peter, she will hope to have events so arranged that she can be as close as possible to him. If Helen is grieving, she will want events to restore her lost object, even though she knows it to be impossible.

If all such generalizing, time-binding behavior is labeled *directive*, the category will be named after its function in the signaling process on the one hand, and in accordance with its cognitive function on the other. In the visual–motor system, directive behavior transmits instructions about the direction in which a person will try to propel the event in which he is or is going to be involved. The stimulus pattern, or *presentation* (now called emotion), is the way in which the message is coded for visual transmission and perceptual processing. On the cognitive side, directive behavior is a category that connects a large set of programs for multiple-referencing of event categories with activity and somatotactical categories in the construction of a scenario. The directive components of the scenarios are subsequently mapped into the linguistic system in a variety of poorly understood ways. Certainly, the lexical tags for the directive components of scenarios—jealousy, embarrassment, etc.—provide only sketchy information about the direction in which a participant to an encounter will actually move. The story must be told—or enacted—to reveal the flow of behavior of which the directive, visual–motor presentation is a forewarning.

A possible line of inquiry for the experiments of this study could have focused on the interrelations between linguistic and visual–motor coding. However, this interesting and much-needed research falls into the areas of psycholinguistics, a discipline for which the investigators lacked the necessary training. The visual aspects of body movement are more inviting to the attentions of the amateur because there is not yet any generally accepted discipline to which they belong, whereas psycholinguistics already commands the disciplined collaboration of well-trained linguists and psychologists.

# NOTES FOR CHAPTER 8

[1] The possibility of an Asyntropic Pattern (no purposeful association between the two figures), while real enough, has been omitted for the sake of this illustration.

[2] It is apparent that the cognitive procedure which we have called "multiple-referencing" is related to the more traditional concept of "an association of ideas." There are two significant differences between the two notions. First, the "association of ideas" is conceived as taking place in an individually determined way in accordance with dominant themes in the mind of the subject, while multiple-referencing is conceived as, at least initially, an obligatory program. Second, data on the "association of ideas" are elicited primarily by verbal stimuli, while data on multiple-referencing make use of visual stimuli.

[3] We use the word *scenario* to refer to the abstract aspect of the story or plot—that part which can be epitomized in a title, for example, or in a brief description, such as "a love story." For the concrete visual imagery stored in the scenario, we retain the word *fantasy* as it is customarily used. Scenarios (fantasies) are obviously grouped together in larger assemblies along associative lines (or, as we would prefer, in accordance with programs) that are related to the major categories of personality description, conceived in psychoanalytic terms. Our conceptualization touches upon, but does not enter, this area.

[4] No particular virtue or increase in specificity attaches to this particular pair of words. We could have used a number of alternative labels, such as "integration" and "function" and "dysfunction." We choose "agreement" and "disagreement" because they combine in one word the ego process of assent (or dissent) with the physical property of fit (or lack of fit).

# Part
# TWO

# 9. An Exploratory Study

Earlier chapters have set forth a group of concepts and categories designed to deal more systematically than previously possible with the expressive aspects of body movement and position. Because the concepts were not explicitly derived from any pre-existing set of research procedures, it was difficult to determine how to test their utility. While intriguing, their very novelty produced a quandary for empirical investigation. How could one find out whether subjects viewing body movement or positions actually made use of cognitive operations that conformed in any way to the categories? So convincing had the categories become to those who formulated them that there was a risk they would be transmitted to naïve subjects in a way that would shape their reporting of perceptions.

It was necessary to find a way for discovering whether observers used body spaces, the steps in the approach–separation continuum, and syntropic positioning as ways of attributing meaning to presentations of the body. It was also necessary to find out what else subjects used in the interpretation of presenting behavior, especially how they made use of context plus somatotactics in constructing haptodes or episodes, that is, sequences of behavior. It seemed possible that asking viewers to look at paintings portraying figures in positions fairly close to the more abstract arrangements of this study might yield useful information. This procedure would not require actual testing of hypotheses. For example, one would not expect to prove that viewers attribute one, and only one, specific meaning to a figure in a diatropic position with open proximal boundaries. One might, however, discover what range of variation in interpretation would occur for figures presented in this posture. By comparing such ranges of interpretations of figures in a diatropic position with those of figures in, say, a paratropic position, one might be able to frame hypotheses about meanings, about cues used to arrive at those meanings, and about the ways in which the cues interact.

Empirical testing of the usefulness of the conceptual scheme was begun by showing to a sample of Harvard and Radcliffe students a series of paintings chosen because of their simplicity and directness with respect to body positions. Although this plan was frankly exploratory, it was initially thought that it might provide all the needed information. Gradually, it became evident that the data obtained in this fashion were unsatisfactory. The findings were intriguing and produced a variety of speculative hypotheses, but they did not provide sufficient control over the many stimuli giving rise to responses in the subjects. Because of this, a different procedure was devised, based on the exploratory study but permitting more precise control over both the visual stimuli and the response categories which they could elicit. This chapter describes the initial exploratory efforts; succeeding chapters will be devoted to the more controlled experiments.

Probably no richer public source of representations of body positions exists than in Western painting since the Italian Renaissance, particularly in the period of the High Renaissance itself. The elaborate studies of the human body, the innumerable instruction and sketch books, the tradition and taste in representing the body, are all well known. It is probably accurate to say that what was known —or at least thought—about the motions of the body was most importantly confined to the observant and inventive corpus of representational schemata in painting. The advent of photography during the nineteenth century doubtless enriched the representational vocabulary,[1] but figures already integrated into settings seemed better for initial investigation, since they permitted assessment of the importance of cues from scenery and scenario. Reproductions of paintings, though in fact as still as photographs, if well constructed, generally imply more motion than randomly taken photographs. What paintings lose in ability to record instant cross-sections of movement, they certainly gain in richness of posture.

The aim was to select paintings that would represent the positions and groupings outlined earlier, and to conduct interviews with a considerable number of subjects to gather their interpretations. Interviewing had to meet several conditions. First, it had to be non-directive and avoid leading the interpretations toward exaggerated activity or stillness. Thus, questions such as, "What is going on here?" or worse, "What are these people doing?" had to be resisted, at least until the subject himself brought up activities. A simple opening question appeared to be, "What do you see here?" Second, interviewing had to avoid direct questions posed too rapidly on those topics in which the investigators were interested, lest the variables the subjects, as opposed to the investigators, deemed important be lost. Third, interviewing had to cover more or less the same variables from subject to subject. Therefore, though directive probes were unavoidable, they could at least be put off until late in the interview, after the subject had been allowed to speak about variables in directions congenial to him. These conditions were not difficult to meet, although it later emerged that meeting them was only half the battle in the investigation.

It was, of course, important to conceal the titles of the paintings from the observers, since titles suggest something about the structure of events that may not be apparent to the viewer. Frequently, a title was revealed toward the end of the interview not only to be merciful to curious subjects, but so that ensuing changes in interpretation could be observed. Another important variation in procedure consisted of masking certain portions of the paintings before presenting the whole; this technique yielded information about the dependence of interpretation on outside cues, such as those from the background or from other figures. The data obtained in this fashion were rich and complex and contained much material not directly related to the original purposes; the investigators learned, in one sense, more than had been hoped but, in another sense, less than was needed. The negative aspects of this richness were a lack of real comparability from subject to subject, and an intrusion of additional variables that could not be controlled. This lack of system and *embarras de richesse* led to the treatment of this part of the research as exploratory and suggestive; it enriched understanding of some of the variables, and it indicated that others should be tested with more precision later.

Here, material is presented painting by painting, in order to preserve some of the richness of the original data; this will contrast with the systematic presentation of variables in the later chapters. Only those paintings whose analysis yields a wealth of data will be discussed in detail; others will be mentioned in passing.[2] The findings of this chapter are derived from interviews with about 40 different subjects who discussed three paintings each—with interviews lasting an hour to an hour and a half. All the interviews were recorded on tape; some were later transcribed for detailed analysis of the process of interpretation (not discussed in this book), and all were analyzed for content on sheets prepared for this purpose. These sheets made direct analysis from tapes relatively rapid, and reliable from the raters' point of view.

The first painting (Fig. 20) was chosen because it represents five persons seated on a bench with bodies in paratropic positions, facing the viewer, heads turned in various directions; a sixth person, standing or coming in from the right, is closer to the viewer and, consequently, larger. She is dressed differently from the others, who are more or less alike in costume. The setting appears to be that of a Pacific Island and is incongruous with the rigid, hieratic poses of the characters. The painter is, of course, Gauguin; his painting is *Ta Matete,* variously translated as *The Bench* or *The Market.*

Of first interest were the subgroupings that subjects would make of the figures portrayed. If the persons from left to right are labeled Numbers 1 through 6, 1 and 2 are looking roughly in the same direction (the position is a near-

**Fig. 20.** Gauguin: *Ta Matete*

protrope) and are dressed in green and blue; 3 is looking out of the picture at the viewer; 4 and 5 look at each other (the heads are diatropic) and are dressed in yellow and orange; 6 apparently looks at the group. Various stiff gestures are puzzling and require interpretation. What are these interpretations and what cues do subjects use in order to make them?

Numbers 1 and 2 were generally [3] seen as belonging together, although their ties are neither obvious nor strong; they might be conversing, or one might be talking and the other listening. Subjects explicitly identified the cues used for the grouping as head position (both are looking in the same direction—a direction which is also different from that of 3) and color (both are dressed in similar dark colors). Number 3 was universally seen as isolated—by the design on her dress, by looking straight ahead, by her bigger lips, her peculiar hand, her central position in the painting, and the fact that the others in that important group of five are looking away from her. Numbers 4 and 5 were very easily grouped together because their heads are turned toward each other (diatropically) and because they are painted in warm colors. Number 6 was seen as clearly separate by her size, her standing position, her distance from the others, her accentuated lips, her very different dress, and, finally, by her possibly more negroid features. Thus, Gauguin uses redundant cues for grouping throughout the painting where fewer might have been sufficient.

The interpretations of the gestures themselves were generally closely tied to the subgroupings within the picture. For example, Number 2 holds her hand straight up in front of her chest, at the tip of a whitish square which may or may not be noticed. Because the palm of her hand faces 3, subjects often said that she was pushing 3 away—shunning her, refusing her. Perhaps because of this pushing-away gesture, her bowed head and lowered eyes made her disdainful and proud (although, as the analysis of Series L will show, this interpretation of the bowed head is by no means the only possible one; see Chapter 15). Here, one can stress the dependence of the interpretation of one gesture, especially when the gesture is ambiguous, on that of other cues in the same person's body position, or on cues in another's body position, or on the construction of an overall scenario in which all the characters play some role. Another way of interpreting Number 2's bowed head is to say that she is subservient to someone—perhaps to 1, with whom she is grouped, or to 6 who stands so high above her and seemingly watches. A third interpretation, one frequently offered for other figures in this ambiguous painting, was that the gesture was a *prescribed* hand position; the subject presumably meant that, failing to see a meaning in it himself, he nevertheless assumed that a conventional meaning existed, probably in some ritual unknown to him. In passing, one might observe that this assumption of meaning is probably one without which a viewer cannot function perceptually in the social world. To what extent the attribution of ritual meaning (or perhaps also of private meaning) is a characteristic way of dealing with somatotactic ambiguity is not yet known.

Since Number 1 is facing no one, and since her hand position is directed away from the group and from herself, the gesture is difficult to interpret; subjects might say that she was catching a fly, or waving good-bye to someone outside the picture on the left. A similar problem arose with the interpretation of Number 3, who was universally seen as isolated. Her isolation was variously understood as that of a leader following precisely the rules of the ceremony and one who did not allow herself to be distracted by more frivolous comrades; or as an outcast. The obvious fact is that subjects could not know and, thus, their role assignments depended on the type of fantasy from which they constructed their scenarios. In any case, she is passive at this moment of viewing her, and the main cues to presentation meaning are the straightforward gaze (whose only property *is* that it is straightforward), her crooked hand, and her central isolation.

Numbers 4 and 5 were generally seen as conversing, although subjects seldom distinguished between the talker and the listener; the only cue to speech is 4's hand motion, but that, too, could be a sign of her reacting to 5. It hides the mouth; and this appeared to indicate that the talking was being done in a whisper. This apparent secrecy further indicated to some of the subjects that the women were gossiping about someone else. Number 5, with her hand on her chest, expressed torment, shock, disbelief, dismay, or an "Oh, no!" reaction. When pressed, subjects said that this interpretation had something to do with the obstacle that the hand put to the access of, or exit from, the breast, as if the gesture were meant to prevent news from entering or feelings from leaving. Thus, in two instances so far, access to body space or its denial played some role in the interpretations of others beside the investigators. In this case, the space in question is internal.

Subjects who made some point of the secrecy of the communications were likely to see secrecy in the meanings of the two whitish squares that Numbers 2 and 4 hold near their chins. Under this interpretation, the squares hid the faces from other people. Those subjects who strove for maximal consistency might link this to their interpretation of Number 6, who then was not merely looking at the group of five, but gazing at them with envy or censoriousness. It is fair to say that all subjects saw her as different from the other figures; she might be comparing herself to them, she might be looking outside the scene, she might be a busybody, she might be more utilitarian; certainly, fantasy supplied the scenario which in turn supplied the event structure and the roles involved in the interpretation.

The second picture does not so much present problems of grouping as of interpretation of active and passive body stances and movements; it is Botticelli's *Birth of Venus* (see Fig. 6). In this painting, Venus stands in the center, at the edge of a large scallop shell bringing her to shore with the aid of two zephyrs on the left; a female figure stands on the right, ready to put a cloak around the nude Venus. A small land mass forms the female figure's background; all the rest is ripply sea.

The picture is interesting here because of Venus's attempts at modestly covering herself with her hands; it appeared ideal for studying the effects of barriers at the proximal–internal boundary. Moreover, it has symmetrically placed figures with teleokinetic movements directed at Venus. It came as a pleasant confirmation that Venus's defensive arm positions played an important role in subjects' interpretations, although the precise nature of the positions' role did not become clear until the results of later studies were analyzed. Thus, the subjects saw the Venus as self-sufficient, oblivious, unconcerned, modest, unnatural, resigned, passive, melodramatic, sometimes unreal and inanimate. While these interpretations were not always consistent, the cues that gave rise to them were uniform: They reside in her hands, shielding her breasts and the genital area. Although the subjects did not say so directly, it is probable that Venus's hand positions are such as to render interactions between her and her environment difficult; she has effectively cut herself off from physical contact with others (in this case, of course, the viewer) and even from the type of *visual* contact which the viewer might wish to make with her. She pays no attention to the attending figures, and her expression, to the dismay of the viewer, is deadpan, unfocused, and staring; by this, she further refuses to make contact with the person looking at her. If she is interested in anyone, it is in herself; she presents only a narcissistic self-concern.

At the same time, few denied that she was beautiful, even sexy (here, the cue was her sensuous, somewhat paunchy belly), although one person remarked that her pale skin made Venus sexy in a cold way. Subjects did not speak of her with warm admiration; men especially appeared angered by her, using a good deal of sarcasm in describing her. Usually, the mythological or at least serious nature of the subject matter tended to be denied and the viewer might, in a down-to-earth, debunking fashion, speak of the zephyrs coming in on motorcycles. The strength of this reaction was surprising enough to lead to further exploration. A hypothesis about this reaction became the idea behind Series H (see Chapter 10)—the hypothesis that there is a contradiction between Venus's attractiveness, which is certain and undisguised, and the defensive barriers she creates with her hands. She makes the observer feel that she would not be interested in any interaction with him; he may reply with anger or sarcasm.

The nature of her isolation was viewed as different from that of Number 3 in Gauguin's painting: Equally unconcerned, Venus nevertheless has the attention of the figures around her and appears not as shunned but as oblivious and self-concerned. She is the only agent of her isolation.

Reactions to the other figures do not add as much to theoretical understanding. The two zephyrs appeared to most people, somewhat ambiguously, as male and female. The male had darker skin, an intent or malevolent expression, was doing the blowing, and was the clearer possessor of a pair of wings. The female had light skin, a gentler expression, a breast. Depending on the malevolence of the scenario, her peculiar wrapped position around the male and especially her energetic legs, might be seen as dangerous to the male zephyr. Her leg position had an unclear significance. The extent to which it was seen to endanger the male might have been a matter of projection of the subjects' own concerns into the scenario; one subject who saw her as especially dangerous sprinkled his interview with many other perceptions of conflict, more or less dangerous. Some subjects remarked that the zephyrs' positions were neither vertical enough for them to be clearly standing, nor horizontal enough to indicate unambiguous flight.

The clothed woman on the right was generally seen as subservient to Venus; the cues which led to that interpretation are the facts that she is clothed, that she is about to place a cloak on Venus, that she has outstretched arms and even legs, that she looks intently at Venus and strains toward her and, finally, that she is active.

A detail from Toulouse-Lautrec's *Marcelle Lender* was the third picture (Fig. 21). Its interest is centered on Mlle. Lender herself, who is an aging, slightly corpulent, though still impressive dancer in a night club, presumably taking a bow before an unseen audience. She wears a dress that is tight around the hips and has a low neckline; one foot is well ahead of the other, revealing a mass of pink petticoats, kicked up as she bows (and possibly whirls just prior to the bow). Minor figures appear dimly in the background.

When asked what they saw in the painting, subjects generally talked about three things: the movement the dancer is executing at the moment, her character, and the scene in which the action takes place. It was not the meaning of the movement that posed the interpretive problem, but the movement itself; the subjects' answers depended heavily on background cues which form the setting. Until a subject perceived that the action is set in a night club, he was likely to see the scene as a procession; in that case, the woman has just taken a normal step but appears quite unbalanced. Her buttocks are too far to the rear for her to be standing, but then she is clearly not sitting either; her forward leg is placed too far in front. Her hand, at the side of her left thigh, does not have a clear function: it may be an aid to her balance; it may be there to hold up (or in the view of another, to hold down) her skirt; or she may be pinching her thigh with it to forget her uncomfortable position. But if the subject made any one of three other scenic interpretations, she was seen as bowing: if all these persons were before a king, or if the setting was for a play, or if the surroundings were a night club. Then her hand became a part of her curtsy, holding her skirt in the proper position. Although the curtsy interpretation is probably the correct one, her movement remained ambiguous and subjects had to have recourse to scenic cues to feel comfortable with their perception. It was, therefore, impossible to gain more precise ideas about the perception of this

**Fig. 21.** Toulouse-Lautrec: *Marcelle Lender*

movement, which could be a pirouette, or to discover what interpretations are put upon such movements. But all subjects seemed to find it necessary to reduce the position's ambiguity, and the interviews demonstrated the use of one of the following three methods: (1) the interpretation of the movement was made to depend on the interpretation of the scene; (2) the movement was physically attempted by the subject himself (which argues for the importance of empathy or identification for understanding body positions); and (3) the interpretation was based on events outside of everyday life—not on ritually prescribed gestures, as in the Gauguin, but on fantasy or play-acting settings.

But it was the interpretations of character and facial expression that aroused the subjects' feelings the most, and this occurred without any prompting. These interpretations took the form of rapid positive, negative, or ambivalent reactions to the central figure. The reactions were not differentiated from straightforward speculations about the nature of her movement but suffused and animated the entire interview. The emotionally toned responses were considerably stronger among the women subjects than among the men. All subjects made remarks about the dancer's physical appearance, but the women seemed the more upset by it. They gave some evidence of identifying with Mlle. Lender and of seeing in her a middle-aged, undesirable version of themselves. Men, too, perceived her sensuality and contrasted it unfavorably with her age, but they were not particularly disturbed by her. Thus, she might be seen as grotesque, cold, tortured, old, sensual, and dissipated; or her expression might be vaguely pained, animated, expressive, sharp, or even delicate. Above all, the subjects perceived a conflict between the sensuality of her low neckline and tightly outlined buttocks, on the one hand, and her evaporating youth, on the other. They felt positively about her warm smile and attempt to please, and negatively about the appropriateness of her doing so. Some subjects shifted from one extreme to the other; some even gave evidence of a heightened pejorative attitude as a way of controlling the attraction they felt toward her. Naturally, these character evaluations were part of and consistent with the perception of the awkwardness of her movement.

There is no question but that the face, when at least vague features are given it by the painter, is looked on as the seat of emotional expression. Rare is the person who sees expressiveness primarily in the whole body. And yet, in this painting as well as in the others, facial expression received so many contrasting interpretations that it is equally clear that the face is highly susceptible to attribution of feeling and expression by projection. While this may not be quite true for the perception of real faces, in representation, it appears well established. Gombrich (1960) has described the history of caricature and concluded that almost any lines inside an oval will give an intended face expression; and Kris (1952), in his analysis of a psychotic sculptor of the eighteenth century, points to the use of the *same* facial arrangement for some sixty presumably different emotions. Singly, the representations are quite successful, as is a simple caricature whose caption or context provides the clue to presentation meaning. It is only when a series of these expressive busts are seen together that the inexactitude (and disquieting repetitiveness) of the representation becomes evident. Thus, also, with the interpretation of represented faces that are ambiguous or complex.

The emotional distance that separates people who are in physical and social proximity is a recurrent theme in many of Picasso's early paintings. Among those of the rose period, it is particularly well portrayed in *La Famille des Saltimbanques* (Fig. 22). In it, five people—four men of different ages and a girl—stand on a barren landscape; the sixth—a pretty woman—sits apart from them and looks away and out of the picture.

As in *Ta Matete*, an important problem in the painting is grouping: Who is related to whom and, perhaps more important for Picasso, who is distant from whom? Placement of the scene, construction of the scenario, and interpretation of facial and bodily expression are present here as everywhere, and interact with judgments about groupings.

The actors are numbered from left to right, 1 through 6. Numbers 1 and 2 were frequently grouped together and opposed to 3 through 6. As reasons for these groupings, subjects gave the apparent direction of talking (1 and 2 are facing the same way, as are, apparently, 4 through 6), and connections between hands (1 and 2 are holding hands, and 3, 4, and 6 have similar hand positions). If the subject attended to the active members of these groups, 1 and 3 were seen as belonging together because they face each other and may be conversing, or indeed disagreeing; in that case, all the others form a group of bored spectators. Still another proposed grouping was that of 1 through 5, since they are all remote from 6, who is, moreover, sitting down and apparently unconcerned with them. Some subjects made their groupings more detailed and talked of pairs; thus, 1 and 2 were almost always seen as father and daughter; 4 and 5 might be father and son, or older and younger brother, or, in the fantasy of one subject, both sons of 6, especially because they appeared to look at 6 in an emotional way; 3 and 6 might be connected because of the similar color of parts of their costumes; finally, 1 and 3 were paired because they interact and possibly clash and make some decision concerning their stranded position in the desert. This clash was reinforced for one of our subjects by the fact that 1 is slender and 3 very rotund. Thus, the important grouping principles here were: direction of gaze— a strategy that groups together all those who look in the same direction (forming a paratrope) or, alternately, groups those who look at each other (in diatropes) and opposes those who are outside this central group; similarity of

**Fig. 22.** Picasso: *La Famille des Saltimbanques*

body position or of position of parts of the body (including similarity of features); proximal contact such as holding hands; physical distance; and, finally, similarity of costume.

With regard to the interpretation of character and presentation meaning, it was evident that all subjects found such interpretation easy, perhaps unavoidable, although agreement on the description was not prominent. Number 1 was described by some with reference to his role: He was called a performer, clown, or dancer because of his costume. Others noted his firm stance, extended chest, and hand held behind the back, and judged him to be a leader. His scarf, his straight-held head, the stiffness of his arm, his firmly planted feet, all made him appear defiant, Napoleonic, and strong; he was facing the situation, standing up to corpulent 3 and refusing to extend himself to him (by his withdrawn hand). The small girl, Number 2, was seldom characterized apart from her role; she was seen as an ordinary small girl in costume, or, judged by her calves, a ballet dancer.

The large, red Number 3 was quite universally disliked; the group of subjects saw him as angry, grouchy, depraved (but efficient), devilish, a symbol of evil. When asked why, they generally pointed to his fatness; one subject saw his deep orange dress as a sign of lustful gluttony. No provision had been made in the conceptual scheme for somatotypical judgments of this nature and these are not further explored in this study. An equally serious shortcoming, however, is the lack of provision in the framework for the presentation meaning of different degrees of bodily tension. The subjects saw Number 1's expressiveness as derived partly from the tautness of his posture. There is every reason to presume that muscular tension and relaxation are important criteria by which positions and movements are judged. Later data will show that a similar hand position without the tautness that characterizes Number 1 leads to quite different ratings on importance, superordination, and haughtiness.

Number 4, the larger of the two young men, received few presentational characterizations; he was seen as a worker or an aide, because of the barrel carried on his shoulder, or, again, as a performer who did tricks on it. His slim figure indicated to one subject that he was a ballet dancer, but he is also slight enough (especially in contrast to 3) to make him appear physically vulnerable. He might not be very clever, as his closed mouth witnessed (to one subject). His small neighbor, Number 5, looked "Chinese" or generally oriental to two of our subjects, who pointed to his "insolent" mouth and low, loose clothing; or, he might be a precocious child. He was probably a tumbler or an athlete, said others, to judge from his close-cropped hair and costume.

The richest characterizations were made of Number 6. She was seen as tied to the group by her physiognomy, which resembled that of several of the others, and by the near-universality of the others' looking at her. But, otherwise, everything points to her isolation, and the character of the isolation seemed an important problem to explain. As far as her activity is concerned, she could be dreaming of the theater or circus; she could be looking back in memory; she could be about to leave the circus or her "family"; or waiting for a train. The meaning of her isolation appeared to be closer to that of Botticelli's Venus than to Gauguin's central woman (Number 3) because here, too, the isolation was seen as self-imposed, the person remaining the center of interest for the others. The activities or thoughts imagined to occupy her pictured her as psychically detached from the group or dreaming of further detachment.

In any event, she was not merely isolated; the hand which played with her hair made her appear self-contained, passive, and narcissistic. Thus, the subjects perceived as self-involved and narcissistic the close attention that one part of the body paid to another; attention given to a part of the self must necessarily take attention away from elsewhere. In this case, narcissism is less a product of the enclosures that one puts up around one's body space, as in the Venus, than it is a result of involvement with a part of the self; but a condition of this interpretation is that others be attempting interaction with the isolated one.

Manet's *Déjeuner Sur l'Herbe* (see Figure 9) is a painting that offers many possibilities of grouping and presentational characterization. Although, at first, it was expected that certain somatotactic groupings would predominate over others, thus providing some understanding of the criteria that determine them, this was not so. There was no grouping that some subject was not willing to make. On the other hand, as should have been expected, this did not make the detection of the criteria impossible. Any one of the subjects was capable of making several intersecting groups by using several criteria; it is the criteria, therefore, that one should examine.

Manet's painting pictures two men and two women, seated or standing in the woods. Food and other objects are strewn in the foreground. A woman (1), on the left and nude, looks at the viewer; next to her, a man (2), fully clothed, looks towards the right side of the picture, almost in the direction of the other gentleman (4); in the background, between 2 and 4, is another woman (3), clad in a long skirt gathered near her knees to keep it out of the stream she has waded in. Number 4 apparently looks at 2 and extends his right arm in his direction.

A popular grouping made by subjects was that of 1 and 2, on the one hand, and 3 and 4, on the other; after all, 1 and 2 were very close together, they were both looking at or near the viewer (their heads are nearly paratropic), the curves described by their bodies were similar, the look in their eyes was similar, 2's leg was close to 1's (they are probably intersecting in each other's axial space), and, from the perspective of the viewer, they overlapped. Numbers 3 and 4 were often seen as forming the other couple—partly by comparison with 1 and 2— and they could have even a more intense relation if one were to judge from 4's gesture and look, which *could* be directed toward 3, who in turn *could* be looking generally toward 4. Or, the relation of 1 and 2 was often seen as intense, because they were so close together and because, in this view, they couldn't care less about 4 (and 3 was too far away to matter). Other pairs were also formed, however. Thus, 1 and 3 are both nearly or completely undressed, while 2 and 4 maintain their street attire; nor did subjects ignore the fact that the undressed figures are females. Then, too, 2 and 4 could really be interacting with each other, involved in some masculine way such as talking politics; this would leave 1 and 3 out of the conversation and quite uninterested. In fact, one subject supposed that 2 and 4 might have been even closer together without 1's presence. Still another grouping, perhaps the most obvious, was that of 1, 2, and 4 against 3, who is farthest away; nevertheless, her separation from the group is mollified by the similarity of her body type to that of the others, by her looking at the others and presumably intending to rejoin them, and by 4's gesture, which, though pointing ambiguously, could be seen as tying the two together. Finally, and very hearteningly from the theoretical point of view, 1 and 4 were sometimes perceived as interacting because their ankles were crossed. One subject, commenting on this tie, said that crossing ankles with a man is a nice, covert, feminine gesture of possession.

With respect to the meaning attributed to body position, there were two dominant problems concerning woman 1: Why is she nude, and, given that she is, what does her position indicate? The most important fact about her nudity appears to be that her clothes are lying nearby, signifying that she has recently taken them off; thus, she is more naked than nude.[4] This gives her presentation a sexual significance that Venus did not have. Clothes taken off, or clothes in the process of being taken off, or clothes that have certain openings, all imply the possibility of a penetration into proximal space that the mere absence of clothes does not invite. It is as if the person were calling attention to the proximal space by removing the boundary which normally denies access to it. The next three chapters will discuss some of the other implications of boundary defenses of clothed and unclothed figures, and will comment on the changes in boundaries that unclothed figures themselves can create.

Subjects frequently found something remarkable about Number 1's staring out of the picture at the viewer. One subject said that the staring eyes created a "jumping off point" for the rest of the picture. The subject seemed to mean that the stare attracted a viewer's attention firmly enough to make further study of the picture likely. The stare may be even more important. It draws the viewer, hitherto a mere observer, into a two-way interaction with the figure. Now, he is himself observed and thus becomes involved in a much closer contact. This may enable him to "enter" the scene somewhat more easily and become more like a participant in it.

The position of this figure was often interpreted similarly to Picasso's woman (6); subjects noted that she had her elbow on her knee and her hand on her chin. Thus, the hand, normally an instrument for the prehension of other objects, here turns back toward another part of the same body, indicating the person's removal from the situation, her unconcern with it, or her meditation. Her knitted brow and pursed lips (another tightened boundary) showed that she was bored.

This lady's neighbor, Number 2, apparently presented fewer problems for interpretation. The subjects commented only on his eyes; though they may be hard to describe, they make the man meditative, fairly interested in what Number 4 may be saying, though he may merely listen, or think, without becoming too involved. A common feature in these descriptions was the uncertain character of his gaze: The eyes were seen as not lit up, and even going in divergent directions, with the right one aimed towards Number 1. The direction of gaze makes the person gazed at central and relevant; what is to be noticed here is the disruption of contact (or, conversely, the creation of a boundary) between actors produced by an averted look. An elaboration of this problem will be presented later.

The lady in the background, Number 3, gave subjects the fewest clues to presentation behavior. She is bent down but raises her head slightly and thus maintains contact with the foreground figures, or at least appears to want to make contact by some such method as by talking to them. Subjects who made this comment pointed out that she has placed one leg forward and is leaning toward the group. To another subject, this meant that she also finds it necessary to conceal herself. It would appear that an averted gaze makes any unclothed condition a more modest and less embarrassing one. Finally, one subject maintained that this woman was not paying any attention to the group.

No subjects saw Number 4 as not paying any attention to the group; he was close to them and faced them squarely. The subjects first commented on a cue which had not been given explicit attention in the scheme. They pointed out that he is not sitting up straight, that his position is relaxed; thus, his presentation is not intense. In the view of one of the subjects, he is probably too relaxed to be making a conversational point. Barely discriminable differences in tautness made much more of a difference to a somatotactic interpretation than had been expected. The second clear problem for interpretation in his posture is his outstretched arm; this position and the movement it implies constitute the popular meaning of the word "gesture." Since he is pointing in the direction of 1 or 2, or even possibly 3, the most likely guess was that he is talking to them; subjects said that he is making a strong point, or making a random expository gesture, explaining or describing; others said implicitly that he is *not* pointing because his finger is bent (thus, his hand negates, by not continuing the direction started by his arm, what his arm had appeared to intend to do).[5] Another subject said that he makes the effort of communication because at the end of his outstretched arm is an open thumb. It is probable that, for this subject, the communication was better defined by openness than by directedness and penetration of another's distal space; and it may not be fanciful to see in this open hand an analogy to the mouth, which, in order to speak, must be open, too. The perceptions of his gesture frequently depended on the response that other characters in the painting seemed to make to it. One subject, for example, said that 4 might have been talking to 1 at first, but was forced to finish the conversation by talking to 2, since 1 has turned away. Another subject thought that 4 was trying to beckon to 1, to pull her towards him (probably again after having noticed 4's bent finger). To be certain of such an interpretation, one would surely have to know what Number 1 herself was presenting.

Analysis of the interpretations of these five pictures became the main source of further elaborations of the theoretical notions. But they represent less than half of the number of paintings shown to subjects, and this discussion has not come close to exhausting even the tropic positions presented in Chapter 7. Of the remaining pictures used, four are especially central to any description of male–female interaction. Another four present relatively straightforward interpretive problems and may be briefly summarized next.

Forain's *Sentenced for Life* (Fig. 23) depicts three figures in a courtroom: A lawyer, presumably at the height of his triumph, having avoided the death sentence for his client, is standing with head thrown back, the right arm extended forward with palm up and the other reposing at shoulder level on the witness box; the defendant, whose torso is extended horizontally along the top of the bar so that he may kiss the lawyer's hand (the two figures thus forming a type of ankylotrope); and a gendarme standing above the accused and putting his arm on the latter's shoulder. Armitage's *The Remorse of Judas* (Fig. 24) shows Judas extending his body and arm towards a fully clothed Jewish priest who turns his back and ignores him (a protropic position [6]); two more priests, facing the observer and at a right angle to Judas, appear surprised by Judas's intense attempt to return his recently earned money. Homer's *Croquet Scene* (Fig. 25) fully lives up to its placid title: A gentleman on one knee concentrates on the ball next to a Victorian lady croquet player who watches him; two similar ladies in the background show some interest in the proceedings.

The masking of some figures in these paintings as an experimental variation eliminated interpersonal interaction as a basis for interpreting the presentation behavior of the figures shown. Although this was done for most of the paintings in the collection, the results of the procedure are especially important in the case of these three paintings, particularly in relation to the scarcity of other interpretive material. Thus, in Forain's painting, when only the lawyer was exposed, subjects interpreted his triumphant gesture in all sorts of other ways: He was

**Fig. 23.** Forain: *Sentenced for Life*

pleading for mercy; his expression was pained; he was weeping. Some saw no reason to assume that he was a lawyer. When only the defendant was shown, a few subjects perceived him as bending down to bite someone. Even when the whole painting was shown without its title, widely diverse interpretations were advanced. There is no escaping the fact that various interpretations are possible and that the facial and bodily expressions are ambiguous; only the title settled the point, and then not to everyone's satisfaction. Until the subject found out the title, his scenario (and the degree to which he required consistency in it) was his main guide.

**Fig. 24.**   Armitage: *The Remorse of Judas*

In Armitage's *Judas*, the title served as a guide not so much to the interpretation of presentation behavior as it did to the particular persons and events depicted. The interpretation of presentation behavior, however, did change with masking of portions of the painting. Judas himself, when shown alone, was quite regularly seen as imploring someone; this is correct and unambiguous, although some mistakes were made (also with the full picture exposed) about whether he was to be defined as offering to give something or asking to receive it. More troublesome was the turned back of the principal priest: Subjects did not understand the significance of his back until they saw what was behind it; this we may take to be general for the protropic position.

Homer's *Scene* offered interesting examples of the dependence of interpretations on interaction. The kneeling gentleman, seen alone, was perceived as doing any number of things such as getting out of a rowboat onto a dock; only the discovery of flat terrain spanning the whole picture confirmed his kneeling posi-

**Fig. 25.**   Homer: *Croquet Scene*

tion, and only the appearance of a ball near one of his feet made it clear that he is concentrating on something at that point. The ladies in the background were generally perceived as ambiguous until the whole picture was seen; then, they assumed presentation meaning consistent with the freshly constructed scenario. Clearly, the perceptual process here deals not only with increasingly clarified interpretation of facial expression as the picture becomes fully exposed, but also with expanding possibilities for the construction of an episode including several characters.

Mary Cassatt's *Young Mother Sewing* (Fig. 26) is of interest because the little girl looks straight at the viewer with big, brown eyes. The effect of a staring figure may be somewhat uncanny. The viewer is suddenly removed from the isolated observation of the painting he has enjoyed and becomes watched himself. In a group picture, he can use the contact that is thus made to "jump into" the picture, as if an opening had been created by which he could enter the scene. Or, more prosaically, the contact just made draws his attention and invites a

**Fig. 26.** Cassatt: *Young Mother Sewing*

more thorough investigation of what the picture contains. In this painting, the child so monopolized the subjects' attention that she became the main focus of interpretation and the mother receded into the background. Another cue dominating attention in the picture is located in the two soft concavities that echo each other and make the child rest comfortably in the mother's lap, the fingers

**Fig. 27.** Rubens: *Venus and Adonis*

pressed into the cheek near the mouth and the elbows leaning into the mother's skirt. Viewers observed that Cassatt's picture integrated these elements into a pleasant whole.

It was Rubens's, Titian's, and Correggio's pictures that, taken together, yielded the most new information about the uses and meanings of body space. They were all chosen to illustrate some aspects of male–female interaction, and two of them in fact portray the same theme and carry the same title: *Venus and Adonis.* Rubens's version (Fig. 27) shows the nude Venus sitting on a high rock leaning toward Adonis; her right hand clasps his right arm, and her left arm extends farther, past the right side of his body to his back. He stands and leans slightly toward her, his right arm extended uncertainly in her direction, his left clasping his spear high up near its point. Thus, his inclination toward Venus is balanced by the opposite and equal inclination of his spear—a perfect portrayal of the ambiguity of his desires, further aided by his dogs, who seem eager to leave the frame toward the left and go hunting. Venus shows no uncertainty in her desire to detain Adonis. In Titian's depiction (Fig. 28), Venus makes clear the same determination; the observer sees her, however, from her back, as she sits and tries to hold back an already departing Adonis. Her arms are more closely wrapped around him and he leans away from her, one foot forward as if he had already started walking. But he shows no more single-mindedness than the Rubens Adonis, because the spear he holds onto leans in Venus's direction. Many subtle differences were formulated by different viewers, and a few of the anticipated ones will be mentioned here. Quite irrespective of differences in the tone of their complexion and tactile differences in their skin (differences which are very important to most viewers), there seemed to be a greater frankness and openness in Rubens's Venus than in Titian's. The former's grasp was seen as open and relaxed; her arms outline a space in front of her body that Adonis may go further into or leave. Titian's Venus has turned toward Adonis so forcibly that part of her body is still not in a diatropic position with respect to him; thus, there is more tension and less frankness in her grasp. And it may be significant, too, that Titian's Venus has turned her back to the observer. An observer facing a picture of a back may be uncertain whether he should react directly to the figure's back or indirectly to its front—which that figure must be exposing to other figures in the picture. This confusion of viewpoints became clear in reactions to a picture not illustrated here;[7] from them, one can assume that in Titian's picture, as well, subjects saw less frankness and openness because they were "affronted" by Venus's back. Finally, for one subject, the brown tones of Titian's version complemented these impressions with the feeling of a stuffy, enclosed atmosphere, while the cool tones of the Rubens provided atmospheric and emotional clarity.

In Correggio's *Jupiter and Antiope* (Fig. 29), Jupiter, in the guise of a satyr, stands behind the sleeping Antiope and removes the veil that had been covering her. She sleeps with her arm folded behind her head and bares her breast to the observer. It came as no surprise that male subjects found her sexually provocative; the surprise was rather that Rubens's Venus should not have been more so, since her bosom, too, is uncovered. It is true that the corpulence and exaggerated pale complexion of Rubens's Venus do not meet today's standards of beauty, but another variable requires introduction here, the extended arms.

**Fig. 28.**   Titian: *Venus and Adonis*

Extended arms seem to act as a channel along which interaction is invited—within what is here called axial space. One would have assumed the same for a breast (either a man's or a woman's) exposed directly. It emerged, however, that the extended arms also remove the promise or threat of immediate interac-

**Fig. 29.** Correggio: *Jupiter and Antiope*

tion at the proximal boundary; they create a space within which interaction may satisfactorily take place, without going further. The space thus created can be called *defined axial space,* and its presentational meaning may be opposed to that of undefined space, or, better, *open proximal access.* In the latter, it is as if any interaction that might take place would occur directly at the proximal boundary; it would therefore be more drastic—either in a sexual or an aggressive sense. Thus, it seems useful to distinguish several (for the present, two) types of axial space, whose meaning depends on the positions that the arms take within it.

To recapitulate briefly, it was asked, first, how figures in a painting were organized: Who was grouped with whom and who interacted with whom? The following criteria were found to be principles of grouping (and, conversely, of isolation):

1. *Protropic, paratropic, and diatropic groups.* These groups could be determined by the head or by the rest of the body. In the paintings, heads and bodies tended to face in the same direction, making it difficult to distinguish between direction of gaze and direction of bodily movement. More than one criterion could be used in any larger assemblage, leading to cross-cutting groupings.

2. *Proximity.* Figures not clearly interacting might nevertheless be seen as a group if they were placed close together and/or if they intersected at least at the axial boundary.

3. *Sex.* Figures of like sex tended to be grouped together, but depending on the scenario, heterosexual pairs could become the grouped units.

4. *Body type.* A fat and a thin figure could belong together by contrast; on the contrary, similar physiognomies could also group people.

5. *Clothing.* Similarly clothed figures would be segregated from differently dressed ones.

6. *Color.* When two figures were colored in a like fashion, they might be grouped; it sufficed for them to match in a small part of their costume.

7. *Overlapping (perspective).* Two figures who intersected in the two-dimensional plane of the picture would thus be brought into sufficient proximity to be grouped.

8. *Outline.* Figures sharing the same outline (again in the two-dimensional plane) could be seen as a group.

9. *Self-concern.* A person showing a primary interest in himself would be segregated from the others. This is the obverse of organization based on protropic, diatropic, and other groupings; and it is similar to the segregation that occurs as a result of withdrawing a part of the body from possible contact with another person (such as a hand held behind the back).

10. *Subtraction.* All those figures left over after other groups have been formed might be seen as belonging together.

11. *Scenario.* Finally, the story constructed by the viewer would reinforce groupings already made, or create groupings where none might have been obvious otherwise.

Second, the presentational meaning of the body positions shown in the paintings was investigated. The following emerged as criteria for interpretation:

1. *Access to body space or its denial.* Important also as a principle of grouping, it was of primary importance in indicating to the viewer what a body position meant. A figure would be approachable or unapproachable by the exposure of its ventral side and by defenses put up against this exposure. A defined axial space created by arms extended toward the front would make interaction likely within the axial space, but not closer. An attractive figure who erected defenses against approach could arouse a viewer's hostility. The observer might confuse interaction between two figures with interaction between one of them and himself; thus, a dorsal view of a character could indicate his rejection of the observer.

2. *Direction of gaze.* A direct look would establish close contact between persons. It could be seen as comparable to a diatropic, undefended body position; an averted gaze could be viewed as an analogue of an erected boundary or of the presentation of the side or back of the body. When several persons directed their gaze at another, the other became central and important. A direct look could also establish a close relation between the observer and the figure observed.

3. *Movement directed towards the self.* Besides segregating the person from others, a self-directed movement indicated self-absorption, meditation, narcissism, and the like.

4. *Nudity.* Subjects found it important to distinguish between a figure that was appropriately or "naturally" nude and one that was naked because its clothes had just been removed. A problem for investigation concerns changes in presentational meaning of a given position with the addition or removal of clothes.

5. *Pointing.* A protrusion from the body (a limb, part of one's clothing) was seen as directing activity at someone, or as generally "expressive" of feelings or thoughts of the actor. Deviations from an extended limb, such as a crooked finger, or variations, such as an open thumb and forefinger, could reinforce or modify the meaning of the gesture.

6. *Tension.* The same body position was interpreted differently when taut or relaxed.

7. *Facial expression.* Subjects looked to the face as the most important clue to expressiveness. At least in the case of paintings, however, the expressiveness

may have been projected into the face by the observer, who would find an interpretation consistent with his other perceptions and his scenario.

Four factors that emerged from the interviews deserve elaboration: (1) the strong affective relation to a figure which is likely to be formed when it stands out from others (this was the case in particular with Toulouse-Lautrec's *Marcelle Lender*); (2) the construction of the scenario, which will provide the viewer with hypotheses about individual figures, which he then may or may not verify by closer observation of the body position; (3) the dependence of individual interpretations on each other, the more so, the more a figure is ambiguous; and (4) the ways in which subjects deal with difficult interpretations—by placing the gesture in a foreign or fantasy setting, by ascribing to it a ritual significance, or by trying the gesture out themselves.

Only a small part of what the interviews yielded can be submitted to systematic exploration in this study. Almost all the principles of grouping will be neglected because they have been deemed secondary to expressiveness. The variable of tension and relaxation is not considered, in part because it is difficult to represent without tactile details of skin and muscle. Facial expression will be eliminated altogether (except when studying problems connected with the direction of gaze), because it is *bodily* presentation that is the prime concern. And background cues that could act as stimuli to the construction of a scenario are ignored.

The chapters that follow will elaborate the meanings of defenses erected against approach: In the nude female body in Chapter 10, in the same body, clothed, in Chapter 11, and in the nude male body in Chapter 12. Chapter 13 will study direction of gaze as a factor determining the perceived importance of persons looked at. Chapter 14 will examine the meanings for leadership of various hand and arm positions, seen singly or in a group. Chapter 15 will give particular attention to a variable not explored in the paintings, that of acrotropic displacement and the variations it undergoes. Chapter 16 will present the most complicated analysis, that of a male and female figure in interaction, with distances, body spaces, and intended actions systematically varied. Chapter 17 will re-examine the presentational meanings discovered in Chapter 16 from the viewpoint of a radically different methodology.

# NOTES FOR CHAPTER 9

[1] See, for example, such photographic studies of the movements of the human figures as Eadweard Muybridge's *The Human Figure in Motion* (1955).

[2] The paintings used were: Gauguin's *Ta Matete*, Toulouse-Lautrec's *Marcelle Lender* (detail), Botticelli's *Birth of Venus*, Picasso's *Famille des Saltimbanques*, Manet's *Déjeuner Sur l'Herbe*, Forain's *Sentenced for Life*, Cassatt's *Mother Sewing*, Armitage's *The Remorse of Judas*, Homer's *Croquet Scene*, Rubens's *Venus and Adonis*, Titian's *Venus and Adonis*, Correggio's *Jupiter and Antiope*, and Tintoretto's *Adam and Eve*. All reproductions were in color and about the size of a sheet of typewritten paper.

[3] Although we say "generally" and the like, we do not have precise proportions in mind. For each painting, the number of subjects varied from three to six, permitting only vague quantitative statements to be made. Such roughness is intentional and appropriate for this suggestive analysis.

[4] For our purpose, we distinguish simply between the body just undressed (naked) and the body that has no clothes and appears complete that way (nude). Kenneth Clark makes the same distinction better when he says, "The English language, with its elaborate generosity, distinguishes between the naked and the nude. To be naked is to be deprived of our clothes, and the word implies some of the embarrassment most of us feel in that condition. The word 'nude,' on the other hand, carries, in educated usage, no uncomfortable overtone. The vague image it projects into the mind is not of a huddled and defenseless body, but of a balanced, prosperous, and confident body: the body re-formed. In fact, the word was forced into our vocabulary by critics of the early eighteenth century to persuade the artless islanders that, in countries where painting and sculpture were practiced and valued as they should be, the naked human body was the central subject of art." (1959, p. 23.) Later, he redefines the nude as an art form, rather than a state of the body; the nude then becomes "an art form invented by the Greeks in the fifth century." (p. 25.)

[5] Picasso himself has paid some attention to the more unconscious meanings of the body positions and gestures in this painting. In a long series of drawings, in which each departs further from the Manet original, Picasso's ever-freer fantasies eventually lead him to see the outstretched arm of Number 4 as an erect phallus. Whether this unconscious meaning is intended or not is a question. See Picasso (1962).

[6] This position is not quite protropic since the actors are not engaged in a similar activity: one is trying to approach another who turns his back. In any case, the position is rarely found in painting. Sensitive to the unifying properties of diatropic and, to a lesser extent, paratropic groupings, painters very seldom portray interactions that are centrifugal. This position, in which the *back* of one of the actors is the dominant cue, is centrifugal and probably tends to disintegrate composition; a fully apotropic grouping disintegrates the composition even more.

[7] In Tintoretto's *Adam and Eve*, Eve leans toward Adam and proffers the apple; he leans away. His front faces her and his back faces the observer; one subject, instead of saying that Adam is recoiling from the apple, maintained that he was "rejecting"—and that the rejection was apparent from Adam's visible back. What Adam seemed to be rejecting, on this interpretation, was the observer's own advance; the observer was reacting to Adam as if he (Adam) were part of the observer's surroundings. This mode of entering a picture we call the *direct viewpoint*; the mode where an observer interprets movements from the way they appear to others in the picture we call the *refracted viewpoint*.

# 10. The Arms of Venus

It was difficult not to notice the hostility shown toward the Venus of Botticelli; the subjects, even when admitting that she was beautiful, would treat her unkindly and ridicule her "dying swan" look. While such abuse was not universal, she was nevertheless seen as self-absorbed, oblivious to others, even narcissistic. The cues that account for this reaction are likely to be only three in number: her facial expression and either of the hands covering her body. The exploratory interviews showed that the face is generally looked to for the most important cues to presentational meaning, but that it is unreliable and requires much projection of the feelings the subject had deduced from other cues—at least in paintings where the head is small enough to lack precision in features. There is every reason to suppose that, in the Venus, the arms themselves are the crucial variable, although the dreamy face is not to be ignored. This chapter, then, asks more precise questions about the effects of this position of Venus's arms. Its hypothesis is that there is a contradiction between Venus's beauty and her unapproachability; its general field of study is the presentational use of arms by the nude woman to permit or deny access to body spaces.

The best test of this hypothesis would consist of examining figures in which the arm positions were varied and the face left identical, or, better, in which the face was left out altogether so as to test only the presentational meaning of the body position itself. Nine pictures were drawn to represent all the combinations of the three arm positions assumed to be important: the right arm (that is, Venus's right arm) extended out away from the body, or resting at the side and parallel to the body, or covering her breast as in the original; similarly, the left arm extended out to the side, or placed in a resting position at the side and slightly behind the body, or covering the genital area as in the original. One might think that a single covering position of each arm and a single un-

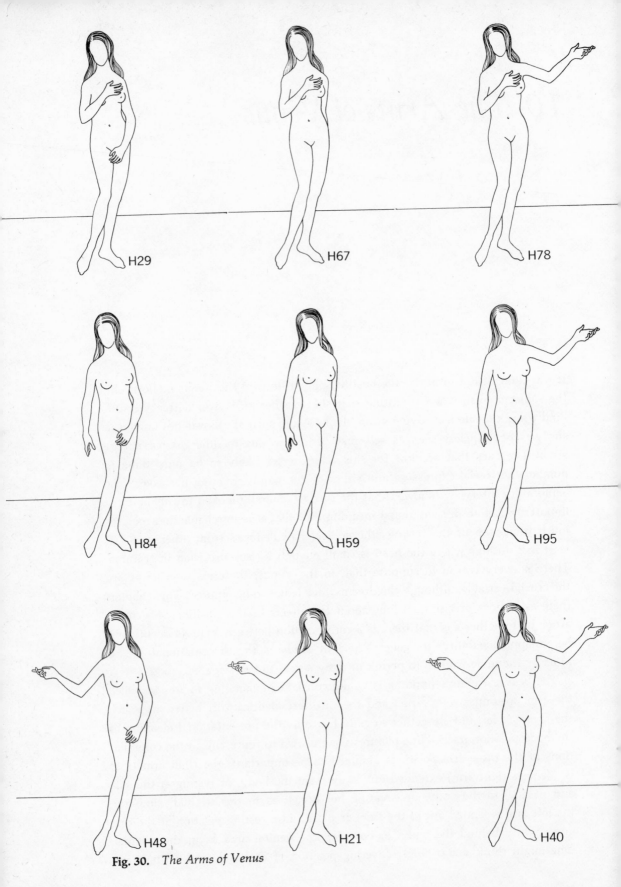

H29　　　　　H67　　　　　H78

H84　　　　　H59　　　　　H95

H48　　　　　H21　　　　　H40

**Fig. 30.**　*The Arms of Venus*

covering one might be enough. Nevertheless, it seemed likely that uncovering itself could be a matter of degree, and that one should study a position that merely uncovers and one that uncovers with a broad, sweeping gesture. All nine positions are shown in Figure 30 and are randomly numbered so as to destroy any feeling of sequence the subjects might be groping for; the whole series is arbitrarily labeled H for convenience. The figures are reduced in scale here; in the test presentation, they were printed separately, each figure about 6 inches high on an 8½″ x 11″ sheet; and, in order to eliminate the possible stroboscopic effects of succeeding arm motions as a factor in the ratings of the whole group, the order of presentations was varied randomly for each subject.

It was crucial to avoid the pitfall of the original interviewing method—that of obtaining very rich and highly unsystematic results that would not be strictly comparable from subject to subject. A paper-and-pencil measure which could be easily administered to a large number of subjects who would select from a finite number of possible answers was devised. What was thus lost in freedom and richness of expression was gained in the strict comparability of the data. Of course, it was important not to sacrifice all flexibility; thus, the use of an adjective checklist as the measuring instrument was rejected in favor of a scale that would allow the subject a choice in the degree to which he would judge a given term as appropriate or not. A bipolar dimensional measure such as Osgood's Semantic Differential Scale seemed ideal; one was constructed with eleven dimensions germane to this problem. (Figure 31 shows a sample answer sheet.) Some of the dimensions directly reflect our interest in the openness and

*Picture identification number H___*

The figure appears to be:

| | | |
|---|---|---|
| natural | : __ : __ : __ : __ : __ : __ : __ : | unnatural |
| immodest | : __ : __ : __ : __ : __ : __ : __ : | modest |
| receiving | : __ : __ : __ : __ : __ : __ : __ : | rejecting |
| self-concerned | : __ : __ : __ : __ : __ : __ : __ : | other-concerned |
| cold | : __ : __ : __ : __ : __ : __ : __ : | warm |
| active | : __ : __ : __ : __ : __ : __ : __ : | passive |
| dramatic | : __ : __ : __ : __ : __ : __ : __ : | calm |
| shy | : __ : __ : __ : __ : __ : __ : __ : | exhibitionistic |
| affected | : __ : __ : __ : __ : __ : __ : __ : | ingenuous |
| unyielding | : __ : __ : __ : __ : __ : __ : __ : | yielding |
| I feel pulled toward | : __ : __ : __ : __ : __ : __ : __ : | I feel pulled away |

**Fig. 31.** Sample Answer Sheet for Series H

approachability of the various positions, and others reflect the comments made by the interview subjects. The last dimension is intended to reflect the degree of attraction or repulsion of the figure. Each dimension has seven positions on which the subject could indicate his judgment; a neutral score, or one reflecting the inapplicability of the dimension to the problem, would be 4. Halo effects were reduced by putting what might intuitively be called the "good" side of each dimension sometimes on the left, at other times on the right.

The subjects were 30 undergraduate volunteers [1] from Harvard and Radcliffe Colleges, 15 men and 15 women. None of these subjects had taken part in the exploratory interview study, nor did they know anything about the theoretical purpose of this one. They were told the manner of using the rating scale and that the study was directed at learning something about the presentational meanings of body positions. After the last person had finished, those subjects who were so inclined stayed for a discussion of the test and the purposes of the research.

This procedure yields two types of data: mean scores on each dimension for each figure for the group as a whole (and for males and females separately); and intercorrelations between the ratings on the different dimensions. The first type of data indicates what the group thought about each painting, dimension by dimension; when analyzed for significance by analysis of variance, it reveals the effect produced by each of the arms in their various positions and thus is directly related to the hypotheses. The correlational data, on the other hand, indicate what dimensions carry which meaning; in a way, they clarify the meaning of each dimension in relation to the other dimensions.[2] This becomes especially useful when males are compared with females.

If the data are ordered according to the drawings in Figure 30, the effects of changes in the left arm from row to row and the effects of movement in the right arm from column to column can be observed. Eleven analyses of variance are appropriate, one for each of the dimensions that can be affected by these changes. The complete tables are presented in Appendix A, but what they reveal can be stated here.

> Changes in the right arm (the one that covers the breast in the original Venus) significantly affect the ratings on all dimensions except "unyielding–yielding" (where $p$ is slightly higher than .05). Variations in the left arm (which covers the genital area) affect the ratings significantly on all the dimensions.

> Specifically, the results indicate that the more the arms cover the body of this figure, the more she is perceived as modest and rejecting, self-concerned and cold, passive and calm, and shy and unyielding. Subjects further

point out that the more her body is covered, the more they feel pulled away from her.

These results are consistent with the point of view presented in the introductory chapters. The covering arms block approach to the body and render it unyielding and rejecting, and the character behind these arms is perceived as self-concerned and cold. That changes in arm positions should act so as to express a psychic "state of being" in the person seems to have importance well beyond anecdotal observations. A person who blocks the avenues of approach by and to others (in the manner of these figures) is seen as concerned only with himself. But, perhaps because of the particular position of the covering hands, a broader hypothesis about self-concern may be suggested: Self-concern is shown not simply by enclosed boundaries, but by a limb's pointing back towards some part of the body. Such a hypothesis would be consistent with the narcissism one may be suspected to display when the object of one's touch is one's own body rather than another's; and it would also follow from the visual direction that is normally established by the limbs, which may be used not only to create spaces around the body but also to point in different directions—in the case under discussion, back towards oneself.

Two other comments seem required by these data. First, effects of changes in the left arm are considerably more significant than those created by the right arm. Since the left arm covered the genital area in the original Venus, perhaps it is natural that changes in its position should do the most to change the figure's perceived approachability, warmth, and even the degree to which one feels attracted to her, particularly if one's fantasy about the figure concerns sexual approach.

Second, the effect of arm changes on two dimensions, "natural–unnatural," and "affected–ingenuous," are not entirely clear. Inspection of the tables in Appendix A shows that, in spite of the overall significance of arm effects, naturalness does not increase or decrease in any simple way with the covering arms; one can note only that the figures with the most asymmetrical arm position (H48–N/OC and H78–N/CO),[3] in which one arm covers while the other is extended, were seen as the most unnatural. Similarly, these two figures, particularly H48–N/OC, were rated as the most affected. What seems likely to explain these ratings is the contradiction between maximum covering and greatest exposure.

With the exception of these two dimensions, the analysis of variance has suggested that most of the attributes associated with arm positions are additive: The more covered the body is, the more of a given effect will one observe. But the two exceptions suggest the desirability of a closer look at the data. Is it inevitable that the maximally closed and maximally open positions will be judged as extreme on all the other dimensions? Table 10–1 brings together the pictures that received the highest and lowest scores on each dimension: The two end columns in the table contain the identification letters of the drawings that are extreme at each end of the dimensions; the two middle columns contain those just short of the extreme. The presentation makes clearer which particular combinations of arm positions create the strongest effects.

TABLE 10–1.  Pictures with Extreme Scores on Each Dimension (All Subjects)

|  | *Most* | *Second* | *Second* | *Most* |  |
|---|---|---|---|---|---|
| *Natural* | N/SS | N/SO | N/CO | N/OC | *Unnatural* |
| *Immodest* | N/OO | N/SO | N/SC | N/CC | *Modest* |
| *Receiving* | N/OO–N/SS | N/SO | N/OC | N/CC | *Rejecting* |
| *Self-concerned* | N/CC | N/SC | N/OO | N/SO | *Other-concerned* |
| *Cold* | N/CC | N/SC | N/OO | N/SS | *Warm* |
| *Active* | N/OO | N/SO | N/CS | N/CC | *Passive* |
| *Dramatic* | N/OO | N/CO | N/SC | N/SS | *Calm* |
| *Shy* | N/CC | N/SC | N/CO | N/OO | *Exhibitionistic* |
| *Affected* | N/CO | N/OC | N/OS | N/SS | *Ingenuous* |
| *Unyielding* | N/CC | N/OC | N/OO | N/SS | *Yielding* |
| *Pulled toward* | N/SS | N/OS | N/CO | N/CC–N/OC | *Pulled away* |

One might have expected the two most covered and uncovered figures, N/CC and N/OO, to pre-empt the extreme positions, but they do not quite do so. They are joined by N/SS, and the trio together accounts for 20 of the 24 extreme appearances. As different as the three figures are, they do have in common a symmetry of arms; their presentational meaning is probably the clearest.

N/CC, to start with the prototypical figure, appears eight times in the table. She is seen as the most modest, shy, and passive, and as the most self-concerned, cold, rejecting, and unyielding. Early interpretations of her position are amply justified: Her proximal boundary is indeed defended against approach (she is rejecting and unyielding), and the personality that hides behind these barriers is self-concerned and cold. If one asks whether the subjects take this defensive position personally and feel rejected as viewers, the answer is affirmative: N/CC shares with N/OC the distinction of being the most repellent.

No greater contrast could be readily imagined than that between N/CC and N/SS. The latter, with both arms at her sides, seems to have received all the admiring comments; she was seen as the most natural and calm; as yielding, warm, and receiving; as ingenuous. Most important, she is the figure subjects felt the most attracted to, which tends to confirm these attributes as the most admired ones. Four groups of criteria seem to appear here: warmth, openness, calm, and lack of affectation. Certainly, the former two are what one should have expected as opposites of $N/CC$'s attributes.

The third most frequent extreme is $N/OO$, the figure with both arms extended away from the body. This arm position gives her a demonstrative quality that the other figures lack: She appears as the most immodest, dramatic, and active of the figures. It may seem strange that she who has not uncovered more of herself than has $N/SS$, should be seen as so exhibiting; perhaps subjects perceived her way of uncovering herself as active and recent; she is more naked than nude, as was Manet's figure who had recently taken off her clothes. $N/SS$, on the other hand, appears natural, calm, and unhurried in her nudity. One might have expected that this would make $N/OO$ the more exciting woman, but, in view of this analysis, it seems more likely that there are strong enough defenses against sexuality in our culture to condemn blatant displays of attractiveness and openness (she is immodest, the ratings indicate), and that the subjects, especially males, may have feared that, in further approaching her, they would become trapped in the next move she was likely to make; that is, to bring her arms together around the approaching person.

Yet a further striking fact about $N/OO$ is that she, like $N/SS$, was perceived as highly receiving, yielding, warm, and other-concerned, but that these qualities did not win the subjects' unhesitating admiration. Apparently, they felt a certain ambivalence towards her—attracted, yet hesitant because she might be too open (she is not extreme on the dimension of attraction). And this ambivalence may be contrasted with the one that subjects seemed to feel when looking at Botticelli's Venus, an ambivalence between physical attractiveness and rejecting position.

Three other figures appear frequently enough in the table to require discussion. $N/SO$ appears five times, and the tables in Appendix A show her to be the third most attractive. She, like $N/OS$, $N/OO$, and $N/SS$, presents no covering gestures to the observer; one might suppose this to account for her attractiveness, and one could support the interpretation with the fact that she was also perceived as quite receiving. But she shares with $N/OO$ the questionable qualities of immodesty and activity which might have sufficed to lower her attractiveness rating. On the other hand, she has two other qualities that could make her desirable: She is other-concerned and natural. Which of these criteria are the determining ones will become clear in the analysis of interdimensional correlations.

Appearing five times in the table is $N/CO$, whose left arm extends away from her body and whose right arm covers her breast. She is one of the figures the subjects felt most repelled by, and she was also rated as the most affected and the second most dramatic, exhibitionistic, and unnatural. Thus, she shares with histrionic demeanor that appears to have repelled subjects; and she is the pole in attraction from the favorite figure *N/SS*, who was seen young and natural. Since *N/CO* was not perceived as rejecting, one presumes that the important differentiating dimension between these figures is naturalness. It appears, tentatively, that among the figures the subjects examined there were two types they felt repelled by: the rejecting figure and the unnatural one.

*N/SC* appears very frequently in *N/CC*'s company (like *N/CC*, she covers her genital area with one arm; unlike her, she leaves the other by her side). The table shows her, accordingly, very modest and shy, self-concerned and cold. The surprising fact is only that she was not repellent in the manner of *N/CC*; she was, after all, perceived as unyielding and self-concerned and (see Appendix A) also highly rejecting. But she was also rated as calm, unlike *N/CC*; this was one of the qualities of the admired *N/SS*.

The remaining two drawings appear in the table only two or three times each. In *N/OC*, one arm covers the genital area and the other is extended toward the right. This figure was seen as the most unnatural and affected, and as the second most rejecting and unyielding; small wonder—in view of her resemblance to the asymmetrical *N/CO*—that she is highly repellent. The meaning of unnaturalness seems to become clearer; it comes either from the contradiction between covering and exposing, or from the incongruity between the hand that points to a sexual area and the hand which directs attention elsewhere. In either case, these positions seem to be bodily analogs of that more commonly understood expression of contrary intentions: the grimace.

Finally, *N/OS* has the left arm by the body's side and slightly behind, while the right points sideways to the right; in this, she is symmetrical with *N/SO*. Like the latter, she was rated as highly other-concerned (see Appendix A); unlike her, she was ingenuous (see Table 10–1) and warm (Appendix A). She was the second most attractive figure.

## MEANINGS OF DIMENSIONS

One can expect that a correlation between the various dimensions would indicate the aura of meaning that surrounds dimensions that correlate with others; the more highly correlated, the more are two dimensions likely to have identical meaning.[4] Further, one can expect to gain a better understanding of the criteria of attractiveness by examining the dimensions that correlate with the dimension "pulled to–pulled away." In Table 10–2 are listed the correlations above ±.41; in each case, for presentational simplicity, only one end of each dimension

TABLE 10–2 (p < .025) Interdimensional Correlations (All Subjects)

| | | |
|---|---|---|
| pulled to: | ingenuous | .49 |
| | natural | .48 |
| | modest | .42 |
| | warm | .41 |
| shy: | passive | .56 |
| | modest | .54 |
| | calm | .50 |
| warm: | receiving | .54 |
| | calm | .51 |
| receiving: | yielding | .50 |
| natural: | ingenuous | .45 |

appears.[5] Positive scores in the table refer to positive correlations between the two dimension ends listed. (For the complete matrix of correlations, see Appendix B.)

In the total sample of subjects, attraction is correlated with ingenuousness and naturalness, and with modesty and warmth; since the most attracting figure (*N/SS*) was natural and two of the least attracting ones (*N/OC* and *N/CO*) were unnatural, this is not surprising. Missing, however, is the other criterion that analysis of mean scores had indicated as important—that of "reception–rejection." (Appendix B shows the "pulled to–receiving" correlation to be .33.) In the analysis of extreme figures, the attracting figures were also rated as receiving, although the repelling ones need not have been rejecting; it is probably this lack of correspondence at the rejecting end of the dimension that prevents a higher correlation. But if attraction is not a question of receptiveness, it is also not one of sexuality; rather, it is a matter of innocence and warmth. Of course, these correlations reflect the criteria that male and female subjects agree on.

If the subjects are attracted to warm figures, one may inquire into the meanings of warmth; in Table 10–2, warmth is related to receiving and to calmness. And calmness itself is related to shyness, which in turn is correlated with modesty and passivity. To the two sexes together, then, a female figure is attractive when she is warm, undramatic, modest, and without affectation.

## SEX DIFFERENCES

The first datum comes from the earlier analysis of variance. As well as examining the data for the significance of the effect of each arm, that analysis pointed up male–female differences; these differences were computed across all

but separately by each dimension. One difference of significant
...erged (see Appendix A): Males are significantly more attracted to
...an are females (p < .05). The data also suggest other differences,
...n, however, do not come up to the usual standard of significance: Men tend
to see the figures generally as colder (p < .10) and as less yielding (p < .20)
than do women; they also see the figures as somewhat less active (p > .20). To
interpret these latter differences, a closer look at the data is necessary.

One can also search for sex differences within each picture; since there are
nine pictures, each rated on 11 dimensions, 99 comparisons can be made for
male–female discrepancies. The full data may be found in Appendix C; the
significant differences appear in Table 10–3. Certainly, the remarkable result is
that the sexes agree on nearly all of the ratings they make; the interpretation of
body positions is made from a common basis of shared meanings, and, indeed,
it is likely that life in society might be more complicated were this not so. But
some consistent differences do appear.

TABLE 10–3. Significant Differences between Male and
Female Ratings, by Picture

| Figure | Dimension | M | F | p |
|--------|-----------|------|------|------|
| N/OO | receiving–rejecting | 3.53 | 2.13 | .025 |
| N/OO | self–other-concerned | 3.80 | 5.00 | .05 |
| N/OC | immodest–modest | 4.87 | 3.73 | .025 |
| N/OC | receiving–rejecting | 4.80 | 3.93 | .05 |
| N/SO | cold–warm | 3.47 | 4.80 | .01 |
| N/OS | unyielding–yielding | 3.80 | 4.87 | .05 |
| N/CO | unyielding–yielding | 3.47 | 4.73 | .01 |
| N/CS | active–passive | 4.33 | 5.33 | .05 |

In the table, two figures, N/OO and N/SO, are perceived by the men as less
approachable and welcoming: N/OO is seen as less receiving and more self-
concerned, while N/SO is viewed as more cold. Both are highly uncovered positions, permitting approach directly to the proximal boundary; therefore, there is
a suggestion in these data that men are in some way wary of the openness. In
addition, the full table in Appendix C indicates that men see the open N/OO
as somewhat less warm (p < .10),[6] less yielding (p < .10), and more affected
(p < .20)—and that they like her more than do women (n.s.). Perhaps the best
way to express these differences in scores is to suggest that men especially (but
women also, though less) feel a strong ambivalence toward the most open figure:
attraction on the one hand, but caution and scepticism about the genuineness of
her warmth, receptiveness, and concern for others.

There are other differences which seem to show that men are generally sensitive to rejection: N/OC was rated as more modest and rejecting, N/OS and N/CO as more unyielding. These differences do not seem related to any particular type of figure, and perhaps may be understood as expressing a greater concern with rejection by men because they are more eager to approach in the first place.

One more difference appears; figure N/CS is seen as less passive by the men than by the women. She is one of the figures that presents a covering gesture to the observer, and it appears that men find the position to require more activity than do women. It may be that men generally perceive the closed, covered state of the female body as one requiring activity to establish, while women may see the same state as a more natural, passive stance.

Is there further evidence in the data for this hypothesis? One instance of support comes from the figure that is indisputably the most closed, N/CC. The full table shows her to be perceived as more passive by the women than by the men (p < .20). But if this reasoning is correct, it should apply generally to all the closed figures in the group and not apply (unless, in fact, it is reversed) to the more open. To test this suggestion, an additional analysis of these same data is presented in Table 10–4; in it appear the means of the five figures that exhibit covering gestures (N/CC, N/OC, N/CS, N/CO, N/SC) and the four that are completely uncovered (N/OS, N/OO, N/SS, N/SO).

**Table 10–4. Sex Differences on Defensive Figures (N/CC, N/OC, N/CS, N/CO, N/SC) and on Open Figures ( N/OS, N/OO, N/SS, N/SO)**

| Dimension | Defensive | | p | Open | | p |
|---|---|---|---|---|---|---|
| | M | F | | M | F | |
| natural–unnatural | 4.65 | 4.93 | | 3.92 | 3.72 | |
| immodest–modest | 4.59 | 4.45 | | 3.38 | 3.67 | |
| receiving–rejecting | 4.19 | 4.19 | | 3.37 | 2.92 | .20 |
| self–other-concerned | 3.25 | 3.01 | | 4.18 | 4.45 | |
| cold–warm | 3.37 | 3.41 | | 4.15 | 4.47 | >.10 |
| active–passive | 3.97 | 4.33 | >.20 | 3.22 | 3.30 | |
| dramatic–calm | 3.71 | 3.52 | | 3.38 | 3.82 | >.20 |
| shy–exhibitionistic | 3.64 | 3.57 | | 4.68 | 4.62 | |
| affected–ingenuous | 3.39 | 3.36 | | 3.73 | 4.35 | .10 |
| unyielding–yielding | 4.07 | 4.03 | | 4.43 | 5.50 | .10 |
| pulled toward–pulled away | 4.17 | 4.64 | >.10 | 3.28 | 3.87 | .10 |

Differences between the sexes do appear, and, although none of them individually reach the usual standard of significance, they are all in the direction predicted by this hypothesis. Men rate the defensive positions as more active than women, and no such difference appears among the open figures. As for the latter, women are likely to see them as more receiving, warmer, more ingenuous, and yielding, while men see them as more dramatic; these differences are similar to those observed for figure N/OO alone.[7]

There is some evidence, then, that, for men and women, the meaning of the proximal boundary is different. Female subjects tend to see the open boundary as open in a more genuine (perhaps even other-concerned) sense than do males; the latter appear to mistrust the openness, calling it more dramatic. When closed boundaries are in question, in the women's view they have been arrived at more passively; it is as if women saw the closed boundary as the more natural one. Further data, complementary to the correlational analysis presented earlier, should be consistent with the male–female differences so far outlined.

The other source of data on masculine–feminine differences are the interdimensional correlations. Table 10–5 presents all correlations above ±.57 (p < .025); only one end of each dimension is listed, as in Table 10–2 above. In parentheses are listed matching correlation coefficients for the other sex where those of only the first were significant.

Only one striking agreement between the sexes results from this analysis: Both males and females are attracted toward arm positions they characterize as warm—and to very much the same degree. This datum is consistent with the supposition about what the two sexes appreciate in common; the quality they

**TABLE 10–5. Significant (p < .025) Interdimensional Correlations, by Sex**

|  | Male (N = 15) | Female (N = 15) |
|---|---|---|
| pulled to: receiving | .67 | (.36) |
| warm | .60 | .59 |
| yielding | .57 | (−.15) |
| natural | (.00) | .72 |
| ingenuous | (.21) | .71 |
| shy | (−.21) | .57 |
| shy: passive | .67 | (.48) |
| modest | (.13) | .88 |
| yielding: receiving | .78 | (−.01) |
| other-concern | (.01) | .57 |
| calm: yielding | .60 | (−.12) |
| warm | (.32) | .66 |
| warm: receiving | .57 | (.45) |

Note: In parentheses, matching dimensions not reaching significance.

agree on does not relate to sexual approachability but specifies rather the sublimated one of warmth.

But the number of disagreements in criteria is even more notable. There is one where the criteria are in fact opposed: While men are pulled toward yielding figures, women are somewhat attracted by unyielding ones. Men seem to show that when they claim to be attracted by a figure they suppose that she permits access to her proximal boundary, or possibly further; women claim greater attraction to figures that deny such access. Nevertheless, women, too, appreciate the possibility of some approach; since they speak of attraction to receiving figures (at an admittedly lower level than the men), they must be attracted by the possibility of approaching at least up to some boundary. Their dislike of yielding figures suggests that the boundary must be located farther from the center of the body than is the boundary the men are speaking of. When men say "receiving," they also mean "yielding," but for women those two words are unrelated.

Warmth, although the one shared criterion, is not the most important (for either sex). Women are more strongly pulled towards figures they characterize as natural and as ingenuous, and somewhat less so to figures they see as shy (while men, if anything, prefer the figures to be exhibitionistic); shy figures, for women, are moreover predominantly modest. And warm figures are calm rather than receiving, while for men they are rather receiving.

The male view of female attractiveness, therefore, is rather uncomplicated: Women (to the extent that these pen and ink drawings can stand for them) are attractive when they are yielding, receiving, and warm. For women, the matter is less sexual: Figures are attractive when they are unyielding, and when their human qualities include warmth, naturalness, shyness, and ingenuousness.

Two possible processes may be operating to determine the correlations obtained on female subjects. On the one hand, it is likely that some defenses are put to use against the suspicion of homosexual attraction; on this hypothesis, women feel that they should claim to be attracted only by figures that present no danger of any close approach. One of the female students did in fact ask after the testing session whether we really expected her to say that she was attracted to the different open figures. It would then also follow that only asexual qualities would be given as criteria for attraction and that women would claim much less attraction to the figures than would men.

Chapter 9 emphasized the emotional relation of the viewer to the person represented; this was particularly important in pictures where one figure stood out conspicuously, as in the paintings by Toulouse-Lautrec and Botticelli. But this relation need not have been one of sexual attraction or repulsion; women who talked about *Marcelle Lender* often became more involved than the men, but the process seemed to be one of identification rather than object-choice. Thus, the second process presumed to operate here is one in which the subject takes as the description of attractiveness qualities which she believes characterize her, too. If this is the case, then one comes up against genuine (rather than defensively determined) sex differences in the criteria of attractiveness. According to this interpretation, women in this culture do not believe that in order to be attractive they need be open and yielding; they are attractive when they retain quite a bit of their boundaries and remain natural, shy, and ingenuous. Evidence already presented supports this interpretation: Men saw the *closing* of the proximal boundary as requiring activity; this suggested differences in the perception of the "natural" state of the feminine body.

## SUMMARY

The exploratory interviews on Botticelli's Venus pointed to some of the presentational meanings of covering arms: They rendered the figure self-centered and rejecting, unnatural and affected. This chapter confirms this description nearly to the letter. As far as openness is concerned, it was most clearly embodied in a figure that was also seen as immodest, exhibitionistic, and active; but it was put to best use in the figure also rated as natural, calm, warm, and receiving. The former figure was as receiving as the latter but did not attract the subjects; either her histrionic mien made her objectionable, or her excessive openness rendered her frightening. Nevertheless, warmth and naturalness were criteria by which a figure was judged attractive; thus, openness as such did not guarantee that the beholder would wish to approach. The effect of openness and enclosure by *both* arms turned out to be generally greater than that produced by one arm; in this sense, the properties determined by each arm position were additive.

The decision to study permission or denial of access to body space as a crucial variable in determining the expressive meaning of body positions now appears justified. Although it is true that most of the ratings were made to deal with this variable, and might be expected to produce an exaggerated view of its importance, it does not seem likely that the effects were arbitrarily created by the choice of dimensions. At the very least, one can say that, when subjects are asked to make discriminations between figures on openness, they are readily capable of doing so and, more importantly, can agree on what properties they derive from it.

The analysis of extreme figures revealed a bodily analog to the deformation of facial expression known as the grimace. Kris (1952) describes grimaces as facial configurations expressing contradictory affects; since the figures here judged as the most unnatural expressed conflict between covering and uncovering, or contradiction between pointing towards and away from the body, their positions may appropriately be called *bodily grimaces*.

The analysis of male–female differences provided information about the explicit sexual meanings these positions convey. Male subjects reported attraction to figures that were yielding, receiving, and warm; that is, to figures that allowed approach and promised to respond with warmth. Female subjects, on the other hand, described themselves as attracted to unyielding, shy, natural, warm, and ingenuous figures, thus removing sexual approach from their criteria. One may wonder that the most attractive figure for each sex turned out to be the same; it is as if she embodied all these criteria, while the other figures allowed the differences to come through. The feminine population made more of an issue of the proximal boundary than did the masculine; they reported greater contrasts between the open and closed positions and thus showed themselves more sensitive to changes in the ways the proximal boundary is handled. For women, a closed boundary also required less activity to establish than it did for men, a fact which suggested that the two sexes assumed different degrees of openness as natural. Finally, the ratings reflected genuine differences in criteria of attractiveness, and suggested the possibility that they represented defenses against homosexual feelings or the implied accusation of homosexual attraction.

It may well be asked at this point whether these findings can be generalized to interaction with real women in real situations. It is certainly difficult to guarantee that these observations apply to concrete interactions. Even in descriptions of paintings, many cues interact with those analyzed here and perhaps alter their presentational meaning, such as cues from facial expression, from the bodily or facial expression of other interacting figures, from clothes, and from the background. None of these played a role in this study. Yet it seems probable that, as far as bodily presentation is concerned, the variables treated here are applicable in social situations, although details may well change. Perhaps a given gesture will be perceived as more or less inviting in different contexts; perhaps its invitingness will appear unnatural or justified; and possibly the same gesture in the "same" context will be rated at a different point on the "open–closed" continuum in different cultures. But, while one would expect both the situation and the cultural meanings to effect changes in the *absolute* level of the meanings of openness and enclosure, one would expect *relative* changes in the openness of positions, particularly in time, to carry very similar meanings with most humans. Quite independently of testing for this type of cross-cultural uniformity, research that more closely approximates social situations should be carried out, *using these variables*. The stimuli could be photographs, cinematographic records, or even observations done through one-way mirrors, or in natural social situations themselves.

# NOTES FOR CHAPTER 10

[1] In fact, some were paid; we ran three other groups of subjects, some paid, some not, well after the first. The second group were tested on Series D, on the comparison of Series H and G, and on a retest of Series S; a small part of this group also judged Series H and are included in this analysis. The third group rated Series L; the fourth, Series K and Series P.

[2] Our reason for using interdimensional correlations was originally to weed out superfluous dimensions. We thought that if two dimensions correlated very highly, their meaning would be nearly identical; hence, one could be eliminated. After the first presentation of the material, which was intended as a pretest, we discovered no correlation above .59 for the total sample, and decided to retain all the dimensions we had started with. Since we changed nothing else in Series H between presentations, we also included the "pretest" results with the final ones. It did, however, become apparent that correlations of the order of .41 (p < .025) and higher would give us some information about the meaning of each member of the correlated pairs; and, in particular, that correlations between the dimension of attractiveness and all the others would tell us what the criteria of attraction were. We shall comment below on the use of intercorrelations for the analysis of meaning.

[3] From here on, we shall use the following descriptive code to label these figures: N will stand for the nude state, C for the clothed; O will refer to the open-arm position, S to the at-side position, and C to the covering position. Thus, N/OC will mean Nude/Open–Covering (arm on viewer's left Open, on the viewer's right Covering, as in figure H48), while N/CO refers to the Nude/Covering–Open figure H78, and C/OO refers to the Clothed/Open–Open figure G40, encountered in the next chapter.

[4] This statement is true only in an ideal sense; that is, when the correlation remains high irrespective of the figure to which it is applied. In practice, the correlation depends on the finite number of contexts in which it is used. Thus, when one examines interdimensional correlations for the different drawings separately, entirely different dimensions may be seen to correlate. The reader should keep in mind that when we say "meaning," we refer to meaning for this population of nine figures.

[5] A problem arises in the selection of the relevant end. In most cases, it does not matter; the meaning is unaltered. In other cases, a choice must be made. We have chosen the end which made "better" sense. The reader may, if he wishes, also read into the table the unmentioned dimension ends; or he may reverse one of the dimensions and read the correlation as negative, as in "pulled to–affected: − .49."

[6] We must explain the conditions under which we use the comparatives "less" and "more." We call a score "less shy" when it is closer to the neutral point from the shy end of a dimension than another score; we say "more exhibitionistic" when it is farther from the neutral point and in the same direction as the first score, or when it crosses to the other side from the first score. This will be our practice throughout.

[7] A more general statement may be made about these sex differences: Because they see the open figures as warmer and more receiving, women perceive the contrast between the open and covered positions as greater than men. Appendix C–1 shows this finding to be general across a number of the dimensions, in that, on 7 of the 11 dimensions, women perceive the greater contrast, while men see a larger contrast on only one. It may be suggested, therefore, that women are the more sensitive to changes in the proximal boundary. That this is not due to the commonly observed tendency of women to make more decisive and extreme ratings (see, for example, Wallach and Kogan, 1959) will be shown in the next chapter.

# 11. Venus Clothed

The previous chapter gathered evidence for the importance of spatial boundaries in determining the expressiveness of the nude body. Clearly, the presence of covering arms transformed an open and receiving figure into a cold, rejecting, enclosed one; and the extreme opening of the arms rendered her immodest and exhibitionistic. Practical considerations lead one to wonder whether all this arm use has any effect, let alone pertinence, in everyday attire, or whether the effect is confined to nude figures.

This question has theoretical as well as practical importance. One may ask, for example, whether the presence of clothes makes any protection of the sort observed in the last chapter unnecessary, and, in the eyes of the observer, superfluous or even ridiculous. Since the covering hand also, in a way, calls attention to the part covered, the pointing might take over and produce awkward effects when the covering function is performed by clothes. Or, possibly, simple "additiveness" of the properties of the clothes and the arms might merely reinforce the effects already observed. There is a theoretical interest in discovering whether one is simply adding effects or creating new forms when one clothes Botticelli's Venus.

Of various possible "plain" styles of clothing one was chosen that avoided a skirt length below the knee (to avoid suggesting a formal occasion), a collar (that could indicate too much "character" of one sort or another), and sleeves (which might present clues to a woman's age or, again, to "character"). All these details of dress and others appeared too closely tied to roles and situations. A dress that was sleeveless, collarless, of knee length, and comfortably straight was chosen for clothing Venus because it was deemed to present a minimum of cultural clues.

It seemed superfluous to repeat the analysis with all nine of the figures previously used. The effects sought would probably be elicited in their fullest range by the extremely open figures (N/OO), the most closed one (N/CC), and two figures in between (N/SS and N/CS). To insure comparability of judgment from the unclothed to the clothed version, each subject was presented with both the nude and clothed figures—but separated, with the unclothed at the beginning of a long test booklet [1] and the clothed at the end; this was intended to lessen the possibility of the nude figures' appearing undressed.[2] The original answer sheet appeared satisfactory although two dimensions had to be added: (1) a further, direct measure of *approachability* that would hopefully discriminate approach to the axial–proximal boundary from receptivity, which could imply progress beyond it; and (2) a measure that would enable the subject to judge whether the presenting position was *appropriate* or not (with the choice of situation left to his imagination). It seemed likely that the dimension of appropriateness might better describe possible incongruities between the presence of clothes and the addition of covering gestures than any of the dimensions already used.

There were 41 subjects, nearly equally distributed between Harvard and Radcliffe college students; all were new to the test. The series is called H and G (G representing the clothed figures), and it retains the same pose identification numbers as before.

Were the ratings of the four unclothed figures substantially the same as in the earlier presentation? It was imperative that the ratings should have substantial repeat reliability. From a comparison of mean scores in the two presentations, one might anticipate this finding: that the absolute level of some scores would shift because of a change in context (only 4 figures in the second series as opposed to 9 in the first), but that the relative rankings of the four figures on each dimension would remain much the same. A one-way analysis of variance for differences between presentations for the 4 figures on the 11 comparable dimensions revealed 11 significant differences of 44 possible ($p < .05$; see Appendix D for complete table). On the other hand, when the four figures were ranked from lowest to highest on each dimension (see Appendix D), strictly identical rankings resulted in each presentation. Thus, the effect of the reduced context in the second presentation was to shift some scores absolutely but to preserve the same ratings relative to the other figures.

Given this stability across presentations, one may analyze the changes in scores that result from the addition of clothes. The comparisons will, in each case, be made between ratings given to the figures only on the second presentation, that is, by the same subjects for series H as for series G. An analysis of variance for correlated means is, therefore, appropriate.

It may be well to begin with the figure that displays the greatest degree of openness: N/OO and C/OO. The comparison is illustrated so that the reader

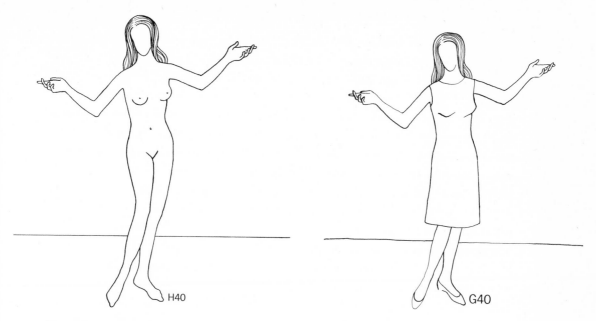

**Fig. 32.** Venus With Open Arms, Nude and Clothed

may form his own idea of the qualitative difference that may exist between the clothed and unclothed versions (see Fig. 32). The mean scores these two figures received appear in Table 11–1.[3] Differences significant beyond that .05

**Table 11–1. Mean Ratings on Unclothed and Clothed Figures OO (All Subjects)**

|  | C/OO<br>N = 20 | N/OO<br>N = 20 |
|---|---|---|
| natural–unnatural | 4.05 | 3.85 |
| immodest–modest | 2.60 | 3.30° |
| receiving–rejecting | 2.85 | 3.30 |
| self-concerned–other-concerned | 4.40 | 3.20* |
| cold–warm | 4.70 | 4.30 |
| active–passive | 2.80 | 2.80 |
| dramatic–calm | 2.40 | 2.20 |
| approachable–unapproachable | 2.55 | 3.30° |
| shy–exhibitionistic | 5.65 | 5.45 |
| affected–ingenuous | 3.15 | 3.10 |
| unyielding–yielding | 5.05 | 4.15° |
| appropriate–inappropriate to situation | 4.16 | 3.63° |
| pulled toward–pulled away | 3.85 | 4.50° |

\* p < .05
° difference of ±.50, not significant

level are marked with an asterisk; those not reaching significance, but above ±.50, are indicated by a circle.

The only significant difference occurs in the dimension of self- or other-concern: The clothed figure C/OO is rated considerably more self-concerned than the nude. A less-than-significant difference occurs on the yielding dimension: Again, the clothed figure is judged as less yielding than the unclothed. So far, then, the expectation of additiveness has been confirmed and the presentation of clothing has indeed added a further barrier to approach. Other (smaller) differences support this interpretation: The clothed figure is seen as more modest and as more unapproachable; and subjects feel more repelled by her than by the nude. But all these differences appear to contribute to the following qualitative one: The clothed figure's position is judged as more appropriate to the situation than that of the nude. This seems consistent with the reduction in her openness; since that was extreme in the original presentation (and carried with it the opprobrium of immodesty), it is here made socially acceptable by the presence of clothes. The clothed figure still retains an air of exhibitionism and drama; in this, her clothes have changed nothing. But the clothing provides the figure with a social role and she becomes accordingly more modest and appropriate.

There are similar differences for a less-open figure, N/CS and C/CS (whose right arm covers her breast while the left hangs at her side); her scores are presented in Table 11–2. The significant difference here is on the modesty dimen-

**TABLE 11–2. Mean Ratings on Unclothed and Clothed Figures CS (All Subjects)**

|  | N/CS | C/CS |
| --- | --- | --- |
|  | N = 21 | N = 21 |
| natural–unnatural | 3.60 | 3.29 |
| immodest–modest | 3.10 | 4.62* |
| receiving–rejecting | 2.71 | 3.19 |
| self-concerned–other-concerned | 4.33 | 4.05 |
| cold–warm | 5.05 | 4.48° |
| active–passive | 3.48 | 3.81 |
| dramatic–calm | 4.19 | 3.48° |
| approachable–unapproachable | 2.38 | 2.76 |
| shy–exhibitionistic | 4.52 | 4.10 |
| affected–ingenuous | 3.62 | 3.48 |
| unyielding–yielding | 5.48 | 4.67° |
| appropriate–inappropriate to situation | 3.48 | 3.00 |
| pulled toward–pulled away | 3.00 | 3.62° |

* $p < .001$

° difference of ±.50, not significant

sion: The clothed version is again seen as more modest than the nude—and by a sizable score. But the former also appears as slightly colder, more unyielding, and more repellent. All these differences again indicate that an added boundary has been established.

One difference not accounted for simply by the addition of boundary properties is the fact that the clothed *C/CS* appears as slightly more dramatic than the nude *N/CS*. If it is true that the defensive intention of her covering gesture has become superfluous, as indicated in Table 11–2, then the main function of that arm position is to point to the area covered by the hand. It is likely that the gesture thus becomes one of exaggerated surprise (the "Oh, no!" reaction in the Gauguin picture). On this interpretation, the gesture may still act as a barrier—to information that a person refuses to take in—although the barrier would be more symbolic than real; or, alternatively, the gesture might serve to point to the breast, where a deep inhalation has just taken place. Or, perhaps more simply, it is perceived as indicating modesty that has become excessive: It would be genuinely modest in function were the figure nude, but here it protests too much. The increase in perceived dramatic quality is not accompanied by an increase in exhibitionism; perhaps the clothed figure is understood as merely calling attention to her modesty without showing off any more of herself.

Another figure, relatively intermediate on openness, by far the most attractive to the subjects of the preceding chapter, was *N/SS*. The scores for the clothed and nude versions are presented in Table 11–3. Surprisingly, there are few differences, although two of the three which do appear are consistent with

**TABLE 11–3. Mean Ratings on Unclothed and Clothed Figures SS (All Subjects)**

|  | *N/SS*<br>*N = 20* | *C/SS*<br>*N = 20* |
|---|---|---|
| natural–unnatural | 3.65 | 3.85 |
| immodest–modest | 4.95 | 5.65° |
| receiving–rejecting | 3.35 | 3.00 |
| self-concerned–other-concerned | 3.65 | 3.00° |
| cold–warm | 4.45 | 4.35 |
| active–passive | 4.80 | 5.05 |
| dramatic–calm | 5.00 | 5.10 |
| approachable–unapproachable | 2.80 | 3.00 |
| shy–exhibitionistic | 2.70 | 2.45 |
| affected–ingenuous | 4.25 | 4.15 |
| unyielding–yielding | 5.40 | 5.10 |
| appropriate–inappropriate to situation | 3.47 | 4.16° |
| pulled toward–pulled away | 3.35 | 3.40 |

° difference of ±.50, not significant

what is now known of boundary properties. Thus, the clothed version is again seen as more modest, on the one hand (this difference approaches the .05 level), and slightly more self-concerned on the other. It would appear that boundaries have again been reinforced by the presence of clothes. But it is also noteworthy that the clothed figure is seen as slightly less appropriate to the situation than the nude, a curious difference. It may be that, as with all the clothed figures, the viewer more readily imagined the figure in a role or a setting and judged accordingly. In such a case, the slightly cocked head may appear somewhat affected or the right hand may appear removed enough from the body to be in readiness for some sort of action. Surprisingly, the scores for attraction remain the same in both versions; here, whatever boundary effect may have existed was clearly nullified by other unknown factors.

The final comparison shows the effect of the presence of clothes on the most rejecting of the previous chapter's figures, $N/CC$ (see Fig. 33). One might expect the meaning of defensive gestures to be the most subject to change with the addition of the boundary of clothes; the data are presented in Table 11–4.

The largest difference occurs in the ratings of the appropriateness of the two positions: The clothed figure is perceived as much more inappropriate to the situation than her nude colleague. A difference of this magnitude goes far towards confirming the speculation made at the beginning of this chapter that defensive gestures may become superfluous in the clothed condition and lead the subject to see them as ridiculous. Further support of this interpretation comes

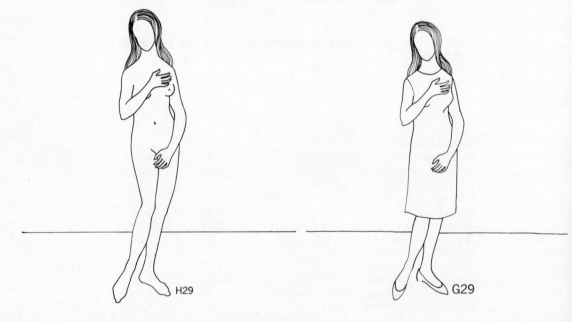

**Fig. 33.** Venus With Covering Arms, Nude and Clothed

TABLE 11–4. Mean Ratings on Unclothed and Clothed Figures CC
(All Subjects)

|  | N/CC<br>N = 21 | C/CC<br>N = 21 |
|---|---|---|
| natural–unnatural | 4.33 | 5.95** |
| immodest–modest | 5.81 | 5.23 |
| receiving–rejecting | 4.47 | 4.90 |
| self–other-concerned | 2.38 | 2.05 |
| cold–warm | 3.43 | 2.76° |
| active–passive | 5.24 | 4.86 |
| dramatic–calm | 4.43 | 2.95** |
| approachable–unapproachable | 3.90 | 4.76° |
| shy–exhibitionistic | 2.48 | 3.05° |
| affected–ingenuous | 4.71 | 3.67° |
| unyielding–yielding | 4.24 | 3.48° |
| appropriate–inappropriate to situation | 3.67 | 5.81*** |
| pulled toward–pulled away | 3.50 | 5.10* |

\* p < .05
\*\* p < .01
\*\*\* p < .001
° difference of ±.50, not significant

from the fact that the clothed version is again rated as considerably more dramatic than the nude. This figure out-does *C/CS*, whose right hand also rested on her breast; she points to her genital area and appears to call attention to it, and the gesture, as a consequence, appears not only more dramatic, but more unnatural and somewhat more affected (p > .05). Finally, the clothed figure moves away from a very shy rating in the direction of an exhibitionistic one. All five differences indicate qualitative changes in the perception of what is being presented by these defensive arm positions.

Conversely, other changes are consistent with the addition of boundary properties. The subjects felt considerably more repelled by the clothed figure and perceived her (though not significantly) as more unapproachable, unyielding, and cold. Thus, both qualitative and quantitative changes may be observed to take place as a result of the changes created by adding a new boundary, a dress. But, here, the qualitative changes in the scores in Table 11–4 generally exceed the quantitative ones; this did not occur with the other figures.

It is interesting to examine again the differences between men and women in the perception of these changes. The clearest measure of these differences and one that does not duplicate the analysis of the preceding chapter is the contribution each sex makes to the changes described above; a one-way analysis of variance can be used to measure the significance of differences in these contributions. The data are presented fully in Appendix E.

Figures without covering gestures (OO and SS) and those with at least one (CS and CC) produce quite different results; the former two show no significant male–female differences and very few of any magnitude whatever. The latter, on the other hand, indicate that men and women perceive the changes from the nude to the clothed state in different but consistent ways: Men see the clothed C/CS as relatively more unapproachable and shy (p < .05) and unyielding (p < .01) than do women; and, if one looks at non-significant differences greater than ±1.00, they also see her as relatively more cold and passive. As for figure C/CC, men again perceive her as relatively more inappropriate to the situation than women (p < .05) and as more unyielding (n.s.). Both figures, when clothed, appear to men as more rejecting and self-concerned; finally, men feel relatively much more repelled by the clothed figures than by the nude (these differences short of significance).[4]

An initial suggestion for interpreting these differences is that men are more sensitive to changes from the nude state to the clothed than women; the additive and qualitative changes discussed earlier in this chapter appear greater to male than to female subjects. In the two drawings where covering gestures are present, the presence of clothing seems to alert the men's sensitivity to greater rejection, unyielding, self-concern, inappropriateness, and lack of attraction on the part of the clothed women. However, there are two possible sources of such differences in the judgments made by men and women. If the differences are greater between sex ratings of the clothed figure, then it would be correct to speak of greater sensitivity (on the part of the male) to the consequences of additional, closed boundaries; if they occur in the nude version, one should speak of greater sensitivity to the openness of boundaries. The data indicate that the sex differences are generally greater for the unclothed figures than for the clothed, thus supporting the latter formulation. But it does remain true that men are more sensitive to the contrast between the clothed and nude states, while women, as the data of Chapter 10 indicate, seem more sensitive to changes in arm positions.

To sum up, clothing Venus has produced the two types of changes anticipated. On the one hand, the proximal boundary was strengthened and this effect elicited attributes associated with stronger boundaries: greater modesty, self-concern, rejection, and coldness. On the other, qualitative changes occurred which were caused by the superfluity of covering gestures when the proximal boundary was already adequately defended: increased inappropriateness, dramatic quality, and unnaturalness. Consistent with these results is the fact that the most open figure (C/OO) gained, rather than lost, in appropriateness to the situation; her completely open proximal boundary only profited from the additional covering. This stresses the change in function of covering arms; those of the original Venus, when superimposed on a covered boundary, appeared to point rather than cover.

Men and women differed consistently in their perception of the differences between the clothed and nude versions of figures *OO* and *SS*; men saw the changes as greater than did women. The differences were best accounted for by differing evaluations of the nude figures rather than divergences in the perceptions of the clothed. Nevertheless, there remained the suggestion in the data that men were more sensitive than women to the consequences of the addition or removal of clothes, an interpretation that contrasts with the importance that the boundary properties of arm positions assumed for women in the preceding chapter.

## NOTES FOR CHAPTER 11

[1] The booklet also contained Series D, a second run on Series P, and an additional run on S. The figures were no longer randomized; in short series, the "stroboscopic" effect would seem to disappear, while in the remaining ones it appeared negligible.

[2] See the discussion of this distinction in Chapter 9.

[3] To shorten the very long test booklets, we split this Series, as well as Series D, in two. Thus, twenty or twenty-one subjects rated each picture. In Tables 11–1 through 11–4, the subjects in the left and right columns are identical.

[4] These differences are not due to any overall sex differences in variability of ratings. Men and women have substantially the same standard deviations of means in the nude and clothed versions, and very much the same standard deviations of differences between those means.

# 12. Presentations of Apollo

The questions that pertain to the presentations of the nude male figure are for the most part the same as those asked of the transformations of Venus, with a few differences suggested by psychoanalytic descriptions of masculinity such as those of Erikson (1963). The common ground consists of the dimensions of defensiveness and self-centeredness which, with the Venus, varied directly with the barriers she erected against approach. These dimensions were in a sense onesided: They emphasized feminine passivity and receptiveness, and, although this emphasis resulted from some of the most striking findings of the exploratory study rather than from any notions we may have entertained about the essential qualities of female body presentation, passivity and receptiveness did, nevertheless, turn out to be attributes that the subjects describing the figures were comfortable with. They were comfortable with them perhaps because feminine nature is indeed more passive, or perhaps because they conceived of feminine nature as passive and found the conception useful, or perhaps because in visual representation the passive feminine body is easy for the artist to portray and for the public to understand. Whatever the reasons may be, it is a remarkable fact that Kenneth Clark, in his excellent analysis of the portrayal of the nude (1959), described very many more female nudes that were passive objects of contemplation rather than active subjects of action.

It is different with the male body. Although the perfection of the male form was also studied, in classical Greek sculpture, in calm athletes (all forms of the theme of Apollo as the god of light, reason, and calm, in Clark's formulation), the most frequent departures from the body-between-two-states-of-motion were males not females. Besides discussing the calm representation of Apollo, Clark presents descriptions of the portrayal of energy and pathos—and most of his examples are male. Energetic figures move through the space they occupy, intrude

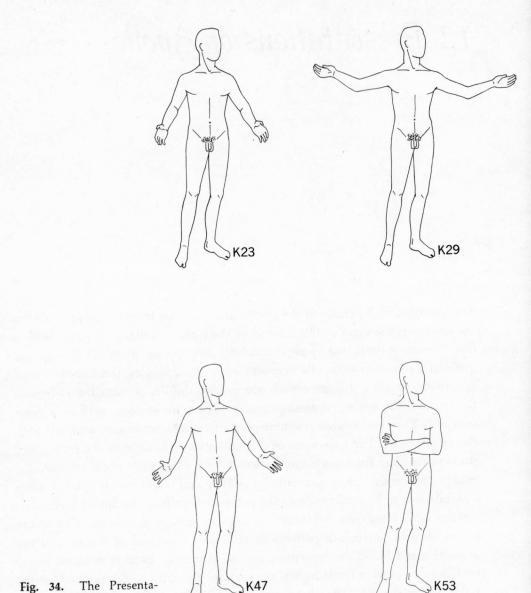

**Fig. 34.** The Presentations of Apollo

into it, command it; pathetic figures frequently put effort into twisting and turning. It is true that some female nudes also move vigorously, especially when dancing (in the representation of what Clark labels ecstasy), but, on the whole, movement and tension seem to be characteristically depicted as masculine qualities.

While the primary aim here was to elaborate on the attributes communicated by display and defense, as with the Venus, the experiment also made some

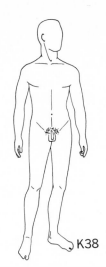
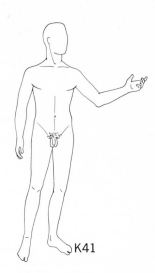

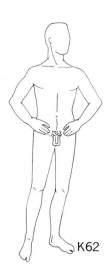

attempt to give the drawn male figures a greater firmness of stance and some intrusiveness into the circumambient space. The figure that is the subject of this chapter is related to the "Apollo" from Eleusis, the Bronze Statuette of Youth in the Louvre, or Agias from Delphi (see pose K38); unlike these prototypes, its stance is reversed from left to right and its hips do not protrude. Its legs differ from those of the Venus by being farther apart with heels to the ground, thus assuring a firmer stance. The arms differ, first, by not covering the chest, second, by occasionally intruding into lateral or anterior space, third, by being at times placed behind the body so as to expose the arm and chest muscles and the genitals, and fourth, by being crossed on the chest in one picture and planted on the hips in another (see poses K53 and K62 in Fig. 34). Eight of the dimensions used in the Venus study were again used here; the central question asked in this chapter is, therefore, whether the body positions communicating those attributes are also similar. One dimension not retained was "affected–ingenuous"; although one can see how a male position may appear affected, one has more difficulty summoning up a body image of male ingenuousness. Another dimension was altered: "receiving–rejecting" became "receiving–giving," in order to give an active scope to the ratings. Three dimensions intended to measure attributes important to male figures were added: "effeminate–virile," "strong–weak," and "imperious–humble." As before, the subjects also rated each figure on attraction, the degree to which they felt pulled toward or away from it.

The subjects were 19 men and 24 women, undergraduates at the University of Colorado (most tables will contain data on only the first 19 women); each rated each of the ten figures. The results will be presented in an order similar to that of the Venus series, with an overall comparison of arm position types first, a discussion of extreme figures second, a presentation of the dimensional intercorrelations third, and a comparison of men and women fourth.

The ten drawings may be divided into three groups according to arm position: those in which the arms cover part of the body (K53, K62, K68), those in which the arms hang at the side or are clasped at the back (K32, K38, K59), and those in which the arms are extended away from the body, either laterally or in front (K23, K29, K41). (Note: K47 is not included because its presence in the series had a special purpose.) This grouping is not as regular as for the Venus pictures, where the increase in the exposure of the anterior proximal space was stepwise; nor is the grouping two-dimensional, since this time the right and left arms were not manipulated systematically. But it does proceed from maximal defense to maximal exposure, at least on visual inspection, and one can examine the mean scores received by these three groups of pictures on each of the thirteen dimensions to see whether the attributes measured are a function of exposure. For tests of statistical significance, t-tests were calculated for each of the possible comparison pairs (covering vs. at-side, covering vs. extended, and at-side vs. extended). The means of the three groups are presented below, while the significance tests are listed in Appendix F.

Table 12–1 shows that, on the dimension "natural–unnatural," the picture groups do not differ appreciably; the covering and at-side positions are judged as equally natural and the extended position is seen as neutral (the extended position differs significantly from the other two). The amount of exposure of

TABLE 12–1. Mean Scores of Groups of Drawings, by Rating Dimensions (N = 38)

| | *"Natural–unnatural"* | *"Immodest–modest"* | *"Receiving–giving"* | *"Self-concerned–other-concerned"* |
|---|---|---|---|---|
| *Covering* | 3.40 | 4.07 | 4.08 | 2.68 |
| *At side* | 3.26 | 4.03 | 3.53 | 3.47 |
| *Extended* | 4.03 | 2.94 | 3.59 | 4.54 |

the anterior proximal boundary *as such* does not determine naturalness, at least in these groups of pictures, although in individual positions it will be seen later to make a difference. On the dimension "immodest–modest," however, the differences are both greater and more systematic. The extended position is the most immodest and differs significantly from the other two positions, which are neutral and do not differ from each other. It is interesting to note that arms at the side (or back) create a more modest position on the whole than extended arms, in spite of the equal exposure of the genital area; therefore, it appears that exposure itself does not determine immodesty so much as the way in which that exposure is called to attention.

The dimension "receiving–giving" again does not differentiate the figure groups appreciably; the extended and at-side positions are somewhat receiving, as one might expect, and the covering position is neutral (and different from the other two). No position appears really giving; it may be suggested tentatively that this is a measure of the degree to which these figures are objects of contemplation for the observers rather than subjects of action, or, more precisely, a measure of the degree to which these arm positions can indicate the passive quality of receptiveness (when open) or its lack (when covering), but not the active attribute of giving. "Self-concern–other-concern," however, is well expressed by these arm positions: Increasing other-concern is shown by increasing exposure of the proximal boundary (all differences are significant). On this dimension, the results are perfectly parallel to those of the Venus series, and, as with Venus, indicate further that the extended arms appear to open up the body more to interaction with the observer than does the merely uncovered proximal boundary.

The dimension "effeminate–virile" (see Table 12–2) provides results that appear straightforward here but will later receive more complex interpretation. Although all figures are judged virile, the more they expose the proximal boundary, the more virile they are judged (all differences are significant). Tentatively, one may suggest that virility here is not merely a question of the exposure of the genital area, since all the at-side positions are exposed but are not judged as possessing as much virility as are the extended positions; rather, virility results from the openness to interaction that the extended arms permit, or from some other factor not yet identified. Coldness and warmth appear to differentiate the figures in the same manner as did self-concern and effeminacy: The covering figures are the coldest, as they were the most self-concerned and effeminate; the at-side positions are in the middle; and the extended figures are the warmest, as they were the most other-concerned and virile (all differences are significant). Increasing openness to approach by others again serves to indicate warmth, as is quite natural; and that dimension tentatively appears closely related to other-concern and virility.

TABLE 12–2. Mean Scores of Groups of Drawings, by Rating Dimensions (N = 38)

|  | "Effeminate–virile" | "Cold–warm" | "Strong–weak" | "Dramatic–calm" |
|---|---|---|---|---|
| Covering | 4.21 | 3.26 | 3.69 | 4.07 |
| At side | 4.54 | 3.90 | 3.54 | 4.63 |
| Extended | 5.36 | 4.73 | 2.72 | 3.00 |

Figures with extended arms also appear the strongest, while those with arms at the side or covering are less strong (the latter two do not differ from each other). Here, it appears that the relation between strength and openness is again not simple; an examination of individual figures will later show that strength may be shown by certain figures with covering arms as well as by figures with arms extended. The dimension "dramatic–calm" shows a curvilinear relation to openness: The most dramatic figures extend their arms, as one would expect, but after them come the figures with arms covering; most calm are those with arms at the side (all differences are significant). The extended arms, it would appear, have a histrionic, declaiming, "theatrical" quality which is well-known but the covering arms are *also* departures from calm. Unlike the covering arms of the Venus, those of the Apollo do not necessarily perform a useful hiding function; when crossed on the chest, or when akimbo, their function may also be "expressive" in some manner not yet clear.

"Activity–passivity" is related to openness of boundaries in the same manner as the preceding dimension: Figures with arms extended are the most active, those with arms covering somewhat passive, and those with arms at the side most passive (see Table 12–3; all differences are significant). One may presume these results to mean that the at-side position takes the least activity to assume, the extended the most, while the covering takes some; or that these differences indicate the amount of "expressing" or "presenting" that the positions imply. Shyness and exhibitionism are related in a clear-cut manner to openness of boundaries, in that the figures with arms extended are (significantly) the most exhibitionistic, while the other two positions are somewhat shy. Here, it is important to note that simple exposure of the genital area, as among the at-side figures, does not suffice to make a figure exhibitionistic, any more than to make it immodest; the latter two qualities, as will be seen later, depend more on the use to which exposure is put than on the fact of exposure itself.

**TABLE 12–3. Mean Scores of Groups of Drawings, by Rating Dimensions (N = 38)**

|  | "Active–<br>passive" | "Shy–exhi-<br>bitionistic" | "Unyielding–<br>yielding" | "Imperious–<br>humble" | "Pulled to–<br>pulled away |
|---|---|---|---|---|---|
| *Covering* | 4.37 | 3.83 | 3.49 | 3.76 | 4.66 |
| *At side* | 4.66 | 3.59 | 4.27 | 4.29 | 4.33 |
| *Extended* | 2.53 | 4.95 | 4.24 | 3.53 | 3.89 |

"Yielding–unyielding" is again linearly related to the use of body boundaries: As the boundaries open, the figure comes to be perceived as increasingly yielding (although the difference between at-side and extended is not significant). On this dimension, the results are parallel to those obtained with the Venus figures. Imperiousness is once more curvilinear, being primarily embodied in figures with extended arms, secondarily in figures with arms covering, and least (but not significantly so) in figures with arms at side; among these groupings of pictures, imperiousness is therefore close to exhibitionism, activity, and drama.

Finally, the "attraction–repulsion" dimension is also directly tied to exposure of proximal boundaries, since the most attractive figures extend their arms, the next most attractive allow the arms to hang at the side (but do not differ significantly from the former), and the least attractive cover the body (and differ from both the former). One may tentatively conclude that the permission or invitation to approach determines the degree to which subjects will feel pulled toward the figure in question.

In summary, as the proximal boundary becomes more open and approach to the body is increasingly permitted, the male figures come to be perceived as more other-concerned, virile, and warm (with full statistical significance); and as more unnatural, immodest, strong, yielding, and attractive (with less than full significance). On other dimensions, the changes in scores are closer to curvilinear, however: the at-side (middle) position is seen as most receiving, calm, passive, shy, and humble, with the other two positions at the opposite poles and sometimes joining. But this analysis is rough and glosses over certain differences between individual figures.

To one who expects a very small number of drawings to account for the extreme positions, as with unclothed Venus, the full table of mean scores received by each figure (in Appendix G) is disappointing. This series lacks the simple additivity of properties which resulted in $N/OO$, the most open figure, and $N/CC$, the most closed, being so frequently perceived as most opposed. With the exception of two male figures, K38 (arms at side) and K47 (palms turned out), each of the drawings receives some extreme rating and only one receives as many as eight.

The first figure, K23 (arms extended toward observer), was intended to appear receptive and welcoming; the scores it received even surpassed these expectations and made of the figure a rather ideally masculine one. It was seen as the most virile, warm, and strong Apollo, as the second most other-concerned and yielding, and as the one to which the subjects felt the most attracted. Most important about the location of its arms is probably the clarity of the space they define; unlike the mere and extreme openness of K29 (arms open), the arms extend toward the viewer and outline a space into which or toward which he may move. The arms do not simply indicate that the anterior proximal boundary is open, they provide an invitation but, at the same time, limit the approach to what might be called "social" distance, and leave the observer feeling comfortable because an invitation was made to him that is welcoming but not drastic enough to arouse defensiveness. In addition, the figure probably indicates a certain amount of effort spent in raising the arms to that height and, at the same time, a measure of restraint in not flailing them about (as does K29). The quality of measured expenditure of energy probably accounts for the figure's virility and for part of its attractiveness.

K29, on the other hand, is the most unnatural and immodest, dramatic and exhibitionistic; he is the second most active and imperious, and, on the whole, he is one of the less attractive figures, although not extremely so. One should point out once more that immodesty and exhibitionism have to do not with exposure of the proximal boundary in general and the genital area in particular, but with the extreme way in which that exposure is called to attention. The unnatural quality is probably caused by the very highly upraised arms, which either have little discernible function or indicate exaggeration (as if the length they were indicating were too large to be encompassed by merely stretching them maximally). Its lack of attractiveness is consistent with the unattractiveness of female figure $N/OO$, and probably may be taken to support the notion, adumbrated above, that the maximally open body discourages interaction by inviting too extreme a form of it.[2]

Figure K32 (hands behind back), fully exposes his proximal boundary but, surprisingly, was rated as the most calm, and as the second most modest and passive, shy and humble. These ratings are the best evidence so far for the unimportance of simple exposure of the front of the body for immodesty and exhibitionism; the genital area is fully visible but the manner in which it is exposed allows the pose to be viewed as passive and modest, one which the figure might strike in order to stand comfortably (as in response to the command, "At ease"). In comparison with a fully clothed figure, it is likely, of course, that this stance would be seen as immodest; in this context, however, no attempt at exhibition is apparent.

The drawing most similar to the preferred female $N/SS$ is K38 (arms at side). It was also similarly perceived: It is the second most natural and virile, and one of the three most attractive ones. Where virility appeared to be the consequence of controlled expenditure of effort in drawing K23 (arms extended toward observer), here, it seems a function of unhurried readiness for action; it is probably not a simple result of the relaxed pose, since the previous picture, K32 (hands behind back), was calm and natural but not virile. It may be suggested that the distance of the hands from the body plays an important role, too. A closer positioning would point back toward the body and probably indicate self-absorption; and it may further be proposed that such self-absorption, particularly when it takes the form of a sensuous interest in one's skin, is characteristically thought to be effeminate, and, therefore, proper for women but strongly censured in men. Such speculation requires further testing.

Picture K41 (one arm at side, one extended) is in the pose of one of the myriad Roman frames to which portrait heads would be added as customers required individual likenesses of themselves; the success of this prototype is attested to by the extreme rating it received on other-concern, and the second highest score it received on activity, giving, and warmth. Although the dimension "receiving–giving" does not differentiate figures very strikingly, it is important to note at least the quality of warmth, activity, and a relatively high (though not extreme) score on virility; insofar as evidence indicates that the latter was prized in the Roman culture, and insofar as this was a position that was also meant to characterize orators, this particular combination of virtues appears well suited to the intent of the pose.

Drawing K47 bears some resemblance to K23 (arms extended toward observer) but differs in the more outwardly turned palms; this small change suffices to make the figure lose character. It received no extreme ratings and only on drama did it obtain a second place rating; its differences with K23 are discussed at greater length below.

The crossed arms of K53 give the figure a vividness that is reflected in the number of extreme ratings it receives. It is judged to be the most self-concerned, cold, unyielding, and unattractive. In most of these scores, this figure resembles the original Venus of Botticelli: The strong barrier to approach renders it unattractive and self-absorbed; the character the pose portrays is cold because it does not make contact with others. But it is also natural and imperious, something the covered Venus was not. One may ask speculatively in what this difference may reside: perhaps, in the fact that Venus merely covered herself while this Apollo intertwines his arms and displays his biceps, thus appearing not only self-concerned but also as taking pains to show others that he has little need for their contact. On this interpretation, imperiousness would imply distance from others; if this interpretation is correct, it is consistent with the imperiousness of K29 (arms open) who, by his extreme openness, also dissuaded subjects from feeling pulled toward him.

Figure K59 differs from K32 (hands behind back) only in a slight displacement of the hands clasped behind the back; but the difference it brings about in presentation meaning is much more than slight. The position was seen as the second most unnatural and effeminate, and the next-to-least strong—qualities that were absent in K32.

The arms-akimbo in K62 were seen as the most imperious and the second most immodest, cold, strong, exhibitionistic, and unyielding. This combination of ratings is instructive because it has not been encountered in the Venus series: On the one hand, the figure shows openness in its high scores on immodesty and exhibitionism, but, on the other suggests strong barriers in its scores on coldness, imperiousness, and refusal to yield. The contradiction between these two effects is more apparent than real and results from a consideration introduced above: The factually open proximal space of this figure leaves little possibility for interaction at a comfortable distance and provokes an encounter directly at the proximal boundary. If it took place, such an encounter would be more drastic and, therefore, threatening; consequently, the position discourages approach instead of encouraging it; hence, the high ratings on the emotional qualities associated with barriers concurrent with rather literal descriptions of the absence of barriers.

The final figure, K68 (hands clasped in front), received the largest number of extreme scores: It was seen as the most modest and shy, passive and yielding, effeminate, weak and humble, and as the second most self-concerned and calm—and the subjects were not very attracted to it. The qualities of modesty and passivity are already familiar from the presence of a strong covering boundary, but effeminacy and weakness are new. On first impression, they might result from the figure's apparent lack of genitals; if the subjects perceived him as castrated, it is no wonder they were alarmed. If they did not, it is possible that they perceived him as merely concerned about his genitals, and that the strength of his concern was interpreted as effeminate and weak. Whether it is the interpreted effeminacy that makes him unattractive or simply his barriers, is impossible to tell.

Two pairs among the figures bear considerable resemblance to each other except in one detail, and that detail generally sufficed to produce large differences in scores. The changes in the drawings were intentional, and the resulting divergent perceptions need to be considered to add subtlety to the discussion above.

Drawings K23 and K47 are alike except for the greater openness of the palms in the second; the first drawing was intended to be welcoming, the second exaggeratedly so. That excess produced the following significantly different scores: The second figure was seen as more effeminate, cold, weak, and yielding, and subjects were more pulled away from it (see Appendix H). It is clear that such differences require other factors as determinants of presentation meaning beside the rough ones that have served so far. The amount of exposure is clearly not sufficient; it might have pushed scores in the direction of yielding and and perhaps in addition toward other-concern, drama, or exhibitionism, but instead it produced quite different qualitative changes. The considerations which impelled the subjects to change their scores might have been of some esthetic order, which is, however, difficult to specify beyond the impression that the second figure may look less natural. Perhaps the changes in scores were produced instead by the feeling that the latter figure protests too much: The open palms appear to indicate that the actor is intent on proving his sincerity to a doubting observer; he presents the fleshy, indefensible palm by way of saying that he could not possibly have any defenses left—and seems, thereby, to show himself as weak, as one who has to resort to this maneuver in order to gain his way. As a maneuver, if it is indeed perceived as such, it may appear particularly feminine.

The other pair in which there is a slight difference consists of K32 and K59, both clasping the hands behind the body, but one just barely exposing the clasp. The latter figure was adapted from a pose frequent in "muscle magazines"; there, it serves to flex one biceps and perhaps to throw the shoulder into better relief. As a position meant to be attractive to the opposite sex (if this is its function), it fails; it was seen as more unnatural, self-concerned, effeminate, and dramatic than its calmer counterpart. Thus, its exhibiting, narcissistic nature is immediately apparent and the passivity of its exhibition (passive because the figure appears to wish to be admired for the way it *looks* rather than for the way it *acts*) seems more pertinent to feminine than masculine displays.

An analysis of dimensional correlations will describe the ways in which the descriptive dimensions are related to each other and to the evaluative rating, "pulled toward–pulled away." The significant correlations are listed below, in Table 12–4, and the complete matrix may be found in Appendix I. (In the table, opposite dimension-ends may be substituted at will.)

TABLE 12–4. Interdimensional Correlations
Significant Beyond .05 Level (N = 43)

| | | |
|---|---|---|
| pulled to: | strong | .46 |
| | warm | .36 |
| | virile | .35 |
| | natural | .33 |
| | other-concerned | .32 |
| strong: | virile | .73 |
| | active | .57 |
| | exhibitionistic | .49 |
| | imperious | .48 |
| | unyielding | .43 |
| | immodest | .38 |
| virile: | active | .51 |
| | exhibitionistic | .40 |
| | imperious | .37 |
| | natural | .31 |
| immodest: | exhibitionistic | .56 |
| | imperious | .49 |
| | dramatic | .33 |
| | active | .32 |
| dramatic: | active | .56 |
| | exhibitionistic | .37 |
| | imperious | .32 |
| exhibitionistic: | imperious | .66 |
| | active | .58 |
| | unyielding | .40 |
| other-concerned: | warm | .54 |
| active: | imperious | .48 |

To judge from the dimensions that correlate with attractiveness, the criteria of attraction are strength, warmth, virility, naturalness, and other-concern. Of these, two had characterized preference for Venus figures also: warmth and naturalness. One should note, on the one hand, that these two criteria apply equally well to figures of both sexes, but, on the other hand, that they are embodied in somewhat different figures. The most natural Venus had her arms at her side, while the most natural Apollo crosses them on his chest; similarly, naturalness correlated with ingenuousness among the female figures and with virility among the male. Thus, while naturalness is appreciated in figures of both types, what is considered natural differs. But warmth appears constant, since it is embodied in both cases in figures that are open (but not too open) to interaction with the viewer.

Two criteria, however, are in each case specific to the figures' sex: for the Venus figures, they were ingenuousness and modesty, while, for the Apollo drawings, they are, almost tautologically, virility and strength. Strength, the most important criterion, in turn relates to virility, activity, exhibitionism, imperiousness, refusal to yield, and immodesty; this, too, suggests that subjects liked the masculine figures to be open but firm. In turn, virility correlates with activity, exhibitionism, and imperiousness, suggesting again that the positive evaluations are strongly determined by openness. Surprisingly, however, imperiousness has only an indirect relation to preference—perhaps because imperious positions maintain a certain distance from the observer.

The Venus chapter (Chapter 10) showed that, on the one hand, males were unambiguously attracted by yielding positions (while women were more attracted by unyielding ones), but, on the other, they perceived the very open positions as less receiving, warm and yielding, and at the same time "distrusted" them more, judging them as more affected and dramatic. Women may have shown more expectable defensiveness in rating the attractiveness of the figures, or perhaps they used different criteria of judgment from the men because they identified with the figures portrayed. One of the interests in the Apollo analysis lies, therefore, in looking for mirror-image results.

As before, for the first comparison, we may well ask whether the two sexes differ in their overall ratings of all the figures. Appendix J lists the thirteen possible differences (one on each of the thirteen dimensions) and shows only that women rated these figures on the whole as more unnatural and as stronger; the table does *not* show women to be more attracted to these figures than men, as men, in Chapter 10, felt themselves more attracted to the female figures than did women. That women did not report more attraction generally may be explained by their claiming both more attraction and more repulsion to individual figures, thus canceling out any possible overall difference, while men, in Chapter 10, never reported greater repulsion than women. But it is not clear why women should generally have seen the male figures as stronger and more unnatural; the difference seems to be confined to a few figures and may be better appreciated by turning to the individual data.

Table 12–5 presents significant differences in the ratings for all 10 figures on all thirteen dimensions; of a possible 130 differences, the table shows that only nine were found (at the probability of .05 or better; for a listing of additional suggestive differences see Appendix K). They scatter over six figures and concentrate on figure K62 (arms akimbo).

Drawing K23 (arms extended toward observer)—the one preferred by both sexes—was seen by women as warmer. Since it received the highest rating on virility, strength, and warmth, this difference suggests that women perceived at least one part of the figure's welcoming openness as more extreme than did men; one would expect, as a consequence, that women would have been more attracted to the figure than men, but this was not the case (see Appendix K). Figure K32, with arms clasped behind the back, was seen by women as unyielding and by men as yielding; it would appear that women paid more attention here to clues

**TABLE 12–5. Significant Differences between Male and Female Ratings, by Picture**

| Figure | Dimension | M (N = 19) | F (N = 19) | p |
|--------|-----------|------------|------------|------|
| K23 | cold–warm | 4.58 | 5.58 | .05 |
| K32 | unyielding–yielding | 5.11 | 3.79 | .05 |
| K53 | unyielding–yielding | 3.21 | 2.16 | .05 |
| K59 | natural–unnatural | 3.47 | 5.05 | .01 |
| K62 | strong–weak | 3.11 | 2.00 | .05 |
|     | active–passive | 3.53 | 2.21 | .01 |
|     | unyielding–yielding | 3.16 | 2.26 | .05 |
|     | imperious–humble | 3.26 | 2.00 | .01 |
| K68 | natural–unnatural | 3.42 | 5.00 | .05 |

indicating firmness while men were more concerned with the figure's exposure. Drawing K53, with arms crossed on the chest, was similarly seen as more unyielding by women; in addition there is a suggestion that women liked the closed proximal boundary less ($p \cong .10$) and that they saw the figure as more imperious (a difference of one full point, but without statistical significance). Thus, so far, women have shown greater sensitivity to the welcoming quality of the defined axial space and the forbidding quality of access that is refused.

Figure K59, which, like K32, clasps the hands behind the back, was seen as more unnatural by the women, and the full data contain the suggestion that women perceived the figure as colder and more passive ($p > .05$). These data may be taken as support for the earlier suggestion that this position, if meant to be attractive to women, fails singularly; the figure protests its openness too strongly and makes clear that it is showing off. K62, on the other hand, with arms akimbo, seems to have more appeal for the opposite sex: It was viewed as more active, unyielding, imperious, and stronger by the women than by the men; in addition, it was rated by them as somewhat more virile and exhibition-istic ($p > .05$). Again these differences suggest, as did those observed with K32, that women are sensitive especially to the figure's firmness, and that they are not particularly unattracted by it here, perhaps since it occurs in conjunction with some exposure (on attraction, men rated the figure as negative and women as neutral, but the difference is not significant). Finally, women saw the highly defensive K68 (hands clasped in front) as unnatural (men perceived the figure as natural!) and as somewhat weaker ($p > .05$).

By way of tentative summary, these differences suggest that women show more sensitivity to the opening and closing of the male proximal boundary than do men: They perceive the completely open boundary (as in K32 and K59) as more dissuasive of approach (unyielding and cold), the boundary with defined axial space as warmer, and the closed boundary as more unyielding and imperious. This difference in sensitivity is the same, then, as that seen in the ratings of Venus.

Further evidence for women's greater concern with the boundary properties of arms comes from sex differences in the ratings of the three familiar figure groups: of figures with arms extended, with arms at side or back, or with arms covering. Of the 39 possible differences, the four significant ones are listed in Table 12–6 (all others appearing in Appendix I). Covering positons were seen by women as more self-concerned, unyielding, and imperious (and as somewhat more unnatural, p < .10, strong, p > .10, and active, p > .10); at-side positions appeared colder (and somewhat more unnatural, p < .10); and arms-extended positions show differences that only approach significance but that go, for the most part, in the anticipated direction (more unnatural, warm, yielding, and shy, at p < .10).

TABLE 12–6. Sex Differences in Male and Female Ratings, by Groups of Pictures

| Figure group | Dimension | M (N = 19) | F (N = 19) | p |
|---|---|---|---|---|
| Covering | cold–warm | 4.19 | 3.61 | .05 |
| At side | self-concerned–other-concerned | 2.98 | 2.37 | .05 |
| | unyielding–yielding | 3.83 | 3.16 | .05 |
| | imperious–humble | 4.07 | 3.46 | .05 |

Additional sex differences may be appreciated from interdimensional correlations. As in Chapter 10, interest centers, above all, on the criteria of attractiveness and on their meaning in relation to other dimensions. While the full correlation matrices are shown in Appendix I, Table 12–7 presents correlations significant beyond the .05 level; in parentheses are listed matching correlations that do not reach significance, and the table may be read equally well with dimension-ends reversed.

Since the number of subjects in the male and female columns is smaller than it was in the table in which all subjects were treated together (Table 12–4), a correlation coefficient does not become significant until it is correspondingly higher; as a result, fewer variables correlate significantly with attractiveness than before. There are only three, and all belong only to female subjects. Women are attracted by figures that are virile, warm, and strong; men, although clearly attracted to some figures more than others, seem confused about the criteria for this attraction. Men do not object to virile, warm, and strong figures,

TABLE 12–7. Interdimensional Correlations Significant
Beyond .05 Level, by Sex

|  |  | M<br>(N = 19) | F<br>(N = 24) |
|---|---|---|---|
| pulled to: | strong | (.41) | .49 |
|  | virile | (.15) | .44 |
|  | warm | (.20) | .43 |
| immodest: | exhibitionistic | .60 | .54 |
|  | imperious | .50 | .48 |
| other-concerned: | warm | (.36) | .62 |
| virile: | strong | .55 | .80 |
|  | active | (.40) | .55 |
|  | exhibitionistic | (.39) | .41 |
| strong: | active | .55 | .58 |
|  | exhibitionistic | (.45) | .51 |
|  | imperious | .50 | .48 |
|  | unyielding | .48 | .41 |
| dramatic: | active | .63 | .52 |
|  | exhibitionistic | .48 | (.30) |
|  | imperious | .49 | (.24) |
| active: | exhibitionistic | .62 | .57 |
|  | imperious | .55 | .45 |
| exhibitionistic: | unyielding | (.38) | .42 |
|  | imperious | .66 | .66 |
| unyielding: | imperious | .57 | .59 |

they merely attempt to make these qualities irrelevant. The defensive process
that may have been observed in women's criteria of attraction to female figures
is differently manifested here. In the Venus series, women reversed one of the
men's ratings and showed some defenses, it seemed, in liking figures that were
unyielding; but, in so doing, they did not seriously impugn the figures'
femininity, nor did they question their own femininity in showing some liking
for them (and for others). On the other hand, men seemed to feel that they
would endanger their masculine selves by claiming, in opposition to women, to
prefer effeminate, cold, and weak male figures. Instead, their ratings appear to
say that they have no sex-related criteria at all.

For the women, virility further correlates with strength, activity, and exhibitionism (and, for the men, considerably less so); warmth is strongly related
to other-concern; and strength is further explained by imperiousness and refusal
to yield. The data indicate, therefore, that, among these figures, women show
a preference for those that show strength, firmness, and activeness, and, at the
same time, exhibit themselves and show concern for them as observers. Men, if
anything, like strong figures, but strength for them means primarily activity,
imperiousness, and refusal to yield, and only secondarily exhibitionism. Women

feel welcomed by a warm figure, such as K23, which extends its arms toward them; men judge the same figure as less warm.

It is interesting to note that the few dimensions that men relate more highly to others than do women form a close pattern: they have to do with immodesty, exhibitionism, drama, activity, and imperiousness. These dimensions may be seen as more descriptive than evaluative, since they do not relate directly to masculinity or attractiveness. Perhaps the suggestion may be put forth that men's greater readiness to cluster *these* dimensions rather than the more evaluative ones is part of the same defensive process that accounted for their having no real criteria for attraction.

In the Venus figures, the attributes on which the figures were rated generally varied directly with the degree of proximal exposure or defense, and this variation was even more pronounced for the left arm, which covered the genital area or exposed it, than for the right. No such universal regularity appeared in the data for Apollo; perhaps because the drawings varied the amount of exposure less systematically, or perhaps, as seems more likely, because the male figure was perceived as an active subject of action more often than the female. If this were so, then its presentation meaning would be less regularly evaluated on simple approachability, making variations in the proximal boundary less of a determining factor in the evaluations. Nevertheless, boundary qualities were directly related to three ratings—other-concern, virility, and warmth—and less directly to five others—unnaturalness, immodesty, strength, yielding, and attractiveness. As they opened up more, the figures assumed more of these qualities. On a number of dimensions, however, the middle (at-side) positions received one type of rating, while both the most open and the most covered positions received the other: The middle positions were seen as the most receiving, calm, passive, shy, and humble.

It is important not to imply that, even in the Venus chapter (Chapter 10), no other determinant of presentational meaning existed than increasing and decreasing openness. The extreme figures yielded exceptions to this rule and indicated, in particular, that attraction was *not* greatest in the most open figure but rather in the one with hands at her sides. Since this finding was repeated in this chapter, perhaps the completely flaunted open proximal access discourages approach instead of encouraging it; it makes possible an approach into proximal space which, whether interpreted as sexual or aggressive, is likely to be seen as threatening.

Some of the other important variables were discovered in the comparison of two pairs of figures that differed only in a small particular. Thus, K47, with palms turned further outward than K23, was seen as more effeminate, cold, weak, yielding, and unattractive than K23; these differences were attributed to the former's attempting to appear defenseless. And K59, who just exposes his clasped hands, while K32 lets them assume a natural position behind his body, appeared as more unnatural, self-concerned, effeminate, and dramatic, supporting the hypothesis that the position is a narcissistic, passive, exhibiting one.

As to criteria of attraction, some repeated those of Chapter 10, while others were specific to the male figures. Among the latter were virility and strength; among the former appeared warmth and naturalness. The repeated criteria seem to emphasize qualities of humanness that need not be sex linked, although, in reality, there were some differences in their meaning: For the female figures, naturalness meant ingenuousness, and warmth meant calm and receptiveness; for the male figures, naturalness meant virility, and warmth meant other-concern.

This study disclosed sex differences that appeared strikingly similar to those for Venus. Primary among them was the women's greater sensitivity to changes in the proximal boundary, which led them to perceive each change as more pronounced; in particular, they emphasized the unapproachability of the completely open boundary, the warmth of the one marked by defined axial space, and the imperiousness and unyieldingness of the closed one. But in contrast to the results of Chapter 10, where men used the less ambiguous criteria of attraction, here it was the women who reported the more straightforward criteria; men showed some (expectable) defensiveness, which appeared, on the one hand, in their inability to agree on criteria of attraction and, on the other, in their propensity to cluster purely descriptive dimensions rather than any of the evaluative ones.

This chapter's results suggest certain hypotheses that need further elaboration and testing. The first arises from an interpretation of the virility of figure K38, resulting in part from the hands' distance from the body. If the hands were closer to the skin of the thighs, the figure might appear less ready for action; and, perhaps more important, the figure might be exhibiting too much sensuous interest in its own skin. The presumed femininity of such an interest seems worth exploring further. The second hypothesis is suggested by the imperiousness of figure K53; since the figure had a very well-defended proximal boundary (and since other imperious figures display the approach–dissuasive, highly open proximal access), imperiousness seems partly a function of distance from the observer, and seems particularly well embodied in positions implying little need of contact with him.

# NOTES FOR CHAPTER 12

[1] T-tests were used rather than the more elegant analysis of variance because programs for the latter were written in a language incompatible with the computer on which this analysis was carried out.

[2] This argument will be elaborated, and further evidence will be adduced in its support, in Chapter 13.

[3] It might be objected that the women may have simply made more extreme ratings no matter what the context. While it is true that women often express very definite judgments on rating tasks (see Wallach and Kogan, 1959), in this study, women rated more extremely in some contexts, men in others.

# 13. Direction of Gaze

The reader will recall that, in discussing Botticelli's Venus and the lone woman in Picasso's *La Famille des Saltimbanques*, our subjects emphasized their isolation. Unlike the central woman in Gauguin's *Ta Matete*, these two were neither shunned nor ostracized but stood alone by choice; their isolation was that of important persons. While this self-willed apartness could have been produced by the self-concern that their arm gestures indicate (the arms and hands point back toward the body), it was clear that in making this interpretation the subjects also used the reactions of other actors in the picture. What differentiated the central Venus and the important woman by Picasso from the ignored Number 3 of Gauguin was the fact that others were looking at them. When you are looked at by others, the subjects seemed to say, you must be important in some way. This chapter will further explore that idea.

Since, in the original pictures, the gaze of other actors only confirmed the self-concerned gesture of the principal figures, drawings were needed in which arm positions did not contribute to the effect—in which the direction of others' gaze could be isolated. It was important to create pictures in which background figures directed their gaze at a principal figure in one picture, and averted it in another. In order not to make matters too patently obvious, the background figures would switch their gaze between different foreground characters. The presence of two people in the foreground also provided an opportunity to vary *them*; one sits down and the other stands up, in order to see whether the gaze would affect figures of varying posture differently. The experiment was designed also to contrast the effects of the directed gaze with those of the direction of the whole body; thus, in one version, the background figures not only look at a foreground one but also fully turn their bodies toward him; in another, their bodies remain facing but their heads are averted (and turned toward the other figure).

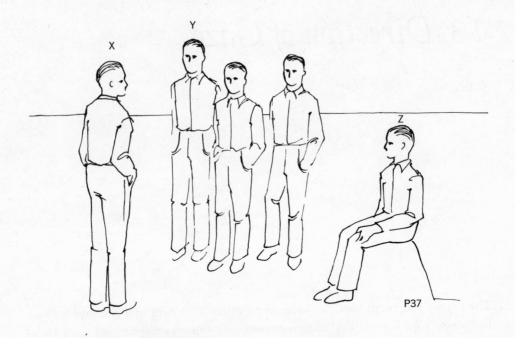

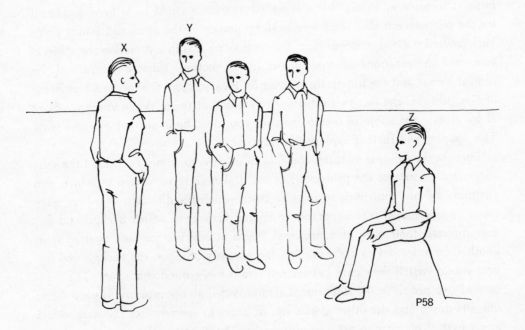

**Fig. 35.**  Gaze and Body Displacements

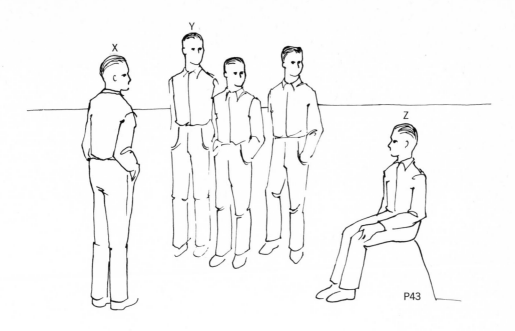

P43

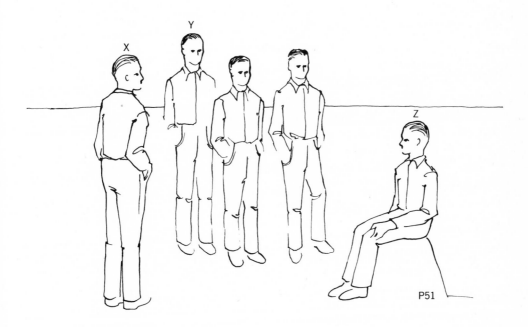

P51

*Picture identification number* P____

## SERIES P

X appears to be:

| | |
|---|---|
| subordinate | : __ : __ : __ : __ : __ : __ : __ :  superordinate |
| haughty | : __ : __ : __ : __ : __ : __ : __ :  humble |
| important | : __ : __ : __ : __ : __ : __ : __ :  insignificant |
| receiving action | : __ : __ : __ : __ : __ : __ : __ :  initiating action |

*In relation to* Y, X *appears to be:*

| | |
|---|---|
| hostile | : __ : __ : __ : __ : __ : __ : __ :  friendly |
| approaching | : __ : __ : __ : __ : __ : __ : __ :  withdrawing |
| intimate | : __ : __ : __ : __ : __ : __ : __ :  distant |

Y appears to be:

| | |
|---|---|
| subordinate | : __ : __ : __ : __ : __ : __ : __ :  superordinate |
| haughty | : __ : __ : __ : __ : __ : __ : __ :  humble |
| important | : __ : __ : __ : __ : __ : __ : __ :  insignificant |
| receiving action | : __ : __ : __ : __ : __ : __ : __ :  initiating action |

*In relation to* X, Y *appears to be:*

| | |
|---|---|
| hostile | : __ : __ : __ : __ : __ : __ : __ :  friendly |
| approaching | : __ : __ : __ : __ : __ : __ : __ :  withdrawing |
| intimate | : __ : __ : __ : __ : __ : __ : __ :  distant |

*In relation to* Z, Y *appears to be:*

| | |
|---|---|
| hostile | : __ : __ : __ : __ : __ : __ : __ :  friendly |
| approaching | : __ : __ : __ : __ : __ : __ : __ :  withdrawing |
| intimate | : __ : __ : __ : __ : __ : __ : __ :  distant |

Z appears to be:

| | |
|---|---|
| subordinate | : __ : __ : __ : __ : __ : __ : __ :  superordinate |
| haughty | : __ : __ : __ : __ : __ : __ : __ :  humble |
| important | : __ : __ : __ : __ : __ : __ : __ :  insignificant |
| receiving action | : __ : __ : __ : __ : __ : __ : __ :  initiating action |

*In relation to* Y, Z *appears to be:*

| | |
|---|---|
| hostile | : __ : __ : __ : __ : __ : __ : __ :  friendly |
| approaching | : __ : __ : __ : __ : __ : __ : __ :  withdrawing |
| intimate | : __ : __ : __ : __ : __ : __ : __ :  distant |

**Fig. 36.** Sample Answer Sheet for Series P

The total number of possibilities is only four, shown in Fig. 35. The two foreground figures (X and Z) are identical in each of the four pictures, as are the types of bodies. The background has been kept free of scenic cues; there is a simple horizon line to locate the figures in space without giving additional information.

To measure changes in perception, dimensional ratings were again devised; and, in addition to X and Z, one of the background figures, Y, was also evaluated. Dominance and activity, of course, were the attributes whose change was of most concern, and dimensions were selected accordingly; X, Y, and Z were rated on "subordination–superordination," "haughtiness–humbleness," "importance–insignificance," and "initiation–receipt of action." All of these dimensions in some way relate to the dominance that may be expressed in the picture. However, further qualitative ratings of the interaction taking place also seemed important to measure: whether the attitude of each of the actors toward the others was hostile or friendly, approaching or withdrawing, and intimate or distant. Because the answer sheet became more complicated than the ones shown so far, it is illustrated in Fig. 36.

As in all the analyses in this study, primary data are the mean ratings on each of these dimensions across all subjects who took the test.[1] In two respects, this presentation of data will differ from the preceding chapters: The extreme-figures analysis will be omitted as redundant, since only four pictures are being studied; and any analysis of the results by sex is ignored, since such an analysis seems useful only where matters closer to the erotic approaches to body spaces are concerned.[2] For the same reason, Series S and L, reported on in subsequent chapters, will also be analyzed only from the point of view of the total sample of subjects.

The method of analysis that the systematic variation of head and body positions makes most useful is again analysis of variance. One can ask of analysis of variance to determine which of these variations (head or body) significantly influences the ratings that the three main figures receive. One finds, for example, whether as Y turns he systematically makes X or Z (or, for that matter, himself) appear more or less superordinate, and whether it is his head or his body that produces this effect.

Table 13–1 presents the mean ratings that X, Y, and Z received on the dimension of "subordination–superordination" in each of the four pictures. (The scores are arranged spatially in the same way as Fig. 34, and a score below 4.00 indicates the left end of the dimension, while a score above 4.00 indicates the right end.) A rough comparison of the three parts of the table shows that X is generally a superordinate figure, that Y is generally subordinate, and that Z's scores are, for the most part, in between. Irrespective of the turns that Y makes, the

**TABLE 13–1. The Scores of X, Y, and Z for Each Position of Y; Dimension: "Subordinate–Superordinate"**

| Body position | X Head position | | | Y Head position | | | Z Head position | | |
|---|---|---|---|---|---|---|---|---|---|
| | LEFT | RIGHT | MEAN | LEFT | RIGHT | MEAN | LEFT | RIGHT | MEAN |
| LEFT | 5.29 | 4.48 | 4.88 | 3.10 | 3.05 | 3.07 | 3.23 | 3.98 | 3.61 |
| RIGHT | 5.19 | 3.83 | 4.51 | 2.95 | 3.33 | 3.14 | 3.90 | 4.07 | 3.99 |
| MEAN | 5.24 | 4.14 | | 3.02 | 3.19 | | 3.47 | 4.02 | |

standing and separate X therefore appears as the protagonist of the action, and Y as the executor of his will; Z, though not so superordinate as X, also helps direct the actions of Y. This result may have been expected from the lone positions that the two end figures occupy, but is not the really interesting one. The finding of greatest interest is that X is most superordinate when Y turns toward him both with his body and with his head, and least superordinate when Y turns away from him altogether; and that, if one looks at the marginal means, a greater difference is produced in X's scores by changes in Y's head position than by changes in his body. (The F ratios expressing the significance of these changes are 18.1 and 5.6 respectively; see Appendix M.) Thus, X's commanding position is strongest when Y concentrates his full attention on him (as if listening to his directives), lesser when he looks at X but turns to Z (as if momentarily distracted from interaction with Z in order to receive further instructions from X), still less when Y looks at Z (as if to pass the instruction on, but necessarily showing attention to Z), and least when paying full attention to Z.

The converse effect is also observed, though much less clearly. Z is in the most superordinate position when Y pays full attention to him, and in the most subordinate position when Y completely turns away from him; but the effect of Y's head and body are about equal and both statistically weak (see Appendix M). And in turn, curiously enough, Y does the most to overcome his own subordination when he turns to pay full attention to the seated Z; it is as if, in that position, he were getting furthest away from the person who gives him orders, X. This effect, however, is not statistically significant and pales in comparison with the fact that Y can do very little to change his ratings, while he determines the superordinate scores of others.

The ratings of these same figures on the dimension "haughty–humble" appear in Table 13–2; there, scores below 4.00 indicate haughtiness. If one looks first at the marginal figures, one experiences some disappointment, because the ratings appear not to vary systematically with Y's head and body position. Only Z's scores show some change (which, as Appendix M shows, are also statistically

TABLE 13–2. The Scores of X, Y, and Z for Each Position of Y; Dimension:
"Haughty–Humble"

| Body position | X Head position | | | Y Head position | | | Z Head position | | |
|---|---|---|---|---|---|---|---|---|---|
| | LEFT | RIGHT | MEAN | LEFT | RIGHT | MEAN | LEFT | RIGHT | MEAN |
| LEFT | 4.17 | 3.40 | 3.79 | 4.36 | 4.07 | 4.21 | 4.57 | 3.74 | 4.15 |
| RIGHT | 3.38 | 3.74 | 3.56 | 4.00 | 4.19 | 4.10 | 3.98 | 3.88 | 3.93 |
| MEAN | 3.77 | 3.57 | | 4.18 | 4.13 | | 4.27 | 3.81 | |

significant, but only for the head turns). As far as Z goes, he appears most humble when Y turns away from him to fully devote his attention to X, and most haughty (though never very much so) when Y looks directly at him. This is in the desirable direction and shows that Y has some power to make at least one figure appear haughty by the direction of his gaze. But the changes in X's scores come as a paradox. Although none of them is significant, X nevertheless appears as the most *humble* when Y pays him full attention, and haughty when Y looks away, turns away, or both. Thus, while Y makes Z appear haughty by looking at him, he makes X haughty by looking away. The difference may be explained in this way: Z is always humbler than X because Z sits while X stands; the ordinarily humble Z can obtain a small reduction in humbleness only when some attention is being paid to him. But X is normally haughty and his haughtiness is challenged only when someone turns to him and looks at him; when that happens, X is establishing contact and can no longer maintain the distant position that haughtiness implies. As the following two chapters will show, superordination implies contact with others (hence, X is most superordinate when Y looks at him), while haughtiness requires distance (hence, X cannot remain haughty when Y looks at him). As before, Y does not markedly influence his own scores in turning this way and that, and remains generally the most humble of the three; as between X and Z, the taller, standing figure is always haughtier than the sitting one.

The third dimension is "important–insignificant," and the pertinent ratings are presented in Table 13–3. Scores below 4.00 are at the "important" end of the dimension. In comparing the scores of the three figures without reference to changes in Y's position, one notices that Y is invariably insignificant, while the two lone figures, X and Z, tend generally to be important, sometimes very much so. Already it is apparent that this dimension refers to a different aspect of dominance than do the previous two: While X was generally both more superordinate and haughty than Z, here, X and Z are equal in importance. It would appear that superordination implies greater height and that haughtiness requires

TABLE 13–3. The Scores of X, Y, and Z for Each Position of Y; Dimension: "Important–Insignificant"

| Body position | X Head position | | | Y Head position | | | Z Head position | | |
|---|---|---|---|---|---|---|---|---|---|
| | LEFT | RIGHT | MEAN | LEFT | RIGHT | MEAN | LEFT | RIGHT | MEAN |
| LEFT | 2.62 | 2.90 | 2.76 | 4.62 | 4.38 | 4.50 | 4.12 | 2.52 | 3.32 |
| RIGHT | 2.50 | 4.00 | 3.25 | 4.50 | 4.33 | 4.42 | 3.12 | 2.67 | 2.89 |
| MEAN | 2.56 | 3.45 | | 4.56 | 4.36 | | 3.62 | 2.60 | |

both height and distance, while importance merely requires one to be the pro-tagonist of action—as either X or Z could be when "giving" orders to the centrally placed Y, who shows that he "receives" them when he looks at the giver.

This interpretation is supported by the fact that both X and Z are important especially when Y is looking at them, and that, under these conditions, their importance is equal. Even more significant is the fact that their importance is the same independent of Y's body position; thus, since gaze—but not the body—determines the ratings, it seems even more likely that subjects perceived Y as the one who receives directions from the protagonists, who have to look at Y while they give directions. (The body position does make a significant difference, as Appendix M shows, though not nearly so great as the head position; but the difference is perceptible only when Y is *not* looking at X or Z. One has the im-pression that X and Z lose importance only when Y turns away from them alto-gether, and that it suffices for either Y's body *or* his head to be turned in the pro-tagonists' direction for them to be important.) Finally, Y himself remains insignificant no matter which direction he turns in; his own gaze has no effect on his ratings of importance.

The last of the four dimensions measuring dominance is "receiving action–initiating action," and the ratings obtained on it are presented in Table 13–4. If

TABLE 13–4. The Scores of X, Y, and Z for Each Position of Y; Dimension: "Receiving–Initiation Action"

| Body position | X Head position | | | Y Head position | | | Z Head position | | |
|---|---|---|---|---|---|---|---|---|---|
| | LEFT | RIGHT | MEAN | LEFT | RIGHT | MEAN | LEFT | RIGHT | MEAN |
| LEFT | 5.45 | 4.00 | 4.73 | 2.55 | 3.10 | 2.82 | 2.69 | 4.21 | 3.45 |
| RIGHT | 5.05 | 3.81 | 4.43 | 2.83 | 3.29 | 3.06 | 3.60 | 4.45 | 4.02 |
| MEAN | 5.25 | 3.90 | | 2.69 | 3.19 | | 3.14 | 4.33 | |

the speculation about the protagonist role played by X and Z is correct, it should be supported directly by these data. Examined from the point of view of the differences between X, Y, and Z, the table confirms the hypothesis and shows Y always to be a receiver of action, while X and Z sometimes initiate it and sometimes receive it; on the whole, X initiates more often than Z.

The circumstances under which X and Z initiate action are the same. When Y is looking at them (Appendix M shows the head effect to be very highly significant, while the body effect reaches significance only for Z), the body can reinforce the gaze, but only slightly. When Y looks at either of the protagonists, he, therefore, expects direction from them and shows to the observer that they are giving these directions to him. It is noteworthy that, on this dimension, Y's head changes also have a significant effect on his *own* scores, in that he is perceived as the most action-receiving when he is looking at X. These data imply that the powerful X seems able to initiate more action in Y's direction than Z can in the same circumstance.

The second intention in this series was to study changes that have less to do with the importance of any one figure than with the affect it might be expressing and the closeness of approach it might be making to others. Thus, under each of the dimensions reflecting dominance were included three expressive ones which refer to the figures' relation to explicit partners. Do these, too, change systematically as Y turns his head and body first to the left and then to the right?

The first dimension measures the amount of hostility or friendliness that X, Y, and Z present to selected others. Table 13–5 presents four different interpersonal relations and their variation with Y's turning movements: X's hostility to Y, Y's hostility to X, then Z's hostility to Y; and Y's hostility to Z. The table is disappointing. Not only is there no appreciable difference among the four rela-

**TABLE 13–5. Interrelations between Figures for Each position of Y; Dimension: "Hostile–Friendly"**

| Body position | X to Y<br>Head position | | | Y to X<br>Head position | | |
|---|---|---|---|---|---|---|
| | LEFT | RIGHT | MEAN | LEFT | RIGHT | MEAN |
| LEFT | 4.40 | 4.38 | 4.39 | 4.19 | 4.52 | 4.36 |
| RIGHT | 4.17 | 4.14 | 4.15 | 3.95 | 4.14 | 4.05 |
| MEAN | 4.29 | 4.26 | | 4.07 | 4.33 | |
| | Z to Y | | | Y to Z | | |
| LEFT | 3.88 | 3.93 | 3.90 | 3.86 | 3.76 | 3.81 |
| RIGHT | 4.14 | 4.07 | 4.11 | 3.83 | 4.00 | 3.92 |
| MEAN | 4.01 | 4.00 | | 3.85 | 3.88 | |

tions as a whole (perhaps X is generally friendly to Y, while Y is generally hostile to Z—but only by the thinnest of hairs), but there appears almost no variation related to Y's changes in position. Analysis of variance (see Appendix N) shows only that a body effect may be observed in Y's relation to X, in that Y is friendlier to X when turning toward him than when not. But since all the scores are very close to the neutral point, 4.00, these positions clearly do not carry much expressive meaning as far as hostility or friendliness is concerned.

Matters are somewhat more decisive in the dimension "approaching–withdrawing." The relevant scores are presented in Table 13–6 with scores below

TABLE 13–6. Interrelations between Figures for Each Position of Y; Dimension: "Approaching–Withdrawing"

| Body position | X to Y Head position | | | Y to X Head position | | |
|---|---|---|---|---|---|---|
| | LEFT | RIGHT | MEAN | LEFT | RIGHT | MEAN |
| LEFT | 3.64 | 3.88 | 3.76 | 4.23 | 4.07 | 4.05 |
| RIGHT | 3.57 | 4.19 | 3.88 | 3.90 | 4.40 | 4.15 |
| MEAN | 3.61 | 4.04 | | 3.96 | 4.24 | |
| | Z to Y | | | Y to Z | | |
| LEFT | 4.64 | 3.95 | 4.30 | 4.62 | 3.84 | 4.18 |
| RIGHT | 4.02 | 3.93 | 3.98 | 4.57 | 3.24 | 3.90 |
| MEAN | 4.33 | 3.94 | | 4.60 | 3.49 | |

4.00 indicating approach, those above 4.00, withdrawal. There are no gross differences among the four relations as a whole, but in three of four cases (see Appendix N), there are differences within these relations produced by changes in Y's head position. Whenever Y faces one of his partners, the partner appears to approach, and when Y looks away, he and the partner appear to withdraw from each other. These scores indicate, then, that two figures looking at each other may, by that fact alone, be presumed to be approaching in some way; Chapter 15 will show that the same effect may be observed in two figures that stand in a relation of vertical inequality. That chapter will also show, as this one does, that changes in body position (among standing figures) produce fewer differences in perceived approach than do changes in head position—or direction of gaze.

One relation forms an exception to the rule that ties direction of gaze and approach: Y's relation to X is withdrawing not just when Y is fully turned away (as is the case with Z), but also when Y faces X with both his head and his body. In view of X's approach to Y under the same circumstance, the result comes as a surprise; one may speculate, however, that, since in this diatropic arrangement *X* is the most important and initiates the most, while *Y* is the least important and receives the most, *Y* will show some resentment about this situation and will tend to withdraw. This interpretation may appear *ad hoc*, but it is consistent not only with the facts about importance and initiation but also with the data concerning distance, about to be discussed.

Table 13–6 also indicates, interesting enough, that *Y* has a greater power to influence his relation to the seated *Z* than to the standing *X*; head changes produce a very highly significant difference in *Y's* relation to *Z*. An asymmetry in the roles of *X* and *Z* has been mentioned before, and, here again, it appears that this difference may be ascribed to *X's* commanding position and *Z's* undistinguished, malleable one. The position of *Z*—because it has so little character of its own—appears to take its expressiveness quite easily from its relation to the stance of *Y*.

The final interpersonal dimension, "intimate–distant," was included to provide subjects with an opportunity to speak of the closeness of the interactants in psychological terms. It was important to find out whether the body or head turns of *Y* could affect the perceived distance between the figures, both *Y's* distance from the others and theirs from him. Table 13–7 presents the relevant information, with scores below 4.00 indicating intimacy.

**TABLE 13–7. Interrelations between Figures for Each Position of *Y*; Dimension: "Intimate–Distant"**

| Body position | *X to Y* Head position | | | *Y to X* Head position | | |
|---|---|---|---|---|---|---|
| | LEFT | RIGHT | MEAN | LEFT | RIGHT | MEAN |
| LEFT | 4.48 | 4.02 | 4.25 | 4.29 | 3.86 | 4.07 |
| RIGHT | 4.26 | 4.50 | 4.38 | 4.21 | 4.40 | 4.31 |
| MEAN | 4.37 | 4.26 | | 4.25 | 4.13 | |
| | *Z to Y* | | | *Y to Z* | | |
| LEFT | 5.07 | 4.40 | 4.74 | 5.07 | 4.21 | 4.64 |
| RIGHT | 4.38 | 4.24 | 4.31 | 4.57 | 4.12 | 4.35 |
| MEAN | 4.73 | 4.32 | | 4.82 | 4.17 | |

One observes, first, that all the relations are quite distant under almost all circumstances; the actors—perhaps because they are standing rigidly or sitting—never strike stances that could be interpreted as intimate. As far as *X's* relation to *Y* is concerned, the marginal figures show no variation, and the analysis of variance (see Appendix N) confirms this lack. There is an indication within the body of the X-to-Y part of the table that X is most distant from Y, not only when Y is fully turned away from him, but also when Y is fully turned toward him; the latter result most likely points out again that X is a commanding figure whose unmoving stance determines the nature of the interaction as much as do Y's turning movements. This is not the first time this result has been observed; in earlier runs with these data, X and Y were most distant when fully facing each other; it was reasoned that their rigid stances must appear as distant in contrast to what one would expect from the approaching possibilities of the fully facing, standing diatrope. Y repays X his distance also, in that his relation to X is quite distant in the full diatrope (though the effect is not significant), and their relation continues to remain symmetrical in that Y is even more distant from X when fully turned away (this effect is significant); the two are least distant when Y turns toward but faces away.

Y and Z maintain an even more distant relation than Y and X, but the effects of Y's turning movements are much more straightforward; the two figures become less distant the more fully they turn toward each other (both the head and body effects are significant for both directions of the Y–Z relation). There is *no* contrast effect here, as there was with X.

The aim of this chapter was to explore the conditions of dominance and superiority in a group setting as a function of the direction of gaze and direction of the anterior part of the body. Observations of subjects' descriptions of paintings suggested that persons become important simply by virtue of the fact that they are looked at.

The results revealed that, as the central, variable figure Y turned toward the standing X, he made X appear as more superordinate, important, and initiating; and that turns of the body produced significant changes only in some cases, but that turns of the head did so every time, and the changes thus created were greater than those the body produced. As Y turned toward the seated Z, he made Z appear more haughty, important, and initiating; again, the head effect was stronger than the body effect. Y generally produced no changes in his own scores, with one exception noted below.

The four dimensions intended to measure dominance were found to differ somewhat in meaning. Superordination was shown both by height (X was almost always superordinate) and by returned gaze (as when Y returned X's instruction-giving gaze); haughtiness was embodied in height and in unreturned gaze (the most haughty figure was X when Y was not looking at him); and both importance and initiation of action were illustrated simply by the returned gaze (either X or Z could be important, depending on whether Y was looking at them or not).

As far as the relations between the actors went, Y's turning movements toward Z made him appear more approaching and intimate, and changed his own scores in the same way. On the dimension of "approach–withdrawal," the head effect was significant, the body's was not; on the dimension of "intimacy–distance," however, the body effect on two occasions proved strong. "Hostility–friendliness" proved inapplicable in the descriptions of these interactions; whether this indicates that emotions are difficult to portray by body movements is not yet clear, but it may be suggested that the major variables of concern in this book (syntropic movements and uses of body spaces) lend themselves more clearly to the presentation of intentions, social statuses, and self- and other-concerns, than to the portrayal of "emotions" as ordinarily understood in psychological theory.

The results of this phase of the investigation also revealed certain exceptions to the regularities in the effects that $Y's$ turning movements had, exceptions that, in some cases, appeared paradoxical, but that were instructive in every case. First, $X$ was made more humble than haughty by $Y's$ directing his gaze at him; an explanation, anticipating the results of Chapter 15, was that $X's$ natural haughtiness became impossible to maintain as soon as he made eye contact with $Y$ (while, with the seated $Z$, there was no haughtiness to maintain, and $Y's$ directed gaze gave him status he did not otherwise have). Second, $X$ and $Y$ were perceived as distant from each other, and $Y$ was withdrawing from $Z$ both when $Y$ faced $X$ fully and turned away fully—probably because subjects perceived a contrast between their rigid stances and the possibilities of approach inherent in the full diatrope. Third, $Y$ was seen as the most action-receiving when his head faced $X$; this seemed a result of the contrast he presents to the dominant $X$, or, in the terms of subjects' possible scenarios, a result of his receiving orders from $X$ to pass on to $Y$. Fourth, $Z$ was more profoundly affected by changes in $Y's$ position than was $X$; his sitting position gave him less command and made his status more susceptible to $Y's$ behavior toward him.

## NOTES FOR CHAPTER 13

[1] The subjects were 18 male and 24 female undergraduates at the University of Colorado. Two earlier samples of subjects failed to give clear results, in the first case because the drawings had not been systematically constructed, and in the second because the central figure, $Y$, wore a severe expression that masked any effects his bodily or head positions might have produced. After two changes in the drawings, this series was finally submitted to the Colorado sample.

[2] We did check for sex differences; only one occurred that was significant at the .05 level—out of 24 tests. This could have come about by chance.

# 14. Arm Positions and Dominance

In Picasso's *La Famille des Saltimbanques* (see Fig. 22), the posture of Number 1 (the circus gentleman of lean proportions who squarely faces the rotund, evil Number 3) includes a left arm bent and comfortably lodged in the small of his back, while his right hand holds the little girl's hand. The subjects said that he looked like a leader: defiant, strong, and Napoleonic (unfortunately, they misplaced his arm from the ventral to the dorsal side); he "faced" the situation, "stood up to," and refused to "extend" himself to Number 3. Of particular interest was the statement describing him as refusing to extend himself; it appeared that the left arm—which he kept to himself—denied others the possibility of interacting within his axial space. It has been suggested that interaction in axial space is social in nature (in the sense that it is not directly sexual or aggressive, and that it is perceived as a mollified form of what could be more drastic), and that this quality of interaction is best invited by arms extending forward from the shoulders toward the interacting partner; the space within these arms is called *defined axial space*. Now, if this circus man exposes his chest and withdraws his arms, he is probably inviting interaction directly at the proximal boundary; anyone approaching him, then, should be prepared to come very close. Such a close approach might be permitted between intimate friends, but, except in specified situations, it might be interpreted as homosexual or aggressive.[1] For this reason, it seems likely that the displayed chest generally discourages *social* interaction in the above sense of the word. Thus, the figures of the preceding chapter and of the Venus series did not attract subjects when their proximal boundary was maximally open, and Picasso's acrobat's arm position served the double function of withdrawing a part of him that could be extended out to others and of displaying his chest in a fashion that dared others to act while discouraging them from doing so.

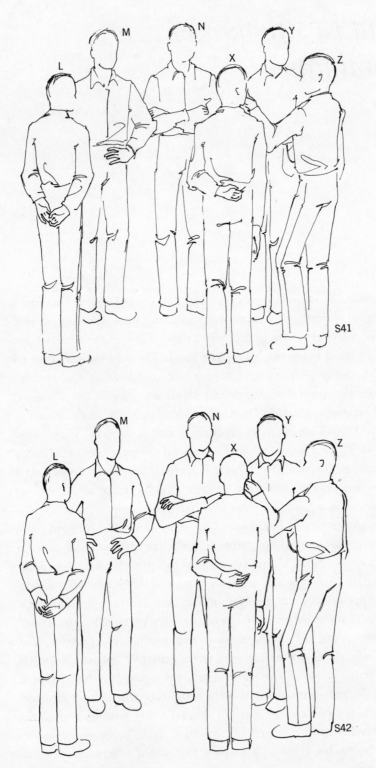

**Fig. 37.** Arm Positions in a Group Setting

Although it would be desirable to find a direct test of the explanation just proposed, this chapter will be content with finding out whether the presentational effects of this out-thrust proximal boundary are the ones described: leading, strong, and distant. And, partly to make up for the inability to test such reasoning directly, other arm positions are added to the series which may broaden understanding of leadership, dominance, activity, and pride as a function of arm position. Thus, the groups in Fig. 37 contain a figure resembling the original Picasso circus man, a person with arms on his hips (to illustrate another position which exposes the proximal boundary at the chest, also quite forcibly, and which penetrates the space at the side with the elbows and points out the secure grasp of the hips), a person with arms crossed on the chest (to cover it and vigorously call attention to the double-strength boundary thus established), one with hands clasped behind the posterior (again exposing the proximal boundary at the chest but without calling attention to the fact that the hand is withdrawn, as in the Picasso stance), a figure with hands simply in the hip pockets (for a relaxed and relatively unexpressive contrast with the others), and, finally, a figure that gesticulates toward the others with an open, extended left arm.

Although these figures offer a good variety of poses in a group setting that appears reasonably natural, it seemed likely that perception of their importance and activity might well be a function of their being set in a group; thus, perhaps by some halo effect, one figure might be picked as leader and receive all the dominant attributes. To prevent this each figure was drawn singly and presented on a separate sheet. These figures will not be shown here because they are excellent copies of the group figures; the perceptible differences between the two versions consisted in the single figures never being partially hidden behind other figures' heads, hands, or bodies. The group and the individual versions were presented to different groups of subjects.

A third version seemed necessary, though its necessity did not become evident until after the first results were obtained. The results were satisfactory but additional confirmation seemed desirable. If the reader looks at group S41 in Figure 37, he will notice that everyone, with the possible exception of the person called N, is looking at Z, the gesticulating gentleman. It would be natural to expect the direction of gaze to have the strong effect analyzed in the last chapter, making Z important without any gestural effort on his part. Therefore, a second group was drawn in which everyone faced a point very near the center of the circle. The artist succeeded in preserving the earlier positions. Group S42 in Figure 37 shows that, aside from the altered direction of gaze, the only appreciable change takes place in M and N's distance from each other. This was purposeful and had the effect of removing M's elbow from its overprominent position in front of N and of exposing his other hand; at the same time, N was slightly displaced to the right. This second version was presented to a third group of subjects.[2]

To measure dominance, as in Series P, the same dimensions were retained; thus, the figures were rated on the same seven-point scales measuring the dimensions: "subordinate–superordinate," "haughty–humble," "initiating action–receiving action," and "important–insignificant." Two other dimensions that seemed appropriate to these gestures were added: "expressive–inexpressive" and "other-concerned–self-concerned." The former was found to discriminate among figures, but the latter was too ambiguous to be really useful.

The presentation of results will talk about the three versions of the pictures together, as if they had been studied at the same time; but in consulting the tables, the reader should remember that the subjects for each of these versions were different.

In Table 14–1, for S41, are listed simply the figures that received extreme (and next-to-extreme) ratings on each dimension, along with their mean scores.[3] As

**TABLE 14–1. Figures with Extreme Ratings in Drawing S41 (N = 11)**

|  | Most | Second | Second | Most |  |
|---|---|---|---|---|---|
| Subordinate | L (2.00) | X (2.64) | M (5.18) | Z (6.64) | Superordinate |
| Other-concerned | X (3.36) | Y (3.45) | L (3.91) | M (4.27) | Self-concerned |
| Haughty | M (2.55) | Z (2.91) | X (4.91) | L (6.09) | Humble |
| Initiating action | Z (1.73) | M (3.91) | X (5.82) | L (6.27) | Receiving action |
| Expressive | Z (1.27) | M (2.82) | X (4.91) | L (6.09) | Inexpressive |
| Important | Z (1.55) | M (2.73) | X (4.73) | L (6.09) | Insignificant |

in Series H, it is interesting to note that a few figures account for almost all of the extreme positions. Thus L, the man with hands clasped behind his back, appears as the most subordinate, most humble, most inexpressive, most insignificant, and least action-initiating of all. He bears little resemblance to Picasso's acrobat; he does not expose his chest in a firm, aggressive manner, and his back is slightly bent and makes the chest retreat into the body. Thus, he has none of the taut ascendance one would associate with qualities of leadership; and the reader will undoubtedly notice that this defect in the design of the picture is consistent with a lack of awareness, discussed earlier, of body tension as a significant variable. X also lacks the required tenseness; thus, his stance has none of the qualities found in Picasso's "Napoleonic" version that were hoped for here.

The "leader" is Z instead; he is the most superordinate, action-initiating, expressive, and important. "Expressiveness" here means the outstretched gesture, but it also makes him initiate the group's action and, thus, become super-ordinate and important.

M (hands on hips) is the most self-concerned and haughty.[4] His high score on self-concern appears to be of particular theoretical significance, because he alone of the six figures redirects the activity of his hands back towards his body; the discussion of Botticelli's Venus and Picasso's lone woman suggested that such redirection is what defines, in body communication, concern with oneself, and that hypothesis seems to be supported here.[5] In addition, he displays his chest, and his high score on self-concern is consistent with the speculation that this stance discourages interaction—perhaps by making possible only a too-close approach. It is instructive that M is the most haughty, not Z; the latter leads, but does not separate himself from the others as does M. Where Z's gesture appears outgoing, M's stance is firm and unyielding; and if the reasoning about the discouragement of approach is plausible, then it is here supported by the "wrong" figure.

The fact that Z is fairly haughty anyway shows that the outgoing nature of his stance is not altogether the sign of contact with others that it has been made to appear. But the gesture is directed less towards the other members of the group than simply out and up away from his body—it is "expressive," though not necessarily directed towards others' axial space. He would probably be less haughty were he to make closer contact with the axial spaces of the other members.

It is important to note the extent to which M and Z appear together in the table, with M taking second place on every dimension but one; he is second to Z in superordination, initiating, expressiveness, and importance. Both figures seem to show superiority or leadership, although quite different in quality: M appears firm, self-contained, perhaps decisive, while Z seems to be energetic, expository, and directs his actions toward the group. The former qualities probably make M the most haughty, with Z only second, and support the suggestion made in the previous chapter that haughtiness is best shown in a stance that maintains distance.

Another frequent pairing is that of X and L, with X again second, this time on subordination, humbleness, action-initiation, inexpressiveness, and insignificance. While X's poor showing would normally be disappointing—since the intention had been to model him on Picasso's circus man—the results have enriched the critical variables by at least one, that of bodily tautness. Moreover, the person who comes second to where it was thought X should be (M) possesses the very attributes hypothesized as important. To this extent, the exploratory results concerning the gestures of "leadership" are supported, although the aggressively exposed chest leads rather to a haughty and firm type of leadership than to the active, outgoing kind exemplified by Z's outstretched arm.

The problematic dimension is that of "other-concern." Since none of the figures differs significantly from the others, and since the range of their mean scores is very low, any generalizations from comparison within this one picture are doubtful. But perhaps larger changes occur between the three presentations—changes that could at least illuminate the meanings of self- and other-concern, and perhaps clarify the dependence of these interpretations on other factors. One must look at the effect produced by the slight changes in the orientations of the heads in version S42 and by the purely individual presentation.

Table 14–2 presents the identifying letters of the extreme figures in all three presentations.

**Table 14–2. Comparison of Extreme Figures in Three Situations**

| Most | S41 | S42 | Individual | S41 | S42 | Individual | Most |
|------|-----|-----|------------|-----|-----|------------|------|
| Subordinate | L | L | L | Z | Z | Z | Superordinate |
| Other-concerned | X | Y | Z | M | M = X | X | Self-concerned |
| Haughty | M | M | M | L | L | L | Humble |
| Initiating action | Z | Z | Z | L | L | L | Receiving action |
| Expressive | Z | Z | Z | L | X | L | Inexpressive |
| Important | Z | Z | Z | L | L | L | Insignificant |

Certainly the most important fact about the table is that so few disagreements appear when the context is changed. L remains the most subordinate, humble, action-receiving, and insignificant; and, with one exception, he is still the most inexpressive. Z retains his rating as the most superordinate, initiating, expressive, and important, while M remains the most haughty throughout. Thus, on 5 of the 6 dimensions, there is only one disagreement out of a possible 30; clearly, there is a high degree of independence of context in the presentational meanings of these arm positions.

There are, nevertheless, some differences, but their significance is likely to remain obscure unless one can assess how large they are in absolute terms. The dimension of "self-concern" was troublesome in version S41 because of the very small range of scores it produced. If that remains the case in the two other presentations, any changes in the relative position of extreme figures will be meaningless. Analysis of variance is particularly well suited for testing the significance of overall differences; therefore, it has been used to find on what dimensions, and on which figures, the three presentations differ. The data, presented fully in Appendix O, are summarized here.

The most important finding is that, of 36 possible differences (between six figures on six dimensions), only 3 are significant at the .05 level; 3 other differences are as large as 1.00 but do not attain significance. Thus, whether alone or in groups, whether facing this or that person, the faceless figures in this study communicate very similar meanings with their arm positions.

The few differences observed are, nevertheless, interesting. Although a discussion of them must remain tentative until supplemented with further studies, the changes shed some light on the effects of context. For individual $L$, one large though non-significant difference appears: In both group situations, he is seen as very inexpressive, but when alone his score comes closer to neutral. Two complementary explanations may be suggested to account for this change. First, in the group situations, $L$ stands the farthest removed from the others, and it is possible that, whatever his natural inexpressiveness may be when alone, it is here reinforced by his being so far removed. Physical interpersonal distance is undoubtedly another important presentational variable to study more systematically (see, for example, the work of Hall, 1959, and Little, 1965), but it will receive attention in this book only in Chapters 16 and 17.

Second, it is possible that some contrasting effect takes place in the group versions; subjects who can look at all the figures simultaneously may come to see the meaning of positions and movements as intensified because the movements appear interpersonal and directed. Support for this suggestion comes from the ranges of mean scores on this dimension in the three versions: for S41, the range is 4.82 points; for S42, it is 3.60; and for the individual version, 3.00 (and these ranges are not related to sample size). Group settings, therefore, create more extreme scores, most probably by contrasting different positions more strongly, or by providing interactants who make their meaning clearer.

Individual $M$ also receives two scores with a difference of this magnitude, but on the dimension "initiating–receiving." In the individual version, he is quite initiating; in S41, he is nearly neutral; but in S42, he is decidedly on the receiving end of the dimension. Here, one probably observes the effect of the group context. In the individual situation, $M$ was the only other initiating figure beside $Z$, and could well remain so because there was no possibility of the latter's competition; but, when put in the group context, he could no longer compete, probably because there was room for only one initiator. This effect is, in all likelihood, reinforced by the fact that he is shown facing $Z$; this makes it likely that he is merely reacting to the other's initiative. He falls further in S42, probably because of the effect intended: He no longer thrusts his elbow into the space within the group. This interpretation is further supported by his less-than-significant loss of superordination, expressiveness, and importance in S42 as opposed to S41.

Individual $X$ undergoes a change (again, it is below significance) from the individual version to S41; in the former, $X$ is somewhat self-concerned, and, in the latter, about equally other-concerned. In this case, the direction of his gaze may be a determinant: When he turns to someone, he can show concern for him, but when no one is present, one can never know what concern he may have. One would expect this explanation to hold especially for figures that are not particularly remarkable or obviously gesticulating, and one *can* observe that the effect occurs, though less strongly, also in figures L and Y (both quiet and unimposing). Further consistent with this explanation is X's score in S42, in which he faces no one in particular (though still giving full attention to the group), and his other-concern score becomes neutral.

Figure Y changes on two dimensions; he shows the same change on other-concern as figure X, and, most likely for the same reason (although the change is below statistical significance), he also receives different ratings (significant this time) on the dimension "haughty–humble." He is humble in the individual version and neutral in the two group versions. In the latter, the hands he is intended to have in his pockets do not show with sufficient clarity; perhaps that fact prevented subjects from being able to determine his haughtiness or humbleness with any certainty—as they seemed to have been prevented from judging his importance or insignificance in the same pictures (see his neutral scores in S41 and S42, and his insignificant rating in the individual version).

Finally, Z's scores undergo some changes—strangely enough, all close to the extreme of superordination. He is highly superordinate in the individual presentation and in S42, but his score jumps even higher in S41. Here, a suggestion of a contrast effect seems insufficient, since what requires explanation is the extreme score in S41 alone. The simplest hypothesis is consistent with the initial reasons for constructing three presentations, that is, that in S41, Z was gazed at by nearly everyone; this should produce exaggerated ratings also on various dimensions measuring dominance. Aside from the observed significant change on superordination, smaller changes do occur in haughtiness, action-initiation, expressiveness, and importance—all in the direction of increase.

To recapitulate the findings, two types of dominant figures have been encountered. Z, the most important figure in the group, was expressive, action-initiating, and superordinate, and seemed to make active contact with the group. M was second to him on these dimensions but surpassed him on haughtiness; he seemed an inflexible and defiant person. It was he who really exhibited his chest as if to dare others to approach. In theoretical terms, he made it impossible for others to interact with him in axial space when he put his hands on his hips; with axial space thus left without definition, interaction with him would most likely have to take place at the proximal boundary, which could cause anyone contemplating it to pause.

Arm positions were largely independent of the context in which they occurred;

there was very high agreement on the figures rated as extreme on each dimension. The few disagreements may have the following relevance: First, the changes in ratings on other-concern show that this dimension was a function of gaze direction, since relatively inexpressive figures would be rated higher on other-concern as soon as they directed their attention to another figure. Second, contrast effects for figures L and M (in both group versions, their scores changed from the individual presentation) showed L more inexpressive (n.s.) in the group situations than before, while M changed from initiating to receiving by contrast with the dominant figure, Z. Third, the normally dominant figure Z became especially dominant in version S41, in which he was the recipient of the others' gaze. Fourth, the experiment again indicated that more attention should be paid to the variable of physical distance; it is one that can probably make a somewhat subordinate figure even more so by increasing his distance from the group.

## NOTES FOR CHAPTER 14

[1] Doubtless, the distance at which comfortable social interaction habitually takes place varies in different cultures, as Hall (1966) has demonstrated. We suggest that what may be common across cultures is the interpretation of *changes* in that optimal distance: approach or withdrawal from it.

[2] The same group that took Series D, and G and I; therefore, 40 in number. The first group version and the individual pictures were rated by eleven and twelve subjects each.

[3] In each row (and, therefore, on each dimension), the scores of the figures are generally significantly different from each other at the .05 level. The exceptions are the following: On the first dimension, L does not significantly differ from X; on the second, none of the figures differ; on the third, M and Z, *and on the fourth*, X and L do not differ.

[4] The table shows M not significantly different from Z in haughtiness; however, since M's mean scores make him haughtiest in all three presentations, we may safely take him to represent the extreme. Z comes second or third.

[5] Again M's score does not differ significantly from the other figures in this table; nevertheless, he is extreme on this dimension in both group presentations (S41 and S42). He becomes somewhat more other-concerned in the individual version, perhaps because of another determinant of "other-concern" that we have not yet stressed: the direction of gaze toward others. In the individual version, he appears to be looking directly at someone else much more clearly than do some of the other individual figures; the others would, if this suggestion is correct, be perceived as less other-concerned than he.

# 15. Acrotropic Superiority and Dominance

The theoretical discussion distinguished two types of positions in which two persons can assume vertical inequality: an acrotrope in which the superior person raises himself above another, and an acrotrope in which the inferior person lowers himself before the partner.[1] In the first type, the superior person is active and strives to assume dominance or endeavors to overcome inferiority; he may have to display active aggression or at least passive haughtiness, depending on whether the other agrees to the inequality or not. In the second type, the source of the inequality is the inferior person; the superior may acquiesce or not. The difference between the two types is that, in the second, the inferior person genuinely humbles himself, while, in the first, he may merely accept subordination tacitly. Similarly in the first type, the superior person creates an aggressive superiority, whereas, in the second, his superiority may be passive —existing, as it were, by default.

Charlie Chaplin, in his portrayal of The Great Dictator, turned an acrotropic situation into comedy by satirizing the sensitivity to height that his dictator displayed. The two principles in the conflict for superiority—caricatures of Hitler and Mussolini—lent surplus meaning to the portrayal because, in reality, both were short. The Hitler figure was forever vigilant for the slightest opportunity to rise above his visitor. Accordingly, when the two visited Hitler's barbershop and sat down to be shaved, Hitler raised his chair slightly above that of the other; the other, equally sensitive, replied in kind. Eventually, both of them, caught in an escalation neither could control by himself, reached the ceiling, from which only an abrupt failure in the raising mechanism could bring them down.

The viewer's satisfaction comes, of course, from the exaggerated nature of this acrotrope and its eventual failure. In more restrained circumstances, acrotropic

259

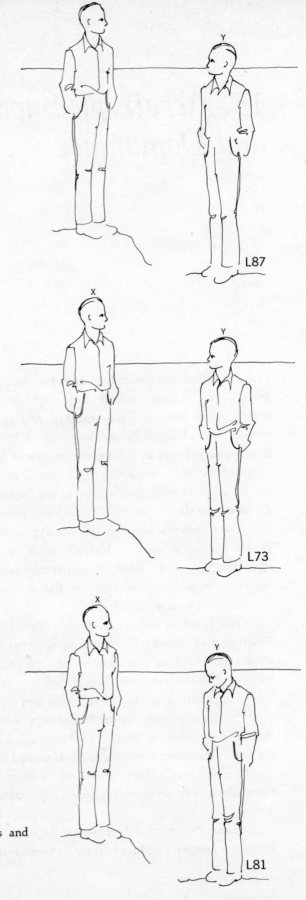

**Fig. 38.** Acrotropic Displacements and Head Positions

L31

L45

L25

L53

L11

L39

inequality is a serious matter which underlies and supports social inequalities of all types.[2] Here, however, only the conditions under which various types of vertical displacements lead to different social meanings in abstracted drawings will be studied. Because the stimuli are drawings, it is impossible to represent people in real motion and, thus, to show unambiguously who is active in producing the acrotrope; there is also a positive reason why the distinction between the two types of acrotropes will not be studied here. The procedure of originally choosing paintings for interviews had revealed that other variables entered into the meaning of the acrotrope beside that of who carries out the vertical displacing. In pictures of the Nativity, for example, shepherds or wise men generally stood higher than the reclining Christ child; nevertheless, they were clearly paying him homage and considered themselves inferior to him. Of course, they frequently bowed their heads, or even lowered their whole bodies by kneeling, and, in spite of their superior location in space, no longer presented the simple acrotropic inequality implied in the description here. One might say that they were attempting to undo the effects of the acrotrope by lowering themselves, or parts of themselves, as much as possible. Thus, by accentuating this departure from the usual, simple acrotrope, it might even be said that they were trying to *reverse* the acrotrope and place the Christ child in the higher position. But to say merely that, in the shepherds' relation to the Christ child, the acrotrope is reversed is to oversimplify the situation, since it ignores the fact that the inferior person is still physically higher and it denies that physical displacement plays any role whatever. One has every reason to suspect that the meaning of a bowed head on a higher person is different from that of a bowed head on a lower; and, in the simple case of two unequal people looking straight ahead, there is no reason to think that the superior is not the higher.

Thus, one still needs to study the conditions under which the usual meaning of the acrotrope does not hold. The subjects for this study rated drawings in which two figures were either acrotropic or not (in the latter case, the position was called an isotrope); beside that, the figures' heads could be bowed or not. In fact, however, the number of drawings needed was higher than the full combination of these two conditions would produce. As soon as one begins to construct the required drawings, one notices that an ambiguity arises in the position of the superior person: If he is looking down, is he looking at the other's head or below it? The meaning that each of these possibilities has seems different; the interaction they imply changes quite markedly.

It was clear that three head positions, not two, could very easily be distinguished for the superior person (head held level, head looking down at the other, and head deeply bowed), but the head positions for the inferior person had to be different. Two lowered positions seemed superfluous because of their apparent similarity in meaning, and only one (head bowed) was retained. On the other hand, a raised position had to be added; since the superior person assumed one position in which he made visual contact with the lower, symmetry demanded that the inferior also assume a position looking at the superior. If the superior person is always placed on the left side of the drawing and the inferior person on the right, and, if they are called $X$ and $Y$ respectively, one obtains the nine possibilities for drawings listed in Table 15–1. This group is called Series L, and there is an identification number for each picture at the intersection of each position of $X$ and $Y$. All the pictures appear in Fig. 38.

**TABLE 15–1. Combinations of Acrotropic Displacements and Head Positions**

| | | Figure X | |
| *Figure Y* | *Looks straight ahead* | *Looks down at Y* | *Bows head* |
| --- | --- | --- | --- |
| *Looks up at X* | L87 | L31 | L45 |
| *Looks straight ahead* | L73 | L25 | L53 |
| *Bows head* | L81 | L11 | L39 |

The isotropic positions could be fewer in number, because, in looking straight ahead, $X$ and $Y$ perforce looked at each other; hence, no distinction could exist between "looking up at," "looking down at," and "looking at." The two positions for each actor became, therefore, "looking at the other" and "bowing the head." This would normally give the four possibilities presented in Table 15–2, but, since the isotropic position was symmetrical, one of the combinations was superfluous. Three isotropic drawings (shown in Fig. 39) sufficed.

**TABLE 15–2. Combinations of Isotrope and Head Positions**

| | Figure X | |
| *Figure Y* | *Looks straight ahead* | *Bows head* |
| --- | --- | --- |
| *Looks straight ahead* | L17 | |
| *Bows head* | L67 | L59 |

To measure the subjects' perception of these drawings, seven-point dimensions were again used; and these dimensions fall roughly into the two categories

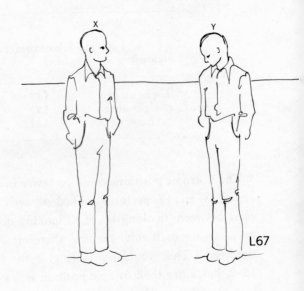

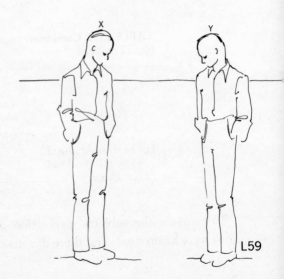

**Fig. 39.** Isotropic Displacements and
Head Positions

264

of theoretical concern with the acrotropic position. Dominance, the first interest, was measured by the following dimensions: "initiating action–receiving action," "subordinate–superordinate," "haughty–humble," and "important–insignificant." The quality of the interaction, the second concern, was assessed on the dimensions: "hostile–friendly," "approaching–withdrawing," "other-concerned–self-concerned," and "intimate with other–distant from other." The reader will recognize that quality of interaction refers to the variables discussed in the theoretical exposition—those referring to the approach–separation continuum. The reader will also notice that the variables are generally the same in each chapter in which the focus of study is interaction; hence, their similarity to the characteristics studied in Chapters 13 and 14. In each of the drawings, the subjects rated both figures, each on the eight dimensions listed. Series L was given to 18 subjects (more men than women). Because body space boundaries were only a secondary concern here, and, because attractiveness was not an issue at all, the results will not be analyzed by sex.

In this chapter the usual extreme-figures analysis will be omitted—it is too unwieldy—and, instead, the principal data will consist of an analysis of variance of figures grouped as types. Each of the head–body combinations listed in Tables 15–1 and 15–2 is represented in the whole collection of pictures by three figures (since each figure had to appear with its three possible partners). The analysis will focus upon the mean ratings that each of these figure types receives on each of the dimensions, and the influence that figures $X$ and $Y$ have on each other.

For the first type of analysis, the figures are grouped as in Table 15–3, with changes in head position appearing on the horizontal axis and changes in acrotropic body displacement varying on the vertical axis. In each cell will appear the mean scores, dimension by dimension, that the three figures received together. As the reader may suspect, some difficulty arises from the lack of

**TABLE 15–3. Figures Grouped by Vertical Displacement and Head Position**

|  | *Looks straight ahead* | *Looks at other figure* | *Bows head* |
|---|---|---|---|
| *Supra* | L87x | L31x | L39x |
|  | L81x | L11x | L53x |
|  | L73x | L25x | L45x |
| *Iso* |  | L17x | L59x |
|  |  | L17y | L59y |
|  |  | L67x | L67y |
| *Infra* | L73y | L87y | L39y |
|  | L53y | L31y | L81y |
|  | L25y | L45y | L11y |

distinction among isotropic figures between looking "straight ahead" and looking "at" the partner, since one must make a choice of the box in which to put them. Since, in an isotropic figure, looking straight ahead implies eye contact with the partner, it is here classified as looking "at" him, whereas, among superior and inferior figures, the straight-ahead gaze misses the partner's eyes altogether.[3] Consequently, one box in the table is left blank.[4]

In Table 15–4 are presented the data for the first dimension: "hostile–friendly." A look at the extreme figures suggests that hostility was an effect of superiority and inattention to the other figure, and that the inferior partners of hostile figures would be friendly. If one looks at the marginal means, one notices that superior figures are indeed seen as the least friendly and that inferior partners are viewed as the most friendly (and significantly so; see Appendix P). The bottom row shows that figures looking straight ahead appear the least friendly, while those looking at the partner or bowing their heads are nearly equally friendly (but these means do not differ significantly). Within the table itself, the superior figures that look straight ahead receive the most hostile rating, and the inferior figures that look up at their partners obtain the most friendly rating. Thus, hostility appears best expressed by a superior inattention, while friendliness is best embodied in what may be inferior supplication.

TABLE 15–4. Mean Scores on "Hostile–Friendly" Dimension, by Position

|  | Looks straight ahead | Looks at other figure | Bows head | Overall mean |
|---|---|---|---|---|
| Supra | 3.22 | 3.65 | 4.04 | 3.64 |
| Iso |  | 4.17 | 4.13 | 4.15 |
| Infra | 4.70 | 4.93 | 4.33 | 4.65 |
| Overall mean | 3.96 | 4.25 | 4.17 |  |

As for the "approaching–withdrawing" dimension, presented in Table 15–5, the marginal means show that figures looking at others are the most approaching and those with heads bowed are the most withdrawing; and further that inferior individuals are rated as the most approaching while the isotropic and superior figures appear about equally withdrawing. Analysis of variance indicates that the head effect is highly significant, while the body effect shows real differences only between the superior and inferior rows. Within the body of the table, the data are more complex: The most approaching figures are the inferior ones that stare straight ahead or look at the partner; the most withdrawing

**TABLE 15–5. Mean Scores on "Approaching–Withdrawing" Dimension, by Position**

| | Looks straight ahead | Looks at other figure | Bows head | Overall mean |
|---|---|---|---|---|
| Supra | 4.72 | 3.06 | 4.96 | 4.25 |
| Iso | | 3.17 | 5.50 | 4.34 |
| Infra | 2.78 | 2.74 | 5.17 | 3.56 |
| Overall mean | 3.75 | 2.99 | 5.21 | |

figures are the isotropic—bowed persons. There seems little doubt that withdrawal is determined—among these figures, and as in Chapter 13—by head position: The lowered gaze is the most averted and most breaks the contact with the partner, especially when the partners are otherwise nearly equal and, therefore, have the best possibility of communicating *inter pares*. But approach, though very much determined by the directed gaze, also seems to be best shown by those figures that have the most *reason* to approach—the inferior ones.

On the "initiating–receiving" dimension, whose data appear in Table 15–6, individuals who look at another are the most initiating and those who lower their heads are the most receiving. The vertical margin shows that acrotropic body displacement plays a *very* small role: Superior figures are only a trifle more initiating than inferior (and the analysis of variance confirms that the head effect is the only significant one). But, in the body of the table, superiority does play a role: Of those looking at others, the superior figures initiate the most, or, conversely, among the superior figures, only those looking down at their partners do any initiating. Therefore, superiority does not guarantee action-initiation; in particular, when it is not used to make eye contact with the inferior person (especially by bowing one's own head), it may indicate the receipt of action. But to show that one is *receiving* action is a very simple matter: One has

**TABLE 15–6. Mean Scores on "Initiating–Receiving" Dimension, by Position**

| | Looks straight ahead | Looks at other figure | Bows head | Overall mean |
|---|---|---|---|---|
| Supra | 4.04 | 2.87 | 4.74 | 3.88 |
| Iso | | 3.20 | 5.04 | 4.12 |
| Infra | 3.30 | 3.56 | 5.09 | 3.98 |
| Overall mean | 3.67 | 3.21 | 4.96 | |

but to lower his gaze, no matter what his relative vertical position. Insofar as head changes play the determining role, these results parallel strikingly those of Chapter 13.

Table 15–7 presents the mean scores for the "subordinate–superordinate" dimension. One might expect subordination to be expressed by a bowed head on an inferior individual, and superordination to be embodied in the superior position with gaze directed straight ahead or down at the partner. The marginal figures in the table show that, among head positions, the bowed heads do indeed create the greatest subordination, but that figures looking straight ahead exhibit slightly more superordination than those looking at others; on the vertical dimension, the inferior figures are, as expected, seen as the most subordinate and the superior as the most superordinate. Both the body and head effects are

TABLE 15–7. Mean Scores on "Subordinate–Superordinate" Dimension, by Position

|  | Looks straight ahead | Looks at other figure | Bows head | Overall mean |
|---|---|---|---|---|
| Supra | 5.37 | 5.44 | 3.85 | 4.89 |
| Iso |  | 4.54 | 3.33 | 3.94 |
| Infra | 3.82 | 3.11 | 2.30 | 3.08 |
| Overall mean | 4.60 | 4.36 | 3.16 |  |

statistically highly significant. The interior of the table clearly points out that the inferior individuals with bowed heads receive by far the most subordinate ratings, and that, among the superior figures, both the directed gaze and the straight-ahead stare obtain the most superordinate ones. Superordination can, then, be expressed in two ways (its precondition, in any case, is the higher position as it was in Chapter 13): with the straight-ahead look, the superordination takes on a haughty, distant quality, while, with a look down at the partner, it appears to be more communicative and perhaps even solicitous. Subordination, on the other hand, is well expressed by the inferior position or by a lowered head, and especially well by both. It is of considerable theoretical interest that on this dimension both the inclination of the head and the vertical displacement play the important roles; it is the first dimension on which this regularity has been observed.

How does one express haughtiness and humbleness? In popular understanding, the former is shown by highly placed people with upturned noses, while the latter requires bowed head, lower position, and wringing of hands or crumpling of hat. Table 15–8 presents the data to verify these images. The marginal means indicate that superior figures appear as the haughty ones and inferior individuals as the humble, and that straight-ahead-looking figures look haughty while persons with bowed heads appear humble; both effects are, for the second time, highly significant. The internal means confirm the conclusion even more strongly, in that the superior, straight-ahead-gazing figures receive the most haughty

**TABLE 15–8. Mean Scores on "Haughty–Humble" Dimension, by Position**

|  | Looks straight ahead | Looks at other figure | Bows head | Overall mean |
|---|---|---|---|---|
| *Supra* | 2.67 | 3.18 | 5.24 | 3.70 |
| *Iso* |  | 3.91 | 5.46 | 4.68 |
| *Infra* | 4.09 | 4.98 | 5.91 | 4.99 |
| *Overall mean* | 3.38 | 4.02 | 5.54 |  |

ratings, and the inferior, bowed figures are rated as the most humble. The distinction, made in Chapter 13, between haughtiness and superordination needs confirmation here: In the former, the superior person consciously avoids contact with the inferior, while, in the latter, he may seek it. It is like the difference between the *parvenu* and the old-moneyed; or between the unforgiving master and the forgiving mother.

Other-concern and self-concern, whose relations to vertical displacement and head position appear in Table 15–9, might be expected to be governed by direction of gaze (see Chapters 13 and 14), in the absence of other bodily changes, such as in arm position. Other-concerned figures, presumably, look at their partners, while self-concerned individuals lower their heads. The marginal means indicate that vertical changes play a small and irregular role, but that changes in head inclination are very important (and significant): In each row, those who look at others are the most other-concerned. Self-concern is somewhat more complicated a matter: It is generally shown by a lowered head, and especially so in an inferior or isotropic individual, but, among superior persons, it seems equally well shown by the straight-ahead look *and* by the lowered head. This result is highly consistent with the theoretical framework, in that it shows self-concern to be expressed by either type of averted gaze, and, consequently, by interrupted communication. (As with Venus, it was expressed by blocked approaches to the body.)

TABLE 15–9. Mean Scores on "Other-concerned–Self-concerned" Dimension, by Position

|  | Looks straight ahead | Looks at other figure | Bows head | Overall mean |
|---|---|---|---|---|
| *Supra* | 4.87 | 3.00 | 4.93 | 4.27 |
| *Iso* |  | 3.35 | 5.26 | 4.30 |
| *Infra* | 3.07 | 2.80 | 5.11 | 3.66 |
| *Overall mean* | 3.97 | 3.05 | 5.10 |  |

As for the dimension "importance–insignificance," one would expect it to be expressed in vertical body displacements and, perhaps, in head-position changes (with the bowed head as the least important). Table 15–10 provides the information relevant to this expectation. In the marginal means, the superior figures are indeed the most important and inferior ones are insignificant; and, among the different head positions, those looking straight ahead are important while those lowering their heads are insignificant. Analysis of variance shows both types of change to effect the ratings strongly and independently. In the body of the table, the data are somewhat more complex for the superior individuals: They express their importance as well by the downward-directed look as by the straight-ahead gaze. In this respect, this dimension strongly resembles that of "subordination–superordination," the latter of which was expressed in the superior person both by communication with the partner and by the level gaze, but these results differ from those of Chapter 13 in that, there, importance of a protagonist was determined solely by the returned gaze of the antagonist. Inferior individuals, however, reduce their subordination (and insignificance) when they look at their partners, and do so still more when they stare straight ahead in their direction. In staring, it is as if they were ignoring the subordinate

TABLE 15–10. Mean Scores on "Important–Insignificant" Dimension, by Position

|  | Looks straight ahead | Looks at other figure | Bows head | Overall mean |
|---|---|---|---|---|
| *Supra* | 2.54 | 2.54 | 4.13 | 3.07 |
| *iso* |  | 3.37 | 4.54 | 3.96 |
| *Infra* | 3.74 | 4.31 | 5.35 | 4.47 |
| *Overall mean* | 3.14 | 3.41 | 4.67 |  |

position that the other placed them in, and, by ignoring it, they were generally successful in reversing it.

The final dimension measures intimacy and distance between figures. It seems reasonable to suppose that, since intimacy between people must be shared, it would generally characterize individuals who look at their partners, and it would be seen particularly in mutually returned gazes—while distance would be created by interrupted eye contact. Table 15–11 shows these qualities to be expressed in complex ways. The most intimate figures do look at their partners (the head differences are very significant) and generally do so from an inferior or an isotropic position (only the "superior–inferior" difference reaches significance); the distant ones tend to be superior or to look straight ahead. But the body of the table indicates that, while the most intimate interaction takes place among isotropic individuals who look at their partners (thus making equality between them important), superior persons can also be very highly intimate, provided they look at the partner; but when they look straight ahead, they receive the highest rating on distance. In summary, since vertical displacement distinguishes only the individuals who look straight ahead, for all other positions, intimacy and distance seem to be determined by the direction of gaze—hence, by the quality of eye communication.

TABLE 15–11. Mean Scores on "Intimate–Distant"
Dimension, by Position

|  | Looks straight ahead | Looks at other figure | Bows head | Overall mean |
|---|---|---|---|---|
| *Supra* | 5.78 | 3.43 | 4.15 | 4.45 |
| *Iso* |  | 3.30 | 4.39 | 3.84 |
| *Infra* | 3.61 | 3.54 | 4.22 | 3.79 |
| *Overall mean* | 4.70 | 3.42 | 4.25 |  |

The superior individual's ability to be seen as either extremely intimate or very distant finds a striking parallel in a study of linguistic expression of inequality. The findings of this study are that the superior individual who looks at his partner is intimate on the one hand, and action-initiating on the other. Brown and Ford (1961), in a study of American modes of address in the expression of status differences, remark that, in an interacting pair, only the socially superior person can control the amount of intimacy that the pair can express. When an increase in intimacy is to take place, it is initiated from above; the superior person can remain distant if he wishes, but the inferior *must* remain so—until the superior approaches him. In this study, the superior's freedom is expressed in his high score on "action-initiation" (when he looks at his partner), and in the choice he has of appearing intimate (when looking) or distant (when not). It is interesting to note the perfect correspondence, in this one realm, between the bodily expression of physical inequality and the linguistic expression of social inequality.

So far, physical inequality has been analyzed only individually, as though no mutual influence existed between the members of the interacting pair. But such influence may safely be supposed to exist, both on the basis of common sense and on the strength of the comparison between individual and social presentation of gestures in Chapter 14. Here, its extent will be analyzed by calculating, picture by picture, the correlations that exist between the scores of $X$ and $Y$ on matching dimensions. The advantage of correlation scores is that they are to a great extent independent of mean levels of the ratings presented already, so that nearly equal mean scores obtained by two figures may still be positively or negatively correlated. The correlations, therefore, measure the interdependence of the scores of $X$ and $Y$ (but only on matching dimensions) in ways that are not always revealed by a more minute examination of mean scores.

The full table of correlations is presented in Appendix Q; for each of the 12 pictures there are 8 scores, one on each of the 8 dimensions. Of the 96 correlations, 33 are significant at below the .05 level, a fact that speaks for rather strong overall interdependence between the two figures. But the specific types of interdependence may be better understood by examining the patterns of correlations, both by individual picture and by dimension. To look at the simpler matter first, the two pictures with a predominance of positive correlations (the criterion is six out of eight, but, for these two pictures, all eight correlations are positive) are L39 and L59; in both pictures, the partners bow their heads deeply, and, if one looks at the scores the partners obtain (see Appendix R), their scores are very similar. The six pictures in which predominantly negative correlations may be observed (L31, L53, L67, L73, L81, and L87) generally show a superior $X$ looking straight ahead or down at his partner $Y$; the two figures' scores generally differ considerably. These inter-picture differences indicate only that the two figures will influence each other's scores positively when they are both humbly bowing their heads, and negatively when the perceived differences between them are large.

But the differences among the *dimensions*, in the predominance of negative or positive correlations, are much more instructive. Five dimensions are mostly negatively correlated across the twelve pictures (criterion: eight out of twelve). Of these, the first is self- or other-concern, which appears inversely related in pictures displaying acrotropic inequality between the partners (and directly related in isotropes and in pictures where both partners bow their heads). The other four dimensions, however, display a marked independence of context, and, whenever their correlations are significant, they are negative: these are the dimensions of action-initiation, superordination, haughtiness, and importance. These dimensions—and only these—measure dominance between the partners, and it may be assumed that the subjects understood the dominance of one partner to be generally antithetical to the dominance of the other.[5] It is as if, in any given situation where dominance must be expressed, only one person could lead.

On only one dimension are the correlations predominantly positive (and exclusively so when one takes into account only the significant ones): that of intimacy. The correlations are significantly high in three very unlike contexts and remain positive in six others, equally unlike; the subjects, therefore, perceived the intimacy of one figure as dependent on that of the other. Brown and Ford's discussion of intimacy, mentioned earlier, provides a clue for explaining this close relation. They found that two people of unequal status had to remain socially distant until the superior took steps towards increased intimacy; when this occurred, the inferior could not very well refuse unless he wanted to break the relation. The pair's degree of intimacy was, therefore, determined by one person, making it unlikely that the two could disagree as to how intimate they were—or, to put it differently, making intimacy the property of a pair, but never of an individual. Thus, it was occasionally possible for the subjects to rate one member as more intimate than the other (which indicates that the member is making the attempt, perhaps unsuccessfully), and to feel, at the same time, that the rating of the one had to reflect, in the same direction, the rating of the other.

The extent to which head position (and consequent eye contact) modified the differences expected to arise from vertical displacement alone is noteworthy. Figures with bowed heads, for example, generally received high ratings on action-receiving irrespective of their vertical position. It is useful to look once more at those tables, more schematically, and attempt to offer a brief but comprehensive review of the disparate results. A consideration of Tables 15–4 through 15–11 makes it possible to construct a summary table in which the dimensions best characterizing each position can be located. The dimension is located at the intersection of a given head and body position, or, when one of these factors makes comparatively little difference, the dimension name is placed in the margin.[6] Table 15–12 has been constructed in this way.

This table makes it possible to form an overview by type of figure rather than by dimension. It shows that the superior figures that look straight ahead (thus avoiding or disdaining the partner) are rated as the most hostile, haughty, and distant, while the superiors looking at their partners appear as the most initiating.

Hostility, haughtiness, and distance, therefore, require absence of eye contact in the superior figure, while action-initiation cannot exist without eye contact. But contact is irrelevant for superordination and importance; these dimensions merely require a superior position that is not tempered by a bowed head. In this sense, superordination and importance are the two most general terms for the dominance that has been the theme of this chapter, while haughtiness is a more special term.

**TABLE 15–12. Dimensions Most Characteristic of Various Positions**

|  | Looks straight ahead | Looks at other figure | Bows head | No difference in head position |
|---|---|---|---|---|
| *Supra* | hostile haughty distant | initiating |  |  |
|  | superordinate important |  |  |  |
| *Iso* |  |  |  |  |
| *Infra* |  | friendly (approaching) | subordinate insignificant humble |  |
| *No difference in vertical displacement* |  | approaching other-concerned intimate | withdrawing self-concerned receiving |  |

There are strong parallels between these results and those of Chapter 13, in spite of differences in their goals: There (in Chapter 13), superordination was also a function of height (the standing $X$ was always superior to the seated $Z$), and, with respect to the movable central figure, of eye contact and diatropic stance. Importance, however, was a function only of the returned gaze, irrespective of height, probably because the pictures were drawn so as to show two figures that give instructions, one of whom was seated. Finally, action-initiation, in Chapter 13 as well as here, was determined by the directed and returned gaze.

Inferior figures, when they look straight ahead (still in the direction of their partners, of course), receive high ratings on approach; when they look up at their partner, too, they receive the highest ratings on friendliness. When they bow their heads, they are perceived as extremely subordinate, insignificant, and humble.

It is remarkable that, of the two margins, only the bottom one contains any entries; all of the figures that look at their partners are seen as most highly approaching, other-concerned, and intimate, while those that bow their heads are invariably seen as very withdrawing, self-concerned, and receiving. It is clear that these dimensions measure eye contact between figures, and eye contact only; and there are no dimensions (among those offered) where large differences are created solely by vertical displacement. This is not to say that vertical displacement makes no difference in scores—it does; but it does not generally act independently, interacting always with head inclination and its direction of gaze.

# NOTES FOR CHAPTER 15

[1] In this chapter, the terms "superior" and "inferior" will refer only to physical position, not to dominance or superordination; for the latter, other terms will be used.

[2] The role of height and/or stature in social interaction has not been studied systematically enough. One would expect a number of social situations to exist in which height confers power, prestige, and status; the reasons for this are doubtless many, including the memory of one's physical inferiority to the parents, the informational superiority that follows from being able to see farther, and others. Where stature fails to (or cannot) produce the necessary height, artificial means, such as elevator shoes and pulpits, may be resorted to. But there is some evidence, though not enough, that taller stature by itself is associated with leadership of groups and the occupancy of higher statuses in organizations. (See Gibb, 1954, p. 885.)

[3] Since $X$'s appear always on the left side of the picture, in nine of twelve cases they will be in the superior position; in those same nine, $Y$'s will be inferior; and, in the remaining three drawings, both figures will be isotropic.

[4] The blank box made it necessary to perform two analyses of variance on these data: one which left out the "looks straight ahead" column, and one which omitted the "iso" row. See Appendix P for the details of this analysis and for the significance levels.

[5] This conclusion is very much strengthened by the one case in which the two unequal figures obtain the same *mean* scores (in L45, on subordination); there, the correlation remains negative and the antithesis continues. But with equal isotropic figures, the correlations sometimes disappear or become positive.

[6] When the means in one row or one column differ by less than about $\pm.50$, we say that they are alike and place the dimension name in the margin; for greater differences, we locate the dimension name within the distinct cell. Both ends of each dimension are located in the table; and when one end appears in parentheses, it means that, although it is properly located in the margin, one location stood out enough for us to call special attention to it in the body of the table.

# 16. Male–Female Encounter

The preliminary study presented to the subjects three paintings of male–female interaction; they were Rubens's and Titian's *Venus and Adonis* (Fig. 27 and 28), and Correggio's *Jupiter and Antiope* (Fig. 29). The first two are relevant here because they vary Venus's relation to the departing Adonis—he shows by his stance, in both cases, that his desire to leave is ambivalent, and she demonstrates by her grasp different modulations of the wish to detain him. In Rubens's version, she extends both her arms towards Adonis and gently curves one hand around his arm; Adonis finds himself just inside her axial boundary, which is made amply evident by the extended arms, but retains some freedom of movement. In Titian's portrayal, Venus hold Adonis back by clasping him around the torso, in this way closing her axial boundary and forcing Adonis to remain within her axial space. The subjects interviewed perceived the former version as relatively more open and airy and saw the latter as stuffy and enclosed. Other cues besides Venus's arm position naturally contributed to this effect— the cool tones of the former and the warm, brown ones of the latter, for example—but it seemed that the arm position was crucial. The subjects who saw Correggio's painting strengthened this belief in the importance of the female figure's arm position. Antiope sleeps with her arms behind her head and flaunts her young bosom.

It seems appropriate to conclude that Antiope's unambiguous attraction is accounted for by the convexity of her torso, or perhaps more simply by the absence of axial space in front of her body. While Rubens's Venus creates a space with her arms within which Adonis can remain but beyond which he is not compelled to go, thus making his presence within that space comfortable and unconstrained, Antiope invites interaction directly at her proximal boundary; given her arm position, there would seem to be no stability for a person attempting to maintain a position at axial length from her. It is natural that male subjects should perceive this position as a welcome invitation—or, on the other hand, to be put off by its frankness. One might say that Rubens's Venus makes it possible for an approaching figure to become involved only up to a certain point, but that Antiope's position is seen as inviting interaction in a more drastic sense.

This distinction between defined axial space and open proximal access has been mentioned in the study of arm positions characteristic of leadership, in Series S; there, the displayed chest was perceived as giving the person an air of haughtiness and firmness. The haughtiness was thought to come from the seemingly paradoxical fact that the exposed chest, by inviting (or permitting) interaction only at the proximal boundary, would discourage approach by threatening an aggressive interpretation of it. Thus, the absence of delineated axial space appears to invite more drastic approach, both in the positive and negative sense.

This chapter asks whether the distinction can be elaborated further, and will compare perceptions of male–female interactions in which the male moves within and without her axial space. Besides analyzing the degree of freedom or constraint or the strength of sexual intention, the study sought to identify the conditions that led subjects to perceive these partners as initiating or receiving action, as aggressive or non-aggressive, as acting with good or evil intentions. Aside from an analysis of perceptions of the different figures, it is crucial to discover the influence that the perception of one figure may have on the perception of the other; whether, and to what extent, the perceived aggressiveness of one actor, say, will affect the attributed aggressiveness of the other.

The model for the drawings became Rubens's painting because it presents the female figure as facing the observer, and, unlike the Correggio, shows the two actors in nearly diatropic interaction. The represented female figure was drawn on a high formless mound, which would give her a place to sit but would still allow her some freedom of movement. The exploratory analysis and the construction of Series H had indicated that at least four arm positions were necessary: both arms down at the side (to open the proximal access), the right arm extended outward (partially to create an axial space, while leaving it open from the observer's view), the left arm extended outward (again, creating axial space partially but presenting it as closed to the observer), and both arms extended (defining the space into which or within which the man can move). In Rubens's painting, Venus is shown with her legs facing away from Adonis, thus making the pelvic region inaccessible to him; it seemed appropriate to explore the meanings of this inaccessibility and create figures whose pelvic region confronts the man in some cases and turns away in others. With legs facing toward the man in some drawings, and away from him in others, one obtains eight different female figures: four arm positions and two leg positions. Only the leg direction changes in the representations; the arms and the head are kept as identical as possible, while the torso leans somewhat forward or backward.

The man, too, was modeled on Rubens's Adonis, although the spear was left out of the picture. Contemporary culture provides few props of spear size and shape for a man to lean on, while, in Rubens's time (or imagination), the spear could point elsewhere than the body and express the figure's wish to move in two directions. To an extent, this difficulty was lessened by a decision to have the man portray unambiguous advance or retreat, the advancing figure leaning towards the woman and extending the right arm partly towards her (this Rubens's figure did, too, the arm extended at the level of Venus's thigh), the receding figure leaning away from the woman and confirming his retreat by extending the left hand slightly in that direction. Each of these two figures was represented both within the woman's axial space and outside it (or at axial distance and farther, in the case of women with arms down). Four male figures could, therefore, interact with the eight females; a total of 32 pictures resulted. Fig. 40 presents a sample of the drawings; these represent each one of the male and female types, in combinations that best illustrate the analysis of extreme figures that will be presented later in this chapter.

Comparability of figures from drawing to drawing was maintained by photographically reproducing each of the male and female types, mounting them on one sheet of paper, and having the whole scene printed by photo-offset. The distance of the male figure from the female, which will simply be called "near" and "far," was determined by measuring the distance between their heads; thus, whatever the position of the bodies, the heads remained apart at one or the other of the two fixed distances.

Ten dimensions were selected to record the subjects' perceptions of the figures, and four additional ones to describe the interaction itself; again, each dimension formed a seven-point scale. The dimensions applicable to the figures measured intensity and determination of the actors ("intense–relaxed," "uncertain–determined"), their activeness ("initiating action–receiving action," "active–passive"), their feelings or motives ("non-erotic–erotic," "warm–cold," "aggressive–unaggressive"), moral qualities associated with their intention movements ("sincere–calculating," "evil–good"), and finally, their freedom of action ("constrained–free"). Each of these dimensions was applied separately to the male and female figures of a picture. After the 20 ratings, subjects made four more to describe the interaction as transient or permanent, satisfactory or unsatisfactory; they rated the atmosphere as enclosed or free, and the movement as about to continue or about to be reversed. Naturally, to make 24 ratings on 32 figures would be a Herculean task; the subjects were split into two groups of 20, each of which rated only 16 of the drawings.

As in preceding chapters, several analyses of these data will be presented;

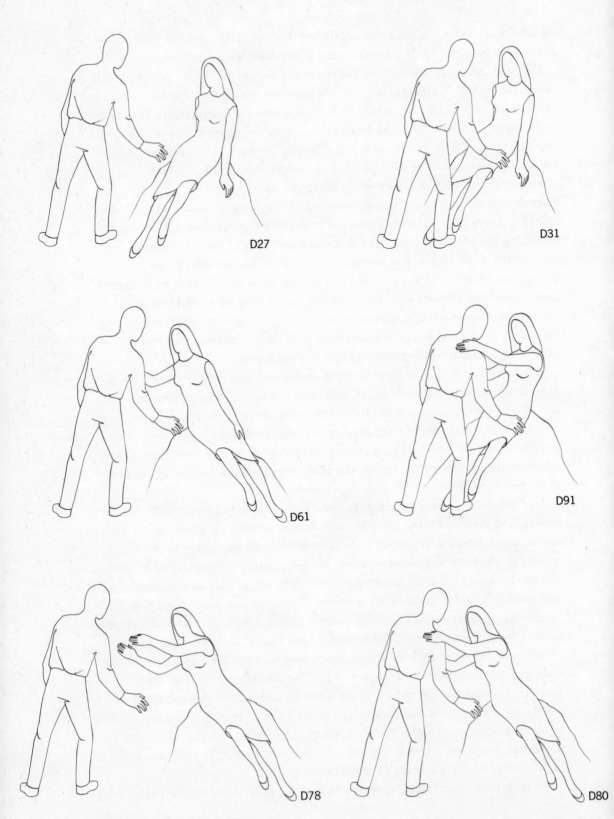

D27

D31

D61

D91

D78

D80

**Fig. 40.**   Male–Female Encounter

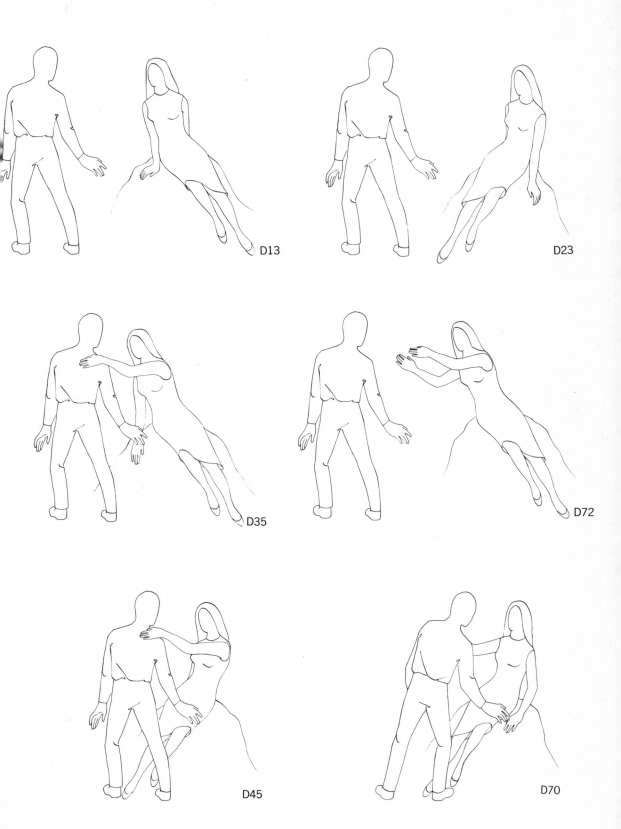

D13

D23

D35

D72

D45

D70

first, the characterizations of each male and female figure (which are means computed across the four presentations of each female and eight presentations of each male, and across all subjects), and the descriptions of the interaction (for each male and female figure); second, an analysis of individual drawings that received extreme ratings and an assessment of the influence of one figure on another; third, a study of sex differences between subjects.

The eight female positions assumed will be grouped in 2 x 4 tables in which the four arm movements and two leg positions intersect; and the rating of each position will be a mean of four identical positions rated by ten subjects each.

The first dimension that appeared on the answer sheet was that of "initiating action–receiving action"; Table 16–1 presents the mean ratings each figure received. It is striking that the upper row, with figures whose legs point toward the man, contains higher scores in every case than the lower row; this leg position was invariably seen as considerably more receiving than the one in which the legs face away from the man. Of all the legs-toward positions, the one with arms down at the sides is the most receiving, and of the legs-away positions, the one with both arms extended is the most initiating. (Analysis of

**TABLE 16–1. Mean Ratings of Female Figures on "Initiating Action–Receiving Action" (40 Observations per Cell)**

|  | Arms down | Right arm extended | Left arm extended | Both arms extended |
|---|---|---|---|---|
| Legs  toward | 5.48 | 3.71 | 2.88 | 2.59 |
| Legs away | 4.58 | 2.39 | 1.56 | 1.51 |

variance confirms the effects produced by changes in the arms and legs as very highly significant; see Appendix S). It would appear that a forward movement of the torso and extension of the arms toward the male figure signify maximally active striving, while the arms-at-side position—in which the ventral side of the body is presented with receding but open proximal access—is seen as the most receiving position. So far, it may be said that the extended arms not only define axial space, but in these figures also serve to indicate the direction in which the whole body would move if it were not stationary.

In Table 16–2 appear the ratings obtained on the dimension "warm–cold." Here, too, all the scores in the upper row are higher than the corresponding ones in the lower, signifying that subjects perceive the legs-away position as warmer and the legs-toward as colder. In fact, the figure with legs away and both arms extended toward the man is the warmest of all, and the one with legs toward him and arms at sides is the coldest (again, with statistical significance for arm and legs changes). It is surprising that the presentation of the undefended ventral side should not be seen as warm in a woman, but, apparently in this series, the subjects connected warmth with active striving.

**TABLE 16–2. Mean Ratings of Female Figures on "Warm–Cold"**

|  | Arms down | Right arm extended | Left arm extended | Both arms extended |
|---|---|---|---|---|
| Legs toward | 4.39 | 3.28 | 2.39 | 2.18 |
| Legs away | 2.61 | 2.38 | 1.79 | 1.69 |

Ratings on "intense–relaxed," in Table 16–3, show that in three of the four arm positions the higher row receives the higher ratings; therefore the legs-toward position is the less intense of the two. (The arm and leg changes are again statistically significant.) Apparently, when the legs point away from the man, the whole body leans toward him in a way that is perceived as directed, striving, and intense, as if its direction of inclination were also a direction of movement forward. Of these four figures, the most intense extends both arms

**TABLE 16–3. Mean Ratings of Female Figures on "Intense–Relaxed"**

|  | Arms down | Right arm extended | Left arm extended | Both arms extended |
|---|---|---|---|---|
| Legs toward | 3.39 | 3.75 | 3.96 | 3.58 |
| Legs away | 3.60 | 3.28 | 3.08 | 2.23 |

as if to supplement the movement her whole body has been perceived as making; but while the four figures whose legs face the man do not differ in any progressive sense, the least intense figure points her legs toward the man and extends her left arm out, in a movement that might have been perceived by the subjects as both backward (with the body) and forward (with the arm)— creating another bodily grimace. It is consistent with this interpretation of her movement that all three of the figures with legs pointing toward the man and arms extended received low ratings on intensity. But no one, in the universe of these pictures, is relaxed.

The "uncertainty–determination" ratings given to the female figures appear in Table 16–4. It is remarkable that the two rows consistently differ from each other (significantly, as do the columns); the higher scores in the lower row indicate that the position in which the woman's legs face away from the man is the more determined of the two. Again, one cannot escape the conclusion that determination was connected in the subjects' minds with activity and striving; the most uncertain position, with arms down and legs facing toward the man, was not judged as one in which the woman could wish to entice the man in a perfectly determined fashion. Nevertheless, all the other legs-toward positions are on the determined end of the mean, suggesting that any extension of the arms toward the man signifies determination; when the body leans in his direction, too (in the legs-away position), the determination is all the more strengthened, culminating in the position in which both arms are extended.

**TABLE 16–4. Mean Ratings of Female Figures on "Uncertain–Determined"**

|  | Arms down | Right arm extended | Left arm extended | Both arms extended |
|---|---|---|---|---|
| Legs toward | 3.44 | 4.45 | 4.93 | 5.21 |
| Legs away | 4.41 | 5.06 | 5.83 | 5.83 |

Table 16–5 presents the ratings on "aggressiveness–unaggressiveness." The trend of scores is as clear as in the preceding table (and even more significant); all the scores in the upper row are higher and show that the legs-toward position is the less aggressive of the two. The most unaggressive position among these has both arms down; and the most aggressive of the eight extends both arms

**TABLE 16–5. Mean Ratings of Female Figures on "Aggressive–Unaggressive"**

|  | Arms down | Right arm extended | Left arm extended | Both arms extended |
|---|---|---|---|---|
| Legs toward | 5.21 | 3.85 | 3.08 | 3.08 |
| Legs away | 4.35 | 2.79 | 2.31 | 1.88 |

toward the man while the legs face away from him. These results are consistent, both generally and in detail, with all the preceding: The body that leans fully toward the man, and the arms that extend its direction, are seen as intensely striving, as determined, and as aggressive.

"Constrained–free" is also a dimension in which all the legs-toward positions differ in score from the corresponding legs-away stances (both the leg effects and arm effects are highly significant). Table 16–6 shows that the former are in every case more constrained than the latter. If the legs-toward position is the more receiving and uncertain of the two, as seen before, it is understandable that

**TABLE 16–6. Mean Ratings of Female Figures on "Constrained–Free"**

|  | Arms down | Right arm extended | Left arm extended | Both arms extended |
|---|---|---|---|---|
| Legs toward | 3.05 | 4.30 | 5.05 | 5.10 |
| Legs away | 4.23 | 4.93 | 5.66 | 5.46 |

it should be perceived as the object of the actions of the man; when the man initiates, he is free, and the receiver of his action is constrained. And, on the contrary, when the woman initiates (as when the legs are facing away and the left arm or both arms are extended toward the man), she is perceived as very free. The extremely free figure does not extend both arms, in this case; she extends her left one only. But the scores of these two are close enough for this change to be counted as slight. The most constrained figure, as one would expect, not only turns her legs toward the man but also keeps both her arms at her side.

Table 16–7 gives the ratings for the dimension "sincere–calculating." Since all the scores are below 4.00, one cannot accuse any of the figures of appearing calculating. Nevertheless, the legs-toward position always receives the higher

**TABLE 16–7. Mean Ratings of Female Figures on "Sincere–Calculating"**

|  | Arms down | Right arm extended | Left arm extended | Both arms extended |
|---|---|---|---|---|
| Legs toward | 3.66 | 3.32 | 3.46 | 3.21 |
| Legs away | 3.21 | 3.05 | 3.27 | 2.60 |

scores and, thus, invariably appears as the less sincere of the two (the leg positions are significantly different, the arm positions are not). One may wonder that the passive, perhaps more enticing, position has the greater air of calculation while the reaching, striving one breathes sincerity; again, sincerity has been linked to activity and initiation of action. While this result may seem surprising, it is quite unambiguous. And as might be expected, the most sincere figure reaches out with both arms, while the least sincere sits with both arms at her side.

The next dimension attempted to measure the sexual quality of the various positions; its analysis appears in Table 16–8. Once again, one row receives scores consistently different from those of the other; the position in which legs face toward the man is consistently perceived as less erotic. And, once again, one may be surprised by the meaning this term had for these subjects; it was the action-initiating, aggressive position that had erotic implications, not the receiving one. It is true that all of the eight positions obtained ratings on the erotic side of the mean, but erotic ratings increase as the legs face away from the male, projecting the torso closer to him and in his direction. Of these positions, the one with both arms out is the most erotic, as one might expect; at the opposite pole is, once more, the figure with legs pointing toward the man and with both arms down. (Statistically, both the leg and arm effects are significant.)

**TABLE 16–8. Mean Ratings of Female Figures on "Non-erotic–Erotic"**

|  | Arms down | Right arm extended | Left arm extended | Both arms extended |
|---|---|---|---|---|
| Legs toward | 4.05 | 4.61 | 5.41 | 5.69 |
| Legs away | 5.04 | 4.91 | 5.72 | 5.98 |

The dimension "active–passive" should, by all expectations, be close to that of "initiating action–receiving action"; a glance at Table 16–9 will confirm this prediction. Figures with legs facing toward the man are in every case more passive than the corresponding figures whose legs face away; the extremes are represented, as before, by the figure with arms down and legs toward, who is the most passive, and by the one with both arms outstretched and legs away, who is the most active. (The same differences are, again, significant.) There is a difference between this dimension and that of "initiating–receiving," in that the scores are wider in range on the latter; perhaps the latter dimension more closely measures differences in actual activity, which may be perceived as large among

**TABLE 16–9. Mean Ratings of Female Figures on "Active–Passive"**

|  | Arms down | Right arm extended | Left arm extended | Both arms extended |
|---|---|---|---|---|
| Legs toward | 5.14 | 3.29 | 2.79 | 2.68 |
| Legs away | 4.41 | 2.66 | 1.79 | 1.78 |

our several figures, while the former ("active–passive") takes into account intentions and feelings of the actor, which can only be assumed. Since there is less evidence for what may be going on inside the actor, there is every reason to expect a lesser spread of scores.

The final dimension attempted to assess the moral qualities that subjects would attribute to the various female figures. If figures could be rated on the dimension "sincere–calculating," one could expect this last dimension to differentiate figures, too. Unfortunately, Table 16–10 shows that this was not the case: There are very few differences among the mean scores; those that exist do not vary systematically with leg or arm position; and, most surprisingly, all the figures were perceived as good! Although one might have expected that figures perceived, say, as calculating, cold, or aggressive could have also been judged as evil, these dimensions bore no relation whatever to moral evaluation. Though later discussion will show that evaluation on the "good–evil" dimension is possible, at this point, one must conclude that it does not characterize the female figures seen individually and whatever traits and intention movements may be perceived in them. This may in itself be an important conclusion.

**TABLE 16–10. Mean Ratings of Female Figures on "Evil–Good"**

|  | Arms down | Right arm extended | Left arm extended | Both arms extended |
|---|---|---|---|---|
| Legs toward | 4.39 | 4.16 | 4.29 | 4.26 |
| Legs away | 4.75 | 4.19 | 4.19 | 4.38 |

What do the female figures contribute to the perception of the interaction itself? Do descriptions of the interaction vary by type of female figure? One can investigate the problem by examining the ratings on the four final dimensions by means of tables set up in the same way as the preceding ones. For the sake of convenience, the data are presented on the four dimensions together in Table 16–11.

TABLE 16–11. Mean Ratings of Interaction on Four Dimensions, by Type of Female Figure

|  | Arms down | Right arm extended | Left arm extended | Both arms extended |
|---|---|---|---|---|
| *Interaction is "transient–permanent"* | | | | |
| LEGS TOWARD | 2.59 | 3.01 | 3.13 | 3.31 |
| LEGS AWAY | 3.05 | 3.24 | 2.80 | 2.99 |
| *Atmosphere is "enclosed–free"* | | | | |
| LEGS TOWARD | 3.69 | 3.86 | 4.16 | 4.16 |
| LEGS AWAY | 4.10 | 3.73 | 4.24 | 3.99 |
| *Movement will "continue–be reversed"* | | | | |
| LEGS TOWARD | 2.88 | 2.70 | 2.36 | 2.48 |
| LEGS AWAY | 2.76 | 2.84 | 2.69 | 2.72 |
| *Encounter is "satisfactory–unsatisfactory"* | | | | |
| LEGS TOWARD | 4.60 | 3.94 | 3.74 | 3.69 |
| LEGS AWAY | 3.59 | 3.92 | 3.75 | 3.90 |

It is both a surprise and a disappointment to find only the smallest differences among the eight figures on each dimension; the scores have a range of more than 1.00 only on the fourth dimension, and one cannot discern any systematic variation among them, by leg or arm position, on any of the dimensions (neither arm nor leg effects are significant). It is clear, therefore, that, whatever differences may exist in the ratings of interaction, they cannot be a consequence of the character of the female participant only. It is impossible to know, of course, whether any differences in the perception of the interaction do occur until one has carried out an analysis of individual extreme drawings; at present, one can assume that, if any do occur, both figures must contribute to them.

Among the female figures, two stood out on almost all the dimensions discussed: the figure with both arms down and legs extended toward the man, and its clearest opposite, the one with both arms outstretched and legs held away from the man. In summary, they may be characterized in this way: The former was rated as most action-receiving and cold, uncertain and unaggressive, constrained and calculating, non-erotic and passive, while the latter was perceived as the most action-initiating and warm, intense and determined, aggressive and sincere, erotic and active. Warmth, sincerity, and erotic demeanor characterize the active, initiating female figure, and, to the extent that a figure becomes passive, her scores tend to move toward the opposite poles of these dimensions. Only two other figures obtained any other extreme scores: the one with left arm and legs extended toward the man, seen as the least intense (probably because of the simultaneous movement backward of her body and forward of her arm), and the one with left arm extended and legs facing away, who was rated as the most free (but whose score was very close to the expected extreme, the figure with both arms extended); the important fact here is their closeness.

It is remarkable that Table 16–11 shows a closeness in ratings between the same two figures (left arm and both arms extended); this result is not limited to that dimension but applies generally. Moreover, a close look also brings out slight similarity in scores between the position with arms down and the position with right arm extended. To be sure, the leg position makes a crucial difference, but, within each leg position, the arm positions may be divided into these two groups. This observation is an important confirmation of the distinction begun in the exploratory analysis using interviews. There, it was found necessary to distinguish between a direct fantasy relation to the person portrayed and a relation by identification; in the former, one understands the meaning of a position or movement by seeing its relation to oneself, as when one calls Tintoretto's Adam "rejecting" because he turns his back to the viewer (ignoring, therefore, Adam's relation to the pictured Eve), while, in the latter, one understands the meaning of the position from its relation to other figures in the picture, as when Picasso's acrobat refuses to "extend" himself to the clown he faces. The same two processes seemed to operate side by side when the subjects viewed the drawings of this series; and, in the case of the two female figures with either the left arm or both arms extended, what made them similar to the observer was the barrier that one of the extended arms erected between the observer and the observed. (The right arm by itself does not erect this barrier because it is on the figure's far side.) In giving these two figures similar ratings, the subject viewed them at least as much from his own point of view as from the seemingly more appropriate one of the male shown in interaction with her. By a similar process, the extended right arm was rated as similar to the arms-at-side position, since, in both cases, the female figure's proximal space was open to the observer. The identification that seems to take place with one or more figures in a painting, which one might think primary for understanding the meaning of interpersonal situations, is only partial; the observer cannot quite relinquish the pleasure of seeing the scene as if he were participating in it.

But the most important theoretical question concerned the qualities of defined axial space and open proximal access; aside from the similarities that the extended near or far arm bears to these two types of space when viewed from the side, what differences exist between figures with outstretched arms or arms at rest? Another look at the tables shows that, when both arms are outstretched, the figure receives certain ratings somewhat irrespective of leg position: She is seen as action-initiating and active, determined, aggressive, warm, erotic, and free. When her legs point away from the man, no more than an accentuation of these attributes takes place. Thus, the quality of this defined axial space is thrusting and active; it appears to indicate the figure's desire to extend herself toward the man. When both arms rest at the sides of the body, leg position seems to make more of a difference; when the legs point toward the man, exposing the proximal space not in front of just the torso but in front of the whole body, the figure receives scores at the opposite ends of these dimensions: passive, cold, unaggressive, and the like. But when the legs point away, making the torso lean farther forward, the scores again move quite far toward what they were with the arms extended (confirming, in effect, that the active and motivated scores arise from the thrust of the body or of its extensions toward the man). Thus, one should say that open proximal access invites intimate interaction at the proximal boundary only when it extends forward, and that when it recedes—and perhaps especially when it is somewhat concave—its provocative quality disappears. In retrospect, this is not surprising in view of its consistency with the differences between the aggressively exposed and merely undefended male chest observed earlier. Defined axial space, however, can also be provocative, most so when both the arms and the body extend toward the person to be provoked.

Since the dimensions describing the male figure were identical to those used for the female figure, the analysis of male positions may be presented in a similar manner. The male could be either receding or advancing, and close to or far from the female figure, so there are four resulting positions. Two dimensions can be presented at one time. This part of the analysis asks only how the individual figures are characterized and ignores the influence that the perception of one figure may have on that of another; nevertheless, it is a necessary base on which the latter study will be built. To arrive at descriptions of the four male figures, the mean of eight separate ratings that the eight presentations of each figure required are calculated.

Table 16–12 lists the mean scores the figures received and on the first two dimensions: "initiating action–receiving action," and "warm–cold." The results are straightforward: The advancing–close position is the most initiating and warm, and the receding–far position is the most receiving and cold. But analysis of variance shows that initiation of action is determined only by the man's direction of movement, not by his distance from the woman, while warmth is determined by both factors (see Appendix T).

Table 16–13 presents the mean scores for the dimensions "intense–relaxed" and "uncertain–determined." Again, the advancing–close male figure obtained both extreme ratings; he is perceived as the most intense and the most deter-

TABLE 16–12. Mean Ratings of Male Figures on Two
Dimensions (40 Observations per Cell)

|  | "Initiating action–receiving action" | | "Warm–cold" | |
| --- | --- | --- | --- | --- |
|  | ADVANCING | RECEDING | ADVANCING | RECEDING |
| *Close* | 3.03 | 4.12 | 2.19 | 3.93 |
| *Far* | 3.39 | 4.31 | 2.74 | 4.50 |

mined. However, while the figure that is receding and far is perceived as the most uncertain, as one would expect, the least intense is the male that is receding and *close*. This outcome parallels that obtained earlier on the female figure, with the difference that, in the female, lack of intensity was expressed by contradictory positions of parts of the body (the arms and torso), while, in the male, it is best shown by a conflict between body movement (retreat) and situation (position close to an attractive woman); the woman's position was spoken of as a bodily grimace, and perhaps this term can also be applied to the man's. On the dimension of determination, both movement and distance create statistically significant differences; on the dimension of intensity, only movement does.

TABLE 16–13. Mean Ratings of Male Figures on Two
Dimensions

|  | "Intense–relaxed" | | "Uncertain–determined" | |
| --- | --- | --- | --- | --- |
|  | ADVANCING | RECEDING | ADVANCING | RECEDING |
| *Close* | 2.57 | 3.11 | 4.52 | 3.08 |
| *Far* | 2.60 | 2.99 | 3.59 | 2.84 |

The scores for "aggressive–unaggressive" and "constrained–free" appear in Table 16–14. The advancing–close figure is once more extreme on both dimensions, receiving the most aggressive and the most free ratings; the male who is receding and far is the most unaggressive and the most constrained. The scores again differ significantly by movement and distance, although more so by movement, especially on aggressiveness.

A similar distribution of scores may be observed in Table 16–15 in which ratings are presented for "sincere–calculating" and "non-erotic–erotic." The most sincere and the most erotic individual again appears to be the male who is

TABLE 16–14. Mean Ratings of Male Figures on Two Dimensions

|  | "Aggressive–unaggressive" | | "Constrained–free" | |
|---|---|---|---|---|
|  | ADVANCING | RECEDING | ADVANCING | RECEDING |
| Close | 3.16 | 4.34 | 4.30 | 3.39 |
| Far | 3.41 | 4.75 | 3.63 | 2.99 |

advancing and close; by contrast, the most non-erotic is the one who is receding and far. The least sincere, however, is receding and close; and the analysis of variance presented in Appendix T indicates that only movement creates significantly different scores on sincerity. Although one may well ask why a retreat is judged as less sincere than an advance, this difference must be accepted as real, especially since it has already occurred in the case of the female figure. Perhaps subjects reasoned that the experimenters used the word to apply to the figure's sexual intentions; if those are low or absent, the figure may be seen as less sincere. Or perhaps activity, when displayed, appears by the fact of its display as straightforward and sincere, while passivity can hide any number of different thoughts which, because they are many, could be calculating.

TABLE 16–15. Mean Ratings of Male Figures on Two Dimensions

|  | "Sincere–calculating" | | "Non-erotic–erotic" | |
|---|---|---|---|---|
|  | ADVANCING | RECEDING | ADVANCING | RECEDING |
| Close | 2.91 | 3.50 | 5.33 | 3.86 |
| Far | 3.20 | 3.38 | 4.58 | 3.37 |

The final dimensions are "active–passive" and "evil–good," and results are given in Table 16–16. The expectable regularity occurs on the first of these dimensions: The advancing figures are rated active, and the receding figures less so (the differences are significant); of these, the advancing–close is the most active, the receding–far the least (but the distance differences, though significant, are less pronounced). On the second dimension, the differences are also significant, because of the high "goodness" rating given to the advancing–close male. It is not certain, however, whether distance or movement is the more important determinant; in any case, the differences are small, and, in their smallness, resemble the very undifferentiated scores obtained by the female figure on this dimension. Whatever differentiations may be possible undoubtedly depend on the relations between the two.

**TABLE 16–16. Mean Ratings of Male Figures on Two Dimensions**

|  | *"Active–passive"* | | *"Evil–good"* | |
|  | ADVANCING | RECEDING | ADVANCING | RECEDING |
| *Close* | 2.74 | 3.52 | 4.67 | 4.26 |
| *Far* | 3.14 | 3.80 | 4.22 | 4.28 |

The ratings on all four of the dimensions that will permit study of variation of interaction according to changes in the male position appear together in Table 16–17. On the dimension "transient–permanent," only small differences appear but they are significant; although all figures portray transient interaction, both the man's advance and his closeness to the woman lead toward some amount of permanence. The dimension "enclosed–free" yields ratings very close to the neutral point, but advance and closeness both produce a certain (significant) freedom in the atmosphere. On the third dimension, it is again both the closeness and the advance of the man that contribute to the movement's being perceived as continuing—and very significantly so. And on the dimension of satisfaction, an identical result is obtained.

**TABLE 16–17. Mean Ratings of Male Figures on Four Interaction Dimensions**

|  | *Interaction is "transient–permanent"* | | *Atmosphere is "enclosed–free"* | |
|  | ADVANCING | RECEDING | ADVANCING | RECEDING |
| *Close* | 3.57 | 2.99 | 4.33 | 3.83 |
| *Far* | 2.88 | 2.63 | 3.93 | 3.78 |
|  | *Movement will "continue– be reversed"* | | *Encounter is "satisfactory– unsatisfactory"* | |
| *Close* | 2.03 | 2.91 | 2.59 | 4.18 |
| *Far* | 2.54 | 3.14 | 3.81 | 4.85 |

How can one explain the power of the male figure to determine the ways in which the interaction will be perceived? One must probably assume that the subjects saw him as the agent of whatever happened in the pair; when he advanced, it was he who began the interaction, and when he receded, it was he who ended it. If one tries to imagine the reasoning that *may* govern the interpretation of the scenes in which the man is close and advancing, one may conclude that the intention movement shown by the advancing male is sexual (all advancing movements were rated warm and erotic—and also aggressive, although one may suppose the aggression displayed to be used as a means for furthering sexual ends), and, when the advance arrives close to the woman, the intention may appear imminently successful. If this is its presumed end, then, this movement should lead to a satisfactory and perhaps continuing meeting.

To summarize, among the male positions, the advancing–close and the receding–far offer the most consistent contrast and appear most frequently at the extremes of the dimensions. The former is perceived as the most action-initiating, warm, intense, determined, aggressive, free, sincere, erotic, and active. The latter appears less frequently among the extremes but is nevertheless seen as the most action-receiving, cold, uncertain, unaggressive, constrained, non-erotic, and finally, as the least active. On dimensions that describe interaction, the advancing–close movement invariably scores as extreme; it is seen as leading to the least transient, most free, and most satisfactory encounter, and the movement appears as the most likely to continue. The receding–far movement is rated the least likely to continue, and as contributing to the most transient and unsatisfactory encounter.

As these results show, distance from the woman does play some role in the description of individual male figures and of the interaction, but the decisive part belongs to intention movements—forward or backward. This is the first study of the series in which intention movements received explicit attention, although their importance has been implied earlier. The paradoxical dissuasion of the extremely open arms of a nude woman (H40 in Chapter 10) has been mentioned with the speculation that she might be perceived as about to close her arms around the person making an approach to her proximal space. Still earlier, the importance of the symmetrical approach that the attendant and the two zephyrs were making toward Botticelli's Venus was noted. Here, one is struck by the extent to which the characteristics of the male figure depend on his intended approach or withdrawal.

The analysis carried out so far had, as its purpose, the description of the actors who made up the interpersonal scene to which subjects were asked to respond. Little has been said about the scene itself or about the way the two actors contribute to each other's characterizations. It is important to clarify the interdependencies among the ratings of the two principals. The first way to proceed is to examine extreme figures, as in preceding chapters; this requires the assumption that, if the aggressive female figure (as judged from the mean scores) obtains the highest aggressive score when her partner is receding and far, her score has risen because of the contrast between her active and his uncertain, unaggressive position. The converse may also occur; *his* ratings on these dimensions may also become more extreme. The scenario constructed by the subjects may also play an important part in affecting the ratings; but, since there are no data recording the scenarists' plots, the investigators' impressions of the scenes will be added.

This method has the advantage of preserving the concrete reality reflected by the subjects' ratings; but there is another method which, though more abstract, has more statistical cogency. The same analysis of variance that measured changes in a figure's presentational meaning with changes in its position may be used to assess the changes in the meaning of *one* figure as a consequence of changes in the position of the *other*.

The table of extreme figures is cumbersome and appears in Appendix U. To one who has read the preceding chapters, the fact that a small number of figures accounts for a majority of the locations in this table will come as no surprise; an observation not possible in the earlier analyses is, however, the repetition of several of the identification numbers among the three parts of the table, which list the scores for the man, the woman, and the interaction. Both the male and female figures in the same drawing often receive extreme scores.

The drawing that appears most frequently in the table is D27. In it, the male figure advances toward the female from afar, and she sits with her arms down and legs facing toward him. The male receives extreme scores on action-initiation, aggressiveness, activity, and evil while the female receives extreme scores on action-receiving, coldness, unaggressiveness, constraint, lack of eroticism, and passivity; and their encounter is among the least satisfactory. Two comments appear pertinent here: First, most of these dimensions characterize these two figures when they are studied singly, but the appearance of the extreme scores in *this* drawing—in which the two actors look so dissimilar—argues that the ratings of one have affected those of the other by simple *contrast*. This suggestion is strengthened by the fact that the figures are unambiguously opposed to each other on a number of the dimensions, such as "initiating–receiving," "aggressive–unaggressive," and "active–passive." One can only suppose that the effect of the ratings on each other has been mutual and in the direction of greater contrast, so that the passivity of one brought out the activity of the other—and vice versa. Second, two important ratings were given the male figure in this setting that he did not receive generally: the highest rating on aggressiveness (which contradicts his general position as second to the advancing–

close figure) and the highest rating on evil (when no figure had been judged as evil by itself). Aside from the apparent contrast with the unaggressive female figure, an important influence on the subjects' ratings seems to have been a brief, privately-constructed scenario, something like this: The distant male figure appears to have designs on the female, which her passive position makes her helpless, at the moment, to accept or resist. The passive but indeterminate reaction of the female figure, therefore, makes the male's designs appear relatively evil and adds to their aggressiveness.

Probably no greater contrast exists than between this picture and one that appeared frequently in the extreme columns but has not been illustrated here. There, the man recedes but is close to the woman; she extends both arms toward him, while her legs face away from him. His scores are extreme on action-receiving, coldness, unaggressiveness, lack of eroticism, and passivity, and hers are very high on warmth, intensity, aggressiveness, and activity; this encounter is the least satisfactory of all. Here, too, the opposition between the two figures on three dimensions shows their ratings as accentuated by a contrast effect; this contrast would appear to affect the male figure the most because, in the general analysis, the receding–close figure received none of these extreme ratings. This meeting shows the woman reaching for the man, possibly with some intensity of feeling, while he is uninterested in her advance and attempts to evade her grasp. If subjects perceived this drawing as one in which one figure's intentions were about to be frustrated, then it is understandable that the inter-action should have been rated as so unsatisfactory. If this view is correct, the high unsatisfactory rating of the preceding picture, D27, came also from the frustration which (in this case) the man's intentions would inevitably meet when faced with the woman's undecided response.

Another type of interaction is presented in D91, in which the male figure advances and is close to the female; she extends both arms toward him and her legs face in his direction, too. He is seen as among the most warm, deter-mined, free, and erotic, and she as among the most erotic and good. Now, in this drawing, it would be difficult to speak of a contrast effect since the figures are both highly erotic; in any case, the accentuations of general ratings that do occur are few. The fact that both figures show familiar intentions is important, however, and determines why these particular dimensions have been selected as extreme from the large number that characterized the advancing–close figure. In D27, the advancing figure was seen as highly aggressive and evil; here, he is rated as warm, free, and erotic. If all these dimensions characterized the advancing figures, then the reason that aggressiveness and evil do not apply in D91 must be related to the woman's warm response. If, in D27, the sexual and other intentions could be attributed only to the man, it might be natural for subjects to see him as aggressive and evil; if, in D91, the woman responds warmly, a negative view of the man's advance would appear highly inappropriate. To state it another way, if the man's intentions are imminently successful, one cannot view his forward movement moralistically; evil in this two-person encounter appears best embodied in pleasurable, egoistic, unshared intentions of a male.

Picture D91, then, strengthens the interpretation of the results obtained from D27 and demonstrates that the woman's response to the man's movement has a strong effect on the way he will be perceived. The next drawing that obtained a large number of extreme scores, D31, further supports this view. D31 is identical to D27 except that the man is now close to the woman. As in D27, the male is seen as aggressive, action-initiating, and active; but, here, he is no longer seen as evil,[1] and he receives instead a high rating on intenseness. The woman is still action-receiving and passive, but she loses her non-erotic and cold ratings; in addition, she is now seen as calculating. Thus, the man's close position to her wrought one important change in the subjects' perception: The evil of the man disappeared, and was replaced by the woman's calculation. The reasons that led the subjects to change their description may be these: If the man is this close to the woman, she must have allowed him to approach, or—what is more serious—has enticed him; although she may not respond warmly, her intention to bring him close to her is evident. But if her response remains passive, then she is still at the level of intention rather than action—or, in the language of the answer sheet, she is calculating. If this interpretation is correct, then another fact about axial space suggests itself: Under normal circumstances, one cannot penetrate the inner boundary of the axial space without acquiescence of the actor whose space is so penetrated. And when this occurs, responsibility for the penetration no longer belongs solely to the penetrator: It is then shared by both partners.

Two further drawings offer the same contrast as have D27 and D31; they are D78 and D80. In both, the female figure extends both arms toward the male and her legs face away from him; and, in both, the man advances, in the first from afar and in the second from close up. In D78, in which the man is far, the woman received extreme scores on action-initiating, sincerity, and eroticism; in D80, she is also sincere, but, in addition, was seen as free and good. Further, in D80, the man was perceived as highly sincere himself, and the interaction received the highest ratings on permanence and satisfactoriness. One important change that the man's close position again brought about, then, was to make the partners' intentions shared: They were both rated as sincere and the woman was no longer rated as highly initiating. As before, penetration into the inner part of axial space seems to have been wished by both actors. Moreover, in the drawing where they are both close, the woman was no longer seen as so highly erotic; earlier, the word was defined as implying activity and intenseness on the woman's part, and now one should add that it also appears to refer to the woman's desire before fulfillment is fully in sight. In D78, the woman seems to be longing for the man; he is moving closer to her, but with less intensity than she shows in her outstretched arms; therefore, she appears initiating and erotic. In D80, her longing and his approach seem about to be rewarded and her apparent initiation has accordingly disappeared.[2] Sincerity, freedom, and goodness now characterize her, and satisfaction and relative permanence describe the encounter. The influence the two figures have on each other's ratings seems better described by the term *complementarity* than by *contrast*. D80 appears the clearest indication that the axial space which the woman's arms so clearly define is one in which the man can move satisfactorily, as the exploratory study suggested. It is perhaps no accident that this is the picture modeled directly on Rubens's *Venus and Adonis*.

But the correspondence between the data and these formulations is more complex, as can be seen in a full comparison of D80 with the two drawings in which the advancing man is close to a woman who has both arms down (D21 with legs away and D31 with legs toward).[3] In D21—the best comparison, since the woman's legs point away as in D80—the woman was seen as receiving action and the man as initiating it; her exposed proximal boundary, therefore, is not inciting here. It becomes so, however, in D31, in which she exposes her proximal boundary not only at the level of the torso but also at the level of the pelvic region and legs, and she receives a high rating on calculation. Thus, the calculating quality of the undefended proximal boundary is higher when it extends over the whole body, although the active, initiating, and erotic qualities are not. In both of the positions with open proximal boundary, it must be added, the interaction was perceived as transient, in contrast to the relative permanence it appeared to have when the man moved within the space defined by the extended arms. To this extent, the earlier formulation has been supported.

A further instance of the manner in which the rating of one figure affects that of the other occurs in drawing D72, in which the woman assumes the same position as in D78 and D80 (both arms extended, legs away from the man), but the man recedes from her and is already quite distant. She received extreme ratings on intenseness, determination, aggressiveness, and activeness. These are dimensions on which she had also received high scores irrespective of the male figure, but what is of interest is the choice, from the larger list, that is made here. In D78, in which the man approached, the erotic, sincere, and free qualities of her position were emphasized; here, the receding man brings out her determined and aggressive qualities. When, in D78 and D80, subjects perceived qualities in her that complemented the man's active approach, D72 seems to deal once more with a contrast. Three of the four dimensions on which this female figure is extreme are opposites of those that characterize the male's receding–far position. A very similar effect of contrast doubtless occurs in another drawing, D35, in which a female figure whose legs point away from the man reaches for him with her left arm; he recedes, but is still close to her. His scores are among the most action-receiving, unaggressive, and the least intense. Since, in the general analysis, this female figure received ratings at the opposite end of these three dimensions, in all probability, contrast pushed his scores away from hers. It is possible that the subjects' brief scenario also played a part in determining these ratings; the woman in D35 looks as if she might be patting the man on the shoulder in a motherly fashion, as if to say goodbye.

Drawing D23 appears to exemplify effects of complementarity rather than those of contrast. The female figure sits with arms down and legs pointing away from the man; he is receding and far from her. Extreme scores were obtained by both figures, with the female rated as very cold, uncertain, constrained, and non-erotic, and the male seen as uncertain and constrained, and the interaction itself viewed as highly transient and unsatisfactory. As far as the woman is concerned, the four extreme characteristics applied to this figure in the general analysis also, and one must explain why only these four were chosen. It may be easier here to construct a very brief scenario. This normally passive woman probably would, like most women, be happy if the man approached closer. But he backs away and she can only watch him escape, so she is likely to feel disappointed and be undecided about what to do next. Therefore, it would not make sense to accentuate her usual qualities, such as passivity or unaggressiveness; it would be more appropriate to stress her disappointment and confusion, and to rate her as uncertain and constrained, cold and non-erotic. Perhaps, at this point, one can define complementarity as the satisfactory completion of one action by another, or the integration of one expression or feeling with another.

This reasoning may not have taken place in the subjects, and it should not be taken completely seriously, but it illustrates the effect of complementarity. It is the fact of complementarity, shown in the similarity of the male and female attributes rather than in their contrast, that matters, and which should be noted.

Finally, picture D70 received five extreme scores: The man was rated as highly warm, determined, aggressive, erotic, and active. He is advancing and close, and the woman sits with her legs toward him and the right arm extended in his direction. It is probable that complementarity accounts for the emphasis on these five dimensions. Without resorting to scenario construction, one might say that this man is intermediate (in the subjects' perception) between the one in D27, who was seen as evil because of his intentions toward a distant, passive woman, and the man in D91, who was perceived as warm, free, and erotic because of the very warm reaction his advance elicited from the woman; the woman's reaction in D70 appears quite warm, too (hence, the rating on warm and erotic), but not so warm as the woman in D97 (hence, high scores on determination, aggressiveness, and activeness).[4]

The figures evinced two types of effects on each other's scores: effects caused by changes in distance, and effects produced by changes in context. As to the first, decrease in distance led to better-shared responsibility for the closer contact. Close figures were rated as more sincere than distant ones, and sometimes as more good; in addition, a female with extended arms could be seen as less erotic when close to the man, while a female with arms at her sides could appear as more calculating. As to the second class of effects, normally differing figures, when placed in the same picture, made each other appear more extreme by contrast; other combinations of figures led to changes in ratings that were best described by the term complementarity. To what extent are these changes general?

One can calculate the mean scores that one figure receives *as a function of the position of the other*, as when one looks at all the female figures' means when the male is close or far, or when one studies all the male figures' ratings when the female extends her arms or puts them down. Marked changes which support the suggestions made in the extreme-figure analysis do appear. The comfortably significant ones are presented in tabular form in Appendix V, and their meaning may be appreciated verbally here.

First, when the male approaches closer to the female, she is judged as warmer, more sincere, more erotic, and more good. It would appear, as suggested, that the greater sincerity and goodness indicate a more even distribution of the intentions that may have brought the two figures together; since the male is the mobile figure, these changes on the part of the stationary female indicate that she has allowed his approach, while her increased warmth and eroticism signal a more active response to his coming closer or, at least, a more evident expression of her feelings.

Second, when the male changes from a receding to an advancing posture, the feminine scores change, very similarly, to the warmer, more erotic, and "better" ends of the respective dimensions. That the same effects (and more) occurred in the male figure itself was apparent earlier, but their generality across all the *female* figures is novel and makes it important not to underestimate their significance. The mere act of turning to face the feminine partner probably radically alters the situation. From centrifugal movement, the action becomes centripetal, as if more were going on between the partners—as if the action were more sexually charged, or at least better provided with positive feelings. Or one might say, to avoid speaking of changes in the situation as a whole, that, as the man's movement becomes one of approach, the woman's position must be seen as a response—and that, as long as she does not actively retreat, her staying may be interpreted as assent. While it is not necessary to decide between these suggestions at present, these changes offer an additional explanation for a phenomenon noted earlier: The rarity of back-to-back (apotropic) situations in painting derives not only from their compositionally centrifugal quality, but also from their emotional coolness and poverty.

Third, changes in the woman's position have a very strong effect on the meaning of the man's—even stronger, since they occur on nearly all of the ten possible dimensions. But they are of a different nature: Thus, as the woman extends, first one, and then the other arm toward the man, he begins to appear as colder and less erotic; as more passive, unaggressive, and action-receiving; and as more relaxed and sincere. As the woman changes her leg position from facing toward to facing away, the inclination of her torso in his direction wreaks the same havoc with his appearance, making him lose apparent activity, aggressiveness, action-initiation, warmth, and eroticism; even certainty, freedom, and sincerity. Thus, all changes that make the woman appear more active and aggressive make the man lose, rather than gain, in these qualities; it is as if her possession of them were incompatible with his.

This incompatibility is in complete contrast to the support that the man's active and centripetal stance gives to the woman's apparent feelings and intentions. Two suggestions may explain this difference. On the one hand, the difference seems to reflect the structure of American society, with its relatively pronounced rivalry between the sexes: men's activity and achievement are generally seen as supportive of women, especially in marriage, where the woman takes her social status and obtains economic sustenance from her husband, while a woman's achievement is too often seen as a threat to the man's social position and masculinity. If this explanation is correct, the discrepancy observed here should not occur in societies in which sexual competition is less or of a different nature; a cross-cultural retest of these results should, therefore, prove fruitful. On the other hand, the difference becomes plausible when one more datum is added to the effects of the female figure's changes on the man's characterizations: As the woman's torso bends in his direction, the male begins to appear not only as less active and warm but also gains in apparent goodness. Perhaps the change in his scores should not be seen as the effect of a competing ("castrating") woman, but rather as a neutralization of his aggressive threat to her; in other words, as she becomes more active, he may be seen as less threatening. A balance may have been restored.

Since this chapter concerns relations between the sexes, it is important to determine, as in Chapters 10 and 13, what can further be learned about the perception of bodily expressiveness by examining sex differences in the subjects' ratings. The remainder of this chapter will be devoted to a study of the characteristics of subjects, rather than of drawings or figures, and will focus on differences between the sexes as the variable. How do the sexes differ on the perception of these interacting figures? What connections do they make between the meanings of words? And how do they differ in their areas of concern with the human body?

Two comparisons between subjects seem appropriate: intercorrelations between dimensions, which indicate what areas of meaning surround each dimension and the ways in which the meanings differ by sex; and the mean scores given by the subjects of each sex to *all* the figures together, dimension by dimension, which uncover the tendencies in each sex to see the figures in characteristic terms.

In Chapter 10, the analysis of sex differences in intercorrelations revealed a number of interesting discrepancies; unfortunately, one cannot report the same for these data. The table of significant correlations is presented in Appendix X, and shows remarkable agreement between the sexes. Two differences, however, do occur: Male subjects link aggressiveness with eroticism quite strongly, while female subjects see the tie as weaker; and men link eroticism to warmth (especially in the female figure) more than women. It is probably correct to explain this difference by saying that men see eroticism as quite aggressive, and warmth as quite erotic, and that women distinguish between them somewhat more fully. Warmth is less sexual for the women than for the men. As for eroticism, its more aggressive meaning for men may relate to the potency and muscularity that seem so important to this culture's definitions of masculinity.

Do the sexes also differ in the mean ratings they assign to the collection of figures as a whole? The relevant data are presented in Table 16–18, and, in part, show important parallels with the analysis of intercorrelations. Thus, there is a significant difference among the subjects in their perception of aggression, which men perceive more in the female figure (and also in the male figure, but not significantly so; see Appendix Y) than do women. Men also rate the figures as more intense and perceive the female figure as more erotic and as more free. There is reason to suppose that, on the one hand, men project more aggression and intensity of feeling into the figures and that, on the other, they are more sensitive to control of the interaction. Their greater readiness to perceive the female figures as free may indicate a vigilance over who is determining the manner and direction of the activity of the pair. But men also perceive both figures as less good than do women; perhaps they do project more aggression, or perhaps they take a more moralistic view of the interaction portrayed; one cannot decide on the present evidence.

Finally, men and women perceive the encounter itself differently; on two of the four dimensions referring to the interaction, their ratings diverge. The men

**TABLE 16–18. Mean Ratings Given to All Figures on Each Dimension, by Type of Figure and Sex (Non-significant Differences in Parentheses)**

|  | *Male subjects* | *Female subjects* |
|---|---|---|
| *Man's figure:* | | |
| intense–relaxed | (2.69) | (2.89) |
| aggressive–unaggressive | (3.71) | (3.91) |
| evil–good | 4.19 | 4.43 |
| *Woman's figure:* | | |
| intense–relaxed | (3.20) | (3.41) |
| aggressive–unaggressive | 3.13 | 3.40 |
| constrained–free | (4.88) | (4.62) |
| non-erotic–erotic | 5.28 | 4.99 |
| evil–good | 4.12 | 4.50 |
| *Interaction:* | | |
| will continue–will be reversed | (2.58) | (2.84) |
| satisfactory–unsatisfactory | 3.70 | 4.18 |

see a greater likelihood of the movement's continuing, and generally perceive the encounters as more satisfactory than do women. The most likely explanations of these differences probably have to do with the use of fantasy in sexuality. One may hypothesize, as a start, that women do not call these encounters satisfactory because, if one views them in the present, one has to admit that they have not yet become so; in the future, they may lead to satisfaction but, unless one is willing to project into the future, one cannot perceive satisfaction in them yet. It would appear that men have a greater ability to use fantasy in relation to their sexuality, and perhaps a greater readiness to resort to it when real satisfactions are absent. Direct evidence exists for this difference, and some indirect support for it comes from subhuman species. Males of most lower mammalian species will cease all sexual activity following deprivation of cortical functions, while females may continue to participate in and even seek sexual activity in spite of decortication; similarly, males of some of these species are particularly sensitive to changes in their environment and to previous unsuccessful sexual experiences.[5] Such evidence points to greater cortical control of sexual behavior in the mammalian male than in the female, which, in the human male, may mean increased reliance on fantasy for sexual arousal and, perhaps, even for satisfaction.

To summarize, the investigation was directed at what seemed to be changes in the quality of axial space by the extensions of the arms in front of it, and designed to inquire into the meanings of the penetration of axial space, both generally and in particular, with reference to changes in the quality of the axial space itself. But, first, the individual actors in the situations had to be characterized. The woman who penetrated the space in front of her by extending her torso and arms into it was judged erotic, active, aggressive, and determined, while the one who sat with legs facing her partner and arms at her sides was seen as the most non-erotic, passive, unaggressive, and uncertain. The man who advanced received all the active, erotic, and aggressive ratings, while the one who backed away obtained the opposite ones; the man's distance from the woman played a lesser role than his advance or retreat. As for the qualities of the defined and undefined axial space itself, all the female figures with out-stretched arms were seen as action-initiating, warm, determined, aggressive, active, free, and erotic, although, when the thrust of the body underlay the extension of arms (when the woman's legs pointed away from the man), all these qualities were accentuated. Arms at the side, on the other hand, produced ratings at the opposite ends of these dimensions only in the legs-toward position.

When the two figures were studied together in particular situations, there was a marked influence of one on the scores of the other; when the male advanced, he made the woman appear more erotic, warm, and good, but when the female leaned toward him and became more active, his scores *fell* in such realms as activity, aggressiveness, eroticism, warmth, and certainty. The man's distance from the woman, too, played some role in changing the woman's ratings: As he came closer, she became warmer, more sincere, more erotic, and more good. As his position became more active and intense, so did hers; as hers changed toward activeness, his diminished.

But some of the cross-figure effects, including those following changes in the man's distance, were more complex. Two conclusions, in particular, emerged from comparisons of individual pictures that had received extreme ratings.

When the female figure was active and highly motivated (with arms extended and legs away from the man) she lost her extreme action-initiating ratings as the advancing man moved closer to her—as if her high activity scores had to be reduced by the fact of the figures' intrusion into each other's axial space; such was the case with drawings D78 and D80. Pictures D27 and D31 gave results that seemed the precise obverse: The passive, action-receiving woman (arms down, legs toward the man) was perceived as more calculating as the man approached closer, while he lost his rating on evil in the approach—as if the woman had to take responsibility for having allowed or incited the man's move toward her. It was concluded that the effect of the mutual intrusion into axial space was to make responsibility for the move shared between the partners.

The second conclusion that resulted from the comparisons of individual draw-ings concerned the two processes by which the figures were found to influence each other's scores within any one picture; the first of these was called complementarity and it, too, was discovered by a comparison of two drawings in which only the distance between figures varied. In both, the female figure sat with arms outstretched and legs away from the man; the man advanced—in D78, from afar and, in D80, from close up. The woman's extreme scores changed from action-initiating and erotic in the first picture to free and good in the second; and, in the second drawing, the man received a high score on sincerity. Besides the sharing of responsibility for this axial space intrusion, the change reflected complementarity (of feeling, action, and intention); the female figure, normally seen as active and intrusive, lost these qualities in favor of merely warm ones as the two forward-pointing figures came into each other's axial space.

The other process by which scores were influenced in the presence of the figure of the opposite sex may accurately be described as contrast; when this occurred, a figure's individual scores were simply accentuated by the presence of another who contrasted with him. Thus, in picture D35, the receding man was close to a woman with an outstretched left arm and legs pointing away; although he was not normally the most passive, here he was perceived as the most action-receiving, unaggressive, and the least intense. Surely, the contrast with the intrusive female partner accounted for this accentuation.

Male–female differences were also of interest. Men were more likely to connect warmth with eroticism and eroticism with aggression than were women. Men also perceived more aggression and intensity of feeling in the figures of both sexes while they perceived less goodness in them. A second difference arose in the men's greater readiness to see the movement as likely to continue, and to perceive the interaction as satisfactory. It seemed best to account for this difference by supposing in men a greater tendency to project into the future and to see the interaction at an imagined subsequent time, and to tie this tendency to the male mammal's greater dependence on cortical activity for sexual behavior. And if the men did, indeed, see these encounters as farther along, perhaps they did have a better opportunity to be moralistic about the goodness of the individual figures.

A final comment seems appropriate. When it is said that the presence of one figure changes the ratings of another, this does not necessarily imply that some "original" perception of one participant is changed by the addition of new elements; in other words, there is no wish to say that the total impression is built up piecemeal from discrete parts. On the other hand, there is no evidence to support the view that an impression of the whole precedes and determines perceptions of the parts. As the exploratory interviews showed, the process by which an interpretation is reached is complex, often deductive, and moves from statements about the whole scene to descriptions of small details—and back again. As far as one can tell, the perceptual process, even in these simpler line drawings, also moves between the whole and its parts in a mutual fashion.


## NOTES FOR CHAPTER 16

[1] His score is 4.32, on the "good" side of the mean.

[2] In D80, her eroticism score is 6.05 and his 5.19, while, in D78, the scores are 6.32 and 4.05 respectively; clearly, when the two penetrate each other's axial space, their intentions appear as much more similar. If we compare ratings on action-initiation, we confirm this statement further: When they are distant, his score is 4.37 (receiving) and hers 1.32 (very highly initiating); when in each other's axial space, the ratings are 3.95 (neutral) and 1.62, respectively.

[3] The complete data for all pictures occupy 32 tables; the reader will, we trust, excuse us if we present only the few ratings we believe relevant.

[4] The ratings subjects assigned to the three women substantiate what we have said about them. In D91, the women's score for warmth is 1.74 (very warm); in D27, it is 5.19 (cold); and, in D70, it is 2.58 (quite warm).

[5] See Ford and Beach (1951, pp. 240–46) for evidence relating to these matters.

# 17. Male–Female Encounter:
## FRESH CONSTRUCTIONS
by Paul Williams

The preceding chapters all used a common method, presenting fixed stimuli and eliciting descriptions in the form of ratings; the stimuli varied systematically in several ways, but their number was always finite. This method asked, in effect, "Of the presentational changes you observe, which ones differ on the rating dimensions that describe them?" If the instructions asked for ratings on "warmth," the investigators discovered which of several figures might be judged warm and which cold, and to what degree—given that collection of figures, and none other. The investigators did not obtain information on the *range* of body positions and movements that might successfully present "warmth."

The method described in this chapter attempted to study that range, by proceeding in the opposite direction—asking subjects to produce body positions, not to describe them. At the same time, the method was designed to verify, modify, or amplify the results obtained in the preceding chapter. Subjects were given a pair of wooden, freely articulating artists' manikins and were requested to construct an encounter in response to certain directions. One of the manikins was given breasts; both could assume a very large number of postures and be supported in them by a wire leading to a stable base. For scenic variety, a simulated rock was provided and allowed, but not necessarily encouraged, to be used. All resulting constructions were labeled and photographed; some thousand photographs thus obtained were then analyzed for the presence of certain attributes and the attributes' tabulations furnish the main data of this chapter.

The flexible and faceless manikins, the plain background, and the single, chair-size rock all furnish possibilities for producing scenes commensurate with those portrayed in the preceding chapter. Why were subjects not asked to act out the instructions using the most natural of all instruments, their own bodies? The possibility appeared impractical; subjects strange to each other might restrict the range of their actual positions even more than the range of manikins' arrangements. Furthermore, the fusing of two different subjects' movements into one scene seemed problematic. After a few pilot trials, it became clear that the manikins and their possible movements permitted the subjects to make a very strong identification between their own bodies and the manikins' wooden ones—an identification strong enough to make one subject request permission to withdraw from the experiment, which she was finding painfully revealing. The manikins' facelessness guaranteed that presentational behavior would be restricted to the body as a whole.

Since this study aimed at obtaining results parallel with those of Chapter 16, the instructions were chosen from the rating dimensions used therein. Not all were used, for reasons of economy—economy of both length and of redundancy. Those retained were: "aggressive–unaggressive," "male initiating–female initiating," "male receiving–female receiving," "erotic–non-erotic," "warm–cold," "sincere–calculating," and "good–evil."

Each subject was asked, first, to manipulate the two manikins so as to produce, for example, an aggressive scene.[1] After it had been produced and photographed, the manikins were moved closer if they were already far (in the sense of "close" and "far" used in the foregoing chapter), and, if they were close, they were moved farther apart. The subject being tested was then asked if the resulting interaction appeared more aggressive (labeled "Alt'd +") or less aggressive (labeled "Alt'd −") than in the original scene. As a third step, the two manikins were isolated from each other and the subject was asked whether the lone manikins were as aggressive as the interaction had been, more so (+2 or +1), or less so (−2 or −1). Then the subject was instructed to change each manikin (if necessary) to make him or her as aggressive as in the original encounter. All constructions were photographed from the same angle as that from which the subject viewed them during his manipulations, save when an additional angle would make it easier to "read" the position of the limbs and the intersection of boundaries. All spontaneous comments were recorded.

The discussion of results will examine the original encounter, the alteration produced by changed distance, and the individual reconstructions—and the differences among the constructions of men and women subjects. The categories of analysis are, for the most part, already familiar, but a few are novel. Synkinetic movements will be categorized as in the preceding chapters (e.g., diatropes, paratropes). An *intention movement* is defined as any interrupted movement that, in the future, may or may not move through space; this movement may be *positive*, as when it moves toward the interacting partner, or *negative*, as when it moves away. When one manikin is said to be *responsible* for the intersection of boundaries, this means that it is the only manikin revealing a positive intention movement; when both display such a movement, they are *jointly responsible.* With regard to body spaces, reference is made especially to *open proximal access* (as when a manikin exposes the anterior projection area by placing his hands at his sides or in the back), *defined axial space* (with one or both arms extended toward the front, creating for the partner the possibility of coming into the space or of remaining within it), *contained axial space* (with the arms joining each other to prevent movement from the inside out), and *closed proximal boundaries* (with arms similarly joined but so close to the body as to make movement within them impossible). Lastly, the frequencies of acrotropes and isotropes will be noted, the superior manikin called *acrotropic* and the equal-height manikin *isotropic*.

Again, the subjects were Harvard and Radcliffe undergraduate volunteers. Most of them specialized in a newly founded program in Visual Studies and could be expected to be particularly sensitive to and versed in visual presentations. Their familiarity with photography and painting, and particularly with the representation of the human body, make their constructions highly vivid and frank, perhaps more so than might occur with a less specialized population. Ten men and women had volunteered; the frequencies with which various categories appear in the relevant tables in the appendix are, therefore, generally parts of a base of 20, or, in the case of isolated constructions (with one manikin of each sex), part of a base of 40. The analysis of each instruction is presented separately.

Under each of these headings, the analysis will seek to discover the characteristics of the interacting pairs and of the individual reconstructions; these characteristics refer to the quality of the intention movement, the type of body space created by the arms, the assignment of responsibility for boundary intersection, the nature of vertical displacements, and the type of horizontal syntropisms. The elaborateness of this analysis will render it cumbersome to read at first; yet, as the analysis proceeds, the terms will become increasingly familiar and the accumulating comparisons between instructions (erotic, initiating, and good, for example) add more and more meaning to the analysis.

*Aggressive.*   Aggressive interactions are characterized by advancing males, receding females, frequent use of defined axial space, primarily male responsibility for intersections at the axial boundary, frequent acrotropic males, and predominantly diatropic, face-to-face, encounters. Figure 41 illustrates most of these characteristics, which are described below.

The active striving of most of the manikins is best substantiated by the 34 of 40 manikin manipulations (see Table 1 in Appendix Z) which show definite intended movements—a movement toward or away from the partner. Of these intention movements, the most are positive (toward the partner) and a few are negative. Males are responsible for about half of the encounters, females for another one-quarter, and about one-quarter show mutual responsibility. Con-

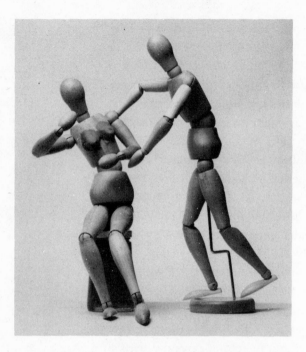

**Fig. 41.** Aggressive Encounter (Subject M2)

**Fig. 42.** Aggressive Encounter (Subject M11) **Fig. 43.** Aggressive Encounter (Subject F7)

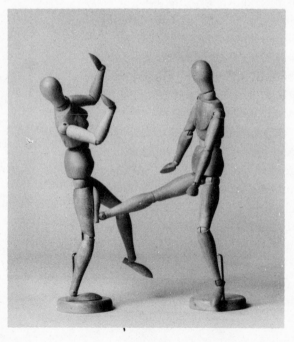 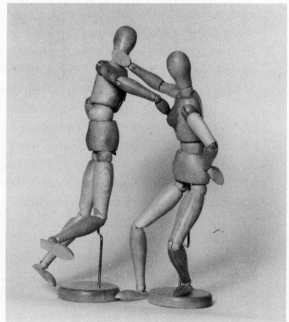

sistent with this picture are, again, the 34 manikins whose arms were put in the position called *defined axial space:* At least one arm is in front, creating a space within which the other manikin may move or rest, or which, in any case, the other manikin must note. Further, most of the partners are close enough to intersect at the axial boundary (18 out of 20 scenes). Fourteen of the 20 encounters show one figure higher than (acrotropic to) the other; of these 14, 11 are male manikins. Lastly, 14 of the 20 confrontations are diatropic, providing maximal exposure of the anterior area to attack, as well as giving the "attacking" manikin the most direct route toward the partner. All in all, then, aggression is generally displayed by the male, who strives actively to reach the female figure, and who is quite close to her and above her; the female generally withdraws (8 of 10 instances of withdrawal are by female manikins), but with her arms defining the axial space in front of her.

Are there differences between the productions of men and women? There are, and they are of considerable interest. For example, men tend to create withdrawing female manikins, while women make the female manikins approach; of the 9 male manikins that are responsible for axial intersection, 7 were produced by men, while all the instances of mutual responsibility were created by women. Thus, not only did the male manikins generally mirror what is thought of as the male role in the culture (aggressive, active, striving), but the men were more likely to portray this role in their constructions than were women (see Figures 42 and 43). It is already worth pointing out that, in responding to the instructions, the subjects proceeded by identifying with the manikin of their own sex. Perhaps identification is present in all the productions, but, at the least, it is visible in those constructions where men and women differ in ways that enhance their own image. Such visible identification may be contrasted with another attitude towards complying with the instructions, that of task involvement, which, for lack of ability to see it elsewhere, shall be assumed to exist at least in instances where men and women do not differ in the encounters they produce.

An additional instance of divergence between men and women appears to come as a paradox: Women produced the larger part of the encounters in which the male was acrotropic, while men produced the majority of instances in which both figures were isotropic. Men, it would seem, produce what they believe are more powerful male manikins without resorting to superiority in height, but women portray the aggressive male as aggressive partly by virtue of his height— which may represent, here, superior size or brute strength. Such a difference may lead to speculation about feminine masochism, sensitivity to an inferior role, and other explanatory mechanisms; while any such suggestions must remain uncertain, it is worth noting that this difference appeared.

Are consistent differences produced by changing distance and, eventually, by isolating each manikin? As to distance, the results are ambiguous: Nine "farther" positions were judged less aggressive, while 11 were judged more so. A farther position could be judged less aggressive because the increased distance provided what could be called protective insulation; but another farther position could be judged more aggressive because the two bodies seemed connected by clearer visual lines, which created better movement between them. It seemed to one subject that the farther position required "more energy to fly through that space," therefore heightening the effect of aggressiveness. As to isolated reconstructions, only one attribute appeared salient: the frequency of intention movements. Thirty-eight of the 40 manikins displayed intention movements, and all 38 movements were positive. Aggression must be displayed *towards* someone.

*Unaggressive.*   Unaggressive scenes present several points of contrast to the aggressive ones; where the latter were full of intention movements, the former are nearly devoid of them (see Table 2 in Appendix Z). This is not to say, however, that all the manikins stand immobile, but that, when the occasional moving manikin is produced, his movement is directed neither toward nor away from the opposite manikin. In Figure 44, a rather typical scene, the male appears to be walking, but neither distinctly toward nor away from his partner. The female figure illustrates another common attribute of unaggressive presentations: a somewhat more frequent use of contained axial space and even closed proximal boundaries, to the detriment of the well-used defined axial space that characterized aggressive encounters. The figures seem to avoid contact by one method or another, and it comes as small surprise that, on another of the tabulations— (that of the total number of intersecting body spaces)—there are fewer intersections than among aggressive productions—either at the axial or at the proximal boundaries. And again contrary to what was observed in aggressive encounters, responsibility for the unaggressive meeting becomes increasingly shared; thus, when aggressiveness was best demonstrated by one member's taking clear initiative, unaggressiveness appears more clearly shown when both members take responsibility for whatever contact they make; it is as if the absence of contrast between them helped make their actions appear unexceptional.

Most striking about the unaggressive encounters is the absence of diatropic positions; against 14 among the aggressive productions, there is only one here. This further supports the notion that, in this instance, the manikins are shunning contact or even the threat of it; they rely more heavily on amphitropes and paratropes, which have in common at least one manikin presenting himself laterally to the other. One has the impression that there is no direct avoidance or flight on anyone's part; rather, there is an absence of passion of whatever sort (see, for example, Figure 45). In the world of art, the tranquil family studies of Henry Moore approximate the tone of these constructions.

Differences among men and women again prove to be illuminating. The instances of shared responsibility for axial contact, more frequent generally, are

 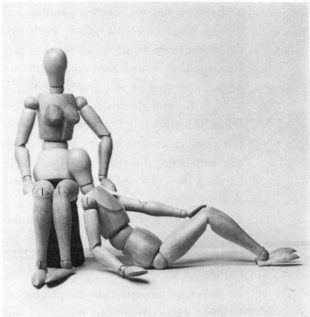

**Fig. 44.**   Unaggressive Encounter (Subject M16)   **Fig. 45.**   Unaggressive Encounter (Subject F20)

mostly produced by women. Therefore, there is evidence to support the conclusion that men prefer to express unaggressiveness by distance and a certain amount of relative isolation, while women tend to see it more as a matter of closeness and mutuality. The quality of unaggressiveness appears to men to be a lack of something; to women, it is a positive and tranquil quality.

One difference between the sexes is less obviously explained. The only two cases in which a female manikin is cast into the acrotrope are produced by women, in contrast to aggressive encounters, in which women produced fewer female acrotropes than men did. There is some reason to believe, then, that, for the purposes of this experiment at least, women do not believe that assuming the physically superior position necessarily means displaying aggression; the superior position may well signify aggression in the male, but may better present responsibility or motherliness in the female.

What does increased distance signify for the perceived unaggressiveness of the manikins? The data show that 13 figures were judged as even more unaggressive when far, while seven were judged as less so. On the whole, distance appears to reinforce the passionlessness that is so much the distinctive quality of unaggressive interactions. When the manikins are completely isolated and remanipulated by the subjects, one can observe a much greater frequency of contained axial space and closed axial boundary, on the one hand—indicating, probably, action and feeling contained close to oneself—and a similar increase in open proximal access, which, perhaps, leaves the manikin perfectly approachable because no danger is assumed to threaten. But a decrease can be seen in the frequency of defined axial space—space which intrudes into that of the partner or tells him that he is being invited or allowed to come within it.

*Male Initiating.* Instructions for this category of encounter differed from those just preceding it and most of those that follow. The subjects were asked to construct a scene in which only one manikin (here, the male) initiates. One can anticipate, therefore, that the subjects would tend to make the contrast between the male and female figures as great as possible. One can also assume that the instructions were too specific here to make it possible for the subjects to display much identification with manikins of their own sex; if the male is to initiate, both men and women have to portray him as an initiator. This may still allow the men to identify, but the identification can never really be perceived. On the whole, one may say that this series of constructions will be guided more by task requirements than by projective identification.

These expectations are not disappointed: Male manikins most characteristically approach the female and define the anterior axial space, while the female figures withdraw (see Table 3 in Appendix Z). In response to instructions, the contrast between the two manikins is drawn much more sharply than in aggressive meetings. Here, every male manikin without exception defines his axial space; the males show almost the only intention movements (with one exception, all positive), while, of the few feminine intention movements shown, almost all are negative. Female manikins seldom define axial space (compared with the males), but more frequently open their proximal access (and sometimes react to the male by altogether closing proximal boundary). As against aggressive encounters, here even more males take responsibility for intersection at the axial boundary; there are fewer mutually responsible intersections, and none for which females are responsible. A large number of meetings are acrotropic, and, in these, most of the superior figures are males. In contrast to the approaching, active, thrusting male manikin, the female remains essentially uninvolved, not actively accepting or rejecting as she might be, were she defining her axial space, but passively suffering the action or closing herself off against it. Figure 46 illustrates a typical production.

The categories of synkinetic movements speak most forcefully for a genuine difference between this and the aggressive dimension. There are no diatropic encounters at all, but eight amphitropic and 12 protropic ones. In the protrope, one manikin presents his back to the other's front (see Figure 47); in the amphitrope, one presents his side either to the other's front or, more rarely, to his back. In both cases, one manikin appears unaware of the other's intended action.

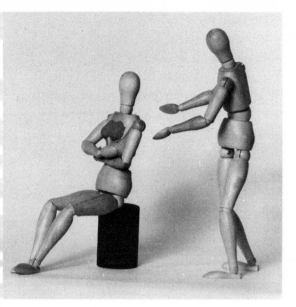

**Fig. 46.** Encounter With Male Initiating (Subject M18)

**Fig. 47.** Encounter With Male Initiating (Subject F15)

Nothing serves so well, it would seem, to call attention to the exclusiveness with which the other figure initiates.

Because of the greater explicitness of the instructions, subjects had less opportunity to differ because of diverging identifications. Their productions are as a result less varied, more stylized and clear-cut. It is not surprising that such a large majority also agree that near encounters are more initiating than the far.

*Female Initiating.* For this task, subjects were again constrained by rather explicit instructions and one might expect them to produce fairly uniform scenes—ones in which the roles of the two figures are merely reversed. Yet, if one tries to imagine a scene in which the female initiates, one experiences a greater difficulty; the scenes that suggest themselves demand more effort—and refuse to be aided by a facile image, such as one conjures up when thinking of male as initiator. Fewer models for female-initiating types exist, probably, than male initiating types. The question to ask of these data is, therefore, not merely how closely do they parallel the male data, but in which ways do they differ?

In four respects, the constructions are mirror images of the previous ones. First, intention movements are primarily reserved for the female manikin, and nearly all of these actions are positive; the female does, then, as did the male, invade some space of the male manikin, or at least threatens to do so (see Table

4 in Appendix Z). Second, among categories of body space, the females are characterized by defined axial space, and by absence of open proximal access, contained axial space, or closed proximal boundary—as were the males. Third, responsibility for intersection at the axial or proximal boundaries here belongs almost exclusively to the female. Finally, changes in relative distance between the figures have the same effect as before: The closer position is most frequently seen as the more initiating one.

But there are two differences between these constructions and the previous ones that illuminate the portrayal of female initiative. Where previously most subjects agreed that the male manikin should be put in an acrotropic position, here, men and women differ. They constructed about the same total number of acrotropic situations, but men cast the male in the superior position while women cast the female. It is here that the absence of a female-initiating stereotype becomes apparent. From the men's point of view, when the female initiates, she does so from a position of physical inferiority, as if the initiative had to be more seductive or insidious than physically overbearing. For the female to initiate—so men seem to think—she has to take the male's "natural" physical or positional superiority into account and work from there; either she tackles the physical superiority directly (and risks the male's determined resistance, as in Figure 48), or she attempts seduction (as in the unsubtle production illustrated in Figure 49). In the first of these, the male attempts to retain the acrotropic position because losing it would make him receive the action rather than initiate it; in the second, the male appears uncertain about retaining the vertical stance which is the embodiment of his ability to resist the female's initiative.

When women place the female manikin into the acrotropic position, they do so for apparently different reasons. The typical production presents a male manikin so tired that he cannot stand, often sitting on a rock. The male is cast as weak and inferior; the female stands capably on her feet, advising the male or giving him aid. In these scenes, the female manikin is superior by virtue of her wisdom, her nurturance, and—in one production in which she is "giving birth" to a male manikin—by virtue of being able to produce life.

As among the male-initiating scenes, the largest number are divided between the protrope and amphitrope (men and women do not differ in this category). These two positions differ from the infrequently used diatrope in that they present a maximal contrast between the initiative shown by one manikin and the inaction displayed by the other; as indicated above, the diatrope is more suited to portrayal of aggressive interaction, in which the advance of one manikin is met by an active response from the other. Yet here, too, the absence of a typed initiating-female image is apparent: Although the protrope and amphitrope predominate, they are used less exclusively than by the male initiators.

*Male Receiving.* When confronted with this instruction, many subjects asked,

 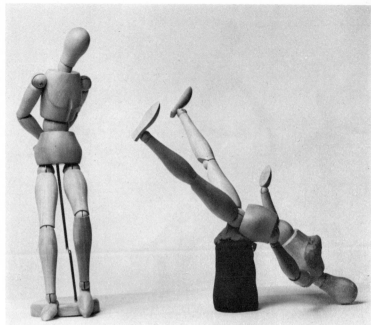

**ig. 48.** Encounter With Female **Fig. 49.** Encounter With Female Initiating (Subject M16)
nitiating (Subject M18)

"Isn't that the same thing as Female Initiating?" Their productions provided an answer that might have surprised them. There are certainly many similarities, but enough differences occur to justify, in retrospect, the choice of both of these seemingly similar dimensions for study. The number and distribution of intention movements remain similar, for example, as does the use of body spaces (open, closed, or defined). That is to say that the female manikins are full of intention movements, that these actions are positive, and that defined axial space (one which the partner has most clearly to take into account) predominates—especially in the female manikin (see Table 5 in Appendix Z).

But among the intention movements, there is a difference: Although the number of female intention movements was high on the female-initiating dimension, it is even higher here. One has the impression that the present male-receiving instructions call for female initiating even more clearly than did the previous female-initiating ones. This impression is further supported by the fact that an even larger number of female manikins is cast into the acrotropic position vis-à-vis the male—and by both men and women (while, in the female-initiating dimension, men made male acrotropes). Thus, not only women, but

 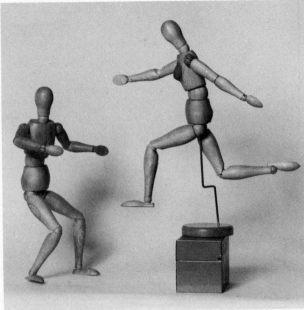

**Fig. 50.** Encounter With Male Receiving (Subject M6)

**Fig. 51.** Encounter With Male Receiving (Subject F15)

also men place the female manikin in a position in which she stands above the male and directs action toward him. What seemed to occur was that, in order to create a scene in which the focus was on the male as the receiver of action, subjects chose to stress female initiation; the male's passive stance took on its clearest meaning from the female's activity.

Two other differences may be observed. The number of instances of *mutual* responsibility for the intersection of boundaries has increased here at the expense of single responsibility (which, when it does occur, naturally remains with the female manikin alone). And consistent with this shift in responsibility is the fact that the number of diatropic interactions has increased dramatically (from zero and three in the two initiating dimensions to ten here). Perhaps these differences best explain why the initiating and receiving dimensions are not portrayed as the same: In the former, initiative is best shown towards a figure that is passive and unaware of the action directed toward it, while, in the latter, the emphasis on the receipt of action requires the receiving figure to acknowledge what it is receiving and from whom. Thus, in Figure 50, the male encourages the female to approach and perhaps sit on his knee; in Figure 51, he prepares to catch her at the end of her leap. The action portrayed in some of the encounters is, expectably, sexual; but its sexuality seems only to be a special case of the more general physical arrangements described here.

One other characteristic of these data requires comment because it completes the sketch presented above: No substantial differences occur between the productions of men and women. Unlike their insistence on male acrotropes in the female-initiating dimension, men here allow male manikins to receive action from acrotropic females. Why do they not feel threatened, as they seemed to before, by the superior female manikin? The answer may be found partly in the prevalence here of the more intimate diatropic encounters and in the feeling-tone of some of the scenes: In those produced by men, the female figure initiates primarily in order to service male intentions or desires.

*Female Receiving.* The productions carried out under this instruction may be best understood by reference to the previous three: male and female initiating, and male receiving. As compared to male initiating, the female-receiving figure approaches and is approached more often (there are more positive intention movements). Instead of "passively" opening her proximal access, she joins the male in "actively" defining axial space and taking responsibility for intersecting at the axial boundary (see Table 6 in Appendix Z). Third, the female manikin almost always faces an acrotropic male, and faces him fully, that is, in a diatrope. As compared to the female-initiating encounters, in these, the female manikin is more often approached by the male, more frequently shares the definition of axial space and responsibility for meeting at the axial boundary with the male, and most often confronts an acrotropic male—again, face to face. Figures 52 and 53 furnish convenient examples.

Is the female manikin here also distinctly different from the male manikin in the male-receiving dimension? On the whole, yes. The female figure here is more approaching than the male was there; she defines her axial space more frequently than did the male; she shares the responsibility for intersecting at the axial boundary more often than he did. Only in a commitment to the male acrotrope is the female manikin a mirror image of the preceding male.

In summary, male and female manikins receive differently: Females receive actively into a well-defined axial space, while males receive passively without defining their axial space. The receiving female is more mutual and active.

*Erotic.* The instruction dimensions that follow once more apply to both manikins without specifying where the emphasis should lie. Accordingly, after presenting an analysis of the positions used in the encounter, the discussion will return to individual reconstructions. From here on, too, it will become increasingly easier to make sense of the various tabulations by reference to the dimensions analyzed previously. In the case of the erotic dimension, it turns out, surprisingly enough, that the most meaningful comparison may be made with the aggressive encounters.

**Fig. 52.**   Encounter With Female Receiving (Subject M12)   **Fig. 53.**   Encounter With Female Receiving (Subject F15)

The many similarities between these two dimensions make the few contrasts appear all the more instructive. Both aggressive and erotic encounters have a high number of positive intention movements (among which, most are made by male manikins), high numbers of intersections at the axial boundary, preference for casting the male manikin into an acrotropic position, a very high number of diatropes (the erotic dimension has 17 of the 20 productions in diatropic synkinesis), and, finally, a very high frequency of defined axial space (see Table 7 in Appendix Z). Thus, in both dimensions, the male is physically superior and reaches towards the female (who, in most cases, responds by extending her own arms towards him); the partners are close to each other and their encounter is face to face.

But unlike the aggressive encounters, none of the erotic ones is characterized by any negative intention movements: All the actions are centripetal. Unlike the one-sided responsibility for the frequent intersections at the axial boundary, the erotic dimension presents a very high number of mutually responsible intersections. From these statistics alone, one has the impression that, while both dimensions present a high degree of involvement of the two partners with each other, in the erotic dimension, the encounter is more mutually agreed upon; if it were not, and in the absence of the other clues, an observer might judge the interaction as initiating or, to a lesser extent, as aggressive.

The effects of increased distance between the manikins, and of their eventual isolation, serve to differentiate this dimension further from the aggressive dimension. Isolated manikins are much more rarely characterized by intention movements than were aggressive manikins; as suggested above, if one is to display aggression, it is easiest to display it toward someone, and eroticism (not autoeroticism) is probably not easily portrayed by a single, active manikin. This interpretation is supported by the use that is made of the anterior body space: While the aggressive individual reconstructions relied almost exclusively on defined axial space, the erotic manikins of both sexes display relatively more open proximal access, and the males show contained axial space; they appear either to invite or expect approach from another, or to pose with relatively closed boundaries.

When the two figures are together, one notes that they are much closer together than under the aggressive instruction; they show by far the largest number of intersections at the proximal boundary. This intersection (the "close" one) is, moreover, almost always judged as more erotic than when the same manikins are farther apart. This effect of changing distance may not cause surprise, but it does serve to explain an inconsistency in the effect of changing distance observed earlier in the aggressive interactions. There, one may recall, about half of the closer positions were judged as more aggressive and half as less so; it was not clear whether this variation was random or whether some general rule could explain it. It appears now that, since contact at the proximal boundary is the hallmark of erotic encounters, aggressive encounters have the aggression taken out of them when the two manikins move close enough to touch proximally.

Differences between the productions of men and women appear again and they help to illuminate several of the observed similarities to the aggressive dimension. The differences may be stated thus: The high frequency of positive intention movements, of the female manikins' defined axial space, and of the male figures' acrotropic superiority is, for the most part, accounted for by the productions of men; and these characteristics were prominent among those who made the aggressive and erotic dimensions appear so close. Therefore, it is men who make these two dimensions seem alike: As in Chapter 10, which analyzed the properties of Venus, women distinguish much more clearly between eroticism and aggression than do men. The contrast between the feminine construction shown in Figure 54 and the masculine encounter portrayed in Figure 55 may be taken as typical.

In the individual reconstructions, these differences disappear; the productions become remarkably similar. It is as if men were on the defensive and took care to present themselves as "masculine" only when in the presence of the female partner, and that, either when alone or when explicitly instructed to see themselves as receiving action, their aggressive superiority appeared no longer required.

**Fig. 54.**   Erotic Encounter (Subject F9)   **Fig. 55.**   Erotic Encounter (Subject M6)

*Non-erotic.* The non-erotic productions of men and women are quite similar, and the similarity argues well for suggestions about the sensitivity men show to certain aspects of the erotic encounter. The non-erotic interaction is a less stressful one and, precisely because it appears not to stress men, it allows them to construct encounters that resemble women's. As a result, the productions offer few surprises (see Table 8 in Appendix Z). There are almost no intention movements. As one might have expected, the frequency of open proximal access is even higher than in the unaggressive encounters. There is less defined axial space, a good deal of contained axial space, and more closed proximal boundaries than in any dimensions except cold and calculating; thus, the manikins seldom reach for each other, instead remaining very open or quite closed—in either case, not involved. The farther position is consistently judged more non-erotic, while proximal contact consistently elicits less non-erotic judgments. Perhaps most significant is the fact that men and women prefer isotropes among the vertical displacements (proving one's superiority, of whatever type, is not required), and avoid the diatropic placement of the erotic encounter in favor of the less exposed, less engaged, and less intimate amphitropic and paratropic configurations (see, for example, Figure 56).

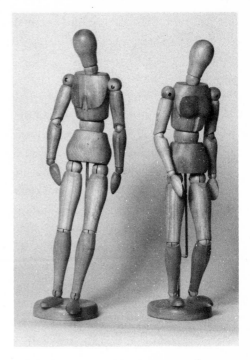

**Fig. 56.** Non-erotic Encounter (Subject F3)

**Fig. 58.** Non-erotic Manikin (Subject M11)

**Fig. 57.** Non-erotic Encounter (Subject M11)

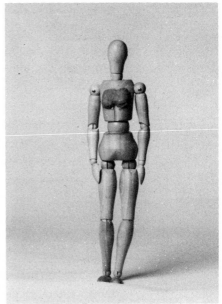

In the isolated reconstructions, one finds little change in body spaces, but a sizable increase in positive intention movements on the part of males. In such cases, the male manikin is running or engaging in some other sporting position such as doing push-ups. But, while the male manikins are consistently rated more non-erotic when alone, the female manikins often as not are judged less non-erotic. A review of the isolated females reveals that the manikins in the original interaction usually actively defined their axial space, and that the same space took on different meaning when the figure was isolated. For example, in Figure 57, the female manikin is merely "shaking hands with a man, as at a party." But when she is removed from the interaction, she appears inviting and distinctly less non-erotic. (To test this, one may cover the male manikin in Figure 57.)

To reconstruct this figure as non-erotic again, the subject felt compelled to bring both her arms to her sides and to compress her legs (see Figure 58). This prompts the observation that, although open proximal access acts as a challenge to approach (as in several of the illustrations in the preceding chapters), in many cases, extreme rigidity can counteract the invitation. In most cases of non-erotic figures with open proximal access, the manikin is either standing exceedingly straight or pathetically drooped over. Such a presentation may withdraw the possibility of intention movements, and open proximal access without a hint of flexibility may not be enticing. Indeed, cold and unaggressive encounters are also characterized by both a low frequency of intention movements and a high frequency of open proximal access.

One other characteristic adds to understanding of non-erotic encounters. It is shown in constructions in which the manikins make contact, but with one of the less prehensile or sensitive parts of the anatomy, such as the feet. An encounter may become non-erotic by displaying lack of contact, as in a paratropic position, or by displaying neutral contact. In the latter case, it may appear non-erotic especially by contrast with what it might have been.

*Warm.* Warm scenes seem most easily understood when compared with erotic ones; the former appear as limited editions of the latter. Among the quantitative differences, one may mention that warm interactions are less active: Defined axial space is still common (in both manikins) but less so than among erotic manikins (see Table 9 in Appendix Z). The figures in warm encounters invite less intimacy and focus more on self-originating feelings: While erotic manikins never contained their axial space, warm figures occasionally do. The male physical superiority that the frequent acrotropic displacements signified in erotic productions drops considerably in warm ones. Although male manikins still approach more frequently than female (again, with total absence of negative intention movements), the total number of such presentations decreases markedly.

One difference is definite enough to constitute a difference in quality. It is

**Fig. 59.** Warm Encounter (Subject F19)

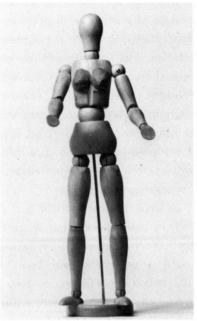

**Fig. 60.** Warm Manikin (Subject F7)

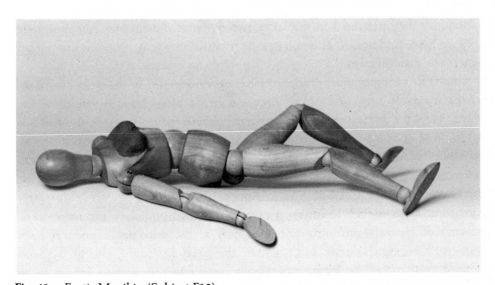

**Fig. 61.** Erotic Manikin (Subject F10)

exemplified in Figure 59, in which the manikins sit with legs parallel, arms around each other, and torsos in an amphitropic position—and, in other similar productions, in which the figures mirror each other and stand in an amphitropic relation. The tabulations show that, as compared with erotic encounters, warm ones show many more amphitropic configurations at the expense of the formerly frequent diatropic ones. When one recalls that the diatrope was favored especially in aggressive and erotic encounters, and very much avoided in unaggressive ones (and, as will be seen, in cold productions), and that the rare back-to-back apotrope is used to portray cold meetings, it seems safe to conclude that the amphitrope is a good presentation of warmth—halfway between the threat or opportunity of the diatrope and the refusal to engage of the apotrope.

Isolated reconstructions are especially instructive about the meanings of defined axial space. That space is used less often in warm *encounters* than in erotic ones, but with the partner absent the proportions are reversed: Lone manikins present warmth by extending one or both arms. The difference is best understood by referring to two illustrations. The warm manikin in Figure 60 appears to invite approach, while the erotic one in Figure 61 seems to dare it; or, in the formulation of Spiegel and Machotka, the former invites approach into axial space, while the latter invites it to the proximal boundary. This difference in subjects' productions is more direct evidence than the dimensional ratings had been for the notion that defined axial space provides a well-limited and subdued area for a partner to move into.

Two more characteristics of warm encounters make them similar to, but cooler than, erotic ones. Men again surpass women in the production of acrotropic males (but acrotropes are generally used less often than in erotic and aggressive encounters); men, it would seem, retain vestiges of the active physical superiority they preferred in the latter two dynamic dimensions, but they tone it down here. And finally, as among erotic productions, near positions are judged as warmer than far ones.

*Cold.* The configurations produced here are as opposed to the preceding ones as the words "warm" and "cold" they are meant to portray. When all of the warm manikins displaying any intention movement moved towards the partner, all the cold ones move away; when warm figures displayed defined axial space, cold ones very rarely do so; and when warm figures at least confronted each other in an amphitrope, cold ones often refuse confrontation and assume the rarely seen apotrope (see Table 10 in Appendix Z). In only one scene do manikins come close enough to intersect even at the axial boundary (an unheard of absence of contact), and only one pair meet at the proximal boundary; even non-erotic encounters took place within the axial boundary, though without defined axial space (see Figure 62). Finally, cold interactions also appear to be at the opposite pole from erotic ones, in that they take place almost exclusively

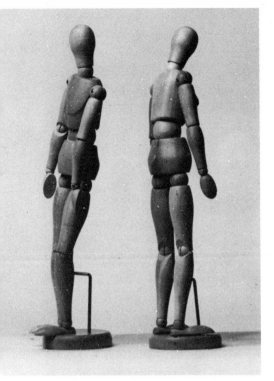

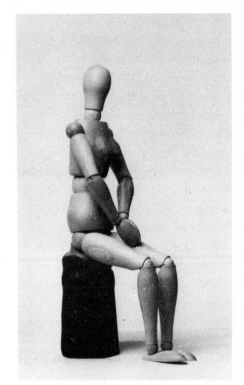

**Fig. 62.**  Cold Encounter (Subject F17)          **Fig. 63.**  Cold Manikin (Subject F15)

in the same horizontal plane; as many isotropes are produced here as in non-erotic encounters. If acrotropes characterize manikins with initiative, among cold figures, very few people initiate.

In their use of body spaces created by the arms, cold constructions resemble unaggressive and non-erotic ones. In both of the latter dimensions there occurred a frequent use of open proximal access—but with infrequent intention movements; here, the frequencies are similar, but the lack of contact is very much strengthened by the apotropic non-confrontation. And, since the manikins stand back-to-back so often, there appears to be little use for defined axial space; and indeed even the non-erotic encounters, very careful to avoid defined axial space, display it twice as often as do cold ones. Instead, these figures rely on contained axial space and closed proximal boundaries, the latter of which subjects judging the Venus of Chapter 10 saw as rejecting, self-concerned—and cold.

Isolated reconstructions throw further light on the uses of axial space, and speak for the only appreciable sex differences observable in cold productions. While the encounters frequently consisted of manikins displaying closed proximal boundaries (and, secondarily, contained axial space), the single figures rely primarily on contained axial space and show the closed proximal boundary but rarely. It would seem that, in lone figures, the fully closed boundary is not required, and that contained axial space presents the self-contained quality of coldness quite adequately (see Figure 63). In reaction to a partner, however, the fully defended proximal boundary seems necessary if the proper degree of coldness is to be portrayed. But in the lone reconstructions, as in the encounters, some open proximal access also appears (though no contact is implied since, in the encounters, it is shared). One finds, however, that men very seldom cast females in this position, while women allow it for both the male and female manikins. The difference is explained, possibly, by referring to the sex differences that appeared in the perceptions of Venus: Since, there, men showed a preference for the open, warm, undefended female figure, it appears natural that they should not produce such female figures if they had to call them cold. Women seem not to operate under this restriction.

One peculiarity of these data deserves mention because it enriches understanding of positions that present coldness. Normally, distance acts to increase coldness between manikins; this is an expectable outcome, and it occurs in the vast majority of instances. But there are three exceptions to this rule. They occur in each case with manikins that had been standing with an open proximal access and in a rigidly immobile stance. The manikins were, therefore, maximally exposed to each other—but when they were close, the encounter was perceived as colder than when they were far. Some of the subjects themselves provided the explanation: There is a contradiction between the closeness and openness on the one hand and the rigidity and lack of action on the other. A situation that is potentially warm, but refuses to be so, must be cold. Similar reasoning explains the one instance in which the male manikin lay on top of the female; since the female was rigid and did nothing to define her axial space, this encounter could very well present coldness.

*Sincere.* No particular set of characteristics distinguishes the sincere dimension. It is very probable that the word "sincere" is more easily applied as a judgment to activity that has already taken place than used as a suggestion for the production of movement; and it is also quite likely that the word usually has very unclear referents regardless of context. In any event, sincere productions are most similar to warm ones, both in the frequencies of the various categories and in the qualitative appearance of the photographs themselves (see Table 11 in Appendix Z). They are characterized, for example, by a moderate frequency of positive intention movements and a virtual absence of negative ones. The manikins face each other fully, that is, in a diatrope, somewhat more frequently than the warm ones but less frequently than the erotic ones. The male figure usually defines his axial space, while the female manikin fairly frequently retains open proximal access. Thus, the male is generally approaching and the female

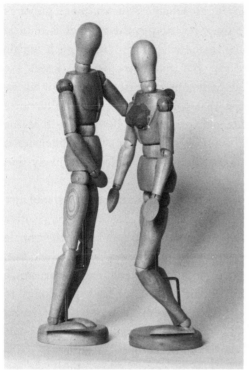

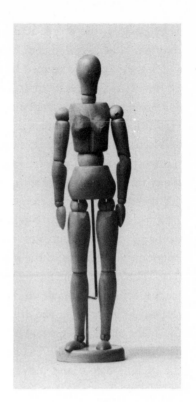

**Fig. 64.** Sincere Encounter (Subject M6)

**Fig. 65.** Sincere Manikin (Subject M1)

receptive—not with any degree of passion, but nevertheless unambiguously so (see Figure 64).

In one respect, the sincere dimension may be best described as a further toned-down version of the warm dimension: The number of male acrotropes decreases progressively from the erotic situation through the warm to the sincere, while the number of isotropes increases proportionately. The preference for isotropes here seems to indicate an emphasis on honest confrontation, less concerned with physical assertion than with conveying a state of mind that refuses to manipulate or influence. The male acrotropes that do exist usually show one manikin sitting or even lying down; the vertical difference portrays a resting position rather than one of unequal power. As in the erotic and warm dimensions, there is a fairly high number of mutually responsible intersections at the axial and proximal boundaries. All in all, the productions have an almost exclusively "good" cast to them and indicate that the subjects seldom thought that one could be sincerely nasty.

Isolated reconstructions furnish the one example of differences between men and women. Men have a greater tendency than women to produce female manikins with open proximal access and male manikins with defined axial space.

They portray, therefore, active males and approachable females. Since previous chapters have revealed that men see the open position in the woman as natural and satisfying, they seemed to fulfill some sexual wish in producing such female figures in response to instructions (see Fig. 65, and note that the knees are apart and one hand is held away from the body—in contrast with the non-erotic Fig. 58). In judging changes in meaning that follow changes in the distance between the manikins, however, the sexes do not differ: Both agree that the changes are ambiguous. It would appear that (among the "positive" dimensions) the more the sexual content of the encounter diminishes, the less is it likely that decreased distance will intensify expressive qualities.

*Calculating.* At first, calculating encounters show some statistical resemblance to their presumed opposites, sincere ones. Both show a predominance of positive intention movements in the male manikin but a very small number in the female (see Table 12 in Appendix Z). Half the vertical displacements are isotropic but, of the acrotropic ones, all show the male as superior; and, whenever single responsibility is assigned for intersection at the axial boundary, it belongs to the male. And, in contrast to the male's positive intended actions, the female most often presents either open proximal access or contained axial space. Thus, the male is active and moving toward the female; she appears either as without defenses or she erects a definite boundary in front of her—but does not define her axial space in a way that would explicitly allow the male to move towards it or within it; in this, the female differs from her sincere counterpart.

But in several ways there is no mistaking calculating encounters for sincere ones. For one, the manikins seldom meet: There are relatively few instances of intersection at the axial boundary and many fewer at the proximal boundary. For another, there is a large number of isotropes (exceeded only by the non-erotic and cold dimensions), suggesting that the subjects saw physical superiority as too direct a presentation to be a sign of calculation, and that, instead, they wished to emphasize the cerebral nature of the encounter. But most important, the encounters differ from the sincere ones (and from all others save non-erotic and warm) in their avoidance of the diatrope and preference for the less direct amphitrope and protrope. A very literal interpretation of this use of the amphitrope suggests itself: When someone is calculating, he does not fully show himself. He approaches a partner who is himself half-turned, or he hides a apart of his body, or he approaches obliquely. The cloak masks part of the face as well as the dagger. In Figure 66, the male manikin hides his approach by attempting to tiptoe past the female; in Figure 67, less anatomically convincing, the torsos are in a diatropic position but the legs carry the figures away from each other; in either case, the calculating encounter is insincere, oblique, or ambiguous in its body message.

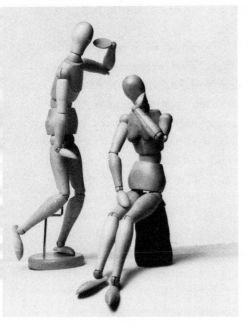 

**Fig. 66.** Calculating Encounter (Subject M8)  **Fig. 67.** Calculating Encounter (Subject M16)

Changes in relative distance between the manikins produce ambiguous changes in meaning; some closer encounters are more calculating, others less so. But men differ radically from women in assigning these meanings, with seven of the ten calling the far position more calculating, while seven women call the near one more so. The reader will recall that, in the preceding chapter, the female figure was in some cases generally seen as more sincere when close. There, the authors theorized that the greater role that fantasy seems to play in the male's sexuality (see pp. 302 and 303) enables him to imagine an encounter-to-be as already sexual, while women appear more to rely on closer (probably proximal) contact before their sexuality is as fully aroused as the male's at greater distance. Here, for the men, a far interaction could be calculating where the near one is already kinetic; for the women, the far encounter might be merely cold. The following quotation from a woman subject supports this interpretation: "He (the distant male) is merely scheming; now (when close) he's trying to brush her unintentionally." The latter contact is what this subject sees as calculating behavior. One can also cite three women who found it easier to portray calculating encounters than sincere ones: One said about sincere interaction, "There's no such thing"; a second said, "Sincere is a fake emotion"; while a third maintained, "Women are much more calculating."

*Good.* In the last chapter, all the male–female encounters were rated "good," although some were seen as more good than others. That experiment and this one used a sample of relatively sophisticated Harvard and Radcliffe students; the utter unanimity of good responses may have to do with the academic community's conscious valuing of relativism. This suggestion is supported by the comments made by some of the subjects when asked to construct a good meeting: "Good is really meaningless unless put in a childish frame of reference, for example, the Bible," or, "You're out of your nut." They were then asked to create an encounter which they would characterize—from their own subjective and relative point of view—as good. Subjects who found this difficult produced ritual scenes, such as prayers, very much in the same way as the subjects of Chapter 9 used ritual or mythological interpretations when all others failed. But generally, in spite of their disclaimers, subjects constructed encounters which were quite consistent when compared with other dimensions as well as among themselves.

Thus, good scenes have fewer intention movements than any other dimension in the study, and there are no instances of withdrawing movements (see Table 13 in Appendix Z). A good encounter tends to be one in which both manikins are quite content with the position they happen to occupy. The partners in Figure 68, for example, appear as if they will continue to look into each other's eyes indefinitely. The few manikins who are "moving" do so neither toward nor away from one another; their activity may be parallel, as in Figure 69, or oriented around one another, as with the manikins "madly twirling around" in Figure 70. In their low frequency of intended actions, good encounters resemble unaggressive and non-erotic ones, but in their distribution of body spaces, they are closest to warm ones. In both warm and good encounters, defined axial space presents an opportunity for a fairly intimate relation. Open proximal access of the female manikin—permitting either drastic approach or discouraging any approach whatsoever—is understandably less frequent than in warm (therefore, slightly erotic) encounters.

Good encounters have high rates of both axial intersection and proximal contact; in this, they also resemble erotic and warm ones. On the other hand, erotic encounters frequently show individual responsibility for the intersection, while good and warm ones are characterized by joint responsibility. As to turning movements in the horizontal plane, there is an almost even distribution of all the configurations except the apotrope, with the manikins assuming diatropes as often as paratropes, and amphitropes as often as protropes. Perhaps most remarkable about this variety is the low number of diatropes—previously so frequent in erotic, aggressive, and receiving encounters. Among vertical dis-

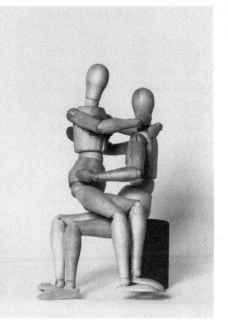

**Fig. 68.** Good Encounter (Subject F20)

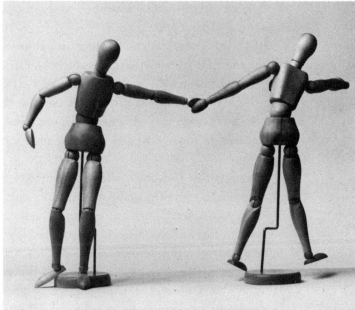

**Fig. 70.** Good Encounter (Subject F19)

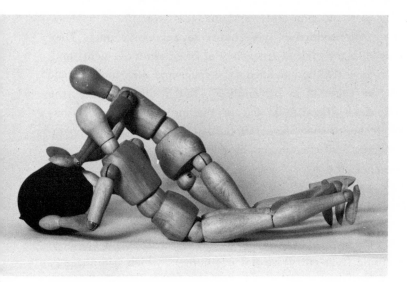

**Fig. 69.** Good Encounter (Subject M8)

placements, both male and female acrotropes are surprisingly frequent; although in this the good interactions seem to resemble aggressive and male-initiating ones, they differ from the latter in their low frequency of approaching movements. Thus, good productions frequently reveal one manikin in a protective or benevolently superior role; they resemble warm encounters in the distribution of body spaces and contacts, and unaggressive interactions in lack of intended movement and infrequent diatropes. In the compact words of one subject, "Good is warmth without sex."

Effects of inter-manikin distance are consistent again, as they were in the erotic and female-receiving dimensions: All but two of the near positions are judged "more good." The two exceptions bear out the discussion of sex differences in the calculating constructions because they both occur in women. Since women more often judge the near distance to be calculating than the far sincere, it is consistent for two women to be the only subjects to call the farther distance "more good."

Finally, isolated reconstructions differ from the encounters in one interesting manner: They avoid the defined axial space that was fairly frequent in the two-manikin productions. Defined axial space seemed consistently to indicate a warm or even erotic relation between the partners—when reinforced by the full face-to-face diatrope; this reinforcement did not occur in good interactions, so the meaning of defined axial space was toned down. But in the isolated reconstructions, no such positional toning down is possible, and subjects indicate the lesser degree of warmth by avoiding the defined space, preferring instead the cooler contained axial space, on the one hand (which keeps intentions inside and partners' movements away) or the open proximal access on the other (which, in most circumstances, is also cold, non-erotic, and unaggressive).

*Evil.* In many ways, evil productions are similar to aggressive ones. They are the two dimensions with the highest frequency of intention movements and, in both, the manikins frequently show defined axial space and occasional female open proximal access (see Table 14 in Appendix Z). But in other respects, the two dimensions differ, both statistically and in the individual constructions themselves. Thus, while aggressive presentations often portrayed both males and females as approaching, evil encounters show approaching males and withdrawing females; this echoes the discovery in the last chapter of the one instance in which a male figure was judged as really evil (that is, in drawing D27; see Fig. 40). In that drawing, the male approached (from afar) and the female leaned away from him, with open proximal access. Evil has been portrayed similarly here, but with the two sexes reversed, as in Figure 71, and it has been portrayed in the protropic (rear-entry) sexual position, in which, significantly enough, one partner is less than a full member of the interaction. It has also been illustrated by highly contradictory body stances, as when the male in Figure 72 invites with his well-defined axial space (and open palms) but kicks the female with his foot.

Vertical displacement in evil encounters is quite different from other dimensions. Subjects exaggerated the acrotrope to make one figure drastically higher than the other, even placing (in half the cases) the lower figure in a helpless

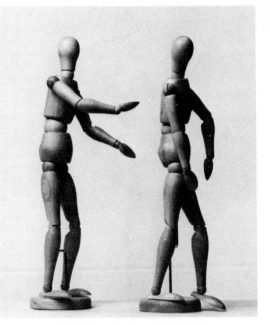

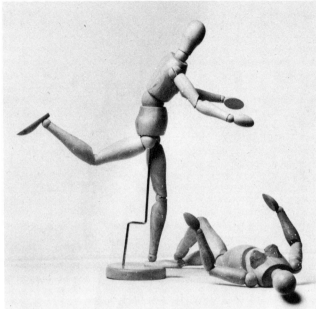

**Fig. 71.**  Evil Encounter (Subject M4)    **Fig. 72.**  Evil Encounter (Subject M5)

horizontal position. The differences in vertical placement are blatant enough to call attention to the injustice of a one-sided encounter. And the one-sidedness is further emphasized by the distribution of horizontal syntropisms: By far the largest number are protropic and a fairly large number are amphitropic. Thus, while the calculating interactions were best shown by the oblique confrontation of the amphitrope, evil ones are better portrayed by the non-confrontation of the back-to-face protrope.

The contradictory nature of the evil encounters (the contradiction exists between the positions of the partners, or within the stance assumed by one manikin) is well brought out by the individual reconstructions. In some, as in Figure 73 the manikin defines his axial space with the left arm, seemingly making approach possible, but brings down his right arm as if to strike. In Figure 74, the manikin makes the Nazi salute; significant about his position is the contradiction between the very open partially defined axial space and the rigidity of the body—the one receptive, the other cold and rejecting. That this contradiction is real is corroborated by the historical observation that, for the Romans, the salute indicated that one came as a friend, unarmed; thus, its original aim, to show that one's partner need not feel threatened, contrasts strangely with its later rigid, militant, and exclusive meaning.

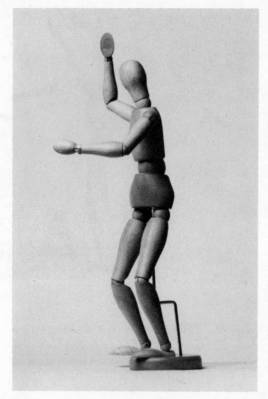 

**Fig. 73.**  Evil Manikin (Subject F20)      **Fig. 74.**  Evil Manikin (Subject M12)

An overview of this chapter is best accomplished by rearranging the data. Until now, the chapter has asked what body movements distinguish various categories of encounters, the "categories" being the one-word instructions given to subjects. As the analysis of the data progressed, interpretation of the various body movement frequencies became less isolated and more comparative; nevertheless, even the comparative (and, therefore, interdependent) interpretations could not pretend overall coherence of presentation. To attempt some additional coherence, one should now ask: What effects result (across instruction dimensions) from distance manipulation between the manikins? What differences can be observed between the encounters and the isolated reconstructions? What regularities exist in differences between men and women subjects?

*Near/Far.* In the preceding chapter, the authors discovered that, although the male figure's distance from the female played a lesser role in determining the way he was perceived than did his advance or retreat, nevertheless, a distance effect could be observed, and it generally consisted of making the male figure appear more erotic, aggressive, warm, and even good when close; and, surprisingly, it also made the (unchanging!) female figure appear more erotic and good.

In the data presented here, nearer manikins were generally judged to be more erotic, good, and warm than the farther ones. In this respect, these data are a welcome confirmation of the preceding conclusions, especially since they result from a different experimental procedure—one in which, to mention one of the less obvious differences, the male manikin was not always the one to advance toward the female. Can one make a more general statement about the near–far differences, and can one propose an explanation for them?

This hypothesis might be advanced: The effect of changing distance is not explained by distance as such but rather by the assignation of mutual responsibility for the encounter. On this hypothesis, the changes in subjects' perception resulted not from how close or far the manikins are but from what they do with the space that they occupy. To test this proposal, a rank ordering of the instruction dimensions on the frequency with which the "meaning" of the interaction is "intensified" by the close position, and a rank ordering based on the frequency of joint responsibility for intersection at the axial boundary are presented in Table 17–1.

**TABLE 17–1. Rankings of Dimensions on Frequency of Near Intense Judgments and Joint Intersection of Axial Boundary (in parentheses: frequency)**

| *Near position more intense* | *Joint responsibility for intersection* |
| --- | --- |
| 1. Good (18) | 1. Erotic (15) |
| 2. Erotic (17) | 2. Warm (15) |
| 3. Female-Receiving (17) | 3. Good (14) |
| 4. Warm (16) | 4. Non-erotic (14) |
| 5. Male-Receiving (16) | 5. Sincere (13) |
| 6. Male-Initiating (16) | 6. Female-Receiving (13) |
| 7. Female-Initiating (15) | 7. Unaggressive (9) |
| 8. Sincere (12) | 8. Male-Receiving (7) |
| 9. Evil (11) | 9. Calculating (5) |
| 10. Calculating (10) | 10. Aggressive (4) |
| 11. Aggressive (9) | 11. Female-Initiating (4) |
| 12. Unaggressive (7) | 12. Evil (2) |
| 13. Non-erotic (4) | 13. Male-Initiating (2) |
| 14. Cold (3) | 14. Cold (1) |

The table shows that, as manikins come close, the good, erotic, and warm nature of the encounter is emphasized, and that the unaggressive, non-erotic, and cold aspects become weakened. On the whole, the other ranking in the table parallels the first; therefore, as joint responsibility for the intersection increases, so does the intensity of the meaning of the encounter, and, as the one decreases, so does the other. There are, however, some exceptions that sharpen understanding of this relation.

One glaring difference (especially in absolute frequency, not just in rank) is the placement of the non-erotic dimension; as manikins come closer and assume joint responsibility for the approach, they become less non-erotic, not more. On reflection, this result would make less sense were it otherwise: If manikins come to appear more erotic when close, they could not very well also come to look more non-erotic at the same time. But can one similarly explain the differences in the positions of the male-receiving, and male- and female-initiating dimensions? Here, the difference appears to be accounted for by another factor: In all three dimensions, one partner leads and presents all the intention movements while the other reacts more passively. Since the interaction is so purposely one-sided, no correlation should have been expected between intensity of meaning and mutual responsibility for intersection (and the fact that the female initiating dimension is not one of these three exceptions supports this interpretation: Here, the male manikin reacts by defining his axial space; hence, both manikins show intended action and the relation is not one-sided). Finally, the evil dimension fails to show the correlation observed elsewhere because it, too, is one-sided; the male generally approaches while the female withdraws.

With the exception of explicitly one-sided interactions, then, it may be said that, as the manikins assume joint responsibility for their contact, the encounter comes to be perceived as more intense.

*Encounters/Isolated Reconstructions.* Perhaps the most dramatic illustration of the difference between encounters and isolated reconstructions is one subject's almost total inability to create an evil situation without two people. "How can you be evil alone?" she asked. She was voicing more forcefully than some of the others the conclusion that the bodily presentations take on their clearest meaning in relation to another person. Even when an isolated manikin is successfully manipulated, one can notice that his position frequently takes an unseen other into account. Emotions and intentions—at least those studied here —are not "expressed" by being channeled outward through a meaningfully compliant body, but are instead presented to a partner for his information.

As a result of the interpersonal nature of these presentations, the distributions of body spaces and intention movements generally differ in the individual and interpersonal versions. Only two dimensions contain similar total distributions. Both aggressive and evil productions are characterized by similar manikins in the two versions—similar both in the body spaces used and in the frequency of intended actions. But the two versions differ in one particular: The withdrawing movements apparent in the encounter are absent in the individual reconstruction, while the approaching movements are present in both. In the two "nasty" dimensions, it appears, one can portray the aggressive approaching movements in the isolated manikin and have them make sense to an observer who himself supplies the missing partner; but if the isolated manikin were withdrawing, the observer would not know what he was withdrawing from. In advertisements for horror films, curiously enough, the horrified reaction to an unseen source of evil is as often portrayed as is the evil itself, but in contrast to the manikins used here, the frightened young woman has facial expression at her disposal. The merely withdrawing body movement of one of the manikins might have illustrated fear or self-defense, but would in all likelihood have drawn attention away from the evil partner.

There is yet another difference between the individual and the paired constructions, and it provides further information on the uses of the anterior body space. Throughout this study, evidence has been found for the notion that, when the anterior space is *defined*, it provides a location toward which the partner may move and within which he may comfortably stop. (There are cases, of course, in which such defined space forbids approach, as in the policeman's traffic-stopping movement, or in which the extended arm moves toward the partner and forces him to react, as in aggressive confrontations.) Open proximal access, on the other hand, may challenge approach (and, thus, either encourage a drastic form of it or discourage it altogether), while contained axial space is a private affair, portraying inwardly originating feelings, rather than reactions to a partner. Supporting these notions is the fact that 238 instances of defined axial space (of 280 possible) occur in the encounters, while only 167 instances (of 400 possible) occur in the individual reconstructions. But contained axial space occurs relatively more frequently (than defined space) in the isolated constructions; there, it is seen in 62 instances, while it can be observed 48 times among the interactions. Further, the highest frequency of defined axial space occurs in aggressive interactions, while the highest number of contained axial spaces appears in the sincere and calculating encounters.

*Differences between Men and Women.* The subjects, as previously suggested, operated under two sorts of overall directives, one coming from the experimenter and the other mostly from the subjects themselves. The first directive (or attitude towards the instructions) was called *task orientation;* under this attitude, the subjects produced encounters that satisfied the demand of the experimental instructions because the instructions were explicit and left little room for freely floating fantasy. The second, inner-inspired attitude was called *identification;* it arose when the instructions were vague and the subjects relied more on personal experience and fantasy to produce their constructions. Under these conditions, it was suggested, differences between male and female subjects would become apparent.

They became apparent, first, in the "aggressive–unaggressive" dimension. When producing aggressive encounters, men created advancing males who took responsibility for the contact and relatively passive females who withdrew; women, on the other hand, made the females approach and share responsibility for the contact with the males—and more often put the male manikins in the vertically superior position than did men. In the aggressive encounters, women emphasized the male's brute strength but also created female manikins who resisted more actively. In unaggressive scenes men created males with open proximal access and females with defined (active, intrusive) axial space and placed the manikins in more isolated positions, while women produced manikins that had more contact and more shared responsibility for the contact; thus, when men emphasized distance and one-sidedness, women stressed mutuality and closeness.

The "initiating–receiving" dimensions allowed the least identification to come through but, nevertheless, did show some sex differences. Under the female-initiating instruction, women created quite a number of females who initiated from the acrotropic position, while men saw the initiation of the female as coming from the inferior location. For the men, the female's initiative was, therefore, more insidious or seductive. But when asked to produce a situation in which the male receives, men reversed this tendency and created superior females—but ones whose superiority existed only to better serve the men's needs and desires.

In erotic and (to a lesser degree) warm encounters, men seemed to find it necessary to produce highly initiating males: ones who stood higher, approached the female, and defined their axial space. While the women stressed their equality (in the isotrope) and the partners' mutuality (shared responsibility for boundary intersection), the men once more confused eroticism and aggression, and accounted for a striking presentational similarity with the aggressive dimension.

Finally, men and women differed in their perceptions of the effect of distance on the calculating quality of the encounters they had produced. For men, the more calculating encounters were the far ones, while, for women, they were the near ones. Speculation was made, as in the last chapter, about the greater role of visual fantasy in men's sexuality, which permitted them to see as calculating an encounter that had not achieved proximal contact; by contrast, in women's sexuality, proximal contact played the greater role and had to be achieved before the calculating nature of the encounter came through.

One may note, in closing, that, when an encounter was removed from the competition of aggression or the uneasy threat of eroticism, the sexes again found little reason to differ; they were brought into harmonious agreement on the desexualized meeting labeled good.

# NOTE FOR CHAPTER 17

[1] An initiating or a receiving interaction appeared to be too ambiguous; therefore, the subjects were asked to create an encounter in which specifically either the male or the female manikin was initiating or receiving. Hence, male initiating, female initiating, and so on.

# 18. Future Directions

This book has been devoted to setting forth a theory of how people communicate with their bodies and to the description of some studies designed to test aspects of that theory. Because of the broad nature of the theory and the narrowly selective nature of the studies, it would be inappropriate to end with a mere summary of the results in the usual fashion. We prefer instead to ask some questions about the place of this work in scientific methodology and about its possible usefulness in the arts. What have we learned from our methods, and what can we conclude after a critical assessment of our initial assumptions, about the empirical study of presentation behavior? To what sorts of problems can the theory be addressed in the future? In what ways can the experimental procedures be improved, or along what lines can new testing procedures be devised?

The *presentational* approach discussed in the initial chapters was designed originally to deal with the visual aspects of non-verbal communication. While experimenting with the theory, it became evident, somewhat unexpectedly, that certain issues transcended the purely visual, body-message concerns with which we started. The most general of these issues, and perhaps the most significant, has to do with ambiguity—ambiguity in the interpretation of presentations and even in their performance.

It is the business of science to decrease ambiguity and to increase certainty. The physical sciences discovered long ago how to go about this, and, their sisters, the biological sciences, have followed suit somewhat more recently. The procedure to be followed in the natural sciences involves discovering what range of "units," "elements," or "forces" are implicated in the phenomenon to be studied, simplifying the investigative process by ruling out of any one inquiry all but a few of these, and by arranging an experimental set-up designed to elucidate what cause-and-effect relations exist within the reduced number of factors so that "initial conditions" lead to "final results." The social sciences have attempted to emulate this model although they have encountered some tough problems concerning the existence of causes and effects. Perhaps because social scientific method relies so much on correlations (mere calculations of the degree of closeness between two phenomena), or perhaps because it has such a difficult time discovering units of analysis which feel natural to all concerned, social scientists have shied away from distinguishing what is cause and what is effect. This does not mean that they do not do so covertly; they do so distinguish, but pretend not to, and call causes "independent variables" and effects "dependent variables." This compromise formulation has become generally accepted, so much so that departure from it appears unprofessional, but it only serves to underscore that the assumptions and procedures of the natural sciences are being followed, even though with some discomfort.

The procedure of the natural sciences, then, is linear, from cause to effect, though it can be manipulated—that is to say, modified—by adding new factors to the initial conditions or by segregating intervening steps or variables. Insofar as its purpose has consisted of eliminating ambiguity, it has been highly successful, an end result to which our technological mastery of nature is adequate testimony. To the extent that we know how effects are caused, we know how to control our natural environment. But do we know ourselves—the goal to which Socrates long ago directed our inquiry? And can we attain this knowledge through the linear procedures of the natural sciences?

Psychologists, in particular, and sociologists, anthropologists, and political scientists somewhat less so, have sought to reproduce the linear procedures of their successful brother scientists by seeking out the variables responsible for the behavioral phenomenon being studied, and by arranging them for experimental manipulation in cause-and-effect sequences. There has been considerable disagreement about how the variables were to be conceived and named ("stimulus" and "response," for example, versus "drive" and "defense"), but, among experimental social scientists, very little controversy over the heart of the procedure. And yet we do not really *know* ourselves, although we know a lot *about* ourselves. Success has eluded us, and ambiguity is still high.

Considering the amount of time, effort, and money expended, it is not implausible to ask whether the elimination of ambiguity—to the degree and by the methods used by the natural sciences—is a proper goal. Perhaps it would be more appropriate to define the nature and the limits of the ambiguity. It is possible that if we elucidate this problem, we will, at once, eliminate our slavish imitation of the natural sciences while harmonizing the dichotomy between the arts and the sciences. If ambiguity is to the arts what certainty is to the sciences, is there not some prospect of a marriage based upon the limits of certainty and the confinement of ambiguity?

Clearly, the presentations of the body are an apt subject for this approach. If human behavior in general is subject to a variety of interpretations depending upon what conceptual system we use, understanding the visual aspects of communicating through the body has been a conceptual wilderness. We do not know (unambiguously) how we interpret body messages and we disagree (to some extent) about the end results of our interpretations. Was so-and-so being defensive, rejecting, or shy? Do vivid gestures indicate lively emotionality and spontaneity, or merely a hysterical and basically shallow search for theatrical effects? Do presentationally still waters run deep? Is it true that a person whose pelvis and lower extremities move awkwardly is emotionally out of touch with his lower body? These are questions to which psychology might want clear answers; but the novel, the drama, film and dance, painting and sculpture, happily make room for ambiguous interpretations and use them to achieve their powerful effects. In the arts, it is rare that clear answers are offered; they appear incompatible with artistic purposes. Moreover, disagreement has also been recognized and systematized in discussion about the arts in the form of "criticism." Until the present, psychology and the social sciences have, on the contrary, expanded the disagreements by elaborating various incompatible technical procedures for eliminating ambiguity. Something parallel to criticism—or a "critical tradition"—in the arts is needed in the social sciences.

For this purpose, we propose presentational psychology as one possible model. Ambiguity is not to be eliminated, though it can be reduced, and more importantly, it is to be made "rational"—that is to say, understandable, or, even, predictable. Given the initial conditions, the end result depends not upon a random constellation of events nor upon the personal vision (needs, values, perceptual defenses) of the individual interpreter—at least not upon these alone—but also upon the fit of the actual presentation into the hierarchically arranged system of categories designed *to place* an interpretation upon the phenomenon. According to the theory we have proposed, for an interpretation to be made fairly accurately, the movements or position of the body must be placed within: (1) the *somatotactical categories* of body movement; (2) an *activity series* capable of giving the sequence of movements a logical ends–means (intentional) structure; (3) a set of *social roles*, along with their associated cultural value and allocative structures, to place the interpretation of the activities within an appropriate interpersonal context; and, finally, (4) an event structure or *scenario*, properly confined to time, place, and scale, and designed to explain what the roles are all about. Labels, titles, captions, or other linguistic aids of course help in the problem of correct category selection at any of these system levels (when they have been furnished), but the process of selection is essentially a non-linguistic, visual–motor affair dependent upon vertical and associative *referencing*.

The theory places the question of ambiguity versus certainty (plus the problem of cause and effect) in a multi-dimensional context. As opposed to the usual, one-dimensional linear chain of cause and effect inherited from the natural sciences, ambiguity enters into explanation (or interpretation) in several ways, of which two are important for our purposes here. The first is connected with the great chance of error or mistake (or simple disagreement) in category selection at any of the four system levels. If the capacity for error in the interpretation of a presentation is great at any one system level, then, possibly, the chance of being correct is much reduced by its having to occur simultaneously at all four system levels. There is the alternative possibility, of course, that referencing across the four levels reduces one's chance of error, because the levels may be correlated with each other and thus offer corrections for one's guesses as one moves across them. This matter, however, is something that can be subjected to empirical inquiry, and should be looked into in the future. Whatever the outcome, it will not alter the conclusion that one aspect of ambiguity in human affairs is an irreducible percentage of error in category selection. If this percentage of error is large enough, then no one can say who is 100% "right," and people will have to go on agreeing-to-disagree without expecting more aid from science than the phenomenon allows. Much, however, may be learned about the process of erroneous category selection (beyond what we already know from psychoanalytical studies) and this may be of some help in reducing error or in making ambiguity more manageable.

The second source of ambiguity is possibly more interesting. It derives from the uncertainty of event structures. As previously pointed out, the behavioral sciences have tended to ignore the *flow* of events, preferring to chop its parodic structure into little pieces in which outcomes are managed in reference to selected variables. Can one predict who will profit from psychotherapy? How well does a personality test predict the future behavior of the individual? The larger "story," of which the outcome is but one facet, is essentially ignored— or treated unsystematically as a "case history." The scenario is considered outside the interests of science although it may be of the essence of history. But scenarios have structure; they are not randomly distributed and they exist only in limited supply. Thus, they can be compared, analyzed, and subjected to probability tests. Ambiguity arises from the likelihood of one versus another scenario actually taking place. A detailed investigation of the interdependence among somatotactical, activity, and role structures, and the fit of all three into possible scenarios, conflict-laden, violent or harmonious, comic or tragic, routine or extraordinary, may well make the ambiguity of events more manageable.

There is a third source of ambiguity, and that resides in the multiplicity of motives that may underlie a single body presentation. We had suggested earlier that body movements seem more useful for portraying social intentions than for revealing emotions. For example, they indicate what an actor intends to do or what qualities he wishes to convey; or they show the status he occupies in relation to another; or they reveal to what extent he wishes to appear open to encounter with another. But they do not very well indicate why he may wish to do so nor what he is feeling at the time. If we look at a person standing with his arms crossed on his chest, we understand that he is keeping a certain distance and signaling us not to approach too close, but we do not know whether he is feeling haughty, modest, or anxious, or whether he is trying to hide some part of his body, or whether he is fighting a desire to embrace someone. If we wish to find out, we may try placing his body arrangement into an activity series, an appropriate social role, or a probable scenario, but it is not certain that any of these will insure success. Or we may go in the opposite direction and search for more microscopic clues, such as in the facial display, since it is agreed that at least some emotions can be adequately coded in facial presentation. But even facial presentation can be intentional, so our attempt to discover the "underlying" emotion may not fare any better when we examine the face.

If we combine these three sources of ambiguity—the uncertainty of category selection, the uncertainty regarding which scenario is most likely to take place or why it took place, and the uncertainty of the underlying emotions—we reach the essential problem in regard to interpretation and perception: the ambiguity of meaning. Though posed in visual–motor terms, it is this problem with which our studies have been centrally concerned. We have not attempted to solve it but merely to propose some conceptual and methodological approaches, thereby providing a fresh perspective.

Just as with respect to interpretation, the issue of ambiguity arises on the performance side of a presentation. Here, we encounter a small terminological problem. Although many of the current words for presentations aim at precision, by attempting to remain free of inappropriate connotations, none of them distinguishes between the interpretation of a presentation and its enactment. We prefer to recognize the difficulty of making this distinction by using the word "presentation" for what people do with their bodies (or their speech)— in other words, their actions. The word "performance" seems the best way to refer to the process through which they come to do what they do in action (or rest), and the word "interpretation" seems best for coded signals received (perception) and meanings imputed to presentations witnessed.

Having recognized and incorporated into our terminology the ambiguity stemming from semantic problems, we are still faced with the ambiguity of the way in which the performance is carried out. Here, we refer to the well-known facts that people are often not only unaware of what they are doing but are frequently not sure why they are doing it. Much of the uncertainty surrounding the performance aspects of presentations has been reduced through the findings of psychoanalytical and psychological research. If there is a good deal of difficulty in reconciling these two research approaches, it may well be due to the fact that the presentation itself (actions taken) has been slighted and, so, the performance aspect of the presentation (as opposed to the interpretive aspect) is difficult to examine in a systematic fashion.

To put the matter differently, neither case histories nor laboratory-type psychological experiments nor participant–observer studies can substitute for a systematic presentational analysis. Case histories deal, on a rather catch-as-catch-can basis, with the structure of events. They are particularly suited for helping order events in time, and they can also describe how activities fit into events. But the event dimension is their primary focus, and a description of the uniqueness of each case seems their foremost aim. Laboratory experiments are aimed at making general conclusions about phenomena, but they deal with subjects in subject roles and experimenters in experimenter roles (as is true of the experiments reported in this book), and are generally designed to study only the most detailed levels of presentations (body movement and activity). Participant–observer studies examine the roles people perform and how the roles fit into scenarios, but they only describe what occurs, in a given circumstance, not what range of activities or body presentations might be permitted to occur under varying conditions; in other words, they can be neither systematic nor experimental.

In this book, we have been concerned (with one exception) with the interpretive side of body presentations, confining our interests mainly to the somatotactical and activity levels of the presentation. The role level has been examined in certain instances—for example, with respect to generalized male–female roles in the Venus–Apollo series and with respect to diffuse leadership roles in the dominance series. The experiments reported are merely beginnings. We make no apologies for using the one-dimensional, linear approach of traditional scientific procedure and, in fact, would defend the procedure as appropriate, provided it is placed in a multi-dimensional, conceptual context. Clearly, many other experiments could be devised on the interpretive side to examine the relation between selected somatotactical categories and activities or roles.

To return to the performance side of the presentation, the one exception to our preoccupation with the interpretive aspect is the chapter reporting Paul Williams's experiments with manikins. He asked subjects to arrange the bodies of manikins to see if they would duplicate the activities and somatotactical properties previously interpreted by subjects in the line-drawing studies. This is one way of approaching the performance side of body presentations and it produced interesting results. The correspondence of somatotactical positions between the completely different subjects involved in the interpretive and the performance studies raises one's confidence in the validity of the conceptual categories. Nevertheless, these conceptual categories still existed only in the minds of the experimenters (where we meant them to remain), and performance mediated by manikins are not the same as the acts of the living human body. Many other experiments on the performance side must be performed to test the usefulness of the somatotactical categories and of the overall conceptualization of the presentational approach.

We can visualize several different lines of investigation for this purpose. We had suggested earlier that the rules for moving from one somatotactical category to another be written out as a program of motions. Similarly, we have suggested that programs of instruction for carrying out activities can be written down, and we believe that the same thing can be done for role patterns. It would be interesting to write out instructions for performances at these three system levels, without providing the subjects with any verbal tags indicating the scenario to which they should belong. We would then ask: Can the written instructions be converted into any semblance of realistic interaction? If not, why? Having witnessed what the subjects have done, can they then place their behavior in a scenario—that is, in an event structure? If so, can they agree upon the scenario? If not, what intervening assumptions interfere with agreement? At what system levels do the intervening assumptions occur?

In such an experiment, the spontaneity of role sensitivity experiments would be absent, and wooden enactments could be expected. However, precisely because of the contrived and artificial nature of the behavior, both the verbal and the visual–motor links between body action and interpersonal communication would become more apparent. We would expect a subject to say, "I wouldn't have done that if I had intended to defy my boss," (in accordance with a suggested scenario). Inquiry as to what he *would* have done with his body under the circumstances would expose an important connection between the image one has of one's behavior and the transformation of that image into physical action through intervening cognitive structures. Since visual–motor imagery would be directly linked to verbal instructions for movement, on the one hand, and to the purpose of movement within a scenario on the other, the connection between words and deeds would become more explicit. Further, the way any person in the experiment had learned to make his moves would come more into the foreground.

Learning how to move (or to avoid moving) within specific somatotactical positions, activities and roles could form the basis for another line of inquiry into the performance aspect of presentations. Using children of different ages as subjects and using age-graded presentations as subject matter, one could investigate the influence of imitation versus instruction on the way performances are carried out. Here, an equally important aspect of body-message learning would be the discovery by the child of how his spontaneous or learned presentations are interpreted within his environment.

Studies could also be carried out to determine the effect of different scenarios on habitual activities and body presentations. Let us assume that we have an inventory of the habitual body presentations of people in informal settings—that we know how they present the intentions of modesty, attractiveness, power, status, and others. We assume that the body presentations required for accurate communication are heavily dependent on the appropriate arrangement of the covering of the body's proximal boundary—that is, clothes. Let us take a setting in which clothes have been eliminated by mutual agreement, such as at a nudist camp. What happens to the formal arrangements of the body under these circumstances? On the one hand, one might assume that, because everyone is totally uncovered, no need for gestures of modesty would be felt; if that were so, the range of usable body presentations would be at least as great as in the clothed state, and probably greater, since, in the clothed state, there exist arrangements of the body which allow the clothes to uncover too much. On the other hand, this assumption might not hold, or at least not altogether; one might then suppose that not all views of all parts of the body would be tolerable, and that rules limiting body presentations exist. What are those rules, if they exist? Or, to look at the matter from the opposite direction, what are the rules for presenting bodily attractiveness and seductiveness? Since, in the clothed state, presentations of attractiveness are implicit and indirect, how does one make implicit statements with an explicitly uncovered body? How can one be suggestive, that is, avoid "speaking" in simple declarative sentences? Doubtless, ways are found to communicate by indirection, but they have not, to our knowledge, been the objects of study.

Inquiries of broader scope can also be suggested by the perspectives of presentational analysis. It is possible, for example, that, when an architect says that a building makes a statement, he is referring to the somatotactical aspects of the way the building presents itself to viewers and users. In addition, it is possible that the aesthetics of an architectural structure rest upon the degree of fit, or congruence, between the somatotactical, activity, role, and event levels hierarchically assembled within its presentation. The role of a building, especially if it is large and important, is of concern to city planners, while its place within a structure of events is of interest to historians and critics. On the same score, it may well be that the often-noted strain existing between architects and clients occurs because the architects' interest in the somatotactical level of presentation may be out of phase with the activities of those who will actually inhabit the building. Again, with respect to the level of roles, the architect-as-designer may be more interested in a future-time orientation, considering himself at the leading edge of style developments, while the client as inhabitant may be more concerned with present-time values.

Studies of the fit between architects' and clients' somatotactical conceptions blur the distinction between performance and interpretive inquiries, and help remind us that further interpretive studies are as necessary as studies of performance. We have in mind not only studies of how different body movements are decoded, but also studies of the process by which interpretation is reached. As an example, we refer to the processes alluded to in our study of the meanings of the arms of Venus, in which we distinguished between identification and object-choice as processes by which presentational meaning becomes apparent. We had suggested, though we had no direct evidence on the matter, that the interpretation of body presentation in the opposite sex had a strong component of object-choice, while interpretation of presentations by figures of the same sex involved a prominent use of identification. By the first process, we meant principally treating the figure as an object of attraction and interpreting its somatotactical arrangement from the approach that it permitted, while, by the latter, we meant interpreting presentational meaning from inside the figure's skin, as if by identifying with the figure and its possible intentions. We would be in a better position to distinguish the processes in practice if we modified the methods used here. For example, we could pay attention to individual differences and contrast the interpretations of presentations indicating, for instance, shyness, of subjects who are shy and those who are not; if the subjects were interpreting the presentation by identification, shy subjects should consider shy presentations natural and exhibitionistic presentations unnatural. Object-choice could be studied by comparing the interpretations of subjects who find a given opposite-sex figure attractive with subjects who find the same figure unattractive; if their interpretations were based on object-choice, they would differ. These are but two examples of what could be done; there certainly exist other methods by which these processes could be studied, and there are probably other processes at work.

At the moment, the future directions of presentational analysis can only be sketched in lightly. At the least, it may well throw fresh light on the non-verbal, visual–motor aspects of body communications. At the most, it may awaken interest in the physical aspects of everyday experience and thus build a bridge between the arts and the behavioral sciences. In the meantime, there is much work to be done.

# Appendices

# Appendix to Chapter 10

## APPENDIX A

### Analysis of Variance by Left and Right Arm Position (N = 30)

Mean scores correspond to figures presented in this order:

| | Right arm | | |
|---|---|---|---|
| Left arm | Cover-ing | At side | Extended |
| Covering | H29 | H84 | H48 |
| At side | H67 | H59 | H21 |
| Extended | H78 | H95 | H40 |

| Ratings on dimension "natural–unnatural" | | | Effect | d.f. | F ratio | p |
|---|---|---|---|---|---|---|
| 4.67 | 4.73 | 5.27 | A (sex) | 1,28 | .06 | |
| | | | B (R arm) | 2,56 | 6.08 | .01 |
| 4.33 | 3.40 | 4.03 | AB | 2,56 | .08 | |
| | | | C (L arm) | 2,56 | 5.81 | .01 |
| 4.97 | 3.47 | 4.37 | AC | 2,56 | .94 | |
| | | | BC | 4,112 | 2.18 | |
| | | | ABC | 4,112 | .17 | |

## APPENDIX A *Cont.*

| Ratings on dimension "immodest–modest" | | | Effect | d.f. | F ratio | p |
|---|---|---|---|---|---|---|
| 5.57 | 4.63 | 4.30 | A | | .04 | |
| | | | B | | 12.89 | .001 |
| 4.33 | 4.20 | 3.77 | AB | | .72 | |
| | | | C | | 24.84 | .001 |
| 3.77 | 3.30 | 2.83 | AC | | .97 | |
| | | | BC | | 1.00 | |
| | | | ABC | | 1.46 | |

| Ratings on dimension "receiving–rejecting" | | | | | | |
|---|---|---|---|---|---|---|
| 4.77 | 4.30 | 4.37 | A | | 1.37 | |
| | | | B | | 4.00 | .05 |
| 3.77 | 2.83 | 3.53 | AB | | 2.36 | |
| | | | C | | 25.88 | .001 |
| 3.73 | 3.37 | 2.83 | AC | | 2.02 | |
| | | | BC | | 2.40 | |
| | | | ABC | | 1.46 | |

| Ratings on dimension "Self-concerned–other-concerned" | | | | | | |
|---|---|---|---|---|---|---|
| 2.30 | 3.00 | 3.47 | A | | .01 | |
| | | | B | | 12.26 | .001 |
| 3.03 | 3.90 | 4.33 | AB | | .10 | |
| | | | C | | 16.55 | .001 |
| 3.87 | 4.63 | 4.40 | AC | | 2.93 | |
| | | | BC | | .79 | |
| | | | ABC | | .60 | |

| Ratings on dimension "cold–warm" | | | | | | |
|---|---|---|---|---|---|---|
| 2.80 | 3.30 | 3.33 | A | | 2.26 | .20 |
| | | | B | | 4.62 | .05 |
| 3.83 | 4.67 | 4.40 | AB | | .61 | |
| | | | C | | 15.93 | .001 |
| 3.70 | 4.13 | 4.63 | AC | | 3.06 | >.05 |
| | | | BC | | .75 | |
| | | | ABC | | .87 | |

# APPENDIX A *Cont.*

| Ratings on dimension "active–passive" | | | Effect | d.f. | F ratio | p |
|---|---|---|---|---|---|---|
| 5.07 | 4.47 | 3.60 | A | | 1.52 | |
| | | | B | | 15.88 | .001 |
| 4.83 | 4.63 | 3.17 | AB | | 1.11 | |
| | | | C | | 51.32 | .001 |
| 2.80 | 2.77 | 2.47 | AC | | .19 | |
| | | | BC | | 3.05 | .05 |
| | | | ABC | | .92 | |

| Ratings on dimension "dramatic–calm" | | | | | | |
|---|---|---|---|---|---|---|
| 3.80 | 4.30 | 3.43 | A | | .20 | |
| | | | B | | 8.06 | .001 |
| 3.97 | 4.77 | 3.80 | AB | | .52 | |
| | | | C | | 16.82 | .001 |
| 2.57 | 3.40 | 2.43 | AC | | 1.03 | |
| | | | BC | | .18 | |
| | | | ABC | | .94 | |

| Ratings on dimension "shy–exhibitionistic" | | | | | | |
|---|---|---|---|---|---|---|
| 2.57 | 3.23 | 3.77 | A | | .10 | |
| | | | B | | 11.21 | .001 |
| 3.33 | 3.77 | 4.20 | AB | | .72 | |
| | | | C | | 86.98 | .001 |
| 5.13 | 4.97 | 5.66 | AC | | .15 | |
| | | | BC | | 1.17 | |
| | | | ABC | | 2.68 | .05 |

| Ratings on dimension "affected–ingenuous" | | | | | | |
|---|---|---|---|---|---|---|
| 3.40 | 3.63 | 3.23 | A | | 1.30 | |
| | | | B | | 3.60 | .05 |
| 3.87 | 4.60 | 4.20 | AB | | .67 | |
| | | | C | | 6.65 | .01 |
| 2.73 | 3.93 | 3.43 | AC | | .47 | |
| | | | BC | | 1.10 | |
| | | | ABC | | 1.05 | |

## APPENDIX A *Cont.*

| Ratings on dimension "unyielding–yielding" | | | Effect | d.f. | F ratio | p |
|---|---|---|---|---|---|---|
| 3.27 | 4.03 | 4.00 | A | | 1.85 | .20 |
| | | | B | | 2.96 | .10 |
| 4.83 | 5.27 | 4.33 | AB | | 1.34 | |
| | | | C | | 12.38 | .001 |
| 4.10 | 4.40 | 4.97 | AC | | 3.75 | .05 |
| | | | BC | | 3.48 | .05 |
| | | | ABC | | 1.35 | |

| Ratings on dimension "pulled toward–pulled away" | | | | | | |
|---|---|---|---|---|---|---|
| 4.67 | 4.13 | 4.67 | A | | 4.78 | .05 |
| | | | B | | 4.06 | .05 |
| 4.03 | 3.13 | 3.63 | AB | | .65 | |
| | | | C | | 8.88 | .001 |
| 4.53 | 3.70 | 3.83 | AC | | .32 | |
| | | | BC | | .58 | |
| | | | ABC | | .12 | |

*Intercorrelations Between Rating Dimensions (All Subjects; N = 30)*

| | Natural | Immodest | Receiving | Self-concerned | Cold | Active | Dramatic | Shy | Affected | Unyielding |
|---|---|---|---|---|---|---|---|---|---|---|
| Immodest | −.25 | | | | | | | | | |
| Receiving | .23 | −.16 | | | | | | | | |
| Self-concerned | −.12 | −.05 | −.08 | | | | | | | |
| Cold | −.14 | .39 | −.54* | .22 | | | | | | |
| Active | .18 | .17 | .20 | −.23 | .15 | | | | | |
| Dramatic | −.37 | .32 | −.23 | .10 | .51* | .36 | | | | |
| Shy | .23 | −.54* | .01 | .22 | −.34 | −.56* | −.50* | | | |
| Affected | −.44* | −.01 | −.19 | −.02 | .34 | .12 | .36 | −.23 | | |
| Unyielding | −.08 | .35 | −.50* | −.28 | .21 | .04 | .22 | −.26 | −.03 | |
| Pulled to | .48* | −.41 | .33 | −.10 | −.41 | .20 | −.39 | .24 | −.47 | −.03 |

\* p < .025

*Intercorrelations Between Rating Dimensions (Male Subjects; N = 15)*

| | Natural | Immodest | Receiving | Self-concerned | Cold | Active | Dramatic | Shy | Affected | Unyielding |
|---|---|---|---|---|---|---|---|---|---|---|
| Immodest | .04 | | | | | | | | | |
| Receiving | .37 | −.40 | | | | | | | | |
| Self-concerned | −.12 | −.04 | −.21 | | | | | | | |
| Cold | .08 | .23 | −.57* | .28 | | | | | | |
| Active | .24 | .10 | .29 | −.33 | .05 | | | | | |
| Dramatic | −.41 | .16 | −.49 | −.04 | .32 | .44 | | | | |
| Shy | −.09 | −.13 | .02 | .07 | −.12 | −.67* | −.53 | | | |
| Affected | .05 | .04 | .08 | .12 | .40 | .22 | .29 | −.44 | | |
| Unyielding | −.23 | .53 | −.78* | .01 | .38 | −.05 | .59* | −.18 | −.19 | |
| Pulled to | .00 | −.47 | .67* | −.36 | −.60* | .35 | −.23 | −.21 | −.21 | −.57* |

\* p < .025

## APPENDIX B Cont.

*Intercorrelations Between Rating Dimensions (Female Subjects; (N = 15)*

|  | Natural | Immodest | Receiving | Self-concerned | Cold | Active | Dramatic | Shy | Affected | Unyielding |
|---|---|---|---|---|---|---|---|---|---|---|
| Immodest | −.45 | | | | | | | | | |
| Receiving | .14 | .14 | | | | | | | | |
| Self-concerned | −.12 | −.05 | .04 | | | | | | | |
| Cold | −.32 | .55 | −.45 | .21 | | | | | | |
| Active | .15 | .33 | .19 | −.14 | .21 | | | | | |
| Dramatic | −.36 | .44 | .05 | .20 | .66* | .32 | | | | |
| Shy | .45 | −.88* | −.03 | .33 | −.52 | −.48 | −.48 | | | |
| Affected | −.63* | −.05 | −.33 | −.06 | .30 | .03 | .39 | −.16 | | |
| Unyielding | .00 | .17 | .01 | −.57* | −.10 | .06 | −.12 | −.33 | −.06 | |
| Pulled to | .72* | −.48 | .36 | .02 | −.59* | −.10 | −.56 | .57* | −.71* | .14 |

* p <.025

# APPENDIX C

*Sex Differences, by Picture and by Dimension*

|  | Dimensions | Males (N = 15) | Females (N = 15) | F ratio (d.f. = 1,28) | p |
|---|---|---|---|---|---|
| H21 | natural–unnatural | 4.27 | 3.80 | .55 | |
| | immodest–modest | 3.60 | 3.93 | .41 | |
| | receiving–rejecting | 3.53 | 3.53 | 0 | |
| | self-concerned–other-concerned | 4.53 | 4.13 | .41 | |
| | cold–warm | 4.13 | 4.67 | .84 | |
| | active–passive | 3.00 | 3.33 | .47 | |
| | dramatic–calm | 3.53 | 4.07 | .87 | |
| | shy–exhibitionistic | 4.27 | 4.13 | .07 | |
| | affected–ingenuous | 3.73 | 4.67 | 2.34 | |
| | unyielding–yielding | 3.80 | 4.87 | 4.41 | .05 |
| | pulled toward–pulled away | 3.20 | 4.07 | 3.07 | |
| H29 | natural–unnatural | 4.47 | 4.87 | .38 | |
| | immodest–modest | 5.40 | 5.73 | .41 | |
| | receiving–rejecting | 4.47 | 5.07 | 1.07 | |
| | self-concerned–other-concerned | 2.47 | 2.13 | .54 | |
| | cold–warm | 2.80 | 2.80 | 0 | |
| | active–passive | 4.67 | 5.47 | 2.07 | |
| | dramatic–calm | 3.93 | 3.67 | .21 | |
| | shy–exhibitionistic | 2.93 | 2.20 | 1.84 | |
| | affected–ingenuous | 3.20 | 3.60 | .32 | |
| | unyielding–yielding | 3.47 | 3.07 | .52 | |
| | pulled toward–pulled away | 4.47 | 4.87 | .45 | |
| H40 | natural–unnatural | 4.53 | 4.20 | .22 | |
| | immodest–modest | 2.73 | 2.93 | .16 | |
| | receiving–rejecting | 3.53 | 2.13 | 7.16 | .05 |
| | self-concerned–other-concerned | 3.80 | 5.00 | 5.56 | .05 |
| | cold–warm | 4.07 | 5.20 | 3.09 | |
| | active–passive | 2.40 | 2.53 | .01 | |
| | dramatic–calm | 2.33 | 2.53 | .17 | |
| | shy–exhibitionistic | 5.80 | 5.53 | .46 | |
| | affected–ingenuous | 3.00 | 3.87 | 2.03 | |
| | unyielding–yielding | 4.40 | 5.53 | 3.32 | |
| | pulled toward–pulled away | 3.47 | 4.20 | .94 | |
| H48 | natural–unnatural | 4.93 | 5.60 | 1.45 | |
| | immodest–modest | 4.87 | 3.73 | 7.36 | .05 |
| | receiving–rejecting | 4.80 | 3.93 | 4.01 | |
| | self-concerned–other-concerned | 3.73 | 3.20 | .70 | |
| | cold–warm | 3.27 | 3.40 | .09 | |
| | active–passive | 3.67 | 3.53 | .06 | |
| | dramatic–calm | 3.73 | 3.13 | .99 | |
| | shy–exhibitionistic | 3.33 | 4.20 | .30 | |
| | affected–ingenuous | 3.20 | 3.27 | 1.18 | |
| | unyielding–yielding | 4.13 | 3.87 | .27 | |
| | pulled toward–pulled away | 4.27 | 5.07 | 2.50 | |

## APPENDIX C *Cont.*

| Dimensions | Males (N = 15) | Females (N = 15) | F ratio (d.f. = 1,28) | p |
|---|---|---|---|---|
| **H59** natural–unnatural | 3.47 | 3.33 | .04 | |
| immodest–modest | 4.13 | 4.27 | .06 | |
| receiving–rejecting | 3.00 | 2.67 | .80 | |
| self-concerned–other-concerned | 4.07 | 3.73 | .49 | |
| cold–warm | 4.93 | 4.40 | 1.34 | |
| active–passive | 4.80 | 4.47 | .33 | |
| dramatic–calm | 4.80 | 4.73 | .02 | |
| shy–exhibitionistic | 3.47 | 4.07 | 2.06 | |
| affected–ingenuous | 4.67 | 4.53 | .07 | |
| unyielding–yielding | 5.20 | 5.33 | .10 | |
| pulled toward–pulled away | 2.93 | 3.33 | .73 | |
| **H67** natural–unnatural | 4.47 | 4.20 | .19 | |
| immodest–modest | 4.13 | 4.53 | .57 | |
| receiving–rejecting | 3.60 | 3.93 | .55 | |
| self-concerned–other-concerned | 3.00 | 3.07 | .02 | |
| cold–warm | 3.87 | 3.80 | .02 | |
| active–passive | 4.33 | 5.33 | 5.43 | .05 |
| dramatic–calm | 4.07 | 3.87 | .21 | |
| shy–exhibitionistic | 3.53 | 3.13 | .74 | |
| affected–ingenuous | 3.87 | 3.87 | 0 | |
| unyielding–yielding | 5.07 | 4.60 | 1.03 | |
| pulled toward–pulled away | 4.00 | 4.07 | .02 | |
| **H78** natural–unnatural | 4.87 | 5.07 | .10 | |
| immodest–modest | 3.87 | 3.67 | .14 | |
| receiving–rejecting | 3.93 | 3.53 | .79 | |
| self-concerned–other-concerned | 3.80 | 3.93 | .04 | |
| cold–warm | 3.53 | 3.87 | .41 | |
| active–passive | 2.80 | 2.80 | 0 | |
| dramatic–calm | 2.53 | 2.60 | .02 | |
| shy–exhibitionistic | 5.00 | 5.27 | .33 | |
| affected–ingenuous | 2.80 | 2.67 | .07 | |
| unyielding–yielding | 3.47 | 4.73 | 9.19 | .01 |
| pulled toward–pulled away | 4.47 | 4.60 | .06 | |
| **H84** natural–unnatural | 4.53 | 4.93 | .59 | |
| immodest–modest | 4.67 | 4.60 | .02 | |
| receiving–rejecting | 4.13 | 4.47 | .62 | |
| self-concerned–other-concerned | 3.27 | 2.73 | 1.03 | |
| cold–warm | 3.40 | 3.20 | .16 | |
| active–passive | 4.40 | 4.53 | .08 | |
| dramatic–calm | 4.27 | 4.33 | .03 | |
| shy–exhibitionistic | 3.40 | 3.07 | .72 | |
| affected–ingenuous | 3.87 | 3.40 | .66 | |
| unyielding–yielding | 4.20 | 3.87 | .36 | |
| pulled toward–pulled away | 3.67 | 4.60 | 3.00 | |

## APPENDIX C *Cont.*

| | Dimensions | Males (N = 15) | Females (N = 15) | F ratio (d.f. = 1,28) | p |
|---|---|---|---|---|---|
| H95 | natural–unnatural | 3.40 | 3.53 | .03 | |
| | immodest–modest | 3.07 | 3.53 | .65 | |
| | receiving–rejecting | 3.40 | 3.33 | .02 | |
| | self-concerned–other-concerned | 4.33 | 4.93 | 1.11 | |
| | cold–warm | 3.47 | 4.80 | 5.48 | .05 |
| | active–passive | 2.67 | 2.87 | .24 | |
| | dramatic–calm | 2.87 | 3.93 | 2.76 | |
| | shy–exhibitionistic | 5.20 | 4.73 | 1.37 | |
| | affected–ingenuous | 3.53 | 4.33 | 1.70 | |
| | unyielding–yielding | 4.33 | 4.47 | .07 | |
| | pulled toward–pulled away | 3.53 | 3.87 | .35 | |

## *Sex Differences on Defensive and Open Figures, by Dimension*

### Series H, defensive figures (29, 84, 48, 67, 78)

| Dimensions | Males | Females | F ratio (d.f. = 1,28) | p |
|---|---|---|---|---|
| natural–unnatural | 4.65 | 4.93 | .93 | |
| immodest–modest | 4.59 | 4.45 | .19 | |
| receiving–rejecting | 4.19 | 4.19 | 0 | |
| self-concerned–other-concerned | 3.25 | 3.01 | .71 | |
| cold–warm | 3.37 | 3.41 | .04 | |
| active–passive | 3.97 | 4.33 | 1.66 | >.20 |
| dramatic–calm | 3.71 | 3.52 | .46 | |
| shy–exhibitionistic | 3.64 | 3.57 | .08 | |
| affected–ingenuous | 3.39 | 3.36 | .01 | |
| unyielding–yielding | 4.07 | 4.03 | .03 | |
| pulled toward–pulled away | 4.17 | 4.64 | 2.72 | >.10 |

### Series H, open figures (21, 40, 59, 95)

| Dimensions | Males | Females | F ratio | p |
|---|---|---|---|---|
| natural–unnatural | 3.92 | 3.72 | .21 | |
| immodest–modest | 3.38 | 3.67 | .49 | |
| receiving–rejecting | 3.37 | 2.92 | 1.94 | .20 |
| self-concerned–other-concerned | 4.18 | 4.45 | .78 | |
| cold–warm | 4.15 | 4.77 | 2.84 | >.10 |
| active–passive | 3.22 | 3.30 | .10 | |
| dramatic–calm | 3.38 | 3.82 | 1.41 | |
| shy–exhibitionistic | 4.68 | 4.62 | .06 | |
| affected–ingenuous | 3.73 | 4.35 | 3.39 | .10 |
| unyielding–yielding | 4.43 | 5.05 | 3.05 | .10 |
| pulled toward–pulled away | 3.28 | 3.87 | 3.06 | .10 |

## APPENDIX C *Cont.*

### *Sex Differences Across All Pictures, by Dimension*

| Dimensions | Males | Females |
|---|---|---|
| natural–unnatural | 4.33 | 4.39 |
| immodest–modest | 4.05 | 4.10 |
| receiving–rejecting | 3.82 | 3.62 |
| self-concerned–other-concerned | 3.67 | 3.65 |
| cold–warm | 3.72 | 4.01 |
| active–passive | 3.64 | 3.87 |
| dramatic–calm | 3.56 | 3.65 |
| shy–exhibitionistic | 4.10 | 4.04 |
| affected–ingenuous | 3.54 | 3.80 |
| unyielding–yielding | 4.23 | 4.48 |
| pulled toward–pulled away | 3.78 | 4.30 |

### *Differences Between Defensive and Open Figures, by Sex and by Dimension*

| Dimensions | Males | Females |
|---|---|---|
| natural–unnatural | .73 | 1.21 |
| immodest–modest | 1.21 | .78 |
| receiving–rejecting | .83 | 1.27 |
| self-concerned–other-concerned | −.93 | −1.44 |
| cold–warm | −.78 | −1.36 |
| active–passive | .75 | 1.03 |
| dramatic–calm | .33 | −.30 |
| shy–exhibitionistic | −1.04 | −1.05 |
| affected–ingenuous | −.34 | −.99 |
| unyielding–yielding | −.36 | −1.02 |
| pulled toward–pulled away | .89 | .77 |

# Appendix to Chapter 11

## APPENDIX D

*Repeat Reliability of H Scores, by Picture and by Dimension*

| Dimensions | $H_1 29$ (N = 30) | $H_2 29$ (N = 21) | F ratio (d.f. = 1,49) | p |
|---|---|---|---|---|
| natural–unnatural | 4.67 | 4.33 | .42 | |
| immodest–modest | 5.57 | 5.81 | .40 | |
| receiving–rejecting | 4.77 | 4.48 | .40 | |
| self-concerned–other-concerned | 2.30 | 2.38 | .05 | |
| cold–warm | 2.80 | 3.43 | 2.26 | |
| active–passive | 5.07 | 5.24 | .19 | |
| dramatic–calm | 3.80 | 4.43 | 1.90 | |
| shy–exhibitionistic | 2.57 | 2.48 | .06 | |
| affected–ingenuous | 3.40 | 4.71 | 6.40 | .05 |
| unyielding–yielding | 3.27 | 4.24 | 5.30 | .05 |
| pulled toward–pulled away | 4.67 | 3.50 | 4.79 | .05 |

| Dimensions | $H_1 40$ (N = 30) | $H_2 40$ (N = 20) | F ratio (d.f. = 1,48) | p |
|---|---|---|---|---|
| natural–unnatural | 4.37 | 4.05 | .20 | |
| immodest–modest | 2.83 | 2.60 | .41 | |
| receiving–rejecting | 2.83 | 2.85 | 0 | |
| self-concerned–other-concerned | 4.40 | 4.40 | 0 | |
| cold–warm | 4.63 | 4.70 | .02 | |
| active–passive | 2.47 | 2.80 | .93 | |
| dramatic–calm | 2.43 | 2.40 | .01 | |
| shy–exhibitionistic | 5.67 | 5.65 | 0 | |
| affected–ingenuous | 3.43 | 3.15 | .35 | |
| unyielding–yielding | 4.97 | 5.05 | .03 | |
| pulled toward–pulled away | 3.83 | 3.85 | 0 | |

## APPENDIX D *Cont.*

| Dimensions | $H_1 59$ (N = 30) | $H_2 59$ (N = 20) | F ratio (d.f. = 1,48) | d |
|---|---|---|---|---|
| natural–unnatural | 3.40 | 3.65 | .27 | |
| immodest–modest | 4.20 | 4.95 | 3.45 | |
| receiving–rejecting | 2.83 | 3.35 | 2.30 | |
| self-concerned–other-concerned | 3.90 | 3.65 | .36 | |
| cold–warm | 4.67 | 4.45 | .31 | |
| active–passive | 4.63 | 4.80 | .15 | |
| dramatic–calm | 4.77 | 5.00 | .34 | |
| shy–exhibitionistic | 3.77 | 2.70 | 10.31 | .01 |
| affected–ingenuous | 4.60 | 4.25 | .64 | |
| unyielding–yielding | 5.27 | 5.40 | .17 | |
| pulled toward–pulled away | 3.13 | 3.35 | .31 | |

| Dimensions | $H_1 67$ (N = 30) | $H_2 67$ (N = 21) | F ratio (d.f. = 1,49) | p |
|---|---|---|---|---|
| natural–unnatural | 4.33 | 3.60 | 2.55 | |
| immodest–modest | 4.33 | 3.09 | 10.73 | .01 |
| receiving–rejecting | 3.77 | 2.71 | 8.86 | .01 |
| self-concerned–other-concerned | 3.03 | 4.33 | 9.00 | .01 |
| cold–warm | 3.83 | 5.05 | 11.57 | .01 |
| active–passive | 4.83 | 3.48 | 12.76 | .01 |
| dramatic–calm | 3.97 | 4.19 | .32 | |
| shy–exhibitionistic | 3.33 | 4.52 | 9.99 | .01 |
| affected–ingenuous | 3.87 | 3.62 | .34 | |
| unyielding–yielding | 4.83 | 5.48 | 2.92 | |
| pulled toward–pulled away | 4.03 | 3.00 | 5.26 | .05 |

* $H_1$ = scores from 30 Ss in Chap. 10; $H_2$ = scores from 20 Ss from Chap. 11.

## Repeat Reliability of H Scores: Four Figures Ranked on Each Dimension, by Presentation

| | $H_1$ Ranks: | | | | $H_2$ Ranks: | | | |
|---|---|---|---|---|---|---|---|---|
| Dimensions | 1 | 2 | 3 | 4 | 1 | 2 | 3 | 4 |
| natural–unnatural | 59 | 67 | 40 | 29 | 59 | 67 | 40 | 29 |
| immodest–modest | 40 | 59 | 67 | 29 | 40 | 59 | 67 | 29 |
| receiving–rejecting | 40 | 59 | 67 | 29 | 40 = 59 | | 67 | 29 |
| self-concerned–other-concerned | 29 | 67 | 59 | 40 | 29 | 67 | 59 | 40 |
| cold–warm | 29 | 67 | 40 | 59 | 20 | 67 | 40 | 59 |
| active–passive | 40 | 59 | 67 | 29 | 40 | 59 | 67 | 29 |
| dramatic–calm | 40 | 29 | 67 | 59 | 40 | 29 | 67 | 59 |
| shy–exhibitionistic | 29 | 67 | 59 | 40 | 29 | 67 | 59 | 40 |
| affected–ingenuous | 29 | 40 | 67 | 59 | 29 | 40 | 67 | 59 |
| unyielding–yielding | 29 | 67 | 40 | 59 | 29 | 67 | 40 | 59 |
| pulled toward–pulled away | 59 | 40 | 67 | 29 | 59 | 40 | 67 | 29 |

# APPENDIX E

*Sex Differences in Changes from H (Unclothed) to G (Clothed) Scores, by Picture and by Dimension*

### Picture 29

| Dimensions | MALES (N = 10) Mean difference | FEMALES (N = 11) Mean difference | F ratio (d.f. = 1,19) | p |
|---|---|---|---|---|
| natural–unnatural | 1.10 | 2.09 | 1.32 | |
| immodest–modest | −0.20 | −0.91 | .75 | |
| receiving–rejecting | 1.00 | −0.09 | 2.01 | |
| self-concerned–other-concerned | −0.90 | 0.18 | 2.06 | |
| cold–warm | −0.80 | −0.54 | .12 | |
| active–passive | −0.20 | −0.54 | .31 | |
| dramatic–calm | −1.80 | −1.18 | .84 | |
| approachable–unapproachable | 1.10 | 0.64 | .23 | |
| shy–exhibitionistic | 0.70 | 0.45 | .07 | |
| affected–ingenuous | −0.90 | −1.18 | .10 | |
| unyielding–yielding | −1.30 | −0.27 | 1.14 | |
| appropriate–inappropriate | 3.20 | 1.18 | 6.84 | .05 |
| pulled toward–pulled away | 2.40 | 0.82 | 1.66 | |

### Picture 40

| Dimensions | MALES (N = 10) Mean difference | FEMALES (N = 10) Mean difference | F ratio (d.f. = 1,18) | p |
|---|---|---|---|---|
| natural–unnatural | −0.50 | 0.10 | .30 | |
| immodest–modest | 0.50 | 0.90 | .30 | |
| receiving–rejecting | 0.20 | 0.70 | .67 | |
| self-concerned–other-concerned | −1.50 | −0.90 | .44 | |
| cold–warm | −0.20 | −0.60 | .34 | |
| active–passive | −0.10 | 0.10 | .08 | |
| dramatic–calm | −0.60 | 0.20 | .90 | |
| approachable–unapproachable | 0.80 | 0.70 | .01 | |
| shy–exhibitionistic | −0.30 | −0.10 | .10 | |
| affected–ingenuous | 0.40 | −0.50 | .92 | |
| unyielding–yielding | −0.60 | −1.20 | 1.08 | |
| appropriate–inappropriate | −0.40 | −0.60 | .03 | |
| pulled toward–pulled away | 1.60 | −0.30 | 3.76 | |

## APPENDIX E *Cont.*

### Picture 59

| Dimensions | MALES (N = 10) Mean difference | FEMALES (N = 10) | F ratio (d.f. = 1,18) | p |
|---|---|---|---|---|
| natural–unnatural | 0.40 | 0 | .59 | |
| immodest–modest | 0.60 | 0.80 | .09 | |
| receiving–rejecting | −0.80 | 0.10 | 1.25 | |
| self-concerned–other-concerned | −0.10 | −1.20 | 2.00 | |
| cold–warm | −0.10 | −0.10 | 0 | |
| active–passive | 0.20 | 0.30 | .03 | |
| dramatic–calm | −0.20 | 0.40 | 1.62 | |
| approachable–unapproachable | 0.30 | 0.10 | .11 | |
| shy–exhibitionistic | −0.10 | −0.40 | .42 | |
| affected–ingenuous | −0.50 | 0.30 | 1.35 | |
| unyielding–yielding | −0.50 | −0.10 | .94 | |
| appropriate–inappropriate | 0.90 | 0.40 | .60 | |
| pulled toward–pulled away | 0.50 | −0.40 | 3.49 | |

### Picture 67

| Dimensions | MALES (N = 10) Mean difference | FEMALES (N = 11) | F ratio (d.f. = 1,19) | p |
|---|---|---|---|---|
| natural–unnatural | −0.80 | 0.09 | 1.09 | |
| immodest–modest | 1.80 | 1.27 | .51 | |
| receiving–rejecting | 1.20 | −0.18 | 3.71 | |
| self-concerned–other-concerned | −0.90 | 0.27 | 2.32 | |
| cold–warm | −1.10 | −0.09 | 2.42 | |
| active–passive | 0.90 | −0.18 | 3.02 | |
| dramatic–calm | −1.00 | −0.45 | .40 | |
| approachable–unapproachable | 1.20 | −0.36 | 6.06 | .05 |
| shy–exhibitionistic | −1.20 | 0.27 | 5.71 | .05 |
| affected–ingenuous | 0.30 | −0.54 | 1.66 | |
| unyielding–yielding | −1.60 | −0.09 | 8.96 | .01 |
| appropriate–inappropriate | 0.30 | −1.18 | 3.05 | |
| pulled toward–pulled away | 1.30 | −0.09 | 3.77 | |

# Appendix to Chapter 12

APPENDIX F

*Significance of Mean Difference Between Types of Figure, by Dimension*

| Dimensions | Arms covering vs. at side $t$ (d.f. = 17) | Arms covering vs. extended $t$ (d.f. = 17) | Arms at side vs. extended $t$ (d.f. = 17) |
|---|---|---|---|
| natural–unnatural | .32 | 3.12** | 3.18** |
| immodest–modest | .49 | 5.43*** | 5.63*** |
| receiving–rejecting | 3.47** | 1.47 | .51 |
| self-concerned–other-concerned | 4.47*** | 7.18*** | 4.60*** |
| effeminate–virile | 2.10* | 5.62*** | 4.96*** |
| cold–warm | 3.67*** | 6.59*** | 4.53*** |
| strong–weak | 1.14 | 4.71*** | 4.54*** |
| dramatic–calm | 3.13** | 4.94*** | 6.81*** |
| active–passive | 2.14* | 7.27*** | 8.22*** |
| shy–exhibitionistic | 1.00 | 5.27*** | 6.76*** |
| unyielding–yielding | 3.05** | 3.00** | .73 |
| imperious–humble | 1.91 | 1.18 | 3.47** |
| pulled toward–pulled away | 2.00* | 3.55*** | 1.92 |

\* p <.05 (two-tailed test)

\*\* p<.01 (two-tailed test)

\*\*\* p<.001 (two-tailed test)

# APPENDIX G

## Mean Scores, by Picture and by Dimension (All Subjects)

| Dimensions | Picture: K23 | K29 | K32 | K38 | K41 | K47 | K53 | K59 | K62 | K68 |
|---|---|---|---|---|---|---|---|---|---|---|
| natural–unnatural | 3.61 | 4.90 | 2.76 | 2.74 | 3.58 | 4.03 | 2.63 | 4.26 | 3.37 | 4.21 |
| immodest–modest | 2.84 | 2.42 | 4.18 | 3.87 | 3.55 | 2.97 | 3.79 | 4.03 | 2.53 | 5.90 |
| receiving–giving | 3.40 | 3.42 | 3.37 | 3.95 | 3.95 | 3.68 | 4.03 | 3.26 | 4.55 | 3.66 |
| self-concerned–other-concerned | 4.68 | 3.87 | 3.63 | 3.76 | 5.08 | 3.84 | 2.47 | 3.03 | 3.00 | 2.55 |
| effeminate–virile | 5.82 | 5.18 | 4.50 | 5.45 | 5.08 | 4.97 | 4.34 | 3.66 | 5.24 | 3.05 |
| cold–warm | 5.08 | 4.24 | 3.63 | 4.42 | 4.87 | 4.24 | 2.87 | 3.67 | 3.37 | 3.55 |
| strong–weak | 2.50 | 2.87 | 3.74 | 2.74 | 2.79 | 3.05 | 3.32 | 4.16 | 2.55 | 5.18 |
| dramatic–calm | 3.42 | 2.21 | 5.55 | 3.82 | 3.37 | 2.84 | 4.45 | 4.53 | 3.08 | 4.68 |
| active–passive | 2.63 | 2.42 | 5.34 | 3.53 | 2.53 | 2.84 | 4.66 | 5.11 | 2.87 | 5.58 |
| shy–exhibitionistic | 4.84 | 5.45 | 3.26 | 4.13 | 4.55 | 4.82 | 4.18 | 3.37 | 5.24 | 2.05 |
| unyielding–yielding | 4.68 | 4.00 | 4.45 | 3.84 | 4.03 | 3.45 | 2.68 | 4.45 | 2.71 | 5.08 |
| imperious–humble | 3.92 | 3.05 | 4.84 | 3.63 | 3.61 | 3.24 | 3.13 | 4.40 | 2.63 | 5.53 |
| pulled toward–pulled away | 3.50 | 4.45 | 4.47 | 3.74 | 3.71 | 4.21 | 4.95 | 4.76 | 4.29 | 4.74 |

# APPENDIX H

*Significance of Differences Between Selected Pictures in K Series, by Dimension*

| Dimensions | 32 vs. 59 t (d.f. = 41) | 32 vs. 38 t (d.f. = 41) | 32 vs. 68 t (d.f. = 41) |
|---|---|---|---|
| natural–unnatural | 3.85*** | .31 | 3.13** |
| immodest–modest | .63 | .84 | 4.14*** |
| receiving–rejcting | .47 | 2.56* | .99 |
| self-concerned–other-concerned | 2.19* | .78 | 3.13** |
| effeminate–virile | 2.87** | 2.81** | 4.15*** |
| cold–warm | 0 | 2.52* | .09 |
| strong–weak | 1.07 | 2.63* | 4.29*** |
| dramatic–calm | 3.06** | 3.54** | 2.31* |
| active–passive | .55 | 4.85*** | 1.24 |
| shy–exhibitionistic | .24 | 1.85 | 4.00*** |
| unyielding–yielding | .07 | 1.21 | 2.33* |
| imperious–humble | 1.18 | 2.63** | 2.73** |
| pulled toward–pulled away | 1.41 | 2.37** | 1.68 |

| Dimensions | 23 vs. 47 t (d.f. = 41) | 23 vs. 38 t (d.f. = 41) | 59 vs. 68 t (d.f. = 41) |
|---|---|---|---|
| natural–unnatural | 1.33 | 2.32* | .37 |
| immodest–modest | .96 | 3.91*** | 3.96*** |
| receiving–rejecting | .80 | 1.40 | 1.29 |
| self-concerned–other-concerned | 1.70 | 2.28* | 1.24 |
| effeminate–virile | 4.01*** | 1.92 | 2.33* |
| cold–warm | 2.68* | 2.51* | .07 |
| strong–weak | 2.20* | 1.17 | 3.28** |
| dramatic–calm | 1.48 | 1.79 | .41 |
| active–passive | 1.27 | 3.21** | 1.75 |
| shy–exhibitionistic | .82 | 3.15** | 3.84*** |
| unyielding–yielding | 2.88** | 2.92** | 2.31* |
| imperious–humble | 1.86 | .85 | 3.64*** |
| pulled toward–pulled away | 3.09** | 1.05 | .75 |

* p <.05 (two-tailed test)
** p <.01 (two-tailed test)
*** p <.001 (two-tailed test)

# APPENDIX I

## Intercorrelations Between Rating Dimensions (All Subjects; N = 43)

| | Natural | Immodest | Receiving | Self-concerned | Effeminate | Cold | Strong | Dramatic | Active | Shy | Unyielding | Imperious |
|---|---|---|---|---|---|---|---|---|---|---|---|---|
| Immodest | −.04 | | | | | | | | | | | |
| Receiving | .03 | −.01 | | | | | | | | | | |
| Self-concerned | −.15 | −.14 | .04 | | | | | | | | | |
| Effeminate | −.31* | −.31 | .03 | .26 | | | | | | | | |
| Cold | −.11 | −.06 | −.08 | .54** | .29 | | | | | | | |
| Strong | .26 | .38* | −.08 | −.26 | −.73** | −.24 | | | | | | |
| Dramatic | −.24 | .33* | −.07 | −.07 | −.16 | −.15 | .24 | | | | | |
| Active | .02 | .32* | −.09 | −.20 | −.50** | −.24 | .57** | .55** | | | | |
| Shy | −.02 | −.56** | −.02 | .02 | .40* | .04 | −.48** | −.37* | −.58** | | | |
| Unyielding | .15 | .26 | −.13 | .16 | −.26 | .26 | .43** | .19 | .28 | −.40** | | |
| Imperious | .07 | .49** | −.06 | .12 | −.37* | .21 | .48** | .32* | .48** | −.66** | .58** | |
| Pulled toward | .33* | .04 | .07 | −.32* | −.35* | −.36* | .46** | .07 | .29 | −.11 | .09 | .04 |

* p < .05
** p < .01

Intercorrelations Between Rating Dimensions (Male Subjects; N = 19)

| | Natural | Immodest | Receiving | Self-concerned | Effeminate | Cold | Strong | Dramatic | Active | Shy | Unyielding | Imperious |
|---|---|---|---|---|---|---|---|---|---|---|---|---|
| Immodest | -.10 | | | | | | | | | | | |
| Receiving | .02 | .01 | | | | | | | | | | |
| Self-concerned | -.24 | -.16 | .04 | | | | | | | | | |
| Effeminate | -.18 | -.30 | -.04 | .35 | | | | | | | | |
| Cold | -.05 | .10 | -.32 | .36 | .20 | | | | | | | |
| Strong | .08 | .36 | -.13 | -.40 | -.55* | -.13 | | | | | | |
| Dramatic | -.28 | .26 | -.05 | -.02 | -.24 | -.02 | .38 | | | | | |
| Active | -.14 | .36 | -.14 | -.27 | -.40 | -.22 | .55** | .63** | | | | |
| Shy | .12 | -.59** | .01 | .16 | .39 | .08 | -.45 | -.48* | -.62** | | | |
| Unyielding | -.03 | .31 | -.19 | -.07 | -.17 | .17 | .48* | .43 | .45 | -.38 | | |
| Imperious | -.07 | .49* | -.13 | -.09 | -.35 | .15 | .50* | .49* | .55* | -.66** | .57* | |
| Pulled toward | .20 | -.02 | -.08 | -.25 | -.15 | -.20 | .41 | .13 | .21 | -.04 | .13 | -.01 |

* p <.05
** p <.01

Intercorrelations Between Rating Dimensions (Female Subjects; N = 24)

| | Natural | Immodest | Receiving | Self-concerned | Effeminate | Cold | Strong | Dramatic | Active | Shy | Unyielding | Imperious |
|---|---|---|---|---|---|---|---|---|---|---|---|---|
| Immodest | .01 | | | | | | | | | | | |
| Receiving | .04 | −.02 | | | | | | | | | | |
| Self-concerned | −.10 | −.13 | .04 | | | | | | | | | |
| Effeminate | −.40 | −.31 | .07 | .22 | | | | | | | | |
| Cold | −.13 | −.13 | .01 | .62** | .34 | | | | | | | |
| Strong | .38 | .38 | −.07 | −.21 | −.80** | −.29 | | | | | | |
| Dramatic | −.22 | .37 | −.08 | −.10 | −.12 | −.20 | .18 | | | | | |
| Active | .10 | .29 | −.07 | −.17 | −.55** | −.25 | .58** | .52** | | | | |
| Shy | −.10 | −.54** | −.04 | −.07 | .41* | .01 | −.51* | −.30 | −.57** | | | |
| Unyielding | .25 | .24 | −.11 | .27 | −.30 | .29 | .41* | .07 | .20 | −.42* | | |
| Imperious | .16 | .48* | −.03 | .23 | −.37 | .23 | .48* | .24 | .45** | −.66** | .59** | |
| Pulled toward | .40 | .07 | .14 | −.35 | −.44* | −.42* | .48* | .04 | .33 | −.15 | .07 | .06 |

* p <.05
** p <.01

# APPENDIX J

*Male–Female Difference in Overall Ratings, by Dimension*

| Dimensions | Males | Females | $t$ (d.f. = 17) | $p$ |
|---|---|---|---|---|
| natural–unnatural | 3.30 | 3.92 | 3.31 | .01 |
| immodest–modest | 3.71 | 3.51 | 1.16 | |
| receiving–rejecting | 3.80 | 3.66 | .76 | |
| self-concerned–other-concerned | 3.63 | 3.56 | .39 | |
| effeminate–virile | 4.67 | 4.78 | .79 | |
| cold–warm | 4.04 | 3.95 | .58 | |
| strong–weak | 3.45 | 3.13 | 2.32 | .05 |
| dramatic–calm | 3.84 | 3.75 | .59 | |
| active–passive | 3.82 | 3.68 | .89 | |
| shy–exhibitionistic | 4.22 | 4.16 | .50 | |
| unyielding–yielding | 3.97 | 3.90 | .45 | |
| imperious–humble | 3.84 | 3.76 | .54 | |
| pulled toward–pulled away | 4.25 | 4.32 | .43 | |

# APPENDIX K

*Additional Suggestive Scores, by Sex, Figure, and Dimension*

| Figure | Dimensions | Males | Females | $t$ $(d.f. = 17)$ | $p$ |
|--------|-----------|-------|---------|-------------------|-----|
| K23 | active–passive | 3.11 | 2.16 | 1.94 | $>$.05 |
|  | pulled toward–pulled away | 3.58 | 3.42 | .26 | no difference |
| K41 | imperious–humble | 3.05 | 4.16 | 1.91 | $>$.05 |
| K53 | pulled toward–pulled away | 4.53 | 5.37 | 1.62 | $\cong$.10 |
|  | imperious–humble | 3.63 | 2.63 | 2.03 | $>$.05 |
| K59 | cold–warm | 4.21 | 3.11 | 1.94 | $>$.05 |
|  | active–passive | 4.68 | 5.53 | 1.98 | $>$.05 |
| K62 | effeminate–virile | 4.74 | 5.74 | 2.06 | $>$.05 |
|  | shy–exhibitionistic | 4.84 | 5.63 | 1.93 | $>$.05 |
|  | pulled toward–pulled away | 4.53 | 4.05 | .86 | no difference |
| K68 | strong–weak | 4.84 | 5.53 | 1.93 | $>$.05 |

# APPENDIX L

## Male–Female Differences on Three Types of Figures, by Dimension

### Figures with arms extended

| Dimensions | Males | Females | $t$ (d.f. = 17) | p |
|---|---|---|---|---|
| natural–unnatural | 3.68 | 4.37 | 1.83 | >.05 |
| immodest–modest | 3.02 | 2.86 | .57 | |
| receiving–giving | 3.84 | 3.33 | 1.35 | |
| self-concerned–other-concerned | 4.33 | 4.75 | 1.15 | |
| effeminate–virile | 5.28 | 5.44 | .68 | |
| cold–warm | 4.47 | 4.98 | 1.88 | >.05 |
| strong–weak | 2.86 | 2.58 | 1.15 | |
| dramatic–calm | 3.07 | 2.93 | .40 | |
| active–passive | 2.60 | 2.46 | .51 | |
| shy–exhibitionistic | 5.16 | 4.74 | 1.86 | >.05 |
| unyielding–yielding | 3.97 | 4.51 | 1.76 | |
| imperious–humble | 3.33 | 3.72 | 1.40 | |
| pulled toward–pulled away | 3.95 | 3.83 | .41 | |

### Figures with arms at sides

| Dimensions | Males | Females | $t$ (d.f. = 17) | p |
|---|---|---|---|---|
| natural–unnatural | 2.93 | 3.58 | 2.05 | >.05 |
| immodest–modest | 4.11 | 3.95 | .48 | |
| receiving–giving | 3.44 | 3.61 | .74 | |
| self-concerned–other-concerned | 3.60 | 3.35 | .88 | |
| effeminate–virile | 4.47 | 4.60 | .48 | |
| cold–warm | 4.19 | 3.61 | 2.13 | .05 |
| strong–weak | 3.70 | 3.39 | 1.17 | |
| dramatic–calm | 4.65 | 4.61 | .14 | |
| active–passive | 4.56 | 4.75 | .70 | |
| shy–exhibitionistic | 3.68 | 3.49 | .72 | |
| unyielding–yielding | 4.42 | 4.07 | 1.16 | |
| imperious–humble | 4.32 | 4.26 | .20 | |
| pulled toward–pulled away | 4.33 | 4.32 | .07 | |

## APPENDIX L *Cont.*

*Figures with arms covering torso*

| Dimensions | Males | Females | *t* (d.f. = 17) | *p* |
|---|---|---|---|---|
| natural–unnatural | 3.11 | 3.70 | 1.77 | |
| immodest–modest | 4.21 | 3.93 | .84 | |
| receiving–giving | 3.98 | 4.18 | .56 | |
| self-concerned–other-concerned | 2.98 | 2.37 | 2.38 | .05 |
| effeminate–virile | 4.18 | 4.25 | .24 | |
| cold–warm | 3.44 | 3.09 | 1.19 | |
| strong–weak | 3.86 | 3.51 | 1.56 | |
| dramatic–calm | 4.16 | 3.98 | .61 | |
| active–passive | 4.60 | 4.14 | 1.70 | |
| shy–exhibitionistic | 3.67 | 3.98 | 1.44 | |
| unyielding–yielding | 3.83 | 3.16 | 2.44 | .05 |
| imperious–humble | 4.07 | 3.46 | 2.38 | .05 |
| pulled toward–pulled away | 4.51 | 4.81 | .97 | |

# Appendix to Chapter 13

*Significance of Y's Head and Body Turns on the Scores of X, Y, and Z, by Dimension*

| | | X | | Y | | Z | |
|---|---|---|---|---|---|---|---|
| | | F ratio | | F ratio | | F ratio | |
| Dimensions | | (d.f. = 1,40) | p | (d.f. = 1,40) | p | (d.f. = 1,40) | p |
| subordinate– | Head | 18.12 | .001 | .92 | | 1.34 | |
| superordinate | Body | 5.61 | .05 | .15 | | 1.88 | |
| haughty– | Head | .89 | | .10 | | 4.84 | .05 |
| humble | Body | .72 | | .60 | | 2.15 | |
| important– | Head | 27.68 | .001 | 1.85 | | 14.58 | .001 |
| insignificant | Body | 5.05 | .05 | .27 | | 6.76 | .05 |
| receiving– | Head | 17.12 | .001 | 13.13 | .001 | 10.11 | .01 |
| initiating | Body | 1.36 | | 1.82 | | 7.42 | .01 |

Significance of Y's Head and Body Turns on Relations
Between Figures, by Dimension

| Dimensions | | X to Y F ratio (d.f. = 1,40) | p | Y to X F ratio (d.f. = 1,40) | p |
|---|---|---|---|---|---|
| hostile– | Head | .02 | | 1.88 | |
| friendly | Body | 1.92 | | 5.03 | .05 |
| | | Z to Y | | Y to Z | |
| | Head | .05 | | .02 | |
| | Body | 1.23 | | .41 | |
| | | X to Y | | Y to X | |
| approaching– | Head | 7.07 | .05 | 2.63 | |
| withdrawing | Body | .59 | | .62 | |
| | | Z to Y | | Y to Z | |
| | Head | 3.83 | | 43.26 | .001 |
| | Body | 3.14 | | 2.40 | |
| | | X to Y | | Y to X | |
| intimate– | Head | .27 | | .36 | |
| distant | Body | .41 | | 5.53 | .05 |
| | | Z to Y | | Y to Z | |
| | Head | 4.27 | .05 | 12.59 | $\cong$.001 |
| | Body | 8.03 | .01 | 4.04 | $\cong$.05 |

# Appendix to Chapter 14

## APPENDIX O

*Significance of Differences Between Figures in Picture S41,*
*by Dimension*

| Dimensions | Figures L and M | | Figures M and Z | | Figures L and Z | |
|---|---|---|---|---|---|---|
| | F ratio $(d.f. = 1,10)$ | p | F ratio $(d.f. = 1,10)$ | p | F ratio $(d.f. = 1,10)$ | p |
| subordinate–<br>superordinate | 71.22 | .001 | 15.80 | .01 | 162.56 | .001 |
| other-concerned–<br>self-concerned | 0.19 | | 0.84 | | 0.08 | |
| haughty–humble | 128.89 | .001 | 0.64 | | 40.29 | .001 |
| initiating action–<br>receiving action | 42.25 | .001 | 12.57 | .01 | 69.44 | .001 |
| expressive–inexpressive | 58.37 | .001 | 55.57 | .001 | 130.04 | .001 |
| important–insignificant | 67.10 | .001 | 15.94 | .01 | 211.86 | .001 |

| | Figures L and X | | Figures M and X | |
|---|---|---|---|---|
| | F ratio $(d.f. = 1,10)$ | p | F ratio $(d.f. = 1,10)$ | p |
| subordinate–<br>superordinate | 3.06 | | 81.66 | .001 |
| other-concerned–<br>self-concerned | 2.57 | | 1.28 | |
| haughty–humble | 9.82 | .05 | 25.03 | .001 |
| initiating action–<br>receiving action | 1.21 | | 19.17 | .01 |
| expressive–inexpressive | 27.25 | .001 | 32.25 | .001 |
| important–insignificant | 16.30 | .01 | 18.33 | .01 |

## APPENDIX O *Cont.*

### *Significance of Differences Between Three Versions, by Figure and by Dimension*

| Dimensions | Figure L | | | | |
|---|---|---|---|---|---|
| | S41 (N = 11) | S42 (N = 40) | Individual (N = 12) | F ratio (d.f. = 2,60) | p |
| subordinate–superordinate | 2.00 | 2.13 | 2.25 | .15 | |
| other-concerned–self-concerned | 3.91 | 3.53 | 4.42 | 1.27 | |
| haughty–humble | 6.09 | 5.70 | 5.92 | .65 | |
| initiating action–receiving action | 6.27 | 5.65 | 6.00 | 1.51 | |
| expressive–inexpressive | 6.09 | 5.35 | 4.75 | 2.21 | |
| important–insignificant | 6.09 | 5.68 | 5.50 | .70 | |
| | Figure M | | | | |
| subordinate–superordinate | 6.18 | 4.38 | 4.25 | 1.60 | |
| other-concerned–self-concerned | 4.27 | 3.93 | 3.75 | .29 | |
| haughty–humble | 2.55 | 2.88 | 2.75 | .31 | |
| initiating action–receiving action | 3.91 | 4.43 | 3.17 | 3.42 | .05 |
| expressive–inexpressive | 2.82 | 3.05 | 2.67 | .42 | |
| important–insignificant | 2.73 | 3.08 | 2.75 | .58 | |
| | Figure N | | | | |
| subordinate–superordinate | 4.09 | 4.33 | 4.17 | .17 | |
| other-concerned–self-concerned | 3.73 | 3.68 | 3.75 | .01 | |
| haughty–humble | 3.64 | 3.15 | 3.17 | .71 | |
| initiating action–receiving action | 4.64 | 4.23 | 4.25 | .29 | |
| expressive–inexpressive | 4.36 | 3.40 | 3.58 | 1.78 | |
| important–insignificant | 3.45 | 3.20 | 3.67 | .68 | |
| | Figure X | | | | |
| subordinate–superordinate | 2.64 | 2.63 | 2.75 | .04 | |
| other-concerned–self-concerned | 3.36 | 3.93 | 4.50 | 1.20 | |
| haughty–humble | 4.91 | 5.05 | 5.25 | .17 | |
| initiating action–receiving action | 5.82 | 5.38 | 5.67 | .72 | |
| expressive–inexpressive | 4.91 | 5.45 | 4.50 | 2.21 | |
| important–insignificant | 4.73 | 4.53 | 5.00 | .43 | |

# APPENDIX O *Cont.*

| Dimensions | S41 | S42 | Indi-vidual | F ratio | p |
|---|---|---|---|---|---|
| | | *Figure Y* | | | |
| subordinate–superordinate | 3.64 | 3.83 | 3.25 | .74 | |
| other-concerned– | | | | | |
|    self-concerned | 3.45 | 3.10 | 4.25 | 2.62 | |
| haughty–humble | 4.00 | 3.78 | 4.75 | 3.60 | .05 |
| initiating action– | | | | | |
|    receiving action | 5.09 | 4.73 | 5.00 | .34 | |
| expressive–inexpressive | 4.27 | 4.25 | 4.17 | .01 | |
| important–insignificant | 3.91 | 3.98 | 4.75 | 1.23 | |
| | | *Figure Z* | | | |
| subordinate–superordinate | 6.64 | 5.53 | 5.25 | 3.18 | .05 |
| other-concerned– | | | | | |
|    self-concerned | 3.64 | 3.38 | 3.42 | .09 | |
| haughty–humble | 2.91 | 3.15 | 3.00 | .23 | |
| initiating action– | | | | | |
|    receiving action | 1.73 | 2.10 | 1.58 | .71 | |
| expressive–inexpressive | 1.27 | 1.85 | 1.75 | 1.81 | |
| important–insignificant | 1.55 | 2.23 | 2.42 | 1.68 | |

# Appendix to Chapter 15

APPENDIX P

*Significance of Body and Head Changes, by Dimension**

| Dimensions | Effect | First split | | | Second split | | |
|---|---|---|---|---|---|---|---|
| | | F ratio | d.f. | p | F ratio | d.f. | p |
| hostile–friendly | body | 28.36 | 1,16 | .001 | 8.48 | 2,32 | .01 |
| | head | 1.15 | 2,32 | | 0.17 | 1,16 | |
| | body/head | 4.18 | 2,32 | .05 | 3.03 | 2,32 | |
| approaching– withdrawing | body | 7.62 | 1,16 | .05 | 1.64 | 2,32 | |
| | head | 51.43 | 2,32 | .001 | 123.80 | 1,16 | .001 |
| | body/head | 17.96 | 2,32 | .001 | 1.30 | 2,32 | |
| initiating action– receiving action | body | 0.11 | 1,16 | | 2.39 | 2,32 | |
| | head | 27.66 | 2,32 | .001 | 42.59 | 1,16 | .001 |
| | body/head | 10.38 | 2,32 | .001 | 0.63 | 2,32 | |
| subordinate– superordinate | body | 67.27 | 1,16 | .001 | 69.58 | 2,32 | .001 |
| | head | 38.47 | 2,32 | .001 | 59.75 | 1,16 | .001 |
| | body/head | 4.37 | 2,32 | .05 | 2.79 | 2,32 | |
| haughty–humble | body | 33.34 | 1,16 | .001 | 16.65 | 2,32 | .001 |
| | head | 53.08 | 2,32 | .001 | 52.83 | 1,16 | .001 |
| | body/head | 6.30 | 2,32 | .01 | 7.50 | 2,32 | .01 |
| other-concerned– self-concerned | body | 6.60 | 1,16 | .05 | 1.77 | 2,32 | |
| | head | 25.57 | 2,32 | .001 | 35.96 | 1,16 | .001 |
| | body/head | 10.25 | 2,32 | .001 | 0.80 | 2,32 | |
| important– insignificant | body | 34.81 | 1,16 | .001 | 26.37 | 2,32 | .001 |
| | head | 54.64 | 2,32 | .001 | 83.79 | 1,16 | .001 |
| | body/head | 2.63 | 2,32 | | 2.38 | 2,32 | |
| intimate to other– distant from other | body | 10.01 | 1,16 | .01 | 0.08 | 2,32 | |
| | head | 20.59 | 2,32 | .001 | 16.37 | 1,16 | .001 |
| | body/head | 14.52 | 2,32 | .001 | 0.38 | 2,32 | |

* Two analyses are presented: the first split, on data only from the two complete columns; the second split, on data only from the two complete rows.

# APPENDIX Q

*Intercorrelations Between the Scores of X and Y on the Same Dimension, by Picture and by Dimension (N = 18)*

| Dimensions | | L11 | L17 | L25 | L31 | L39 | L45 | L53 | L59 | L67 | L73 | L81 | L87 |
|---|---|---|---|---|---|---|---|---|---|---|---|---|---|
| | | | | | | *Picture* | | | | | | | |
| hostile–friendly | | .13 | .46 | .31 | .20 | .36 | .08 | −.21 | .64** | −.11 | −.24 | −.37 | −.33 |
| approaching–withdrawing | | .36 | .01 | .25 | −.28 | .65** | .02 | .15 | .73** | .02 | −.25 | −.23 | −.51* |
| initiating–receiving | | −.85** | .30 | −.32 | −.55* | .08 | −.79** | −.76** | .31 | −.57* | −.71** | −.28 | −.53* |
| subordinate–superordinate | | −.56* | −.28 | −.59** | −.18 | .30 | −.75** | −.42 | .03 | −.26 | −.44 | −.53* | −.58* |
| haughty–humble | | .02 | −.02 | −.39 | −.84** | .36 | −.38 | −.48* | .35 | −.34 | −.37 | −.47* | −.53* |
| other-concerned–self-concerned | | −.62** | .41 | −.13 | −.69** | .57* | −.19 | −.53* | .85** | −.74** | −.09 | .01 | −.34 |
| important–insignificant | | −.62** | −.14 | −.32 | −.17 | .32 | −.49* | −.54* | .39 | −.57* | .10 | −.54* | −.55* |
| intimate–distant | | .53* | −.03 | .40 | .25 | .36 | .26 | −.18 | .93** | .10 | .66** | .34 | −.20 |

* p < .05
** p < .01

# APPENDIX R

## Mean Scores of X and Y, by Picture and by Dimension

| Dimensions | Picture L11 | | Picture L17 | | Picture L25 | |
|---|---|---|---|---|---|---|
| | X | Y | X | Y | X | Y |
| hostile–friendly | 3.56 | 4.22 | 4.67 | 4.33 | 4.17 | 5.44 |
| approaching–withdrawing | 3.11 | 5.44 | 3.22 | 3.44 | 3.17 | 2.94 |
| initiating action–receiving action | 3.00 | 5.50 | 3.33 | 3.83 | 2.94 | 4.06 |
| subordinate–superordinate | 5.78 | 2.11 | 4.05 | 4.17 | 5.33 | 3.17 |
| haughty–humble | 3.28 | 6.11 | 4.22 | 4.06 | 3.33 | 4.78 |
| other-concerned–self-concerned | 2.94 | 5.33 | 3.78 | 3.33 | 2.78 | 3.39 |
| important–insignificant | 2.44 | 5.28 | 3.56 | 3.89 | 2.67 | 4.17 |
| intimate–distant | 3.11 | 4.33 | 2.89 | 3.67 | 3.72 | 3.39 |

## Mean Scores of X and Y, by Picture and by Dimension

| Dimensions | Picture L31 | | Picture L39 | | Picture L45 | |
|---|---|---|---|---|---|---|
| | X | Y | X | Y | X | Y |
| hostile–friendly | 3.22 | 5.28 | 4.17 | 4.39 | 3.94 | 4.67 |
| approaching–withdrawing | 2.89 | 3.22 | 4.39 | 5.11 | 5.11 | 2.22 |
| initiating action–receiving action | 2.67 | 4.17 | 3.89 | 5.00 | 4.89 | 3.06 |
| subordinate–superordinate | 5.22 | 3.06 | 4.17 | 3.00 | 3.78 | 4.00 |
| haughty–humble | 2.94 | 5.00 | 4.94 | 5.50 | 5.33 | 4.28 |
| other-concerned–self-concerned | 3.28 | 3.33 | 4.72 | 5.44 | 5.06 | 2.83 |
| important–insignificant | 2.50 | 4.44 | 4.06 | 5.11 | 4.11 | 3.44 |
| intimate–distant | 3.44 | 3.00 | 3.56 | 3.89 | 4.33 | 4.00 |

## APPENDIX R Cont.

### Mean Scores of X and Y, by Picture and by Dimension

| Dimensions | Picture L53 | | Picture L59 | | Picture L67 | |
|---|---|---|---|---|---|---|
| | X | Y | X | Y | X | Y |
| hostile–friendly | 4.00 | 3.56 | 4.00 | 4.22 | 3.50 | 4.17 |
| approaching–withdrawing | 5.39 | 2.83 | 5.28 | 5.39 | 2.83 | 5.83 |
| initiating action–receiving action | 5.44 | 2.61 | 4.39 | 4.67 | 2.44 | 6.05 |
| subordinate–superordinate | 3.61 | 4.89 | 3.94 | 3.44 | 5.39 | 2.61 |
| haughty–humble | 5.44 | 3.11 | 5.00 | 5.61 | 3.44 | 5.78 |
| other-concerned–self-concerned | 5.00 | 3.28 | 5.00 | 5.39 | 2.94 | 5.39 |
| important–insignificant | 4.22 | 2.94 | 4.11 | 4.78 | 2.67 | 4.72 |
| intimate–distant | 4.56 | 3.83 | 4.50 | 4.56 | 3.33 | 4.11 |

### Mean Scores of X and Y, by Picture and by Dimension

| Dimensions | Picture L73 | | Picture L81 | | Picture L87 | |
|---|---|---|---|---|---|---|
| | X | Y | X | Y | X | Y |
| hostile–friendly | 3.67 | 5.11 | 2.89 | 4.39 | 3.11 | 4.83 |
| approaching–withdrawing | 4.44 | 2.56 | 4.89 | 4.94 | 4.83 | 2.78 |
| initiating action–receiving action | 4.22 | 3.22 | 3.39 | 4.78 | 4.50 | 3.44 |
| subordinate–superordinate | 5.00 | 3.39 | 5.61 | 1.78 | 5.50 | 2.28 |
| haughty–humble | 3.06 | 4.39 | 2.44 | 6.11 | 2.50 | 5.67 |
| other-concerned–self-concerned | 4.94 | 2.56 | 4.44 | 4.56 | 5.22 | 2.22 |
| important–insignificant | 2.83 | 4.11 | 2.17 | 5.67 | 2.61 | 5.05 |
| intimate–distant | 5.28 | 3.61 | 6.17 | 4.44 | 5.89 | 3.61 |

# Appendix to Chapter 16

## APPENDIX S

Effect of Female Arm and Leg Positions on Female Figure,
by Dimension

| Dimensions | Effect | d.f. | F ratio | p |
|---|---|---|---|---|
| initiating action– | A (arm) | 3,114 | 149.80 | .001 |
| receiving action | B (leg) | 1,38 | 88.07 | .001 |
| | AB | 3,114 | 0.88 | |
| warm–cold | A | | 62.13 | .001 |
| | B | | 30.09 | .001 |
| | AB | | 8.54 | .001 |
| intense–relaxed | A | | 6.54 | .001 |
| | B | | 16.79 | .001 |
| | AB | | 7.92 | .001 |
| uncertain–determined | A | | 46.87 | .001 |
| | B | | 39.73 | .001 |
| | AB | | 0.78 | |
| aggressive–unaggressive | A | | 69.71 | .001 |
| | B | | 51.77 | .001 |
| | AB | | 1.35 | |
| constrained–free | A | | 40.93 | .001 |
| | B | | 31.55 | .001 |
| | AB | | 1.69 | |
| sincere–calculating | A | | 2.55 | $>.05$ |
| | B | | 16.41 | .001 |
| | AB | | 0.77 | |
| non-erotic–erotic | A | | 39.64 | .001 |
| | B | | 7.41 | .01 |
| | AB | | 3.16 | .05 |
| active–passive | A | | 97.51 | .001 |
| | B | | 49.32 | .001 |
| | AB | | 0.98 | |
| evil–good | A | | 3.04 | |
| | B | | 0.76 | |
| | AB | | 1.78 | |

## APPENDIX S *Cont.*

*Effect of Female Arm and Leg Positions on Ratings of Interaction, by Dimension*

| Dimensions | Effect | d.f. | F ratio | p |
|---|---|---|---|---|
| transient–permanent | A | 3,114 | 2.17 | |
| | B | 1,38 | 0.00 | |
| | AB | 3,114 | 3.62 | .05 |
| enclosed–free | A | | 2.85 | |
| | B | | 0.16 | |
| | AB | | 1.18 | |
| will continue– | A | | 1.78 | |
| will be reversed | B | | 1.04 | |
| | AB | | 0.66 | |
| satisfactory–unsatisfactory | A | | 1.70 | |
| | B | | 0.74 | |
| | AB | | 7.51 | .001 |

# APPENDIX T

*Effect of Male Advance and Distance on Male Figure,
by Dimension*

| Dimensions | Effect | F ratio (d.f. = 1,78) | p |
|---|---|---|---|
| initiating action–receiving action | A (advancing–receding) | 72.97 | .001 |
| | B (close–far) | 2.34 | |
| | AB | 0.80 | |
| warm–cold | A | 301.32 | .001 |
| | B | 42.45 | .001 |
| | AB | 0.04 | |
| intense–relaxed | A | 29.50 | .001 |
| | B | 0.40 | |
| | AB | 1.09 | |
| uncertain–determined | A | 43.32 | .001 |
| | B | 41.86 | .001 |
| | AB | 0.97 | |
| aggressive–unaggressive | A | 143.85 | .001 |
| | B | 5.77 | .05 |
| | AB | 1.21 | |
| constrained–free | A | 58.31 | .001 |
| | B | 18.36 | .001 |
| | AB | 2.34 | |
| sincere–calculating | A | 16.80 | .001 |
| | B | 1.09 | |
| | AB | 8.76 | .01 |
| non-erotic–erotic | A | 163.49 | .001 |
| | B | 19.77 | .001 |
| | AB | 2.95 | |
| active–passive | A | 34.05 | .001 |
| | B | 6.81 | .05 |
| | AB | 0.61 | |
| evil–good | A | 6.43 | .05 |
| | B | 7.98 | .01 |
| | AB | 20.89 | .001 |

## APPENDIX T *Cont.*

*Effect of Male Advance and Distance on Ratings of Interaction, by Dimension*

| Dimensions | Effect | F ratio (d.f. = 1,78) | p |
|---|---|---|---|
| transient–permanent | A | 14.41 | .001 |
| | B | 17.28 | .001 |
| | AB | 5.33 | .05 |
| enclosed–free | A | 8.07 | .01 |
| | B | 5.83 | .05 |
| | AB | 2.11 | |
| will continue–will be reversed | A | 60.90 | .001 |
| | B | 17.15 | .001 |
| | AB | 1.88 | |
| satisfactory–unsatisfactory | A | 174.22 | .001 |
| | B | 59.60 | .001 |
| | AB | 6.79 | |

# APPENDIX U

*Figures Receiving Extreme Ratings, by Dimension (in parentheses: mean scores)*

|  | Man's figure | | | | |
|---|---|---|---|---|---|
|  | *Most* | *Second* | *Second* | *Most* | |
| initiating action | D31(1.21) | D27(1.33) | D35(5.52) | D75(5.85) | receiving action |
| warm | D91(1.63) | D70(1.74) | D82(5.35) | D75(5.40) | cold |
| intense | D18(1.86) | D31(2.00) | D63 = D35(3.62) | | relaxed |
| uncertain | D13(2.11) | D23(2.29) | D70(5.47) | D91(5.58) | determined |
| aggressive | D27(1.95) | D31 D70(2.05) | D35(5.33) | D75(5.60) | unaggressive |
| constrained | D23(2.57) | D13 D33(2.79) | D50 = D91(4.95) | | free |
| sincere | D80(2.38) | D39(2.43) | D25 = D85(4.00) | | calculating |
| non-erotic | D75(2.25) | D82(2.70) | D70 = D91(6.26) | | erotic |
| active | D31(1.79) | D27 D70(1.95) | D75(4.50) | D33(4.53) | passive |
| evil | D27(3.71) | D65(3.74) | D39(5.05) | D15(5.10) | good |

|  | Woman's figure | | | | |
|---|---|---|---|---|---|
|  | *Most* | *Second* | *Second* | *Most* | |
| initiating action | D78(1.32) | D37(1.37) | D31(5.79) | D27(6.14) | receiving action |
| warm | D75(1.45) | D35(1.52) | D23(5.14) | D27(5.19) | cold |
| intense | D75(1.70) | D72(1.95) | D48(4.24) | D63(4.38) | relaxed |
| uncertain | D23(2.95) | D25(3.42) | D33(6.06) | D72(6.26) | determined |
| aggressive | D72(1.53) | D75(1.65) | D25(5.16) | D27(5.67) | unaggressive |
| constrained | D23(2.57) | D27(2.81) | D39 D80(5.95) | D35(6.05) | free |
| sincere | D80(2.14) | D78(2.37) | D48(4.10) | D31(4.21) | calculating |
| non-erotic | D27(3.29) | D23(3.67) | D85 D91(6.26) | D78(6.32) | erotic |
| active | D72(1.60) | D75(1.62) | D27(5.19) | D31(5.26) | passive |
| evil | D57(3.68) | D33 D65(3.84) | D91(4.68) | D80(5.00) | good |

|  | Interaction | | | | |
|---|---|---|---|---|---|
| transient | D23(1.95) | D35(2.29) | D55 = D80(4.24) | | permanent |
| atmosphere enclosed | D72(2.74) | D25(3.05) | D91(4.84) | D39(4.86) | atmosphere free |
| will continue | D39 = D80(1.57) | | D75(3.60) | D82(3.85) | will be reversed |
| satisfactory | D80(2.00) | D39(2.14) | D23 D27(5.43) | D75(5.50) | unsatisfactory |

# APPENDIX V

## Effect of Man's Distance on Female Figure, by Dimension

| Dimensions | Close | Far | F ratio (d.f. = 1,78) | p |
|---|---|---|---|---|
| warm–cold | 2.25 | 2.79 | 12.96 | .001 |
| sincere–calculating | 3.08 | 3.31 | 7.17 | .01 |
| non-erotic–erotic | 5.44 | 4.99 | 15.33 | .001 |
| evil–good | 4.51 | 4.10 | 24.84 | .001 |

## Effect of Man's Advancing–Receding on Female Figure, by Dimension

| Dimensions | Close | Receding | F ratio (d.f. = 1,78) | p |
|---|---|---|---|---|
| warm–cold | 2.45 | 2.60 | 10.54 | .01 |
| sincere–calculating | 3.14 | 3.26 | 3.15 | >.05 |
| non-erotic–erotic | 5.37 | 5.06 | 20.60 | .001 |
| evil–good | 3.32 | 3.25 | 6.53 | .05 |

## Effect of Woman's Arm Position on Male Figure, by Dimension

| Dimensions | Arms down | Right arm extended | Left arm extended | Both arms extended | F ratio (d.f. = 3,114) | p |
|---|---|---|---|---|---|---|
| initiating action–receiving action | 2.31 | 3.77 | 4.21 | 4.12 | 56.21 | .001 |
| warm–cold | 2.74 | 3.38 | 3.48 | 3.66 | 20.05 | .001 |
| intense–relaxed | 2.44 | 2.87 | 2.96 | 2.91 | 7.66 | .001 |
| aggressive–unaggressive | 3.12 | 3.86 | 4.28 | 4.11 | 25.30 | .001 |
| sincere–calculating | 3.42 | 3.44 | 2.98 | 3.25 | 5.26 | .01 |
| non-erotic–erotic | 4.74 | 4.21 | 4.26 | 4.15 | 5.37 | .01 |
| active–passive | 2.46 | 3.35 | 3.58 | 3.58 | 24.13 | .001 |

## APPENDIX V *Cont.*

*Effect of Woman's Leg Position on Male Figure,*
*by Dimension*

| Dimensions | Legs toward | Legs away | F ratio (d.f. = 1,38) | p |
|---|---|---|---|---|
| initiating action–receiving action | 3.07 | 4.14 | 65.80 | .001 |
| warm–cold | 3.17 | 3.46 | 4.52 | .05 |
| uncertain–determined | 4.04 | 3.36 | 13.79 | .001 |
| aggressive–unaggressive | 3.46 | 4.23 | 33.07 | .001 |
| constrained–free | 3.90 | 3.35 | 9.37 | .01 |
| sincere–calculating | 3.45 | 3.10 | 10.73 | .01 |
| non-erotic–erotic | 4.73 | 3.95 | 20.99 | .001 |
| active–passive | 2.89 | 3.59 | 29.28 | .001 |
| evil–good | 4.22 | 4.48 | 7.04 | .05 |

# APPENDIX X

### Selected Intercorrelations Between Rating Dimensions, by Sex, Figure, and Dimension

| Man's figure | Males | Females |
|---|---|---|
| initiating: aggressiveness | .68 | .65 |
| active | (.56)* | .68 |
| aggressive: active | (.61) | .64 |
| erotic | .64 | (.58) |
| erotic: warm | .67 | (.60) |
| determined: free | .74 | (.59) |
| | | |
| *Woman's figure* | | |
| initiating: aggressive | .70 | .73 |
| active | .65 | .74 |
| aggressive: determined | ..67 | (.62) |
| erotic | (.61) | (.32) |
| active | .65 | .82 |
| warm | .67 | (.50) |
| erotic: warm | .77 | (.44) |
| | | |
| *Both figures* | | |
| man initiating— | | |
| woman receiving | (.61) | .63 |

* In parentheses: non-significant matching r's

# APPENDIX Y

## Significance of Sex Differences in Mean Ratings of All Figures, by Figure and Dimension

| Man's figure | F ratio (d.f. = 1,634) | p |
|---|---|---|
| intense–relaxed | 3.73 | >.05 |
| aggressive–unaggressive | 2.28 | |
| evil–good | 7.19 | .01 |
| *Woman's figure* | | |
| intense–relaxed | 2.29 | |
| aggressive–unaggressive | 3.87 | .05 |
| constrained–free | 3.66 | >.05 |
| non-erotic–erotic | 5.30 | .05 |
| evil–good | 16.47 | .001 |
| *Interaction* | | |
| will continue–will be reversed | 3.58 | >.05 |
| satisfactory–unsatisfactory | 7.09 | .01 |

# Appendix to Chapter 17

## APPENDIX Z

**Table 1. Characteristics of Aggressive Encounters** (absolute frequencies)

| | Intended actions M | | Intended actions F | | Open proximal access | | Defined axial space | | Contained axial space | | Closed proximal boundary | | Responsible for intersection at axial boundary | | | Responsible for contact at proximal boundary | | | Near | Far |
|---|---|---|---|---|---|---|---|---|---|---|---|---|---|---|---|---|---|---|---|---|
| | Pos. | Neg. | Pos. | Neg. | M | F | M | F | M | F | M | F | M | M/F | F | M | M/F | F | M | F |
| Male | 7 | 1 | 4 | 5 | 1 | 3 | 9 | 7 | 0 | 0 | 0 | 0 | 7 | 0 | 3 | 4 | 0 | 1 | 4 | 6 |
| Female | 7 | 1 | 6 | 3 | 0 | 1 | 10 | 8 | 0 | 1 | 0 | 0 | 2 | 4 | 2 | 1 | 1 | 4 | 5 | 5 |
| Total | 14 | 2 | 10 | 8 | 1 | 4 | 19 | 15 | 0 | 1 | 0 | 0 | 9 | 4 | 5 | 5 | 1 | 5 | 9 | 11 |

| | Vertical displacement Acro-trope | | Iso-trope | Horizontal syntropism Dia-trope | Para-trope | Pro-trope | Amphi-trope | Apo-trope |
|---|---|---|---|---|---|---|---|---|
| | M | F | | | | | | |
| Male | 4 | 2 | 4 | 8 | 0 | 1 | 1 | 0 |
| Female | 7 | 1 | 2 | 6 | 0 | 0 | 4 | 0 |
| Total | 11 | 3 | 6 | 14 | 0 | 1 | 5 | 0 |

| | Individual evaluation M | | | | | Individual evaluation F | | | | |
|---|---|---|---|---|---|---|---|---|---|---|
| | +2 | +1 | 0 | −1 | −2 | +2 | +1 | 0 | −1 | −1 |
| Male | 0 | 6 | 2 | 0 | 2 | 1 | 3 | 5 | 0 | 1 |
| Female | 2 | 5 | 2 | 0 | 1 | 0 | 6 | 3 | 1 | 0 |
| Total | 2 | 11 | 4 | 0 | 3 | 1 | 9 | 8 | 1 | 1 |

| | Intended actions M | | Intended actions F | | Individual reconstruction Open proximal access | | Defined axial space | | Contained axial space | | Closed proximal boundary | |
|---|---|---|---|---|---|---|---|---|---|---|---|---|
| | Pos. | Neg. | Pos. | Neg. | M | F | M | F | M | F | M | F |
| Male | 10 | 0 | 10 | 0 | 0 | 3 | 10 | 7 | 0 | 0 | 0 | 0 |
| Female | 9 | 0 | 9 | 0 | 0 | 2 | 10 | 8 | 0 | 0 | 0 | 0 |
| Total | 19 | 0 | 19 | 0 | 0 | 5 | 20 | 15 | 0 | 0 | 0 | 0 |

**Table 2. Characteristics of Unaggressive Encounters** (absolute frequencies)

| | Intended actions M Pos. | M Neg. | F Pos. | F Neg. | Open proximal access M | F | Defined axial space M | F | Contained axial space M | F | Closed proximal boundary M | F | Responsible for intersection at axial boundary M | M/F | F | Responsible for contact at proximal boundary M | M/F | F | Near M | Far F |
|---|---|---|---|---|---|---|---|---|---|---|---|---|---|---|---|---|---|---|---|---|
| Male | 2 | 0 | 1 | 0 | 7 | 3 | 2 | 6 | 1 | 1 | 0 | 1 | 3 | 2 | 1 | 1 | 2 | 0 | 3 | 7 |
| Female | 2 | 0 | 3 | 0 | 3.5 | 3.5 | 4.5 | 5 | 1 | 0 | 1 | 1.5 | 1 | 7 | 1 | 1 | 1 | 1 | 4 | 6 |
| Total | 4 | 0 | 4 | 0 | 10.5 | 6.5 | 6.5 | 11 | 2 | 1 | 1 | 2.5 | 4 | 9 | 2 | 2 | 3 | 1 | 7 | 13 |

| | Vertical displacement Acro-trope M | F | Iso-trope M | F | Horizontal syntropism Dia-trope | Para-trope | Pro-trope | Amphi-trope | Apo-trope |
|---|---|---|---|---|---|---|---|---|---|
| Male | 5 | 0 | 5 | 5 | 1 | 4 | 0 | 5 | 0 |
| Female | 5 | 2 | 3 | 4 | 0 | 3 | 2 | 4 | 0 |
| Total | 10 | 2 | 8 | 9 | 1 | 7 | 2 | 9 | 0 |

| | Individual evaluation M +2 | +1 | 0 | −1 | −2 | F +2 | +1 | 0 | −1 | −2 |
|---|---|---|---|---|---|---|---|---|---|---|
| Male | 4 | 4 | 1 | 1 | 0 | 6 | 3 | 0 | 1 | 0 |
| Female | 2 | 8 | 0 | 0 | 0 | 5 | 5 | 0 | 0 | 0 |
| Total | 6 | 12 | 1 | 1 | 0 | 11 | 8 | 0 | 1 | 0 |

Individual reconstruction

| | Intended actions M Pos. | M Neg. | F Pos. | F Neg. | Open proximal access M | F | Defined axial space M | F | Contained axial space M | F | Closed proximal boundary M | F |
|---|---|---|---|---|---|---|---|---|---|---|---|---|
| Male | 3 | 1 | 0 | 1 | 5 | 2 | 2 | 4 | 2 | 1 | 2 | 3 |
| Female | 1 | 1 | 3 | 0 | 5 | 4 | 1 | 3.5 | 1 | 1 | 3 | 3.5 |
| Total | 4 | 2 | 3 | 1 | 10 | 6 | 3 | 7.5 | 3 | 2 | 5 | 6.5 |

**Table 3. Characteristics of Male-Initiating Encounters** (absolute frequencies)

| | Intended actions M | | Intended actions F | | Open proximal access | | Defined axial space | | Contained axial space | | Closed proximal boundary | | Responsible for intersection at axial boundary | | | Responsible for contact at proximal boundary | | | Near | Far |
|---|---|---|---|---|---|---|---|---|---|---|---|---|---|---|---|---|---|---|---|---|
| | Pos. | Neg. | Pos. | Neg. | M | F | M | F | M | F | M | F | M | M/F | F | M | M/F | F | M | F |
| Male | 6 | 0 | 0 | 3 | 0 | 3 | 10 | 4.5 | 0 | 1 | 0 | 1.5 | 7 | 2 | 0 | 3 | 1 | 0 | 7 | 3 |
| Female | 9 | 1 | 1 | 3 | 0 | 5.5 | 10 | 3 | 0 | .5 | 0 | 1 | 9 | 0 | 0 | 4 | 0 | 0 | 9 | 1 |
| Total | 15 | 1 | 1 | 6 | 0 | 8.5 | 20 | 7.5 | 0 | 1.5 | 0 | 2.5 | 16 | 2 | 0 | 7 | 1 | 0 | 16 | 4 |

| | Vertical displacement Acrotrope | | Iso-trope | Horizontal syntropism Dia-trope | Para-trope | Pro-trope | Amphi-trope | Apo-trope |
|---|---|---|---|---|---|---|---|---|
| | M | F | | | | | | |
| Male | 4 | 2 | 4 | 0 | 0 | 7 | 3 | 0 |
| Female | 5 | 3 | 2 | 0 | 1 | 5 | 5 | 0 |
| Total | 9 | 5 | 6 | 0 | 1 | 12 | 8 | 0 |

**Table 4. Characteristics of Female-Initiating Encounters** (absolute frequencies)

| | Intended actions | | | | Open proximal access | | Defined axial space | | Contained axial space | | Closed proximal boundary | | Responsible for intersection at axial boundary | | | Responsible for contact at proximal boundary | | | Near | Far |
| | Pos. Neg. | | Pos. | Neg. | | | | | | | | | | | | | | | | |
| | M | F | | | M | F | M | F | M | F | M | F | M | M/F | F | M | M/F | F | M | F |
|---|---|---|---|---|---|---|---|---|---|---|---|---|---|---|---|---|---|---|---|---|
| Male | 2 | 1 | 7 | 0 | 4 | 0 | 3.5 | 10 | 2 | 0 | .5 | 0 | 0 | 0 | 6 | 0 | 1 | 5 | 7 | 3 |
| Female | 2 | 2 | 5 | 1 | 4.5 | 0 | 3 | 10 | 1.5 | 0 | 1 | 0 | 0 | 0 | 8 | 0 | 1 | 5 | 8 | 2 |
| Total | 4 | 3 | 12 | 1 | 8.5 | 0 | 6.5 | 20 | 3.5 | 0 | 1.5 | 0 | 0 | 0 | 14 | 0 | 2 | 10 | 15 | 5 |

| | Vertical displacement | | | Horizontal syntropism | | | | |
| | Acro-trope | | Iso-trope | Dia-trope | Para-trope | Pro-trope | Amphi-trope | Apo-trope |
| | M | F | | | | | | |
|---|---|---|---|---|---|---|---|---|
| Male | 6 | 2 | 2 | 2 | 1 | 4 | 3 | 0 |
| Female | 1 | 6 | 3 | 1 | 0 | 2 | 6 | 1 |
| Total | 7 | 8 | 5 | 3 | 1 | 6 | 9 | 1 |

**Table 5. Characteristics of Male-Receiving Encounters** (absolute frequencies)

| | Intended actions M | | Intended actions F | | Open proximal access | | Defined axial space | | Contained axial space | | Closed proximal boundary | | Responsible for intersection at axial boundary | | | Responsible for contact at proximal boundary | | | Near | Far |
|---|---|---|---|---|---|---|---|---|---|---|---|---|---|---|---|---|---|---|---|---|---|
| | Pos. | Neg. | Pos. | Neg. | M | F | M | F | M | F | M | F | M | M/F | F | M | M/F | F | M | F |
| Male | 1 | 2 | 8 | 0 | 2 | 0 | 4.5 | 8 | 2 | .5 | .5 | .5 | 0 | 3 | 5 | 0 | 3 | 3 | 8 | 1 |
| Female | 2 | 1 | 9 | 0 | 3.5 | 0 | 4.5 | 9 | 2 | 0 | 0 | 1 | 0 | 4 | 3 | 0 | 1 | 5 | 8 | 2 |
| Total | 3 | 3 | 17 | 0 | 5.5 | 0 | 9 | 17 | 4 | .5 | .5 | 1.5 | 0 | 7 | 8 | 0 | 4 | 8 | 16 | 3 |

| | Vertical displacement Acro-trope | | Iso-trope | Horizontal syntropism Dia-trope | Para-trope | Pro-trope | Amphi-trope | Apo-trope |
|---|---|---|---|---|---|---|---|---|
| | M | F | | | | | | |
| Male | 2 | 5 | 2 | 6 | 0 | 1 | 2 | 0 |
| Female | 3 | 6 | 1 | 4 | 0 | 1 | 5 | 0 |
| Total | 5 | 11 | 3 | 10 | 0 | 2 | 7 | 0 |

**Table 6. Characteristics of Female-Receiving Encounters** (absolute frequencies)

| | Intended actions | | | | Open proximal access | | Defined axial space | | Contained axial space | | Closed proximal boundary | | Responsible for intersection at axial boundary | | | Responsible for contact at proximal boundary | | | Near | Far |
| | M | | F | | | | | | | | | | | | | | | | | |
| | Pos. | Neg. | Pos. | Neg. | M | F | M | F | M | F | M | F | M | M/F | F | M | M/F | F | M | F |
|---|---|---|---|---|---|---|---|---|---|---|---|---|---|---|---|---|---|---|---|---|
| Male | 8 | 0 | 4 | 0 | 1 | 1 | 9 | 8.5 | 0 | .5 | 0 | 0 | 1 | 9 | 0 | 5 | 4 | 0 | 9 | 1 |
| Female | 6 | 0 | 2 | 1 | 1 | 2.5 | 7 | 6 | 0 | 1 | 1 | .5 | 2 | 4 | 0 | 2 | 3 | 0 | 8 | 2 |
| Total | 14 | 0 | 6 | 1 | 2 | 3.5 | 16 | 14.5 | 0 | 1.5 | 1 | .5 | 3 | 13 | 0 | 7 | 7 | 0 | 17 | 3 |

| | Vertical displacement | | | Horizontal syntropism | | | | |
| | Acro-trope | | Iso-trope | Dia-trope | Para-trope | Pro-trope | Amphi-trope | Apo-trope |
| | M | F | | | | | | |
|---|---|---|---|---|---|---|---|---|
| Male | 8 | 1 | 1 | 8 | 0 | 1 | 0 | 0 |
| Female | 9 | 0 | 1 | 6 | 0 | 1 | 3 | 0 |
| Total | 17 | 1 | 2 | 14 | 0 | 2 | 3 | 0 |

**Table 7. Characteristics of Erotic Encounters** (absolute frequencies)

| | Intended actions M | | Intended actions F | | Open proximal access | | Defined axial space | | Contained axial space | | Closed proximal boundary | | Responsible for intersection at axial boundary | | | Responsible for contact at proximal boundary | | | Near | Far |
| | Pos. | Neg. | Pos. | Neg. | M | F | M | F | M | F | M | F | M | M/F | F | M | M/F | F | M | F |
|---|---|---|---|---|---|---|---|---|---|---|---|---|---|---|---|---|---|---|---|---|
| Male | 9 | 0 | 6 | 0 | 0 | 1 | 10 | 9 | 0 | 0 | 0 | 0 | 1 | 9 | 0 | 1 | 8 | 1 | 7 | 3 |
| Female | 6 | 0 | 3 | 0 | 1 | 4 | 9 | 5.5 | 0 | 0 | 0 | 0 | 4 | 5 | 0 | 4 | 5 | 0 | 10 | 0 |
| Total | 15 | 0 | 9 | 0 | 1 | 5 | 19 | 14.5 | 0 | 0 | 0 | 0 | 5 | 14 | 0 | 5 | 13 | 1 | 17 | 3 |

| | Vertical displacement Acro-trope M | Acro-trope F | Iso-trope | Horizontal syntropism Dia-trope | Para-trope | Pro-trope | Amphi-trope | Apo-trope |
|---|---|---|---|---|---|---|---|---|
| Male | 8 | 0 | 2 | 9 | 0 | 1 | 0 | 0 |
| Female | 4 | 3 | 3 | 8 | 0 | 0 | 2 | 0 |
| Total | 12 | 3 | 5 | 17 | 0 | 1 | 2 | 0 |

| | Individual evaluation M | | | | | F | | | | | Intended actions M | | F | | Individual reconstruction Open proximal access | | Defined axial space | | Contained axial space | | Closed proximal boundary | |
| | +2 | +1 | 0 | -1 | -2 | +2 | +1 | 0 | -1 | -2 | Pos. | Neg. | Pos. | Neg. | M | F | M | F | M | F | M | F |
|---|---|---|---|---|---|---|---|---|---|---|---|---|---|---|---|---|---|---|---|---|---|---|
| Male | 0 | 7 | 3 | 0 | 0 | 0 | 7 | 1 | 1 | 0 | 3 | 0 | 0 | 1 | 4 | 2.5 | 3.5 | 6 | 1.5 | 0 | 0 | .5 |
| Female | 0 | 9 | 1 | 0 | 0 | 1 | 9 | 1 | 0 | 0 | 4 | 0 | 2 | 0 | 4.5 | 2.5 | 4.5 | 6 | 1.5 | .5 | 0 | 1 |
| Total | 0 | 16 | 4 | 0 | 0 | 1 | 16 | 2 | 1 | 0 | 7 | 0 | 2 | 1 | 8.5 | 5 | 8 | 12 | 3 | .5 | 0 | 1.5 |

**Table 8. Characteristics of Non-Erotic Encounters** (absolute frequencies)

| | Intended actions M Pos. | M Neg. | F Pos. | F Neg. | Open proximal access M | F | Defined axial space M | F | Contained axial space M | F | Closed proximal boundary M | F | Responsible for intersection at axial boundary M | M/F | F | Responsible for contact at proximal boundary M | M/F | F | Near M | F | Far F |
|---|---|---|---|---|---|---|---|---|---|---|---|---|---|---|---|---|---|---|---|---|---|
| Male | 1 | 3 | 1 | 1 | 5.5 | 3.5 | 3 | 1.5 | 0 | 2 | 2 | 1.5 | 0 | 8 | 0 | 0 | 2 | 0 | 2 | | 8 |
| Female | 0 | 1 | 0 | 0 | 5 | 4 | 3 | 3.5 | 2 | 2.5 | 0 | 0 | 0 | 6 | 1 | 0 | 3 | 0 | 2 | | 8 |
| Total | 1 | 4 | 1 | 1 | 10.5 | 7.5 | 6 | 5 | 2 | 4.5 | 2 | 1.5 | 0 | 14 | 1 | 0 | 5 | 0 | 4 | | 16 |

| | Vertical displacement Acrotrope M | F | Isotrope | Horizontal syntropism Diatrope | Paratrope | Protrope | Amphitrope | Apotrope |
|---|---|---|---|---|---|---|---|---|
| Male | 2 | 1 | 7 | 2 | 3 | 1 | 3 | 1 |
| Female | 1 | 1 | 8 | 2 | 5 | 0 | 2 | 1 |
| Total | 3 | 2 | 15 | 4 | 8 | 1 | 5 | 2 |

| | Individual evaluation M +2 | +1 | 0 | -1 | -2 | F +2 | +1 | 0 | -1 | -2 | Intended actions M Pos. | Neg. | F Pos. | Neg. | Individual reconstruction Open proximal access M | F | Defined axial space M | F | Contained axial space M | F | Closed proximal boundary M | F |
|---|---|---|---|---|---|---|---|---|---|---|---|---|---|---|---|---|---|---|---|---|---|---|
| Male | 8 | 1 | 0 | 0 | 0 | 4 | 4 | 0 | 2 | 0 | 4 | 0 | 0 | 0 | 4.5 | 4 | 4 | .5 | 0 | 1.5 | 1.5 | 3.5 |
| Female | 9 | 1 | 0 | 0 | 0 | 6 | 4 | 0 | 0 | 0 | 2 | 0 | 1 | 0 | 4 | 3 | 3 | 5.5 | 2 | 1.5 | 0 | 1 |
| Total | 17 | 2 | 0 | 0 | 0 | 10 | 8 | 0 | 2 | 0 | 6 | 0 | 1 | 0 | 8.5 | 7 | 7 | 6 | 2 | 3 | 1.5 | 4.5 |

406

**Table 9. Characteristics of Warm Encounters** (absolute frequencies)

| | Intended actions M Pos. | Neg. | Intended actions F Pos. | Neg. | Open proximal access M | F | Defined axial space M | F | Contained axial space M | F | Closed proximal boundary M | F | Responsible for intersection at axial boundary M | M/F | F | Responsible for contact at proximal boundary M | M/F | F | Near M | Far F |
|---|---|---|---|---|---|---|---|---|---|---|---|---|---|---|---|---|---|---|---|---|
| Male | 4 | 0 | 3 | 0 | .5 | 1.5 | 9.5 | 6 | 0 | 2 | 0 | .5 | 1 | 9 | 0 | 1 | 7 | 0 | 8 | 2 |
| Female | 4 | 0 | 2 | 0 | 1.5 | 3 | 8 | 6.5 | .5 | .5 | 0 | 0 | 1 | 6 | 0 | 1 | 6 | 0 | 8 | 2 |
| Total | 8 | 0 | 5 | 0 | 2 | 4.5 | 17.5 | 12.5 | .5 | 2.5 | 0 | .5 | 2 | 15 | 0 | 2 | 13 | 0 | 16 | 4 |

| | Vertical displacement Acro-trope M | F | Iso-trope | Horizontal syntropism Dia-trope | Para-trope | Pro-trope | Amphi-trope | Apo-trope |
|---|---|---|---|---|---|---|---|---|
| Male | 6 | 1 | 3 | 5 | 1 | 1 | 3 | 0 |
| Female | 3 | 2 | 5 | 1 | 1 | 0 | 8 | 0 |
| Total | 9 | 3 | 8 | 6 | 2 | 1 | 11 | 0 |

| | Individual evaluation M +2 | +1 | 0 | -1 | -2 | F +2 | +1 | 0 | -1 | -2 | Intended actions M Pos. | Neg. | F Pos. | Neg. | Individual reconstruction Open proximal access M | F | Defined axial space M | F | Contained axial space M | F | Closed proximal boundary M | F |
|---|---|---|---|---|---|---|---|---|---|---|---|---|---|---|---|---|---|---|---|---|---|---|
| Male | 0 | 8 | 2 | 0 | 0 | 1 | 8 | 1 | 0 | 0 | 4 | 0 | 3 | 0 | .5 | 2 | 7.5 | 7 | 0 | 1 | 2 | 0 |
| Female | 0 | 8 | 2 | 0 | 0 | 0 | 8 | 1 | 1 | 0 | 4 | 0 | 3 | 0 | 2 | 0 | 7 | 8.5 | .5 | 1.5 | .5 | 0 |
| Total | 0 | 16 | 4 | 0 | 0 | 1 | 16 | 2 | 1 | 0 | 8 | 0 | 6 | 0 | 2.5 | 2 | 14.5 | 15.5 | .5 | 2.5 | 2.5 | 0 |

**Table 10. Characteristics of Cold Encounters** (absolute frequencies)

| | Intended actions — M | | Intended actions — F | | Open proximal access | | Defined axial space | | Contained axial space | | Closed proximal boundary | | Responsible for intersection at axial boundary | | | Responsible for contact at proximal boundary | | | Near | Far |
|---|---|---|---|---|---|---|---|---|---|---|---|---|---|---|---|---|---|---|---|---|
| | Pos. | Neg. | Pos. | Neg. | M | F | M | F | M | F | M | F | M | M/F | F | M | M/F | F | M | F |
| Male | 0 | 3 | 0 | 2 | 2.5 | 3 | .5 | 2 | 4 | 2.5 | 3 | 2.5 | 0 | 0 | 0 | 0 | 0 | 0 | 0 | 10 |
| Female | 0 | 3 | 0 | 3 | 6 | 6 | 3 | 1 | 0 | 1 | 2 | 1 | 0 | 1 | 0 | 0 | 1 | 0 | 3 | 7 |
| Total | 0 | 6 | 0 | 5 | 8.5 | 9 | 3.5 | 3 | 4 | 3.5 | 5 | 3.5 | 0 | 1 | 0 | 0 | 1 | 0 | 3 | 17 |

| | Vertical displacement — Acrotrope | | Isotrope | Horizontal syntropism — Diatrope | Paratrope | Protrope | Amphitrope | Apotrope |
|---|---|---|---|---|---|---|---|---|
| | M | F | | | | | | |
| Male | 2 | 1 | 7 | 0 | 0 | 1 | 1 | 8 |
| Female | 2 | 0 | 8 | 2 | 1 | 0 | 3 | 4 |
| Total | 4 | 1 | 15 | 2 | 1 | 1 | 4 | 12 |

| | Individual evaluation — M | | | | | Individual evaluation — F | | | | | Intended actions — M | | Intended actions — F | | Individual reconstruction — Open proximal access | | Defined axial space | | Contained axial space | | Closed proximal boundary | |
|---|---|---|---|---|---|---|---|---|---|---|---|---|---|---|---|---|---|---|---|---|---|---|
| | +2 | +1 | 0 | -1 | -2 | +2 | +1 | 0 | -1 | -2 | Pos. | Neg. | Pos. | Neg. | M | F | M | F | M | F | M | F |
| Male | 1 | 8 | 1 | 0 | 0 | 1 | 8 | 1 | 0 | 0 | 1 | 3 | 2 | 1 | 5 | .5 | 1 | 3 | 2.5 | 5 | 1 | 2 |
| Female | 0 | 7 | 2 | 1 | 0 | 2 | 4 | 3 | 1 | 0 | 0 | 0 | 1 | 0 | 6 | 5 | 0 | 1 | 3 | 1 | 1 | 3 |
| Total | 1 | 15 | 3 | 1 | 0 | 3 | 12 | 4 | 1 | 0 | 1 | 3 | 3 | 1 | 11 | 5.5 | 1 | 4 | 5.5 | 6 | 2 | 5 |

# Table 11. Characteristics of Sincere Encounters (absolute frequencies)

| | Intended actions M | | Intended actions F | | Open proximal access | | Defined axial space | | Contained axial space | | Closed proximal boundary | | Responsible for intersection at axial boundary | | | Responsible for contact at proximal boundary | | | Near | | Far |
|---|---|---|---|---|---|---|---|---|---|---|---|---|---|---|---|---|---|---|---|---|---|
| | Pos. | Neg. | Pos. | Neg. | M | F | M | F | M | F | M | F | M | M/F | F | M | M/F | F | M | F | F |
| Male | 4 | 0 | 3 | 1 | .5 | 2.5 | 8 | 5.5 | 1.5 | 2 | 0 | 0 | 2 | 7 | 0 | 1 | 6 | 0 | 6 | 4 | |
| Female | 4 | 0 | 3 | 0 | 1 | 4.5 | 7 | 3 | 2 | 2.5 | 0 | 0 | 1 | 6 | 0 | 2 | 3 | 2 | 6 | 4 | |
| Total | 8 | 0 | 6 | 1 | 1.5 | 7 | 15 | 8.5 | 3.5 | 4.5 | 0 | 0 | 3 | 13 | 0 | 3 | 9 | 2 | 12 | 8 | |

| | Vertical displacement | | | | Horizontal syntropism | | | | |
|---|---|---|---|---|---|---|---|---|---|
| | Acro-trope | | Iso-trope | | Dia-trope | Para-trope | Pro-trope | Amphi-trope | Apo-trope |
| | M | F | M | F | | | | | |
| Male | 3 | 1 | 6 | 2 | 8 | 1 | 0 | 1 | 0 |
| Female | 4 | 2 | 4 | 0 | 3 | 1 | 1 | 5 | 0 |
| Total | 7 | 3 | 10 | 2 | 11 | 2 | 1 | 6 | 0 |

| | Individual evaluation M | | | | | Individual evaluation F | | | | | Open proximal access | | Defined axial space | | Contained axial space | | Closed proximal boundary | | Intended actions M | | Intended actions F | |
|---|---|---|---|---|---|---|---|---|---|---|---|---|---|---|---|---|---|---|---|---|---|---|
| | +2 | +1 | 0 | -1 | -2 | +2 | +1 | 0 | -1 | -2 | M | F | M | F | M | F | M | F | Pos. | Neg. | Pos. | Neg. |
| Male | 2 | 6 | 0 | 2 | 0 | 1 | 9 | 0 | 0 | 0 | 1 | 5 | 8 | 3 | 1 | 1 | 0 | 0 | 3 | 0 | 3 | 1 |
| Female | 1 | 6 | 3 | 0 | 0 | 0 | 5 | 4 | 1 | 0 | 1 | 2 | 5 | 4 | 3 | 1 | 0 | 2 | 3 | 0 | 3 | 0 |
| Total | 3 | 12 | 3 | 2 | 0 | 1 | 14 | 4 | 1 | 0 | 2 | 7 | 13 | 7 | 4 | 2 | 0 | 2 | 6 | 0 | 6 | 1 |

(Individual reconstruction comprises: Open proximal access, Defined axial space, Contained axial space, Closed proximal boundary)

**Table 12. Characteristics of Calculating Encounters** (absolute frequencies)

| | Intended actions M Pos. | M Neg. | Intended actions F Pos. | F Neg. | Open proximal access M | F | Defined axial space M | F | Contained axial space M | F | Closed proximal boundary M | F | Responsible for intersection at axial boundary M | M/F | F | Responsible for contact at proximal boundary M | M/F | F | Near M | Far F |
|---|---|---|---|---|---|---|---|---|---|---|---|---|---|---|---|---|---|---|---|---|
| Male | 6 | 2 | 0 | 2 | 0 | 3 | 6 | 3 | 1 | 3 | 3 | 1 | 0 | 3 | 0 | 0 | 1 | 0 | 3 | 7 |
| Female | 4 | 0 | 2 | 2 | 2.5 | 3 | 6 | 3.5 | 1 | 3 | .5 | .5 | 3 | 2 | 0 | 0 | 2 | 0 | 7 | 3 |
| Total | 10 | 2 | 2 | 4 | 2.5 | 6 | 12 | 6.5 | 2 | 6 | 3.5 | 1.5 | 3 | 5 | 0 | 0 | 3 | 0 | 10 | 10 |

| | Vertical displacement Acrotrope M | F | Isotrope | Horizontal syntropism Diatrope | Paratrope | Protrope | Amphitrope | Apotrope |
|---|---|---|---|---|---|---|---|---|
| Male | 4 | 0 | 6 | 3 | 2 | 1 | 4 | 1 |
| Female | 4 | 1 | 5 | 0 | 1 | 3 | 5 | 1 |
| Total | 8 | 1 | 11 | 3 | 3 | 4 | 9 | 2 |

| | Individual evaluation M +2 | +1 | 0 | −1 | −2 | F +2 | +1 | 0 | −1 | −2 | Intended actions M Pos. | Neg. | F Pos. | Neg. | Individual reconstruction Open proximal access M | F | Defined axial space M | F | Contained axial space M | F | Closed proximal boundary M | F |
|---|---|---|---|---|---|---|---|---|---|---|---|---|---|---|---|---|---|---|---|---|---|---|
| Male | 3 | 5 | 1 | 1 | 0 | 2 | 6 | 2 | 0 | 0 | 4 | 1 | 0 | 0 | 2 | 2 | 4.5 | 4 | 1 | 1.5 | 1.5 | 2.5 |
| Female | 2 | 6 | 2 | 0 | 0 | 2 | 4 | 4 | 0 | 0 | 4 | 0 | 2 | 0 | 2 | 2 | 3 | 3 | 4.5 | 3 | 0 | 2.5 |
| Total | 5 | 11 | 3 | 1 | 0 | 4 | 10 | 6 | 0 | 0 | 8 | 1 | 2 | 0 | 4 | 4 | 7.5 | 7 | 5.5 | 4.5 | 1.5 | 5 |

**Table 13. Characteristics of Good Encounters** (absolute frequencies)

| | Intended actions | | | | Open proximal access | | Defined axial space | | Contained axial space | | Closed proximal boundary | | Responsible for inter-section at axial boundary | | | Responsible for contact at proximal boundary | | | Near | Far |
|---|---|---|---|---|---|---|---|---|---|---|---|---|---|---|---|---|---|---|---|---|
| | M Pos. | M Neg. | F Pos. | F Neg. | M | F | M | F | M | F | M | F | M | M/F | F | M | M/F | F | M | F |
| Male | 2 | 0 | 1 | 0 | 2 | 1 | 7 | 7.5 | 1 | 1.5 | 0 | 0 | 1 | 7 | 1 | 1 | 7 | 0 | 8 | 2 |
| Female | 2 | 0 | 1 | 0 | 1.5 | .5 | 7.5 | 7 | 0 | 1 | 1 | 1.5 | 1 | 7 | 0 | 1 | 7 | 0 | 10 | 0 |
| Total | 4 | 0 | 2 | 0 | 3.5 | 1.5 | 14.5 | 14.5 | 1 | 2.5 | 1 | 1.5 | 2 | 14 | 1 | 2 | 14 | 0 | 18 | 2 |

| | Vertical displacement | | | Horizontal syntropism | | | | |
|---|---|---|---|---|---|---|---|---|
| | Acro-trope M | Acro-trope F | Iso-trope | Dia-trope | Para-trope | Pro-trope | Amphi-trope | Apo-trope |
| Male | 5 | 2 | 3 | 3 | 2 | 4 | 1 | 0 |
| Female | 5 | 2 | 3 | 2 | 2 | 1 | 5 | 0 |
| Total | 10 | 4 | 6 | 5 | 4 | 5 | 6 | 0 |

| | Individual evaluation | | | | | | | | | | Intended actions | | | | Individual reconstruction | | | | | | | |
|---|---|---|---|---|---|---|---|---|---|---|---|---|---|---|---|---|---|---|---|---|---|---|
| | M +2 | M +1 | M 0 | M −1 | M −2 | F +2 | F +1 | F 0 | F −1 | F −2 | M Pos. | M Neg. | F Pos. | F Neg. | Open proximal access M | Open proximal access F | Defined axial space M | Defined axial space F | Contained axial space M | Contained axial space F | Closed proximal boundary M | Closed proximal boundary F |
| Male | 2 | 7 | 1 | 0 | 0 | 3 | 5 | 2 | 4 | 1 | 0 | 0 | 3 | 0 | 4 | 2 | 0 | 4 | 4.5 | 3 | 0 | 1 |
| Female | 1 | 6 | 3 | 0 | 0 | 1 | 4 | 4 | 1 | 5 | 4 | 0 | 5 | 0 | 5 | 5.5 | 1.5 | 2.5 | 5 | 1.5 | 0 | .5 |
| Total | 3 | 13 | 4 | 0 | 0 | 4 | 9 | 6 | 5 | 6 | 4 | 0 | 8 | 0 | 9 | 7.5 | 1.5 | 6.5 | 9.5 | 4.5 | 0 | 1.5 |

**Table 14. Characteristics of Evil Encounters** (absolute frequencies)

| | Intended actions M | | Intended actions F | | Open proximal access | | Defined axial space | | Contained axial space | | Closed proximal boundary | | Responsible for intersection at axial boundary | | | Responsible for contact at proximal boundary | | | Near | Far |
|---|---|---|---|---|---|---|---|---|---|---|---|---|---|---|---|---|---|---|---|---|---|
| | Neg. | Pos. | Pos. | Neg. | M | F | M | F | M | F | M | F | M | M/F | F | M | M/F | F | M | F |
| Male | 8 | 1 | 1 | 5 | 0 | 1.5 | 9 | 6 | 1 | 2 | 0 | .5 | 5 | 0 | 1 | 4 | 0 | 1 | 6 | 4 |
| Female | 8 | 1 | 3 | 4 | 0 | 1.5 | 10 | 8 | 0 | 0 | 0 | .5 | 4 | 2 | 1 | 5 | 1 | 0 | 5 | 5 |
| Total | 16 | 2 | 4 | 9 | 0 | 3 | 19 | 14 | 1 | 2 | 1 | 1 | 9 | 2 | 2 | 9 | 1 | 1 | 11 | 9 |

| | Vertical displacement Acro-trope | | Iso-trope | Horizontal syntropism Dia-trope | Para-trope | Pro-trope | Amphi-trope | Apo-trope | Individual evaluation M | | | | | F | | | | |
|---|---|---|---|---|---|---|---|---|---|---|---|---|---|---|---|---|---|---|
| | M | F | | | | | | | +2 | +1 | 0 | -1 | -2 | +2 | +1 | 0 | -1 | -2 |
| Male | 7 | 2 | 1 | 1 | 0 | 6 | 3 | 0 | 0 | 6 | 2 | 1 | 0 | 0 | 5 | 4 | 0 | 0 |
| Female | 5 | 1 | 4 | 4 | 0 | 3 | 2 | 1 | 1 | 7 | 3 | 0 | 0 | 0 | 6 | 4 | 0 | 0 |
| Total | 12 | 3 | 5 | 5 | 0 | 9 | 5 | 1 | 1 | 13 | 5 | 1 | 0 | 0 | 11 | 8 | 1 | 0 |

| | Intended actions M | | F | | Individual reconstruction Open proximal access | | Defined axial space | | Contained axial space | | Closed proximal boundary | |
|---|---|---|---|---|---|---|---|---|---|---|---|---|
| | Pos. | Neg. | Pos. | Neg. | M | F | M | F | M | F | M | F |
| Male | 6 | 0 | 5 | 1 | 1 | 1.5 | 8 | 6 | 0 | .5 | 1 | 2 |
| Female | 6 | 0 | 5 | 1 | 2.5 | 2.5 | 4.5 | 4 | 1 | 1.5 | 1 | 1 |
| Total | 12 | 0 | 10 | 2 | 3.5 | 4 | 12.5 | 10 | 1 | 2 | 2 | 3 |

412

# References

**Agee, J.** *Agee on Film.* Boston: Beacon Press, 1964.

**Allport, F. H.** *Theories of Perception and the Concept of Structure.* New York: Wiley, 1955.

**Allport, G. W.** "Historical Background of Modern Social Psychology," in G. Lindzey, Ed., *Handbook of Social Psychology.* Cambridge, Mass.: Addison-Wesley, 1954, Chapter I.

**Allport, G. W.** *Pattern and Growth in Personality.* New York: Holt, Rinehart and Winston, 1961.

**Allport, G. W.,** and **P. Vernon.** *Studies in Expressive Behavior.* New York: The Macmillan Co., 1933.

**Andrew, R. J.** "The Origins of Facial Expression," *Scientific American,* 213 (4), 1965, pp. 88–94.

**Antrobus, J. S., Judith S. Antrobus,** and **J. L. Singer.** "Eye Movements Accompanying Daydreaming, Visual Imagery, and Thought Suppression," *Journal of Abnormal and Social Psychology,* 69 (3), 1964, pp. 244–52.

**Arbeau, T.** *Orchesography,* translated by C. W. Beaumont. New York: Dance Horizons, n.d., paperback, based on the first London edition of Beaumont's translation, 1925.

**Argyle, M.** "Non-Verbal Communication in Human Social Interaction," in *Non-Verbal Communication,* R. A. Hinde (Ed.), London: Cambridge U. Press, 1972, pp. 243–69.

**Arnheim, R.** "The Gestalt Theory of Expression," *Psychological Review,* 56 (3), 1949, pp. 165–71.

**Arnheim, R.** *Art and Visual Perception.* Berkeley: University of California Press, 1954.

**Aubert, C.** *The Art of Pantomime,* translated by Ed. Sears. New York: Henry Holt, 1927.

Bailey, M. "An Introductory Treatise on Elocution," in G. S. Hilliard, Ed., *The Sixth Reader*. Boston: Brewer and Tileston, 1866.

Bandura, A. "Social Learning Through Imitation," in M. R. James, Ed., *Nebraska Symposium on Learning*. Lincoln: University of Nebraska Press, 1962, pp. 219–27.

Barker, R. G. "Explorations in Ecological Psychology," *American Psychologist*, 20 (1), 1965, pp. 1–14.

Barker, R. G., Ed. *The Stream of Behavior*. New York: Appleton-Century-Crofts, 1963.

Barker, R. G., and H. F. Wright. *Midwest and Its Children*. New York: Harper and Row, 1955.

Bartenieff, I. "Effort-Shape Analysis of Movement: The Unity of Expression and Function," Unpublished monograph. Bronx, N.Y.: Albert Einstein College of Medicine, 1965. 71pp. (Copies from Dance Notation Bureau, 8 E. 12th St., New York, N.Y. 10003.)

Bateson, G., R. L. Birdwhistell, H. W. Brosin, C. F. Hockett, and N. A. McQuown, *The Natural History of an Interview*. New York: In press.

Beardsley, M. C. *Aesthetics: Problems in the Philosophy of Criticism*. New York: Harcourt, Brace and Co., 1958, pp. 221–37.

Bell, C. *The Anatomy and Philosophy of Expression as Connected with the Fine Arts*, Third Edition. London: John Murray, 1844.

Birdwhistell, R. L. "Redundancy in Multichannel Communications Systems." *Family Process*, 1, 1962, pp. 194–201. Reprinted in Birdwhistell, R. L. *Kinesics and Context*. Philadelphia: U. of Pennsylvania Press, 1970.

Birdwhistell, R. L. *Introduction to Kinesics*. Louisville: University of Kentucky Press, 1952.

Birdwhistell, R. L. *Introduction to Kinesics*. Washington, D.C.: U. S. Department of State Foreign Service Institute, 1952. Reprinted by University of Louisville, 1954.

Birdwhistell, R. L. "The Kinesic Level in the Investigation of the Emotions," in P. H. Knapp, Ed., *Expression of the Emotions in Man*. New York: International Universities Press, 1963, p. 131.

Blasis, C. *The Code of Terpsichore*. (Translated by R. Barton) London: Edward Bull, 1830, p. 76. (First published 1828.)

Bournonville, A. *Études Choréographiques*. Copenhagen: 1861. Quoted in Van Praagh and Brinson, 1963, p. 320.

Brigance, W. N., and K. R. Immel. *Speechmaking: Principles and Practice*. New York: F. S. Crofts & Co., 1938.

Brown, R. *Social Psychology*. New York: The Free Press, 1965. p. 626.

Brown, R., and M. Ford. "Address in American English," *Journal of Abnormal and Social Psychology*, 62, 1961, pp. 375–85.

**Bruner, J. S.** "On Going Beyond the Information Given," *Contemporary Approaches to Cognition*. Cambridge: Harvard University Press, 1957, pp. 41–69. Reprinted in R. J. C. Harper, *The Cognitive Processes*, Englewood Cliffs, N.J.: Prentice-Hall, 1964, pp. 293–311.

**Bruner, J. S., J. M. Mandler, D. O'Dowd,** and **M. A. Wallach.** "The Role of Overlearning and Drive Level in Reversal Learning," *Journal of Comparative Physiological Psychology*, 51, 1958, pp. 607–713. Reprinted in R. J. C. Harper, *The Cognitive Processes*, Englewood Cliffs, N.J.: Prentice-Hall, 1964, pp. 279–93.

**Bruner, J. S.,** and **R. Tagiuri.** "The Perception of People," in G. Lindzey, Ed., *Handbook of Social Psychology*. Cambridge, Mass.: Addison-Wesley, 1954, Chapter II, pp. 643–54.

**Buhler, C.** *The First Years of Life*. New York: John Day, 1930.

**Burke, K.** *A Rhetoric of Motives*. New York: Prentice-Hall, 1950.

**Calmette, M. G.** "Un Faux Pas," *Figaro*, May 30, 1912. Quoted in R. Nijinsky, *Nijinsky*, New York: Simon and Schuster, 1934, p. 175.

**Chomsky, N.** "Deep Structures and Grammatical Transformations," *Aspects of the Theory of Syntax*. Cambridge, Mass.: M.I.T. Press, 1965.

**Clark, K.** *The Nude: A Study in Ideal Form*. New York: Doubleday, 1959.

**Clark, K. B.,** and **M. P. Clark.** "Racial Identification and Preference in Negro Children," in G. E. Swanson, T. M. Newcomb, and E. L. Hartley, Eds., *Readings in Social Psychology*. New York: Holt, 1952.

**Coleman, J. C.** "Facial Expression of Emotion," *Psychological Monographs*, 63 (1), 1949, pp. 1–16.

**Cooley, C. H.** *Human Nature and the Social Order*. New York: Scribner's, 1922.

**Darwin, C.** *The Expression of Emotion in Man and Animals*. New York: Philosophical Library, 1955.

**Davis, M.** *Understanding Body Movement: An Annotated Bibliography*. New York: Arno Press, 1972.

**Davitz, J. B.,** Ed. *The Communication of Emotional Meaning*. New York: McGraw-Hill, 1964.

**Descartes, R.** "The Geometry," in J. R. Newman, Ed., *The World of Mathematics*. New York: Simon and Schuster, 1956.

**Deutsch, F.** "Analytic Posturology and ‚Synesthesiology," *Psychoanalytic Review*, 50, 1963, pp. 40–67.

**Deutsch, F.** "Analytical Posturology," *Psychoanalytic Quarterly*, 21, 1952, pp. 196–214.

**Diebold, A. R., Jr.** "Psycholinguistics: A Book of Readings," *Language*, 40 (2) (April–June), 1964, pp. 197–260.

**Dittman, A. T.** "Kinesic Research and Therapeutic Process," in *Expression of the Emotions in Man*. P. H. Knapp, Ed., New York: International Universities Press, 1963, p. 144.

**Dittman, A. T.** "The Relationship between Body Movements and Moods in Interviews," *Journal of Consulting Psychology,* 25 (5), 1962, p. 480.

**Dodd, E. R.** "The Blessings of Madness," *The Greeks and the Irrational.* Boston, Mass.: The Beacon Press, 1957.

**Dorcy, J.** *The Mime.* New York: Robert Speller & Sons, 1961.

**Duncan, I.** Quoted in Olga Maynard, *American Modern Dancers: The Pioneers.* Boston: Little, Brown, 1965, p. 52.

**Duncan, S.** "Nonverbal Communication," *Psychological Bulletin,* 72, 1969, pp. 118–137.

**Durkheim, E.** *Suicide: A Study in Sociology.* Glencoe, Ill.: The Free Press, 1951.

**Effron, D.** *Gesture and Environment.* New York: Kings Crown, 1941.

**Ehrensweig, A.** "The Undifferentiated Matrix of Artistic Imagination," *The Psychoanalytic Study of the Child.* New York: International Universities Press, 1964.

**Ehrensweig, A.** "Conscious Planning and Unconscious Scanning," in G. Kepes, Ed., *Education of Vision.* New York: Braziller, 1965.

**Einstein, A.,** and **L. Infeld.** *The Evolution of Physics.* New York: Simon and Schuster, 1938.

**Ekman, P.** "Body Position, Facial Expression, and Verbal Behavior During Interviews," *Journal of Abnormal and Social Psychology,* 68 (3), 1964, pp. 295–301.

**Ekman, P.** "Communication Through Nonverbal Behavior: A Source of Information about an Interpersonal Relationship," in S. S. Tompkins and C. E. Izard, Eds., *Affect, Cognition and Personality.* New York: Springer, 1965.

**Ekman, P.,** and **W. V. Friesen.** "Head and Body Cues in the Judgment of Emotion: A Reformulation," *Perceptual and Motor Skills,* 24, 1967, pp. 711–24.

**Ekman, P.,** and **W. V. Friesen.** "Nonverbal Behavior in Psychotherapy Research," in J. Schlien, Ed., *Research in Psychotherapy.* Washington, D.C.: American Psychological Association, 1968.

**Ekman, P.,** and **W. V. Friesen.** "The Repertoire of Nonverbal Behavior: Categories, Origins, Usage, and Coding," *Semiotica.* 1 (1), 1969, pp. 49–98.

**Ekman, P., W. V. Friesen,** and **Phoebe Ellsworth.** *Emotion in the Human Face.* New York: Pergamon Press, 1972.

**Ekman, P., E. R. Sorenson,** and **W. V. Friesen.** "Pan-Culture Elements in Facial Displays of Emotion." *Science,* 1969, pp. 86–3.

**Ekman, P.,** and **W. V. Friesen,** "Constants Across Cultures in the Face and Emotions," *Journal of Personality and Social Psychology,* 17, 1971, pp. 124–129.

**Ekman, P.,** "Universals of Cultural Differences in Facial Expressions of Emotion," in *Nebraska Symposium on Emotion,* J. K. Cole (ed.), Lincoln, Nebraska: University of Nebraska Press, 1972.

**Eldred, S. H.** "A Linguistic Analysis of States of Feeling in Psychotherapy," *Psychiatry,* 21, 1958, pp. 115–21.

**Eibl-Eibesfeldt, I.** "Similarities and Differences Between Cultures in Expressive Movements," in *Non-Verbal Communication*, R. A. Hinde, Ed. London: Cambridge U. Press, 1972.

**Ellsworth, P. C.,** and **J. M. Carlsmith.** "Effects of Eye Contacts and Verbal Content on Affective Response to a Dyadic Interaction," *Journal of Personality and Social Psychology*, 10, 1968, pp. 15–20.

**Emerson, R. W.** Holograph Journal (H) October 16, 1841. Houghton Library, Harvard University, Cambridge, Mass., pp. 65–66. Quoted with the permission of the Houghton Library and the Ralph Waldo Emerson Memorial Association.

**Erikson, E.** *Childhood and Society*, Second Edition. New York: Norton, 1963.

**Exline, R.** "Explorations in the Process of Person Perception: Visual Interaction in Relation to Competition, Sex, and Need for Affiliation," *Journal of Personality*, 1963, 31, 1–20.

**Exline, R., D. Gray,** and **D. Schuette.** "Visual Behavior in a Dyad as Affected by Interview Content and Sex of Respondent," *Journal of Personality and Social Psychology*, 1 (3), 1965, pp. 201–9.

**Feldman, S. S.** *Mannerisms of Speech and Gesture in Everyday Life.* New York: International Universities Press, 1959.

**Fokine, M.** *Memoirs of a Ballet Master*, A. Chujoy, Ed. Boston: Little, Brown, 1961.

**Ford, C. S.,** and **F. A. Beach.** *Patterns of Sexual Behavior.* New York: Harper, 1951.

**Frank, L.** "Tactile Communication," *ETC.*, 16, 1958, pp. 31–79.

**Frankfort, H.** *Ancient Egyptian Religion.* New York: Harper, 1961.

**Frankfort, H.** *Kingship and the Gods.* Chicago: University of Chicago Press, 1948.

**Freud, S.** *Group Psychology and the Analysis of the Ego.* New York: Bantam, 1960. (First published in 1921.)

**Freud, S.** "The Moses of Michaelangelo," *The Complete Works of Sigmund Freud*, Volume 23. London: Hogarth Press, 1955.

**Freud, S.** *Delusion and Dream*, translated by Harry Zohn, with an introduction by Philip Rieff, Boston, Mass.: Beacon Press, 1956.

**Fryjda, N. H.** "Recognition of Emotion," in L. Berkowitz, Ed., *Advances in Experimental Social Psychology*. New York: Academic Press, 1969.

**Fuller, R. B.** "Conceptuality of Fundamental Structures," in G. Kepes, Ed., *Art and Science.* New York: Braziller, 1965, pp. 66–88.

**Galilei, G.** "The Mathematics of Motion," *Dialogues Concerning Two New Sciences*, in James R. Newman, Ed., *The World of Mathematics*, New York: Simon and Schuster, 1956.

**Giedion, S.** "The Supremacy of the Vertical," *The Eternal Present: The Beginnings of Architecture.* New York: Pantheon Books and The Bollingen Foundation, 1964.

**Gibb, C. A.** "Leadership," in G. Lindzey, Ed., *Handbook of Social Psychology.* Cambridge, Mass.: Addison-Wesley, 1954.

**Gibson, J. J.** "Constancy and Invariance in Perception," in G. Kepes, Ed., *The Nature and Art of Motion.* New York: Braziller, 1965.

**Goffman, E.** *The Presentation of Self in Everyday Life.* New York: Anchor Books, 1959.

**Gombrich, E. H.** *Art and Illusion.* New York: Bollingen, 1960.

**Grinker, R. R.,** Ed. *Toward a Unified Theory of Human Behavior.* New York: Basic Books, 1956.

**Guest, I.** *The Ballet of the Second Empire, 1847–1858.* London: Adam and Charles Black, 1955.

**Haggard, E. H.,** and **K. S. Isaacs.** "Micromomentary Facial Expressions as Indicators of Ego Mechanisms in Psychotherapy," in L. A. Gottschalk and A. H. Aurbaack, Eds., *Methods of Research in Psychotherapy.* New York: Appleton-Century, 1966.

**Hall, E. T.** "The Anthropology of Manners," *Scientific American,* 192, 1955, pp. 85–89.

**Hall, E. T.** *The Hidden Dimension.* New York: Doubleday, 1966.

**Hall, E. T.** "The Language of Space," *Journal of American Institute of Architects,* February, 1961.

**Hall, E. T.** *The Silent Language.* New York: Doubleday, 1959.

**Hall, E. T.** "A System for the Notation of Proxemic Behavior," *American Anthropologist,* 65 (5), 1963, pp. 1003–26.

**Hardwick, E.** "Auschwitz in New York," a review of *The Investigation* by Peter Weiss. *The New York Review,* November 3, 1966, p. 5.

**Haring, D. G.** *Racial Differences and Human Resemblances.* Syracuse: Syracuse University Bookstore, 1947. Reprinted under the title, "Contemporary Human Types," in A. M. Lee, Ed., *Readings in Sociology.* New York: Barnes and Nobel, 1951.

**Harper, R., C. Anderson, G. C. Christensen, M. Clifford,** and **S. M. Hunka.** *The Cognitive Processes.* Englewood Cliffs, N.J.: Prentice-Hall, 1964.

**Hayes, A. S.** "Paralinguistics and Kinesics: Pedagogical Perspectives," in T. A. Sebeok, A. S. Hayes, M. C. Bateson, Eds., *Approaches to Semiotics.* The Hague: Mouton, 1964, pp. 145–72.

**Hayes, F.** "Gestures: A Working Bibliography," *Southern Folklore Quarterly,* 21, 1957, pp. 218–317.

**Hebb, D. O.** "Emotion in Man and Animal: An Analysis of the Intuitive Processes of Recognition," *Psychological Review,* 53, 1946, pp. 88–106.

**Hewes, G. T.** "The Anthropology of Posture," *Scientific American,* 196, 1957, pp. 123–32.

**Hewes, G. T.** "World Distribution of Certain Postural Habits," *American Anthropologist,* 57 (2), 1957, pp. 231–44.

**Hinde, R. A.** "Epilogue," in R. A. Hinde, Ed., *Non-Verbal Communication.* London: Cambridge U. Press, p. 395.

**Hochberg, J.** Unpublished materials, 1964.

**Holton, G.** "Conveying Science by Visual Presentation," in G. Kepes, Ed., *Education of Vision.* New York: Braziller, 1965.

**Holton, G.** "Presupposition in the Construction of Theories," in H. Woolf, Ed., *Science as a Cultural Force.* Baltimore: The Johns Hopkins Press, 1964.

**Hunt, D.** and **Kari.** *Pantomime: The Silent Theater.* New York: Atheneum, 1964.

**Hutchinson, A.** *Labanotation: The System for Recording Movement.* New York: New Directions, 1954.

**Jacobs, T. J.** "Posture, Gesture, and Movement in the Analyst," *Journal of the American Psychoanalytic Association,* 21, 1973, pp. 77–92.

**Jammer, M.** *Concepts of Force.* Cambridge, Mass.: Harvard University Press, 1957.

**Jammer, M.** *Concepts of Space.* Cambridge, Mass.: Harvard University Press, 1954.

**Kanfer, F.** "Verbal Rate, Eyeblink, and Content in Structured Psychiatric Interview," *Journal of Abnormal and Social Psychology,* 61 (3), 1960, pp. 341–47.

**Katz, R.** "Body Language: A Study in Unintentional Communication." Unpublished Ph.D. Thesis, Department of Social Relations, Harvard University, 1964.

**Kavolis, V.** *Artistic Expression: A Sociological Analysis.* Ithaca, N.Y.: Cornell U. Press, 1968.

**Kendon, A.** "Some Functions of Gaze Directions in Social Interaction," *Acta Psychologica,* 26, 1967, pp. 22–63.

**Kepes, G.** Ed. *Vision and Value Series: The Nature of Art and Motion; Education of Vision; Structure in Art and in Science.* New York: Braziller, 1965.

**Kestenberg, J. S.** "The Role of Movement Patterns in Development: I. Rhythms of Movement," *Psychoanalytic Quarterly,* 34, 1965, pp. 1–36; "The Role of Movement Patterns in Development: II. Flow of Tension and Effort." *Psychoanalytic Quarterly,* 34, 1965, pp. 517–63. "The Role of Movement Patterns in Development: III. The Control of Shape." *Psychoanalytic Quarterly,* 36, 1957, pp. 356–409.

**Kirstein, L.** *Dance: A Short History of Classic Theatrical Dancing.* New York: G. P. Putnam's Sons, 1935. (See especially, pp. 221–22, 236.) Quoted in F. R. Rogers, Ed., *Dance: A Basic Educational Technique.* New York: Macmillan, 1941, pp. 225–26.

**Kirstein, L.,** **M. Stuart,** and **G. Balanchine.** *The Classic Ballet: Basic Technique and Terminology.* New York: Knopf, 1952.

**Kluckhohn, F. R.,** and **R. Strodtbeck.** *Variations in Value Orientations.* Evanston, Ill.: Row, Peterson & Company, 1961.

**Knapp, R. H.** "The Language of Postural Interpretation," *Journal of Social Psychology,* 67, 1965, pp. 371–77.

**Koner, P.** *The Language of Dance.* Middletown, Conn.: Wesleyan University Press, 1964.

**Kretschmer, E.** *Physique and Character.* New York: Harcourt, Brace, 1925.

**Kris, E.** *Psychoanalytic Explorations in Art.* New York: International Universities Press, 1952.

**Krout, M. H.** "Autistic Gestures," *Psychological Monographs,* 46 (208), 1935, pp. 1–26.

**Krout, M. H.** "An Experimental Attempt to Produce Unconscious Manual Symbolic Movements," *Journal of General Psychology,* 51, 1954, pp. 93–120.

**Krout, M. H.** "The Social and Psychological Significance of Gestures," *Journal of Genetic Psychology,* 47, 1935, pp. 385–412.

**Kruse, H. D.** *Integrating Approaches to Mental Disease.* New York: Hoeber–Harper, 1957. See Chapter 6, "Areas of Interdoctrinal Unacceptance," and Chapter 7, "Further Interdoctrinal Differences."

**Kuethe, J. L.** "Social Schemas and the Reconstructions of Social Object Displays from Memory," *Journal of Abnormal and Social Psychology,* 65, 1962, pp. 61–74.

**Kuethe, J. L.** "Social Schemas," *Journal of Abnormal and Social Psychology,* 64, 1962, pp. 31–38.

**Kuethe, J. L.** "Pervasive Influence of Social Schemata," *Journal of Abnormal and Social Psychology,* 68, 1964, pp. 248–54.

**Kuhn, T. S.** *The Structure of Scientific Revolutions.* Chicago: University of Chicago Press, 1962.

**Laban, R.** *The Mastery of Movement.* Second Edition, revised by Lisa Ullman. London: MacDonald and Evans, 1960.

**Laban, R.,** and **F. C. Lawrence,** *Effort.* London: MacDonald and Evans, 1947.

**LaBarre, W.** "The Cultural Basis of Emotions and Gestures," *Journal of Personality,* 16, 1947, pp. 49–68.

**LaBarre, W.** "Paralinguistics, Kinesics, and Cultural Anthropology," in T. A. Sebeok, A. S. Hayes, M. C. Bateson, Eds., *Approaches to Semiotics.* The Hague: Mouton, 1964.

**Lamb, W.** *Posture and Gesture: An Introduction to the Study of Physical Behavior.* London: Gerald Duckworth & Co., 1965.

**Langer, S. K.** *Philosophy in a New Key.* Cambridge, Mass.: Harvard University Press, 1942. New York: Mentor Books, 1959.

**Lasswell, T. E.,** and **P. F. Parshall.** "The Perception of Social Class from Photographs," *Sociology and Sociological Research,* 45, pp. 417–24.

**Lavater, J. C.** *Essays on Physiognomy,* translated by H. Hunter. London: John Murray, Volume 1, 1789, p. 27.

**Lawler, L. B.** *The Dance in Ancient Greece.* Middletown, Conn.: Wesleyan University Press, 1964.

**LeBon, G.** *The Crowd.* London: E. Benn, 1952.

**Le Corbusier.** "The Core as a Meeting Place of the Arts," in J. Tyrwhitt, J. L. Sert, and E. N. Rogers, Eds., *The Heart of the City* (CIAM 8). New York: Pellegrini and Cudahy, 1952. Quoted in "Views on Art and Architecture: A Conversation," arranged by John E. Burchard, in *Daedalus*, Special Issue, "The Visual Arts Today," Winter 1960, p. 70.

**Levi-Strauss, C.** *Structural Anthropology.* New York: Basic Books, 1963.

**Little, K. B.** "Personal Space," *Journal of Experimental Social Psychology,* I, 1965, pp. 237–47.

**Little, K. B., J. Ulehla,** and **C. Henderson.** "Value Congruence and Interaction Distances," *Journal of Social Psychology,* 1968, 75, pp. 249–53.

**Lomax, A.** *Folk Song Style and Culture.* Washington, D.C.: American Association for the Advancement of Science, Publication No. 88, 1968, pp. 222–273.

**Lombroso, C.** *L'uomo Delinquente,* 1876. *The Man of Genius.* New York: Scribners, 1891.

**Lorenz, K.** *On Aggression.* New York: Harcourt, Brace & World, Inc. 1966.

**Lott, D. F.,** and **R. Sommer.** "Seating Arrangement and Status," *Journal of Personality and Social Psychology,* 7, 1967, pp. 90–94.

**Lucian.** *On the Dance (De Saltatione), The Works of Lucian of Samosata,* translated by H. W. Fowler and F. G. Fowler, four Volumes. 1905, Volume 2.

**MacCurdy, E.** *The Notebooks of Leonardo Da Vinci.* New York: Braziller, 1956, p. 1144.

**Machotka, P.** "Esthetic criteria in childhood," *Child Development,* 1966, 37, pp. 877–85.

**Machotka, P.** "Defensive style and esthetic distortion," *Journal of Personality,* 1967, 35, pp. 600–22.

**Machotka, P.** "Visual esthetics and learning," *Journal of Aesthetic Education,* 1970, 4, pp. 117–30.

**Machotka, P.** "Ego defense and esthetic distortion: Experimenter effects," *Journal of Personality,* 1970, 38, pp. 560–80.

**Magill, M. T.** *Pantomimes or Wordless Poems,* Revised and Enlarged Edition. New York: Edgar S. Werner, 1895.

**Mandler, G.** "Emotion," in R. Brown, E. Galanter, E. H. Hess, and G. Mandler, Eds., *New Directions in Psychology.* New York: Holt, Rinehart, and Winston, 1962, p. 307.

**Mandler, J. M.,** and **G. Mandler.** "Thinking and the New Psychology: Imageless Thought," *Thinking: From Association to Gestalt.* New York: Wiley, 1964. (See, especially, pp. 132–67, on the Wurzburg Group.)

**McLuhan, M.** *Understanding Media: The Extensions of Man.* New York: McGraw-Hill, 1965.

**McQuown, N. A.** "Linguistic Transcription and Specification of Psychiatric Interview Material," *Psychiatry*, 20, 1957, pp. 79–86.

**Mead, G. H.** *Mind, Self and Society: From the Standpoint of a Social Behaviorist*, Charles W. Morris, Ed. Chicago: University of Chicago Press, 1934.

**Mead, M., and C. F. Macgreggor.** *Growth and Culture: A Photographic Study of Balinese Childhood.* New York: Putnam, 1951.

**Mehrabian, A.** *Nonverbal Communications.* Chicago, Ill.: Aldine-Atherton, 1972.

**Mehrabian, A.** "Significance of Posture and Position in the Communication of Attitude and Status Relationships," *Psychological Bulletin*, 71, 1969, pp. 359–72.

**Merleau-Ponty, M.** *The Structure of Behavior.* Boston: Beacon Press, 1963.

**Meyer, L. B.** *Emotion and Meaning in Music.* Chicago: University of Chicago Press, 1956.

**Meyer, M. F.** "That Whale Among the Fishes—The Theory of Emotion," *Psychological Review*, 40, 1933, pp. 242–300.

**Miller, G. A., E. Galanter,** and **K. H. Pribram.** *Plans and the Structure of Behavior.* New York: Holt, Rinehart and Winston, 1960.

**Miller, N. E.,** and **J. Dollard.** *Social Learning and Imitation.* New Haven: Yale University Press, 1941.

**Mittelmann, B.** "Mobility in Infants, Children, and Adults: Patterning and Psychodynamics," in R. S. Eissler, A. Freud, H. Hartmann, and E. Kris, Eds., *The Psychoanalytic Study of the Child*, Volume 9. New York: International Universities Press, 1954, pp. 142–77.

**Morris, D.** *The Naked Ape.* New York: Dell Publishing Co., 1969.

**Muybridge, E.** *The Human Figure in Motion.* New York: Dover, 1955.

**Neisser, U.** *Cognitive Psychology.* New York: Appleton-Century-Crofts, 1967.

**Neisser, U.** "The Multiplicity of Thought," *British Journal of Psychology*, 54 (1), 1963, pp. 1–14.

**Newell, A., J. C. Shaw,** and **H. A. Simon.** "Elements of a Theory of Human Problem-Solving," in R. J. C. Halper, C. C. Anderson, C. M. Christensen, and S. M. Hunka, Eds., *The Cognitive Process.* Englewood Cliffs, N.J.: Prentice-Hall, 1964.

**Nicoll, A.** *Masks, Mimes, and Miracles: Studies in the Popular Theater.* London: George G. Harrup & Co., 1931.

**Nielsen, G.** *Studies in Self-Confrontation.* Copenhagen: Munkagaard, 1962.

**Nijinsky, R.** *Nijinsky.* New York: Simon and Schuster, 1934.

**Niklaus, T.** *Harlequin.* New York: Braziller, 1956.

**Nikolais, A.** "No Man from Mars," in Selma Jeanne Cohen, Ed., *The Modern Dance: Seven Statements of Belief.* Middletown, Conn.: Wesleyan University Press, 1966, pp. 64–65.

**Noverre, J. G.** *Lettres sur la Danse et les Ballets.* St. Petersburg: Schnoor, 1803. *Letters on Dancing and Ballets*, translated by C. Beaumont. London: Beaumont, 1930. Paperback reprint, New York: Dance Horizons, 1966.

**Oliver, R. T., R. L. Cortright,** and **C. F. Hager.** *The New Training for Effective Speech*, Revised Edition. New York: Dryden Press, 1946.

**Ostwald, P. F.** "How the Patient Communicates about Disease with the Doctor," in T. A. Sebeok, A. S. Hays, and M. C. Bateson, Eds., *Approaches to Semiotics.* The Hague: Mouton and Co., 1964.

**Oyama, M.** *What is Karate*, Revised Edition. Yokohama: Tokyo News Co., 1959.

**Park, R. E.** and **Burgess, E. W.** *Introduction to the Science of Sociology.* Chicago: University of Chicago Press, 1924 (2nd Edition).

**Parsons, T., E. A. Shils, G. W. Allport, C. Kluckhohn, H. A. Murray, R. R. Sears, R. C. Sheldon, S. A. Stouffer,** and **E. C. Tolman.** "Some Fundamental Categories of the Theory of Action: A General Statement," in Parsons and Shils, Eds., *Toward a General Theory of Action.* Cambridge, Mass.: Harvard University Press, 1951.

**Pelles, G.** *Art, Artists, and Society: Origins of a Modern Dilemma.* Englewood Cliffs, N.J.: Prentice-Hall, 1963.

**Piaget, J.** *The Construction of Reality in the Child.* New York: Basic Books, 1954.

**Picasso, P.** *Les déjeuners*, Text by Douglas Cooper. Paris: Editions Cercle d'Art, 1962.

**Pittenger, R.** "Linguistic Analysis of Tone of Voice in Communication of Affect," *Psychiatric Research Reports*, 8, 1958, pp. 41–54.

**Pittenger, R.,** and **H. L. Smith.** "A Basis for Some Contributions of Linguistics to Psychiatry," *Psychiatry*, 20, 1957, pp. 61–78.

**Pribram, K. H.** "Discussion," in P. H. Knapp, Ed., *Expression of the Emotions in Man.* New York: International Universities Press, 1962.

**Renneker, R. E.** "Some Methodological Considerations Regarding Kinesic Research," and "Kinesic Research and Therapeutic Processes," in P. H. Knapp, Ed., *Expression of the Emotions in Man.* New York: International Universities Press, 1963.

**Riddleberger, A. B.,** and **A. B. Motz.** "Prejudice and Perception," *American Journal of Sociology*, 62, 1957, pp. 498–503.

**Riley, A. W.** *A Guide to Effective Speaking.* New York: Van Nostrand, 1931.

**Rosenthal, R.** *Experimenter Effects in Behavioral Research.* New York: Appleton-Century-Crofts, 1966.

**Rosenthal, R.** "On the Social Psychology of the Psychological Experiment," *American Scientist*, 51, 1963, pp. 268–73.

**Ross, W. T.** *Voice Culture and Elocution.* New York: Baker and Taylor, 1890.

**Rueusch, J.** and **W. Kees.** *Non-Verbal Communication.* Berkeley: University of California Press, 1956.

**St. Denis, R.** "Dance as Spiritual Expression," in F. R. Rogers, Ed., *Dance: A Basic Educational Technique.* New York: Macmillan, 1941.

**Schafer, R.** *Psychoanalytic Interpretation in Rorschach Testing.* New York: Grune and Stratton, 1954.

**Scheflen, A. E.** "Communication and Regulation of Psychotherapy," *Psychiatry,* 26, 1963, pp. 126–36.

**Scheflen, A. E.** "Quasi-Courtship Behavior in Psychotherapy," *Psychiatry,* 28, 1965, pp. 245–57.

**Scheflen, A. E.** *Communicational Structure: Analysis of A Psychotherapy Transaction.* Bloomington, Ind.: Indiana University Press, 1973.

**Scheflen, A. E., O. E. English, W. W. Hampe,** and **A. Auerbach.** *Strategy and Structure: Three Research Approaches to Whitaker and Malone's Multiple Therapy.* Philadelphia: Commonwealth of Pennsylvania Monograph Press, 1965.

**Schilder, P.** *The Image and Appearance of the Human Body.* New York: Wiley, 1950.

**Schlosberg, H.** "The Description of Facial Expressions in Terms of Two Dimensions," *Journal of Experimental Psychology,* 44, 1952, pp. 229–37.

**Schoggen, M., L. S. Barker,** and **R. G. Barker.** "Structure of the Behavior of American and English Children," in R. C. Barker, Ed., *The Stream of Behavior.* New York: Appleton-Century-Crofts, 1963.

**Selfridge, O.,** and **U. Neisser.** "Pattern Recognition by Machine," *Scientific American,* 203 (2), 1960, pp. 60–68.

**Shawn, T.** *Every Little Movement.* Published by the author, 1963.

**Sheets, M.** *The Phenomenology Dance.* Madison: University of Wisconsin Press, 1965.

**Sheldon, W. H., C. W. Dupertius,** and **E. McDermott.** *Atlas of Men.* New York: Harper, 1954.

**Sheldon, W. H., S. S. Stevens,** and **W. B. Tucker.** *The Varieties of Human Physique.* New York: Harper, 1940.

**Sheldon, W. H., S. S. Stevens,** and **W. B. Tucker.** *The Varieties of Temperament.* New York: Harper, 1942.

**Simmel, G.** "Sociology of the Senses," in R. E. Park and E. Burgess, Eds., *Introduction to the Science of Sociology.* Chicago: University of Chicago Press, 1924.

**Sommer, R.** "Small Group Ecology," *Psychological Bulletin,* 67, 1967, pp. 145–52.

**Sommer, R.** "The Ecology of Privacy," *The Library Quarterly,* 36, 1966, pp. 234–48.

**Sommer, R.** "Further Studies of Small Group Ecology," *Sociometry,* 28, 1965, pp. 337–48.

**Sommer, R.** "Leadership and Group Geography," *Sociometry,* 24, 1961, pp. 99–110.

**Sommer, R.** *Personal Space.* Englewood Cliffs, N.J.: Prentice-Hall, 1969.

**Sommer, R.** "The Significance of Space," *AIA Journal,* 1965, pp. 63–65.

**Spiegel, J. P.** "Conflicting Formal and Informal Roles in Newly Acculturated Families," *Disorders of Communication*, Vol. 42. Research Publications, Association for Research in Nervous and Mental Diseases, 1964.

**Spiegel, J. P.** "Interpersonal Influences Within the Family," in B. Schaffner, Ed., *Group Processes*. New York: The Josiah Macy, Jr. Foundation, 1956.

**Spiegel, J. P.** "The Resolution of Role Conflict Within the Family," *Psychiatry*, 20 (1), 1957, pp. 1–16.

**Spiegel, J. P.** "Some Cultural Aspects of Transference and Countertransference," in Jules H. Masserman, Ed., *Individual and Familial Dynamics*. New York: Grune and Stratton, 1959.

**Spiegel, J. P.** *Transactions: The Interplay Between Individual, Family and Society.* J. Papajohn, Ed. New York: Science House, 1971.

**Spitz, R. A.** *No and Yes.* New York: International Universities Press, 1957.

**Stanislavski, C.** *An Actor Prepares.* New York: Theater Arts Books, 1936.

**Stanislavski, C.** *My Life in Art.* Cleveland: The World Publishing Company (Meridian Books), 1965.

**Tagiuri, R.** "Person Perception," *Handbook of Social Psychology*, G. Lindzey, Ed. Cambridge, Mass.: Addison-Wesley, 1958.

**Tagiuri, R.,** and **L. Petrullo.** *Person Perception and Interpersonal Behavior.* Stanford, Cal.: Stanford University Press, 1958.

**Tinbergen, N.** *Social Behavior in Animals.* London: Methuen, 1953.

**Trager, G. L.** "Paralanguage: A First Approximation," *Studies in Linguistics*, 13, 1958, pp. 1–2, Department of Anthropology and Linguistics, University of Buffalo.

**Van Praagh, P.,** and **P. Brinson.** *The Choreographic Art.* New York: Knopf, 1963.

**Verdenius, W. J.** *Mimesis: Plato's Doctrine of Artistic Imitation and Its Meaning to Us.* Leiden: E. J. Brill, 1949.

**Vermeule, C.** "The Survival of the Ancient World," *European Art and the Classical Past*. Cambridge, Mass.: Harvard University Press, 1964.

**Vishnudevananda, S.** *The Complete Illustrated Book of Yoga.* New York: The Julian Press, 1960.

**Wallach, M. A.** "Art, Science, and Representation: Toward an Experimental Psychology of Aesthetics," *Journal of Aesthetics and Art Criticism*, 18, 1959, pp. 159–73. Reprinted in R. J. C. Harper, *The Cognitive Process*. Englewood Cliffs, N.J.: Prentice-Hall, 1964.

**Wallach, M. A.** "On Psychological Similarity," *Psychological Review*, 65, 1958, pp. 103–16; reprinted in R. J. C. Harper, *The Cognitive Processes*.

**Wallach, M. A.,** and **N. Kogan.** "Sex Differences and Judgment Processes," *Journal of Personality*, 27, 1959, pp. 555–64.

**Watanabe, J.,** and **L. Avakian.** *The Secrets of Judo.* Rutland, Vermont: Charles E. Tuttle Company, 1960.

**Weaver, J.** *The History of the Mimes and Pantomimes.* London: J. Roberts and A. Dod, 1728.

**Weaver, J.** "Of the Modern Dancing," *An Essay Toward a History of Dancing.* London: Jacob Tonsin, 1712.

**White, H. C.,** and **A. C. White.** *Canvases and Careers: Institutional Change in the French Painting World.* New York: Wiley, 1965.

**White, H. C.,** and **A. C. White.** "Institutional Change in the French Painting World," in R. N. Wilson, Ed., *The Arts in Society.* Englewood Cliffs, N.J.: Prentice-Hall, 1964.

**Whitehead, A. N.** "Science and the Modern World," in F. S. C. Northrup and M. S. Gross, Eds., *Alfred North Whitehead: An Anthology.* New York: The Macmillan Company, 1953.

**Whorf, B. L.** "Linguistic Relativity and the Relation of Linguistic Processes to Perception and Cognition," in John Carroll, Ed., *Language, Thought, and Reality.* Cambridge, Mass.: Technology Press, Wiley, 1956, pp. 207–19. Reprinted in *Psycholinguistics: A Book of Reading,* S. Saporta, Ed. New York: Holt, Rinehart, and Winston, 1961.

**Whyte, L. L.** *Accent on Form: An Anticipation of the Science of Tomorrow.* New York: Harpers, 1954.

**Wigman, M.** *The Language of Dance.* Middletown, Conn.: Wesleyan University Press, 1966.

**Wilbor, E. M.** *Delsarte Recitation Book.* New York: Edgar S. Werner, 1889.

**Wilson, A. E.** *Christmas Pantomime.* London: Allen and Unwin, 1934.

**Worth, S.** "Film as Non-Art," The American Scholar, 35 (2), 1966, pp. 322–34.

# Index